the MODERN PIONEER COOKBOOK

the **MODERN PIONEER** COOKBOOK

Nourishing Recipes from a Traditional Foods Kitchen

MARY BRYANT SHRADER

Publisher Mike Sanders
Art & Design Director William Thomas
Senior Editor Brook Farling
Designer Lindsay Dobbs
Photographer (Austin) Kimberly Davis
Food Stylist (Austin) Susan Gebhard
Photographer and Food Stylist (Indianapolis) Lovoni Walker
Recipe Tester Irena Shnayder
Proofreaders Lisa Starnes, Monica Stone
Indexer Johnna VanHoose Dinse

First American Edition, 2023
Published in the United States by DK Publishing
6081 E. 82nd Street, Suite 400, Indianapolis, IN 46250
DK, a Division of Penguin Random House LLC

Note: This publication contains the opinions and ideas of its author.
It is intended to provide helpful and informative material on the subject
matter covered. It is sold with the understanding that the author and publisher
are not engaged in rendering professional services in the book. If the reader
requires personal assistance or advice, a competent professional should be consulted.
The author and publisher specifically disclaim any responsibility for any liability, loss,
or risk, personal or otherwise, which is incurred as a consequence, directly or indirectly,
of the use and application of any of the contents of this book.

A catalog record for this book
is available from the Library of Congress.
Library of Congress Catalog Number: 2022950800
ISBN 978-0-7440-7742-1

DK books are available at special discounts when purchased
in bulk for sales promotions, premiums, fund-raising, or educational use. For details,
contact: DK Publishing Special Markets (SpecialSales@dk.com).

Photographs © 2023 DK Publishing, with the exception of the
following pages: 104, 107, 119, 219, 237, and 252 © Mary Bryant Shrader

Printed and bound in China

For the curious
www.dk.com

This book was made with Forest
Stewardship Council ™ certified
paper – one small step in DK's
commitment to a sustainable future.
For more information go to
www.dk.com/our-green-pledge

DEDICATION

To my amazing husband, Ted. You have made my life a dream come true. And to Ben, the best son in the whole wide world. I love you both with all my heart!

ACKNOWLEDGMENTS

I want to share my sincerest thank you and gratitude to those who made this book possible:

My amazing husband, Ted, for your infinite love, encouragement, and support, not only for this cookbook but for everything in my life. You are my dream come true!

My wonderful son, Ben, for the unconditional love you have always showered upon me and for trusting me as I encouraged you to try beef liver nuggets with fermented ketchup!

My sweet mother, Gloria, the consummate homemaker, who lovingly and patiently taught me how to be a traditional home cook and to proudly embrace the gentle domestic arts of caring for my family.

My late father, James, who taught me from a very early age that I could achieve anything I wanted through hard work and determination.

My welcoming mother-in-law, Michele, who exposed me to a whole new world of traditional Asian culinary delights.

My late father-in-law, Thomas, who as an agronomist and a naturalist was the original Modern Pioneer inspiring me every day with his knowledge.

My editor, Brook Farling, for believing in me right from the beginning and holding my virtual hand as you walked this first-time author through all that is involved in writing a cookbook.

My publisher, Mike Sanders, and the entire team at DK Publishing for all your support throughout this entire process.

Lindsay Dobbs for creating a visually beautiful book. It's more than I ever imagined!

Kimberly Davis for the gorgeous photography throughout this book and Susan Gebhard for making my traditional food recipes look amazing!

Lovoni Walker and Ashley Brooks for adding even more glorious photography.

Irena Shnayder for making sure that all the recipes would come out perfectly.

Kelsey Curtis and her team at DK and Marika Flatt and her team at PR by the Book for helping to make this cookbook a success.

To all my sweet friends around the world who I have been blessed to get to know through Mary's Nest. You made this possible, and I will always be eternally grateful for the love and support you have shown me throughout the years. I look forward to continuing our traditional foods journey together in the many years to come!

And to the dear Lord above, thank you for all the gifts you have given me—my life, my family, the knowledge to write this book, and the opportunity to share my talents to help others.

THANK YOU, ALL!
Love and God bless,
Mary

Table of Contents

ABOUT THE AUTHOR

Mary Shrader is the founder of the Mary's Nest website and the popular *Mary's Nest* YouTube channel. With over 40 million views and counting, her in-depth videos teach traditional cooking skills to those longing to be modern pioneers. Her detailed recipes provide step-by-step instructions on how to make nutrient-dense foods, including bone broth, cultured dairy, ferments, and sourdough. She also shares a video series showing how to stock a pantry with a wide variety of homemade staples.

Mary learned how to make traditional foods from her loving and patient mother, who was skilled in all the gentle domestic arts. Eventually, when Mary married and became a mom, she discovered her passion for teaching other moms how to make traditional foods. Twenty years ago, she started sharing simple lessons as moms and nursing babies gathered around her kitchen island. Then in 2018, she launched her YouTube video channel and discovered that hundreds of thousands of people worldwide longed to learn how to become modern pioneers and make traditional foods!

Through her gentle and encouraging manner, Mary shows how anyone can begin their traditional foods journey and become a modern pioneer in the kitchen by creating nutritious and delicious foods. She shares traditional recipes with whole ingredients that make use of every last kitchen scrap, with the goal of creating a no-waste kitchen, just like our ancestors.

Mary lives in the Texas Hill Country outside of Austin with her sweet husband, Ted, and their lovable yellow lab, Indy. Their son, Ben, is just a drive away and often visits for holiday celebrations, board games, and cozy family meals by the kitchen fireplace.

Find out more about Mary at marysnest.com and @MarysNest.

INTRODUCTION

Greetings, sweet friend, and welcome to The Modern Pioneer Cookbook!

As you work your way through this book, I will be with you every step of the way, teaching you how to become a modern pioneer in the kitchen as you learn to make traditional foods, just like our ancestors.

Let me reassure you. Learning to make traditional foods is not a daunting task. It's actually quite easy and very achievable, even for those completely new to cooking. Nothing in this cookbook is difficult to make. Much of the work is often simply done by time. And it's not time on your part. It's time on nature's part with a little help from a stovetop or oven.

And rest assured, none of the ingredients used to make the recipes in this cookbook are going to bust your grocery budget. It's just the opposite, in fact. I am going to show you how to make real traditional foods while also making use of every scrap of food you have and come as close as possible to creating a no-waste kitchen. Over time, you are going to find you are actually saving money, buying less processed or prepackaged food, and learning to make most foods homemade.

Now chances are if you picked up this book based on the title, you might have some ideas of what traditional foods are. When we think of the pioneers, foods that often come to mind are biscuits, beans, cornbread, lard, pumpkin, sourdough bread, simple broths made from scraps of meat and bones, and foraged wild greens, as well as poultry and meat roasted on the bone. Those are, in fact, foods they did eat. But they ate a lot of other foods, as well. What all the foods they ate had in common was that they were prepared in a traditional way, which is the best way that food can be prepared to extract the maximum amount of nutrition.

Unfortunately, today, when we look at modern recipes for traditional foods, the actual traditional ways in which they were originally prepared are often stripped from the recipes. This is basically done for the convenience of modern cooks who have a grocery store and electrical appliances at their disposal. However, these more modern recipes often contain an extensive list of ingredients and require more involved preparation than how our ancestors would have made the original versions.

Take bread, for example. Our ancestors often had little time to spend on tasks like kneading bread. Instead, they let their sourdough starter (and time) do the kneading for them. All they did was spend a few minutes to shape their loaf and then bake it. And it was a much better tasting bread than any bread that was excessively kneaded. But don't worry if you have never made bread. And if you are concerned about jumping right into making sourdough, don't worry. I start you out with baking a yeast-based sandwich bread, which I promise will be the easiest bread you will ever make. And it's no-knead, too!

In this book, you'll begin learning basic skills by roasting a whole chicken. For me, learning how to be a traditional foods cook started with learning how to make a roast chicken. Once you are comfortable with that skill, you'll feel empowered and ready to forge ahead and learn how to make more traditional foods.

Together, we'll make bone broths, yogurt (no machine required), kefir, ginger "bug" and homemade ginger ale, sauerkraut, foolproof sourdough starter, no-knead sourdough bread, and more. I'll even teach you how to become a home canner. And that's just the beginning. I have a rich and diverse assortment of recipes to share with you!

One of my main goals, since I started teaching these traditional cooking skills to others over 20 years ago, was not only to keep traditional cooking methods alive but to empower others to become more self-sufficient by showing them how to make and eat nutritious real food that would sustain them through the seasons. As you work your way through the chapters that follow, I wish the same for you. My hope is that this book will be your road map, in essence, to creating a traditional foods kitchen—a reference book that you can turn to time and time again as a resource for traditional cooking wisdom.

I'm so happy we are on this traditional foods journey together. Here's to self-sufficiency and becoming modern pioneers in the kitchen!

Love and God bless,
Mary

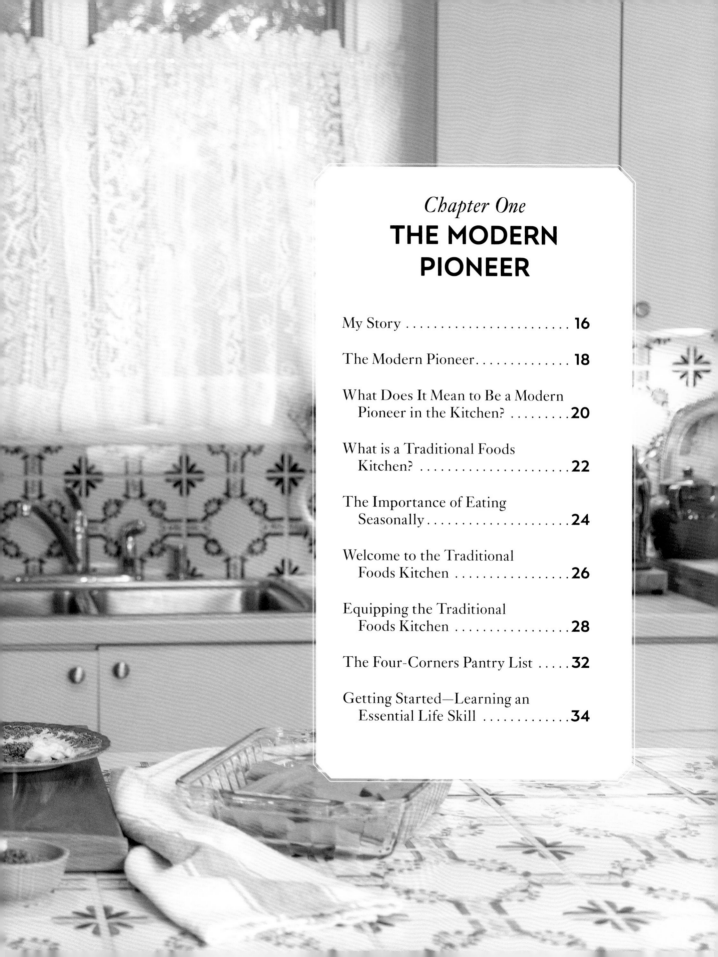

Chapter One
THE MODERN PIONEER

MY STORY

My journey learning how to make traditional foods started many years ago and continues to this day. I started learning how to cook at a very young age, but it wasn't all about white flour and lots of sugar. My mother, who is currently in her late nineties, is fond of repeating the popular saying: you are what you eat! She believed in buying real foods, as close to their natural state as possible, and then preparing them in a way to maximize their nutrition. My father and mother lived through the Great Depression of the 1930s and World War II. They knew hard times, but they always persevered. My mom was not about to let the long stressful days the world threw at us take over our lives and defeat us! She turned her back on the conveniences of the ever-growing selection of packaged foods offered in the many aisles at the ever-growing-in-size grocery store chains. She knew better. Those foods would not nourish us mentally or physically or help us cope with the ever-greater demands of a modern society. We needed real food, properly prepared, making it as nutritious

as possible, just as our ancestors had before us. And I learned everything I could from her while she created our traditional foods kitchen. By the time I was a teenager, I had become more proficient at what my mother referred to as "the gentle arts of domesticity," with home cooking being at the forefront. I loved to bake, and I also enjoyed preparing dinner for my parents.

I'm originally from New York and have lived and worked in New York City and Washington, D.C. As a young single woman, Saturdays and Sundays often found me cooking in my little New York City apartment kitchen and then later in my Alexandria, Virginia, townhouse kitchen. Oh how I loved that kitchen in my townhouse! It seemed massive to me compared to what I had been used to. I went from a sliver of a kitchen to one that could actually accommodate a small table and two chairs! I was regularly calling friends and neighbors to come over and eat a roast chicken with all the fixins'. And it was that roast chicken, thanks to a carcass with which I could make bone broth, that would sustain me throughout the week in the form of lots of homemade soups.

So how exactly did this former New Yorker wind up in Texas? It all started the day after I walked away from a near-fatal car crash. I was driving home from work on a rainy night when a teenager ran a stop sign and plowed into me at full speed. Amazingly, I was unharmed. My car, on the other hand, was not. It may sound a bit crazy, but as I sat on the curb in the rain waiting for the tow truck to arrive, I decided it was time for a much-needed change. It was right around Christmas, and by the new year, my East Coast home went up for sale. Soon after, my furniture went into storage, the dogs were loaded into my car, and together we headed west to Texas, eventually settling in Austin. Then something wonderful happened to me ... something quite serendipitous! One day while traveling, I met a charming man—10 years my junior —at the airport. He swept me off my feet, we married, and 9 months later we were blessed with one of our greatest joys— a healthy and happy baby boy!

Rather suddenly, I now found myself in my early forties, a new wife and mother, and living in an old-but-charming white stone house nestled amongst the bluebonnet-covered rolling hills and peaceful lakes of the Texas Hill Country. Once our son was born, I was determined to feed my sweet little family the same nutritious home-cooked food my mom had served me and my dad. So I rolled up my sleeves and got to work, implementing all my mom had taught me by cooking from scratch, just like her and our ancestors. I was roasting meats on the bone and whole chickens, making bone broth and homemade yogurt, fermenting an assortment of vegetables, baking sourdough bread, and home canning jams, pickles, and tomatoes. I was beginning my journey to become a modern pioneer in the kitchen! My parents lived about 5 minutes from us, and so my mom would stop by to see how I was progressing. She approved. Truth be told, she was thrilled I had returned to the gentle arts of domesticity!

Eventually, I developed a nice social circle of younger moms who enjoyed home cooking and whose interests were piqued by how I appeared to make everything homemade. And not just homemade. They were fascinated with the unique ways that I prepared food. I would tell them that this is the proper way to prepare food for maximum nutritional absorption. I guess I sounded a little bit like a schoolmarm, but I assured them that everything was tasty, too!

Before I knew it, Saturday mornings found my kitchen filled with moms and their nursing babies. We were a group of suburban ladies becoming modern pioneers in the kitchen, learning how to properly prepare real foods throughout the seasons just like our ancestors did. As a result, my Mary's Nest Cooking School, as I affectionately called it, was born, and I soon found myself traveling to other moms' homes on Saturday mornings, teaching traditional cooking skills.

In time, my husband and son encouraged me to put my traditional cooking classes online so that I could reach and teach a broader audience. With their support, I forged ahead and started a YouTube channel, *Mary's Nest*, where I focus on teaching traditional cooking for the modern pioneer. As of this writing, my channel has grown to over 850,000 subscribers (and counting!), who are excited to learn how to make traditional foods. And best of all, I'm so happy to bring the world of traditional foods to you through this book.

THE MODERN PIONEER

Often when we hear the term *modern pioneer*, we think of people who leave city life behind and set up an off-grid homestead in the wilderness. Or maybe we think of individuals who are innovators, bringing new technologies to the forefront. Being one of these modern pioneers might not be attainable for most of us, but there is a facet of modern pioneering that most of us can experience, and that is becoming modern pioneers in the kitchen.

We live in a very fast-paced world that runs on internet time. And since so many of us are often in a perpetual state of rushing around, it can be easy today to find ourselves reaching for expensive, preservative-laden packaged convenience foods at the grocery store or running through the drive-thru line at a fast-food restaurant. If at times we feel overwhelmed with life, it's certainly understandable. In many ways, having a stress-filled life is nothing new. I can remember my father feeling overwhelmed at times about what he called the "rat race." His days consisted of very early mornings commuting into New York City by train and then a long walk, encompassing many city blocks, to the office where he worked, no matter what the weather was like. During the winter months, he often referred to his long walks as "bone chilling." There was even a comedian who made a joke about it all. When asked how the rat race was going, he responded, "The rats are winning!" However, we can still slow down, at least in the kitchen, when it comes to preparing our meals. We can learn from our ancestors and follow in their footsteps to simplify mealtime by preparing foods in traditional ways.

We may lead busy lives, but our ancestors were busy too. They had none of the modern conveniences we have, so their days were often filled with hard physical labor from sunup to sundown. But they had to eat. Yes, making traditional foods takes time, but it is often simply just that—time. With traditional techniques, time does much of the work for you, so there is not much additional work on your part. Bone broth will simmer for hours, sourdough takes time to rise, vegetables take days to ferment, dairy often takes a day or more to culture, and whole chickens roast slowly.

That's okay! Because once you take a few minutes to set the preparation of these traditional foods in motion, you can move on to other tasks. Maybe that task is simply sitting down, taking a deep breath, and basking in the knowledge that you are making wholesome and nutritious foods that are considerably more nutrient-rich and more affordable than anything you can buy. By starting out with real food ingredients and their proper preparations, you'll know that you are able to make a complete and nutritious meal that honors your traditional foods kitchen.

There are certainly times when many of us get that itch to ditch the fast-paced life and dream about being a real modern pioneer, to buy some land and move off-grid, away from it all. It can be fun to fantasize about this, but living off-grid can have its stresses too! That doesn't mean we can't be modern pioneers in our own homes. We can be modern pioneers in the kitchen by doing as our ancestors did and properly preparing real food in simple ways that flow with the seasons. Our ancestors knew that meat cooked with the skin on and the bone in was where it was at, nutritionally. And it still is. We're going to prepare real food, including roasting whole chickens, making bone broths, rendering animal fats, making cultured dairy, naturally fermenting vegetables, and getting the bubbliest sourdough starter going to make sourdough bread. I'm also going to share with you how easy it is to become a home canner, starting with the basics of water bath canning. Before you know it, you'll be making traditional foods with ease and stocking your pantry with an assortment of nourishing and tasty homemade foods. You'll save time and money, and eat better in the process!

Most of us have a kitchen, even if it's not much more than a sink and a hot plate in a college dorm room. No matter what your situation, you can still learn the skills necessary to make traditional foods. These are skills you will carry with you for a lifetime. And hopefully you'll carry them into slightly bigger and better kitchens in time. But no matter the state of our kitchens, we will awaken our modern pioneer spirits and bring back to life the cooking traditions of the many generations of people who came before us. We'll be modern pioneers … if only just in the kitchen!

WHAT DOES IT MEAN TO BE A MODERN PIONEER IN THE KITCHEN?

To be a modern pioneer in the kitchen means to bring back those traditional kitchen skills that our ancestors used as a matter of common everyday practice. They ran what we call today a *traditional foods kitchen*. They used every scrap of food at their disposal, cooking *nose to tail* and never wasting. Cooking this way was all part of the daily or seasonal rhythms of their kitchens. They were as self-sufficient as they could be while properly preparing traditional foods with care so as to extract the maximum amount of nutrition possible from every last bit of food.

The key word in being a modern pioneer in the kitchen is "modern." Although my friends and I create foods like those our ancestors made, we are blessed with the conveniences of the twenty-first century. None of us live off-grid, and we are grateful for the luxuries of modern appliances, electricity, and kitchen sinks with running water! We also have the luxury of being able to shop at local grocery stores and farmers' markets. But the foods we bring into our kitchens should be as close as possible to the foods our ancestors brought into their kitchens. We shop for real food that is as close to its natural state as possible and as free of chemicals and preservatives as possible. Your ultimate goal as you embark on this journey will be to search out meat on the bone, whole chickens, fresh fruits and vegetables, whole grains, dry beans, and milk that is as unadulterated as possible.

Initially, bringing some of these foods into your kitchen may seem a bit unfamiliar, almost intimidating. But not to worry! You will be creating a kitchen rhythm. As a modern pioneer in the kitchen, you will begin to develop a system of soaking your beans or grains before going to bed, feeding your sourdough starter, leaving your milk out on the counter to culture, and "burping" your jars of vegetable ferments as they bubble away in a corner of your kitchen. Before you know it, you will find that it's all actually quite easy to do. It will become quite familiar and comforting to know that you are properly preparing real food. You control the ingredients, creating food that is not only nutritious, but rich in flavor—so much more than anything you can buy that has been commercially prepared for you.

Anyone can be a modern pioneer in the kitchen. It doesn't matter where you live. You can be a city dweller, a suburbanite, or actually live in the country. You can be heading off to a weekday 9-to-5 job or working in the home while also homeschooling six children. You may make a quart of bone broth once per week or 6 quarts every day. It doesn't matter. You can have a little windowsill garden growing a few herbs and cherry tomatoes or a quarter-acre garden with a whole variety of fruits and veggies. You can have a hundred jars of home-canned food in your pantry or just six small jars of home-canned strawberry jam. All that matters is your desire and can-do spirit to begin your journey to becoming a modern pioneer in the kitchen!

And this journey is not to be rushed, but instead, should be taken one step at time. Learning these time-honored skills at your own pace is the secret to success.

WHAT WE CAN LEARN FROM OUR ANCESTORS

Learning to be self-sufficient in the kitchen is more important than ever. We want to learn everything we can from our ancestors so we can implement these skills in our own daily kitchen routines. We may not be raising our own animals, and many of us might not even have a garden—although I recommend that you start one, even if it's on a windowsill—but we can still create a self-sufficient traditional foods kitchen. The common expression of living paycheck to paycheck can, in a way, be modified and applied to our pantries. Does your pantry only hold a week or two worth of food? If you couldn't go shopping, would it be completely bare at the end of the month? This is the antithesis of running a traditional foods kitchen.

If you want to be self-sufficient and create a traditional foods kitchen, you'll want to look to what generations before us did. They ate fresh food in season, stored whole grains and beans, and preserved other foods through culturing or fermentation for times when fresh food was no longer in season or in short supply. This was especially important when food was scarce. They would not starve because they planned ahead and could turn to their stored food when in need. Sourdough bread could be baked from whole grains and served with cultured butter. Beans mixed with dried vegetables could be turned into a nourishing soup. Together, this humble meal would keep families well fed.

WHAT IS A TRADITIONAL FOODS KITCHEN?

The traditional foods kitchen is many things. But how is it different than today's modern kitchen?

The Processed Foods Kitchen

Before we can even address what is a traditional foods kitchen, we need to take a minute to talk about what I call a *processed foods kitchen*. A processed foods kitchen is where most of the food has been purchased from a grocery store in a packaged or preprepared form. This includes the variety of shelf-stable boxed dinners, as well as frozen dinners, boxed rice and grain dishes with seasoning packets, boxed cereals, bottled salad dressings and other condiments, packaged crackers and cookies, and basically pretty much anything that is sold in the interior of your local grocery store. These packaged foods are often loaded with chemicals and preservatives, with names most of us can't pronounce. And I think I can say with certainty that these packaged foods contain ingredients like mold inhibitors that our ancestors were not adding to their traditionally prepared foods.

Why would we even want mold inhibitors in our bread? Or in any of our other food, for that matter? We want our food to be free of preservatives so that it can naturally go stale or spoil. Now, we wouldn't eat any spoiled food, however, the fact that it can start to break down indicates that we have real food that has not been commercially tampered with to last. We want to enjoy our real food while it is fresh. The modern ways of increasing the shelf life of food, such as pasteurization or the addition of chemical and preservative enhancements, often involves decreasing its nutritional value. Our ancestors knew to eat certain foods fresh and in season, before they spoiled. But they also knew how to preserve food in ways to increase its nutritional value and extend its shelf life. This provided them with nutritious food throughout the seasons, when fresh food may not have been available.

The Traditional Foods Kitchen

Now that we understand what a processed foods kitchen is, it's easy to differentiate this from a traditional foods kitchen. A traditional foods kitchen is one in which we make most of our foods homemade using whole, real food ingredients. And we properly prepare these foods using time-honored methods, including slow roasting, simmering, culturing, fermenting, and souring. When real foods are properly prepared in these ways, we maximize their nutritional profiles and make those nutrients easier for our digestive tracts to absorb.

Take sauerkraut, for example. You can easily preserve this food through fermentation. But fermenting cabbage does much more than simply preserve it. When you ferment cabbage to make sauerkraut, you preserve the cabbage and also create a food that is rich in probiotics, which are the beneficial bacteria that keep our digestive systems healthy. Additionally, fermentation also increases sauerkraut's nutritional profile.

Sauerkraut, which our ancestors would have consumed during the winter months, is much richer in vitamin C than fresh cabbage. It is vitamin C that can often be lacking in one's diet when certain fresh fruits and vegetables are not available. Since the human body does not make its own vitamin C, we need to rely on getting it from foods in our diet, since this vitamin plays an important role in maintaining good health and contributing to the body's healing process. Sauerkraut is an outstanding example of a traditionally prepared food.

Creating a traditional foods kitchen goes beyond making properly prepared homemade foods. As home cooks, we also want to use every available scrap of food and never waste, always striving toward creating a low-waste or even a no-waste kitchen. All real food has nutritional benefits and we want to extract every last bit! So as you make the recipes throughout these coming chapters, I will occasionally remind you to save whatever little bits and bobs that might be leftover. I'll then share how to use those scraps for adding to bone broths or making other traditional foods. Before you know it, you'll be looking at every piece of food twice before tossing it into the garbage or the compost pile.

Multiple Streams of Food for the Traditional Foods Kitchen

Our ancestors had what I call "multiple streams of food," which means they had enough food in various forms to see them through difficult times. For example, they may have purchased some foods from the general store, but they also raised or grew and then preserved a lot of their food. For the modern pioneer creating a traditional foods kitchen, these foods can include those you buy and also those you make. You'll want to stock a variety of foods and make sure that you build up a supply of food that can last you more than a few weeks. We can do this by stocking up, little by little, on limited ingredient canned foods, as well as dried foods from our local grocery store, while also preserving fresh food which we grow or buy, through dehydration and fermentation, as well as home canning. When we stock different types of food, we create our own multiple streams of food. We may have dried beans, which can be purchased in bulk (most likely at a discount) and will store well, but we also have canned beans that are extremely convenient for those times when we forget to soak our dried beans. No matter what, if you run out of one type of bean, you will have the other. Having multiple streams of food is like having an insurance policy of food. You are always prepared, won't run out, and no one will go hungry.

The difficult times we are experiencing today might be different from what our ancestors went through, but if we learned anything from the year 2020 and its aftershocks, we need to be prepared for whatever might come our way. However, being prepared doesn't mean stocking up on a lot of junk food. As modern pioneers in the kitchen, being prepared means that we create a traditional foods kitchen in which we stock real food that has been or can be properly prepared to provide us with significant nutrition and not just empty calories.

THE IMPORTANCE OF EATING SEASONALLY

One of the most important things we can learn from our ancestors is how they properly prepared food while also eating with the seasons. There was no running out to the store and buying strawberries in the middle of winter! If we truly want to eat the way our ancestors did, by consuming properly prepared traditional foods, we want to eat them in season.

Finding Foods in Season

It's easy to find what foods are in season on the internet or from your local agriculture-extension service, but there is an even better way. For fresh produce, pay attention to what is in abundance at your grocery store from your local region. This abundant food will most likely be more reasonably priced compared to other produce. And this food is likely to be what is in season. You will notice this seasonal pattern clearly when it comes to fresh fruits and vegetables, but other areas of the grocery store that sell fresh food offer clues too. If you look closely at what the fishmonger has to sell, you will notice that some fish is sold fresh and not "previously frozen" at certain times of the year (usually during the summer months), and that's usually what is in season. Pastured beef, on the other hand, will be in abundance and the most reasonably priced in the fall, usually starting around October. Taking the time to heed these seasonal rhythms is an important first step to creating a traditional foods kitchen.

Properly Preparing Seasonal Foods

Not only is there a seasonal pattern to raising and growing food, there is also a seasonal pattern to preparing many traditional foods. Food needs to be properly prepared so that you can not only digest your food, but so you can absorb all its nutrients. Beans are best soaked and sprouted at certain times of the year, dairy is best cultured during warmer months, and most fresh vegetables are best fermented during the fall season. Following the seasonal rhythms of traditional food preparation will ensure that you have success when making these foods by maximizing their nutritional impact, while at the same time avoiding failed attempts. When we look to how our ancestors prepared their foods and follow their wisdom, it's then that we will have the most success. Does this mean that you can't make homemade yogurt or ferment foods in the winter? Not at all. As modern pioneers in the kitchen, most of us are blessed with modern appliances and temperature-controlled homes. However, even minor fluctuations in temperature can affect the preparation of traditional foods. Following in the footsteps of our ancestors and trying to do things as close as possible to the seasonal rhythms that they followed will help ensure that the foods turn out how we want them to turn out. With time and experience, you will learn when and where foods are best prepared. You will discover the times of year that certain foods just seem to naturally be easier to make. You'll find that exact spot in your kitchen where ferments do best or where your newly fed sourdough starter likes to hang out when it's not in the refrigerator. Over time, this knowledge you develop will prove invaluable. It's all part of the process of creating your traditional foods kitchen.

By following this seasonal rhythm of food preparation, you will be rewarded with rich and gelatinous bone broths, bubbling ferments, silky-smooth homemade yogurt, sourdough bread that rises without commercially packaged yeast, and so much more.

Eating with the seasons might also prove to have another benefit. There are scientific studies that indicate that the microbiome in our digestive systems may change ever so slightly with the seasons. This means that the beneficial or good bacteria in our "gut" might actually adjust to digest certain foods—foods in season—at certain times of year. It's fascinating and something worth further study, but it's certainly another reason to focus on properly preparing our food and eating it in season!

STAYING ON BUDGET

Eating properly prepared foods in season brings us to another important element of creating a traditional foods kitchen: staying within your grocery budget and not overspending! When we eat seasonally, this is certainly easier to do. Food in season will cost less than when it is out of season.

Do not stress yourself over the food you buy. One of the main points in creating a traditional foods kitchen is to eat nutritiously to improve our health. But overspending only causes stress, and stress hurts our health. Buy what you can afford. Can you afford pasture-raised, grass-fed, organic, local, and all that, and more? If so, great. But if you can't, don't worry; just buy the best real food you can.

My mother is of Italian heritage, and she refers to traditional cooking as simply "home cooking" or *la cucina povera*, which loosely translates to the cooking of the poor or peasant cooking. But there is nothing poor about these delicious foods prepared for centuries by traditional cultures. Today, many of the foods served at fancy restaurants are the product of peasant cooking from all over the world. These foods have become quite fashionable! The good news for those of us who strive to create a traditional foods kitchen is that it is a budget-friendly process. We will be creating our own la cucina povera, but there won't be anything poor or lacking about it. We will be preparing and cooking the food of our ancestors that is extremely nutritious and delicious too!

WELCOME TO THE TRADITIONAL FOODS KITCHEN

As a modern pioneer in the kitchen, you are beginning a journey in which you will be transitioning away from a processed foods kitchen and heading toward creating a traditional foods kitchen. It's a journey that is not to be rushed, but is one that should be taken one step at time. Taking your time to learn these time-honored skills is the secret to success.

Embracing Trial and Error

When it comes to creating a traditional foods kitchen, one of the best skills you will learn is to embrace trial and error! If you are accustomed to buying most foods preprepared or packaged from your local grocery store, you need to be prepared to make a mistake ... or two. But that's okay. It's part of the learning curve. (I am fond of saying that traditional foods can sometimes be persnickety!)

Traditional foods are homemade, and whenever you are making something that isn't produced under standard factory conditions, there is always the possibility for error. But don't throw in the proverbial kitchen towel! Keep trying. I promise that each time you try to make a food that is new to you, you will learn something new about the process, your skills will improve, and so will your outcomes. By your second try, things might be turning out quite nicely. And by your third try, I'm confident you will be pleased with your results, whether you are making bone broth, a ferment, or sourdough bread. It's all about trial and error.

The Low-Waste/No-Waste Kitchen

"Waste not, want not" may be an old saying, but it has become a mantra of our century. Or at least it should be. We should all strive to create as little waste as possible. A low-waste kitchen is definitely achievable. And a no-waste kitchen can certainly be a goal to eventually reach for.

You should always do your best to never throw out food. Food is an expensive commodity, especially these days. And if you are going to stay within your grocery budget, you are going to have to stop throwing food into the trash. Those of us living in industrial societies throw out considerably more food than those who still live in traditional cultures. Much like the early pioneers, the traditional cultures that still exist today rarely waste food. Food is not abundant for them, so every last scrap must be eaten. It's our responsibility as modern pioneers in the kitchen to look at food, especially scraps of food, in a new light.

Every time you toss something in the trash, pause and ask yourself if it can be added to one of your "scrap bags," used in a soup or a stew, sprinkled over a salad, or used to make bread crumbs or croutons. Try to train yourself at doing this. It can almost become a little bit of a game to challenge yourself to see how little you can actually put in your garbage can, recycling bin, or compost pile.

Using Scrap Bags

The concept of creating scrap bags may be new to you, but this is one of the best ways to ensure that you stop wasting food. A scrap bag, from a kitchen perspective, as the name implies, is just that—a bag that holds scraps of food. There are a number of ways you can do this. You can use a freezer-safe plastic bag or you can use a freezer-safe container. My preference is actually a combination of the two. I like to line a freezerproof container with a plastic bag. I do this only because it helps me have a defined shape that is easy to store and find in my freezer.

The reason I like to have a definitive shape and size is because I like to have a place for everything and everything in its place. A little compulsive? Maybe. But trust me—the more organized you can be when running a traditional foods kitchen, the better. I fear that if I start throwing a bunch of bags filled with scraps into my freezer, I will forget what I have. Not to mention that the bags will freeze in odd shapes and take up too much precious room needed for other things. If I just throw bags of scraps into my freezer, they may be hard to identify and possibly forgotten. The last thing I want to do is be well intentioned and save my scraps, only to discover them freezer burned a year later and I then have to toss them into the compost pile or—worst-case scenario—the trash!

When it comes to saving scraps, I have a variety of scrap bags. My first scrap bag holds chicken carcasses, along with any chicken scraps; another holds vegetable scraps, including such things as carrot peelings and onion skins; and a third usually holds bits and bobs of stale bread. Also, if you are in the habit of eating a lot of meat on the bone, a scrap bag to save used beef bones can also come in very handy. In time, you might find you have one full area of your freezer devoted to scraps. But this is a great thing because you will find yourself grabbing for those scraps regularly to make all kinds of things, sometimes even full meals!

Keeping a Kitchen Journal

This brings us to the usefulness of keeping a kitchen journal. Your kitchen journal can be as simple as a spiral notebook or as fancy as a three-ring binder. What matters is that as you begin your journey of transitioning away from a processed foods kitchen and begin making traditional foods, you will want to take notes. Copious notes. These notes will guide you each time you return to making a particular traditional food.

For example, if you are making a sourdough starter for the first time, you'll want to include details like what ingredients you used, what time of year it was when you made it, what the weather was like outside, the approximate temperature in your kitchen, the temperature of the area where you decided to let your starter rest, how often and how much you fed your starter, and when you began to see it bubble. All of these notes will increase your level of success each and every time you make a traditional food. And I will be here with a host of tips and tricks to keep your period of trial and error to a minimum.

EQUIPPING THE TRADITIONAL FOODS KITCHEN

Chances are if you have some semblance of a kitchen with a few kitchen tools and a few pieces of equipment, you are probably pretty well-equipped to prepare traditional foods. Our ancestors didn't have kitchens packed full of gadgets that were rarely used. Every kitchen tool served a purpose. And you will find that your kitchen will become the same way. You will turn time and time again to your tried-and-true-friends: a cast-iron skillet or Dutch oven, a stockpot, a large bowl, a few glass jars, and a wooden spoon are some of the essential kitchen equipment and tools you'll need to get started.

Essential Equipment and Tools

As a modern pioneer in the kitchen, there are a few pieces of kitchen equipment and tools that you will want to keep on hand to make preparing traditional foods as easy as possible. But there is something else that you'll need. It's a necessary fashion item that no proclaimed traditional foods cook would be without. And that's an apron! It will put you in the modern pioneering frame of mind, and you will suddenly find that you can tackle any job in the kitchen. To me, it is the equivalent of a superhero's cape! Now that we've got that covered, let's move on to the list of kitchen equipment and tools that will help you out. Put on your apron and read on.

Chef's Knife

A high-quality chef's knife will prove invaluable in your kitchen. It does not need to be expensive, but it should have what is called a *full tang*, which means the blade runs all the way up through the handle of the knife. This makes for a secure, well-balanced knife.

I recommend that you shop for your chef's knife in person so that you can find a knife that fits nicely into your hand and feels well balanced. For example, I have a small hand and have found that a chef's knife with a 7- to 8-inch (18 to 20cm) blade is the perfect size for me. Anything longer is hard for me to control. If I had not shopped for my knife in person, I would have not discovered this.

Large Cutting Board

If you are buying a cutting board for the first time, buy a large one. You can add smaller ones in time for various specialized tasks, but starting out with a nice large board will provide you with sufficient workspace.

Like your chef's knife, cutting boards do not have to be expensive. Certainly having a maple cutting board would be wonderful; however, today many are made from bamboo, which holds up quite well. Plus, bamboo is often considered an invasive plant that can crowd out native plants, which harms biodiversity. Cutting down bamboo and being able to turn it into something useful, such as a cutting board, helps control its spread.

Glass Mixing Bowls

You should have two mixing bowls: one large and one medium, and they should be glass, preferably. Mixing bowls serve so many purposes in your kitchen, from their obvious uses like mixing bread dough and other batters, to making homemade yogurt and straining bone broth. I prefer glass because it is clear as well as nonreactive, meaning that it does not react with any type of food. Stainless steel bowls and pottery bowls are also an option. In the case of pottery bowls, make sure they are lead free. (Lead testing kits are affordable and readily available online.)

10- to 12-inch Cast-Iron Skillet

No modern pioneer in the kitchen worth their salt would be without a cast-iron skillet! A well-seasoned cast-iron skillet will serve as a workhorse in your kitchen. You can use it in place of a roasting pan and use it to cook a variety of foods, from simple eggs to a skillet apple pie. You can also use your cast-iron skillet to bake bread.

SEASONING A CAST-IRON SKILLET

"Seasoning" means a cast-iron pan has developed a coating that makes it basically nonstick. Today, many cast-iron pans are sold preseasoned, but if you are blessed to find a high-quality cast-iron pan at a garage sale or thrift store, you might need to clean it up and reseason it.

To reseason a cast-iron skillet, use a steel wool pad to remove any rust and then wash the skillet well. Once washed, dry it and then very lightly smear it inside and out with bacon grease. Next, place the skillet upside down on the middle rack in a 450°F (232°C) preheated oven and leave it in there for about 1 hour. (To make sure that none of the bacon grease drips down to the bottom of the oven, place some aluminum foil on the lower rack of the oven.) After 1 hour, turn off the heat and let the skillet cool in the oven. Once cool, wipe off any bacon grease residue. It is now ready to store away or use. Over time, as you cook with your skillet, the seasoning will become stronger and stronger. I often use my cast-iron skillet to cook bacon. Trust me: once you start cooking bacon in a cast-iron skillet, it will develop a wonderful nonstick coating!

6- to 8-quart Large Dutch Oven (Cast Iron or Enameled Cast Iron)

A regular Dutch oven is a great addition to the traditional foods kitchen, and enameled cast iron is usually my first choice because it is nonreactive with all foods. It will last you a lifetime as well as the lifetime of future generations!

A plain cast-iron Dutch oven will generally be much more affordable and will also last a lifetime. However, if you decide to go with plain cast iron, I recommend a cast-iron "combo cooker." This combo cooker is a great option if you want to forgo buying a separate cast-iron skillet and a Dutch oven. This cooker is a 2-in-1 pan in that it is a Dutch oven with a lid that when turned upside down actually serves as a cast-iron skillet!

Half-Size Sheet Pan

A half-size sheet pan, or what some call a *baking sheet* or *jelly roll pan,* is an aluminum or stainless steel pan with a rim, and measures approximately 18 x 13 inches (46 x 33cm). This multipurpose pan can stand in for a traditional roasting pan. You can use this pan to cook a spatchcocked chicken, to roast vegetables, to bake cookies, or to make croutons, and it comes in handy for roasting bones when making bone broth.

Stockpots

You'll want to have two stockpots on hand. They should be enameled or stainless steel, and you'll want to have one large pot (at least 10 quarts) and one medium pot (approximately 6 to 7 quarts).

Although a large Dutch oven can stand in for a stock pot, eventually add at least one large stockpot to your kitchen equipment—it will be the perfect vessel for making bone broth. It can also stand in as a water bath canner if you do not have one. Having a second stockpot works well when you need to strain bone broth from one stockpot to another. And a medium-size stockpot is often easier to fit into a refrigerator with the strained bone broth for chilling.

Spider Strainer

A spider strainer is the perfect tool for lifting out bones and vegetables before straining bone broth. A slotted spoon or mesh strainer could certainly work in a pinch, but once you start using a spider strainer, it will be hard to use anything else. Plus, these are very reasonably priced, which makes them easy to add to your kitchen tool collection.

Colander or Mesh Strainer

If you have a mesh strainer, it can stand in for a colander but you might find that a colander will be handier when draining certain foods like pasta. Pasta can easily get caught in a mesh strainer and be quite a job to clean. But you will never run into that problem with a colander. Also, a colander lined with a flour-sack towel makes straining bone broth a breeze. More importantly, a colander is indispensable when sprouting grains or beans.

Assorted-Size Canning Jars with Canning Lids, Bands (Rings), and Reusable Storage Lids

These jars will not only serve the purpose of home canning, but will also serve as a place to house your sourdough starter, as well as leftovers in your fridge. They are also the main vessels for fermentation. Most fermentation recipes in this book will call for using a half-gallon jar or two quart-size jars, plus a small 4-ounce jar to use as a weight. You can certainly use any jars you have on hand for fermentation, but a selection of canning jars can serve multiple purposes. Jars collected from grocery store items might be fine for storing leftovers, but they shouldn't be used for home canning.

If you are a novice to home canning, canning lids and canning bands (sometimes called *rings*), might be something new to you. These are often sold along with canning jars or separately in boxed sets in the canning section of your local grocery store or kitchen store. If you take good care of your canning jars, they should last you quite a long time. Canning rings can be used over and over again, but if you find that you like home canning, you will need to stock a large supply of canning lids since they can't be reused.

Reusable storage lids are also made to fit canning jars once the canning lid and ring has been removed. They are also perfect to use with your jars when making ferments or storing your sourdough starter.

Flour-Sack Towels

Flour-sack towels come in handy for many uses, but my favorite way to use them is when straining bone broth. They are great at catching all those little bits of debris that, once filtered out of your bone broth, make for a simple clarified liquid that can be used in any way you like, including as a sipping broth or in place of water when cooking grains. You can certainly stock cheesecloth instead of flour-sack towels, but cheesecloth disintegrates after a few uses and needs to be discarded. A flour-sack towel, on the other hand, is easy to rinse out and wash along with your other dish towels.

Kraut Pounder

This is a wooden tool used to compress your ferments once they are in a jar. Technically, this could be categorized as an "extra" as opposed to an essential, but if you decide to make a lot of vegetable ferments, this will make your life so much easier! You can certainly use a wooden spoon to do this, but a kraut pounder is more efficient.

Other Essential Equipment to Have on Hand

- Food-safe, sealable, freezerproof bags and plastic containers
- Kitchen twine
- Ladle
- Loaf pans, various sizes
- Measuring cups for both wet and dry ingredients
- Measuring spoons
- Microplane grater or box grater
- Parchment paper
- Spatula
- Spoonula (a cross between a spoon and a spatula)
- Whisk
- Wooden spoon

Nice Equipment to Have (as Your Budget Allows)

As time goes by and you build your traditional cooking skills, there may be equipment or appliances that you'll want to add to your kitchen. What you decide to add will be based on what types of traditional foods you find you are making the most and which of those need a little extra help to prepare.

Equipment:

- Cake and pie pans
- Candy thermometer (for checking liquid temperatures)
- Fat separator
- Fermentation crock
- Food mill
- Meat mallet/hammer
- Meat thermometer
- Ovenproof glass baking dishes
- Pastry brush
- pH strips
- Roasting pan with rack, large
- Rolling pin
- Splatter screen

Appliances:

- Blender (standard, high powered, or immersion)
- Electric handheld mixer or stand mixer
- Food dehydrator
- Food processor
- Grain mill (electric or manual)
- Pressure canner
- Pressure cooker
- Rice/grain cooker
- Slow cooker
- Spice grinder
- Water bath canner

THE FOUR-CORNERS PANTRY LIST

If the term "four-corners pantry" is new to you, it simply refers to the four common places that most home cooks store food:

- **Working pantry**
  (where you store nonperishable food that you access daily)
- **Refrigerator**
- **Freezer**
- **Extended "prepper" pantry**
  (where you store backup nonperishable food for restocking your working pantry)

It's my hope that the following list will help you develop confidence in transitioning from a processed foods kitchen to a traditional foods kitchen. This is just a starting point for what I consider the beginning essential list of traditional foods for stocking your four-corners pantry. But keep in mind that you will want to stock what you know you will eat or drink. What I share here is simply where to start and is by no means an exhaustive list, so you can delete or add items to this list to make it your own.

ANIMAL PROTEINS:

- Assorted cuts of bone-in beef, beef liver, and a variety of beef bones for making bone broth
- Eggs
- Frozen and canned wild fish, including salmon, anchovies, sardines, and herring
- Whole chickens and assorted collagen-rich chicken parts (feet, etc.) for making bone broth

BAKING SUPPLIES:

- All-purpose flour, bread flour, and whole-grain flours (regular or sprouted)
- Baking powder
- Baking soda
- Commercially packaged yeast
- Cornmeal or masa
- Diastatic malt powder
- Old-fashioned rolled oats
- Sourdough starter
- Vanilla extract (preferably homemade)
- Vital wheat gluten

BEVERAGES:

- Beet or rye bread kvass
- Herbal tisanes (herb teas)
- Loose tea (black and/or green)
- Milk kefir (if tolerated)
- Whole coffee beans

CONDIMENTS:

- Fortified wines (for making bone broth)
- Ketchup, mustard, salsa (preferably all fermented)
- Mayonnaise (preferably homemade, but if store-bought, make sure it is free of soybean oil)
- Salad dressings (assorted and homemade)
- Tomato paste (canned, tubed, or homemade)
- Vinegars (raw apple cider vinegar and assorted fruit scrap vinegars, preferably homemade)

DAIRY AND DAIRY ALTERNATIVES:

- Cheese (full fat and preferably made from raw milk)
- Coconut milk or cream (full fat and canned)
- Heavy cream (raw, if available)
- Milk (full fat and preferably raw, if available)
- Milk kefir grains
- Sour cream (preferably homemade)
- Yogurt (full fat and preferably homemade)

FATS AND OILS:

- Beef tallow (rendered beef fat)
- Coconut oil
- Cultured butter and homemade clarified butter or ghee
- Extra virgin olive oil
- Leaf lard or regular lard (rendered pork fat)
- Schmaltz (rendered chicken fat)
- Sesame oil (untoasted and cold pressed)
- Walnut oil (cold-pressed)

FRESH AROMATICS:

- Carrots
- Celery
- Italian (flat-leaf) parsley
- Onions (yellow and red)

FRUITS AND VEGETABLES:

- Fermented vegetables (preferably homemade)
- Fresh fruits and vegetables, in season
- Jams (preferably homemade or store-bought, low-sugar varieties)
- Store-bought canned fruits, packed in their own juices (best saved for emergencies)
- Store-bought canned vegetables (best saved for emergencies)
- Tubers (assorted)
- Water bath home-canned fruits, pickles, and tomatoes
- Winter squash (assorted, in season)

LEGUMES AND PULSES:

- Beans, dried (all varieties)
- Canned beans (all varieties)
- Lentils (dried)
- Split peas

NUTS AND SEEDS:

- Nut butters or seed butters ground from soaked nuts and seeds
- Soaked and dried nuts
- Soaked and dried seeds

SEASONINGS:

- Assorted fresh and dried herbs and spices
- Bouillon powder (preferably homemade)
- Seasoning blends (preferably homemade)
- Unrefined sea salt or "real" salt, fine or coarse ground and free of anticaking agents or other chemicals
- Whole black peppercorns

SWEETENERS:

- Coconut sugar or coconut syrup
- Date sugar or date syrup
- Honey, pourable (preferably raw)*
- Maple syrup or maple sugar
- Unrefined whole cane sugar (sold as Sucanat or Rapadura)
- White cane sugar (to be used sparingly)

WHOLE GRAINS:

- Barley groats
- Buckwheat groats
- Einkorn berries
- Kamut berries
- Oat groats
- Rice (brown or white)
- Rye berries
- Spelt berries
- Sprouted whole grains
- Wheat berries

*Never give honey to infants under 12 months of age.

GETTING STARTED— LEARNING AN ESSENTIAL LIFE SKILL

When my son was young and would accompany me to the grocery store or be cooking alongside me in the kitchen, I would occasionally pause, turn to him, and say, "This is a life skill that you need to learn." To this day, he remembers these little life skill lessons and will often recount them for me. Some sound funny now, being retold by a grown man, but he assures me they have served him well. And while other lessons are more serious and instructional, probably one of the best essential life skills he learned from me was how to roast a whole chicken. He will often recite back to me those words from so long ago: "If you learn how to roast a whole chicken, you will never go hungry."

That is why today, whenever someone asks me, "Mary, I am new to making traditional foods and I feel so overwhelmed! What should I do?" My immediate response is "Just start with a roast chicken." As you transition away from processed and prepackaged foods— and dare I say those boneless, skinless chicken breasts—the first thing you want to do in creating your traditional foods kitchen is learn how to roast a whole chicken. So roll up your sleeves—and if you really need to, don some disposable gloves—and learn this essential life skill. You'll be glad you did!

The Right Way to Roast a Whole Chicken

Is there really a right way to roast a whole chicken? Well, to make it succulent and rich with flavor, there is, and it all comes down to time. Don't rush it. Don't blast it with high heat. A roast chicken is probably one of the original *slow* foods, but *slow* doesn't mean it will require a lot of work on your part. It really only requires about 15 minutes of prep time and then the oven will do the rest of the work. You will be rewarded for your patience with the best-tasting chicken you've ever had.

PREP TIME: **15 MINUTES**
COOK TIME: **1 HOUR 45 MINUTES TO 2 HOURS 30 MINUTES**
TOTAL TIME: **2 HOURS TO 2 HOURS 45 MINUTES**
YIELD: **4–6 SERVINGS**

INGREDIENTS

6 carrots (peeled or unpeeled)

1 (5–6lb/2.25–2.75kg) uncooked whole roasting chicken

1 tsp fine ground sea salt, divided

1 tsp ground black pepper, divided

1 tsp dried mixed herbs, divided

4 tbsp unsalted butter, melted

1 large yellow onion, peeled and quartered

1 Preheat the oven to 350°F (177°C).

2 If using a cast-iron skillet, place the carrots in the bottom of the skillet. If using a roasting pan with a rack, chop each carrot into three logs and place them in the bottom of the roasting pan and underneath the rack. Set aside.

3 Place the chicken on a cutting board and remove the giblets. (The giblets can be simmered in a saucepan on the stovetop with a small amount of water and enjoyed as a side dish.) Coat the chicken cavity with ½ teaspoon salt, along with a ½ teaspoon black pepper and ½ teaspoon of dried herbs.

4   Place the onion in the cavity of the chicken.

5   Bend the wing tips underneath the body of the chicken and tie the legs together with kitchen twine. (This is a quick and easy way to truss a chicken without actually tying the entire chicken with twine.)

6   Place the chicken on top of the carrots in the cast-iron skillet or onto the rack of the roasting pan.

7   Using a pastry brush, brush the exterior of the chicken with the melted butter.

8   Sprinkle the chicken with the remaining ½ teaspoon of salt, black pepper, and dried herbs.

9   Place the chicken on the middle rack of the preheated oven.

10 Roast the chicken for 20 to 25 minutes per pound or until the thigh reaches an internal temperature of 165°F (74°C). Insert the thermometer into the thigh of chicken and away from the bone. (If you do not have a meat thermometer, make a small incision where the chicken leg meets the chicken breast. If the juices run clear, the chicken is cooked.) If at any time the chicken appears to be overbrowning before it is fully cooked, tent it with aluminum foil.

11 Once the internal temperature of the thigh reaches 165°F (74°C), remove the chicken from the oven and set it aside to rest for 10 minutes. After 10 minutes, transfer the roasted chicken along with the carrots and onion to a serving platter. Carve, serve, and enjoy!

········· **COOK'S NOTES** ·········

The United States Department of Agriculture (USDA) recommends that you do not wash the chicken. This can easily spread salmonella, which may go undetected when cleaning up. Any impurities that may reside in the chicken will be thoroughly cooked away in the hot oven.

Although the USDA considers a roast chicken fully cooked once an internal temperature of 165°F (74°C) is reached, some may prefer to cook their chicken to an internal temperature of 180°F (82°C). Roasted to this higher temperature, the white meat might be slightly drier, but the dark meat will be very well cooked, which can be more appetizing to some. Roasting to this higher internal temperature will take closer to 25 minutes per pound.

WHAT TO DO WITH THE LEFTOVERS

After you've enjoyed your roast chicken, you may have some leftovers. The first thing you'll want to do is remove any meat from the chicken that you find appetizing, including both the light meat and the dark meat. Although some people may not like the dark meat, it is actually the tastiest and also the most nutritious. The dark meat from the chicken can be turned into many tasty dishes; it can be tossed into a soup or stew, and it's exceptionally tasty for chopping up and mixing with diced onions, herbs, spices, and maybe some tomato sauce to turn it into a mixture for tacos, hand pies, cannelloni, or casseroles that call for a meat filling.

You can make a quick chicken gravy by combining 2 tablespoons of the pan drippings and 2 tablespoons of all-purpose flour in a small saucepan over medium heat. Whisk together for 2 minutes and then add 2 cups chicken broth or chicken bone broth and then bring up to a boil while continuing to whisk. Once thickened, add salt to taste and serve.

Once all the meat is removed from the chicken, you will be left with the carcass and maybe some skin and various scraps. These are all worth their weight in gold! Do not throw any of this into the trash. Now is the time to start your first of many scrap bags. You can save your chicken carcass, scraps, and pan drippings in your scrap bag to make Roast Chicken Bone Broth (p. 48). Can you throw the carcass into a stockpot right then and there? Sure, but I generally recommend that you wait until you've accumulated three chicken carcasses, which will make a bone broth that is both richer tasting and more gelatinous, which will also make it richer in protein. So throw that carcass into your scrap bag and start building the makings of a nutritious bone broth. You will find that a tasty chicken bone broth only costs pennies to make and it will be head and shoulders—both in taste and nutrition—over any pricey bone broth you can buy at the grocery store.

Chapter Two
BONE BROTHS

BONE BROTH—THE BACKBONE OF THE TRADITIONAL FOODS KITCHEN

When it comes to creating your traditional foods kitchen, one of the first things you'll want to learn is how to make bone broth. It's the backbone of the traditional foods kitchen because it allows the home cook to create a nutritious high-protein liquid, often from nothing more than kitchen scraps. Learning how to make bone broth is the beginning to creating or expanding the concept of a low-waste or no-waste kitchen.

Bone Broth, Simple Broth, and Stock—How Are They Different?

As you learn how to make bone broth, it's important to understand what exactly it is and how it is different from a simple broth or a stock. All three can be made with a wide variety of meats and/or bones that come from assorted poultry, beef, and bison, as well as other ruminants, including pork, and even fish. But it's important to understand the differences between each.

Simple Broth

A simple broth is made by simmering a whole chicken or meaty beef bones, such as beef shanks, along with some vegetables. When making chicken broth, you'll place the raw chicken into a stockpot filled with water. When making beef broth or other red meat broth, you can roast the meat first, but it's not required. Broth is generally used as a base for soups, stews, and gravies, and can also be used in place of water when cooking grains. A simple broth will have somewhat of a gelatinous nature once it's cooled but less so than bone broth due to the shorter simmer time and the fact that it uses the meat of the animal as a primary ingredient. The flesh of a chicken, cow, or other ruminant is not rich in collagen like the bones and cartilage of the animals. A simple broth is made primarily from just the actual meat of the animal.

Stock

Stock is primarily made with bones, such as from a well-stripped chicken carcass, or beef marrow bones that have little or no meat on them. You will usually roast the bones before putting them into a stockpot filled with water. The vegetables used in making a stock can also be roasted along with the bones. Like broth, stock is rich in protein, but it differs from a simple broth in that the bulk of the protein comes in the form of collagen, which is released into the water when the bones are simmered, rendering the stock somewhat gelatinous when cooled. Although the amount of collagen in bones is generally not as high as the amount of collagen in cartilage, the bones used to make stock contain enough collagen to produce a nutritious, semigelatinous liquid that soothes our digestive tracts and nourishes our joints, skin, hair, and nails.

Bone Broth

And then there is bone broth, which is simmered longer than a simple broth or stock. In many ways, bone broth is a combination of both broth and stock, as it's made from both meaty bones and bones with little or no meat on them. But what makes bone broth special is that it also includes a third type of bone: high cartilage, which helps create the very rich gelatin that's associated with this highly nutritous liquid. Gelatin is simply cooked collagen, which is a protein from animal bones, marrow, and cartilage.

The benefits of consuming liquids high in gelatin are multifold. Most importantly, gelatin is rich in protein, which is one of the building blocks for repairing and making human cells. Gelatin protein, when warmed to its liquid form, is easy to digest. This makes it easy for our bodies to assimilate its nutrients, including vitamins, minerals, and antioxidants. Plus, it is soothing to our digestive system while bringing much-needed gelatin-rich protein to our bones, skin, hair, nails—and especially important—our joints.

Using Bone Broth

Bone broth can be used in so many ways in the traditional foods kitchen. You can sip it as is or use it in place of water in many recipes, including grains. This is especially important when cooking white rice. Since white rice has had the bulk of its nutrition stripped away, using bone broth (along with some butter and sea salt) in place of water when cooking it will increase its nutritional profile. Bone broth can also be used in place of water or a simple broth when making a soup or stew. And it can be especially nourishing if we fall ill with a flu or a cold. We might not have much of an appetite when we're under the weather, but the bone broth we can consume will nourish us.

Since bone broth is high in gelatin (cooked collagen), which is high in protein, you can stop buying expensive protein powders or collagen powders and simply use your homemade bone broth instead. From soups to smoothies (yes, smoothies), you'll find that there are many ways to use bone broth and enjoy its taste and nutritional benefits in a variety of recipes.

MAKING BONE BROTH

Bone broth is simple to make, but there are a few steps to follow to ensure your bone broth will achieve optimal flavor and you'll have a finished product that, once refrigerated, will gel significantly.

You can make bone broth anytime of the year, but the fall and winter months are an ideal time to make it because you're most likely roasting chickens and other meats during this time, so you will usually have a ready supply of bones on hand. Here are the steps for making bone broth.

Step 1: Roast the Bones

Generally, bone broth is made by roasting some or all of the bones before adding them to a stockpot or slow cooker. When starting with raw bones, the roasting process will guarantee that the bone broth will have an appetizing color and rich flavor.

Step 2: Cover the Bones in Water

Once the bones have been roasted sufficiently to achieve a golden brown color, they are transferred to the cooking vessel and then just enough water is added to cover the bones. It's important that you only cover the bones with enough water to ensure they are all submerged. The water should come no higher than approximately 1 inch (2.5cm) above the bones. Adding any more than that may make it difficult for the gelatin to form.

Step 3: Acidulate the Water

Once you have added sufficient water to cover the carcass or bones, you will add some type of acid to the water. We acidulate the water to help begin the process of extracting as much collagen out of the bones as possible. This acid can consist of wine, fortified wine, vinegar, or even a bit of citrus juice. I prefer to use some sort of fortified wine for this process because it is very rare that I have a bottle of regular wine on hand. Fortified wines do not sour nor do they become vinegar, as can happen with opened bottles of regular wine, so they make a wonderful addition to any traditional foods pantry. If you prefer using regular wine, you can replace the fortified wine at a 1:1 ratio with regular wine. (You can also use nonalcoholic alternatives as outlined in the recipes.) The bones are generally soaked for 1 hour in the acidulated water to help jump start the process of extracting the collagen.

Step 4: Simmer the Bones

The sweet spot for simmering bone broth, and specifically gelatin, is 180°F (82°C). This temperature is achievable on the stovetop, and in most slow cookers when they are set to their lowest settings. It's the perfect temperature for extracting the maximum amount of collagen from the bones and then simmering the collagen until it becomes a rich gelatin. (You won't notice the gelatin while your bone broth is warm, but once you chill it, it will look like Jell-O!)

How long you should simmer bone broth is determined by what type of bone broth you are making. The process of making fish bone broth is similar to making a simple stock; it really only needs to be simmered for 45 minutes to 1 hour. Chicken bone broth, on the other hand, should be simmered for 6 hours, while beef bone broth is generally simmered for 12 hours. I've frequently found it stated in various recipes that you should simmer any type of poultry or beef bone broth for 24 to 48 hours and even as long as 72 hours. But there are drawbacks to simmering bone broth for this long. First, trying to supervise a long simmer can be precarious for the home cook. Second, there is always the chance that too long a simmer may cause the fat in the bone broth to become rancid, resulting in a bone broth that is neither tasty nor healthy to consume. But the most significant problem is that such a long simmer may actually "break" the gelatin, meaning the bone broth will still contain protein and be nutritious, but it will no longer have the benefit of the gelatin.

Step 5: Strain and Store the Bone Broth

When your bone broth is done simmering, you'll strain, decant, and refrigerate it. To strain the finished bone broth, use a spider strainer or slotted spoon to remove as many solids as possible from the liquid. Next, place a colander (or mesh strainer) over a stockpot or large bowl. Line the colander with a flour-sack towel or cheesecloth. Pour or ladle the liquid through the lined colander and then set the colander aside.

At this point, you have two options: You can decant your bone broth directly into jars, leaving the fat intact. The fat will create a "cap" that will insulate your bone broth and help extend its refrigerated shelf life. If you choose this option, simply place a lid on the jar and refrigerate the bone broth. If you prefer to remove the fat from your bone broth, allow it to cool, uncovered, in the refrigerator overnight. Once cooled, the fat will congeal on the top of the bone broth and can then be removed. Alternatively, you can use a fat separator to remove the fat. Either way, once the fat is removed, transfer the bone broth to a jar, place a lid on the jar, and refrigerate it. You can also freeze it with or without the fat. Just make sure that you use a freezerproof container and allow sufficient headspace for expansion once the bone broth freezes.

FREQUENTLY ASKED QUESTIONS

Sometimes your bone broth may not turn out the way you expected. Here are some common problems, along with some explanations and solutions.

What if the bone broth is not gelatinous the next day?

Chances are you might have simmered it for an exceedingly long time or at too high a temperature, and as a result, you have broken the gelatin. For collagen to be extracted from bones and cartilage, it likes a nice gentle simmer where you see an occasional bubble come to the top of the broth every few seconds. So make sure you don't have any extended rolling boils. It's also possible you simply added too much water to cover the bones. This problem is generally easy to rectify. To do so, simmer the bone broth in a saucepan on your stovetop, keep the temperature very low, and allow some of the bone broth to evaporate. After a while, remove a bit of the broth from the saucepan and place it on a shallow plate that you then place in your refrigerator. If this liquid gels, you are all set. If it still doesn't gel, let it evaporate a bit longer in the saucepan and see if that makes a difference. If the broth still doesn't gel after trying this test a few times, don't throw it out! Your bone broth is still rich in protein and definitely worth consuming. Chances are, with each batch you make, your skill will improve and your bone broth will increasingly become more gelatinous!

Do you really use chicken feet?

I have a little secret that I want to let you in on that might just guarantee perfect bone broth every time, even if you make a few mistakes: chicken feet! I know this may not be for the faint of heart, but if you add chicken feet to basically any type of bone broth, you are generally ensured a very gelatinous bone broth. The credit goes to the chicken feet's rich amount of cartilage. And the nice thing about chicken feet (also known as *chicken paws*) is that they are very inexpensive.

How can you increase the mineral content in bone broth?

Although any type of bone broth is rich in collagen protein, bone broth made just from bones is not particularly rich in minerals. That is why you'll always want to add various vegetables (or vegetable scraps) to your bone broth when simmering it—the vegetables will add important minerals. You can also add eggshells to the soaking and simmering processes. Just give the shells a rinse and put them in your scrap bag in the freezer. And if the membrane is still inside the shell, don't remove it—the eggshell membrane is rich in collagen. When you're ready to make bone broth, simply throw the eggshells in with the bones during the soaking phase and then leave them in the pot as you simmer your bone broth.

Should you add salt or garlic?

I do not add garlic or salt to any of my bone broths. I find that the long simmers required for making bone broth can cause the garlic to develop an off flavor. I also don't add any salt. When I'm using bone broth in various recipes, I like to have the flexibility of starting with a salt-free broth. However, if you use bone broth as a sipping broth, I highly recommend adding a pinch of sea salt when you warm it for drinking. It will help enhance the flavor and add additional minerals.

Can you remove the fat from bone broth without refrigeration?

If you prefer not to have to refrigerate the entire pot of bone broth, you can defat bone broth using a fat separator device and then transfer it immediately to the storage containers. (Fat separator devices are readily available at most kitchen stores or online.) If you prefer to leave the fat in your bone broth, you can pour the strained bone broth directly into your storage containers. The fat will rise to the top and provide a "fat cap." This cap will insulate your refrigerated bone broth, extending its freshness for an additional 3 to 4 days until the cap is removed or cracked.

Can you reuse the bones?

You can make a second batch of bone broth immediately or wrap the bones well and store them in the refrigerator to use within a few days, or store them in the freezer to use within a few months. When you are ready to make the second batch of bone broth, you can reroast the bones and add fresh vegetables. How gelatinous the second batch of bone broth will be is governed by how much collagen is left in the bones and how much cartilage is left on the exterior of the bones. If the bones appear to have some cartilage that has not dissolved, you can reuse them to make a second batch.

How long will bone broth stay fresh?

How long bone broth stays fresh depends on how it is stored. Bone broth that has had the fat removed and is refrigerated in an airtight container (my preferred method) will stay fresh for about 3 to 4 days. If the fat cap is left in place, bone broth will generally stay fresh for about 1 to 2 weeks, but once you remove the fat cap it will only stay fresh in the refrigerator as if it was originally stored without the fat cap, about 3 days. If you freeze bone broth, it will stay fresh for approximately 6 months. However, it is generally at its peak when used within 2 to 3 months. After that time, it can begin to take on ice crystals, which can slightly affect its flavor.

With all of this said, you will always want to use the nose-and-eye test. If the bone broth ever develops an off odor or appearance, it should be discarded.

Bone Broth Master Recipe

Most bone broths follow a relatively simple and similar formula. You can make many varieties of bone broth following this master recipe. If there are any variations, I specify them in the specific recipes that follow.

1   Preheat the oven to 425°F (218°C).

2   If you're making a bone broth that uses raw bones, place the bones on a large baking sheet. Bake until the bones have browned, about 30 minutes. (If you're making a recipe that does not call for roasting the bones, such as Roast Chicken Bone Broth, Turkey Bone Broth, or Beautiful Skin Bone Broth, skip this browning step and simply place the scraps or hocks into the stockpot or slow cooker.)

3   Transfer the browned bones to a large stockpot or large slow cooker.

4   Deglaze the baking sheet with water and scrape up all the fond. (The "fond" is those browned bits that form on the baking sheet as the bones brown.) Add the water from the deglazing and the fond to the stockpot or slow cooker.

5   Pour the fortified wine, apple cider vinegar, or lemon juice over the carcass or bones and then cover everything with water. (Do not add any more water than is necessary to cover. And do not worry if some bones float to the top of the water.) Allow the carcass or bones to soak in the acidulated water for 1 hour. (This soak will help jump start the process of extracting the collagen from the bones.)

6   After the soak, bring the mixture, uncovered, to a boil over high heat and then immediately reduce the heat to the lowest setting. Use a slotted spoon to skim off any foam that has risen to the top of the liquid. If you're using a slow cooker, turn it to the high setting for 1 hour and then turn it down to the low or keep warm setting. Remove the slow cooker lid and use a slotted spoon to skim off any foam that has risen to the top of the liquid.

7   To either the stockpot or the slow cooker, add the selected vegetables, seasonings, and enough additional hot water to just cover all the ingredients. (Any additional hot water should be hot water from a tea kettle or water that has been simmered in a saucepan on the stovetop.) If using a stockpot, place the lid in a tilted position on the stockpot to allow steam to escape. If your slow cooker does not have a keep warm setting, turn it down to the low setting. Tilt the slow cooker lid to allow some steam to escape and prevent the bone broth from boiling.

8   For beef bone broth, turn off the slow cooker or stove after 12 hours of simmering time. For chicken or pork bone broths, turn off the slow cooker or stove after 6 hours of simmering time. Allow the bone broth to cool slightly and then remove any remaining solids with a slotted spoon. If the bones still have some undissolved cartilage on them, reserve them for making a second batch.

9   Once all the solids have been removed from the bone broth, place a colander or mesh strainer over a large, deep pot or large bowl. Line the colander with a cheesecloth or a flour-sack towel that has been moistened with water and then rung out. Use a ladle to transfer the broth from the slow cooker or stockpot to the lined colander. (The broth will drain through the lined colander and into the deep pot.)

10 Once all the bone broth has been strained, transfer the pot, uncovered, to the refrigerator. Leave the pot in the refrigerator until the fat rises to the top and congeals. This will take approximately 12 hours.

11 After 12 hours, use a slotted spoon to skim off the congealed fat and transfer it to a separate container and refrigerate. (You can use this fat in any recipe calling for a cooking fat, such as when sautéing.)

12 Transfer the defatted bone broth to one or more airtight containers that can then be refrigerated or frozen and then cover tightly with a lid. If freezing the bone broth, leave at least 1 inch (2.5cm) of headspace in the container to allow for expansion as the bone broth freezes. For best quality, store the defatted bone broth in the refrigerator for 3 to 4 days. If frozen, the bone broth generally remains fresh for approximately 6 months, but for best quality, it should be used within 2 to 3 months.

The Best Bones for Making Beef Bone Broth

With the current popularity of bone broth, the price of beef bones has increased. The good news is that there are still some reasonable options to choose from when making beef bone broth. You will be looking for three types of bones: meaty bones, marrow bones, and high-cartilage bones.

A meaty bone simply refers to a bone that has some meat on it. A common example would be a shank. Other meaty bones include ribs and meaty, peeled knuckle bones, generally with 6 to 8 ounces of meat on the knuckle.

Medium or long marrow bones are wonderful for making beef bone broth because, as the name implies, they contain bone marrow. During the simmering time, the collagen will leach out of the bones, making the bone broth rich in gelatin. The marrow is also rich in collagen and, once cooked, the marrow can be easily extracted from the bones and stirred back into the bone broth, or it can be removed and eaten. Not only is bone marrow rich in collagen, it is also rich in glucosamine, which can assist in alleviating joint pain. Bone marrow is a powerhouse of nutrients because it also contains vitamins A and B, iron, magnesium, phosphorus, potassium, selenium, and zinc.

The final type of bone is high-cartilage bones. These are the bones that are going to make your beef bone broth very gelatinous. When it comes to this category, you have a variety of options. Oxtails are a wonderful choice, but they can be pricey. More affordable options include less meaty knuckle bones and patellas, beef feet, tendons, and ligaments.

You have a bit of wiggle room with the combination of bones you can use. You may just want to use one meaty bone, such as a beef shank, for flavor and color; one or two marrow bones for the collagen and marrow they add; and have the bulk of the bones be made up of less expensive high-cartilage bones, including knuckles, patellas, feet, tendons, and ligaments. Experiment with different bones that are in your budget, and you will discover affordable combinations that you like.

Bison bones can also be a wonderful option. They are generally less expensive than beef bones, and most bison are both grass fed and finished. (Some are fed grain prior to slaughter, but the label will indicate if they were grass fed and finished.) The taste of broth made from bison bones is almost indistinguishable from broth made using beef bones.

········· **WHAT ABOUT BEEF NECK BONES?** ·········

Neck bones are high in cartilage, so they could possibly be an excellent option to use when making bone broth. They are also affordable. There is only one concern. Although the chances of humans contracting a disease known as bovine spongiform encephalopathy (mad cow disease) are low, it is caused by a protein known as a *prion*. The disease occurs in the central nervous system of the animal (not the muscle meat), so the Center for Science in the Public Interest recommends avoiding eating any part of the cow originating from the nervous system, including beef neck bones. It's important to be aware of this when buying any beef bones.

Rich & Flavorful Beef Bone Broth

Making homemade beef bone broth is so rewarding! It's much less expensive—and of a superbly better quality—than what you can buy at the grocery store. And once you learn to make bone broth, you'll find so many ways for using it in soups, stews, and gravies, not to mention drinking it warm and steaming—sprinkled with a little sea salt—straight from a mug.

PREP TIME: **1 HOUR 30 MINUTES**
COOK TIME: **12 HOURS**
TOTAL TIME: **13 HOURS 30 MINUTES**
YIELD: **APPROXIMATELY 1 GALLON (3.75ML)**

INGREDIENTS

2lb (907g) meaty beef bones (see **Cook's Notes**)

2lb (907g) medium to long marrow bones

2lb (907g) high-cartilage bones (see **Cook's Notes**)

1 cup red vermouth (see **Cook's Notes**)

3 medium yellow onions, quartered with skins on

3 celery stalks with leaves, roughly chopped

3 carrots, roughly chopped

2 bay leaves

10 black peppercorns

Enough water to cover the ingredients

1 Follow the **Bone Broth Master Recipe** (p. 44) to prepare this bone broth.

VARIATIONS

Anti-Inflammatory Bone Broth: Add 3- to 5-inch (7.5 to 12.5cm) pieces each of fresh ginger and fresh turmeric to the bone broth as it simmers. If you cannot find these fresh, powdered versions will do, but I recommend starting with 1 teaspoon of each and see how you like the flavor. You can always add more to your next batch.

Herbal Beef Bone Broth: Add fresh herbs during the last 10 minutes of simmering time. (This will keep their flavors from dissipating during a long simmer.) Some herbs to consider are basil, lemon balm, lemon verbena, marjoram, oregano, parsley, sage, and thyme. (I do not recommend adding rosemary unless it's only a sprig, as it can cause the bone broth to develop a soapy flavor.)

Fall Fruit Beef Bone Broth: Add fruits or fruit scraps during the simmering time. The peels from three or more apples are wonderful, as are pear scraps. These additions are especially nice in the fall, since they provide a lovely in-season fruit-flavored base for soups made with pumpkin and squash.

Citrus-and-Spice Beef Bone Broth: Add the zest and juice from three oranges along with a cinnamon stick or two to your simmering bone broth to give it a delightful seasonal flavor. Alternatively, add a small handful of cloves or allspice berries or even a few star anise. A citrus-and-spice bone broth makes for a comforting sipping broth on a chilly day or to open up your nasal passages when coping with a cold.

Simple Keto Bone Broth: You can lower the carb count by using leeks or spring onions (green onions) in place of the sweeter yellow onions. Romaine lettuce is a nutrient-rich addition if you need to omit the carrots.

········ COOK'S NOTES ········

Choosing meaty beef bones: These can include beef shanks, beef ribs, or meaty knuckle bones.

Choosing high-cartilage bones: These can include beef knuckle bones, patellas, neck bones, oxtails, feet, tendons, or ligaments.

Using alcohol: If you don't want to use red vermouth, you can use another fortified wine, such as Madeira, Marsala, or port. If you don't want to use alcohol, you can substitute ¼ cup apple cider vinegar or 2 tablespoons lemon juice.

Using the leftovers: After you strain your beef bone broth, remove any meat from the meaty bones and reserve this to use in soups or recipes calling for a meat filling.

Reusing the bones: Inspect the high-cartilage bones. If any cartilage is still intact, reserve these bones for making future batches of bone broth.

Roast Chicken Bone Broth

Harness the last bit of goodness from your chicken carcasses to create a delicious broth that is abundant in nourishing vitamins, minerals, and protein-rich gelatin. Enjoy this broth by itself or use it as a base when making tasty soups, stews, gravies, and sauces or in place of water when cooking grains.

PREP TIME: **1 HOUR 30 MINUTES**
COOK TIME: **6 HOURS**
TOTAL TIME: **7 HOURS 30 MINUTES**
YIELD: **APPROXIMATELY 1 GALLON (3.75ML)**

INGREDIENTS

3 roast chicken carcasses and scraps, including skin (see **Cook's Notes**)

Roast chicken pan drippings (if available)

6 raw chicken feet or 6 chicken wing tips or 3 chicken necks or 3 chicken backs (optional) (see **Cook's Notes**)

1 cup white vermouth (see **Cook's Notes**)

3 medium yellow onions, quartered with skins on

3 celery stalks with leaves, roughly chopped

3 carrots, unpeeled and roughly chopped

2 bay leaves

10 black peppercorns

Enough water to cover the ingredients

1   Follow the **Bone Broth Master Recipe** (p. 44) to prepare this bone broth.

········· COOK'S NOTES ·········

Preparing chicken bones: You can use a meat mallet to crack the chicken leg bones and thigh bones in half before adding them to the stockpot or slow cooker. This will help release some of the nutritious bone marrow into the bone broth as it simmers.

Using chicken feet, wings tips, necks, or backs: No need to brown these parts since you have roast chicken carcasses.

Using alcohol: If you prefer not to use alcohol, you can substitute ¼ cup apple cider vinegar or 2 tablespoons lemon juice.

Reusing the parts: Generally, chicken carcasses will not lend themselves to being used to make a second batch of bone broth. However, if you use feet, necks, or backs in the broth, they may still contain some undissolved cartilage and can be wrapped well and refrigerated for 3 to 4 days or frozen for 3 to 4 months and then reused to make another batch.

Why you use three chicken carcasses: You can certainly make Roast Chicken Bone Broth with one or two carcasses but your highest quality end product will be created with three. If you have more than three carcasses, save the extras for your next batch.

Beautiful Skin Bone Broth

This pork bone broth is a nutritional powerhouse of gelatin that will nourish your skin, nails, hair, and digestive system. And you'll be in for quite the treat if you like bacon, because some say if you make this with smoked ham hocks, it tastes like liquid bacon! It also makes a great ramen broth.

PREP TIME: **1 HOUR 30 MINUTES**
COOK TIME: **6 HOURS**
TOTAL TIME: **7 HOURS 30 MINUTES**
YIELD: **APPROXIMATELY 1 GALLON (3.75ML)**

INGREDIENTS

4lb (1.80kg) smoked ham hocks or a mix of pork bones (see **Cook's Notes**)

1 cup red vermouth (see **Cook's Notes**)

3 medium yellow onions, quartered with skins on

3 celery stalks with leaves, roughly chopped

3 carrots, roughly chopped

2 bay leaves

10 black peppercorns

Enough water to cover the ingredients

1 Follow the **Bone Broth Master Recipe** (p. 44) to prepare this bone broth.

Follow the **Bone Broth Master Recipe** (p. 44) to prepare this bone broth.

········· COOK'S NOTES ·········

Using raw ham hocks: Raw ham hocks can be used in place of smoked ham hocks, but you will want to brown them in the oven first.

Using pork bones: The pork bones you use might include ham shanks and ham bones that have been browned in the oven.

Using alcohol: You can use other fortified wines, such as Madeira, Marsala, or port, in place of the red vermouth. If you prefer not to use alcohol, you can use ¼ cup apple cider vinegar or 2 tablespoons lemon juice.

Reusing ham hocks and ham bones: Hocks and ham bones will usually have undissolved cartilage on them, so they are worth reserving and reusing to make a second batch of broth. If wrapped well, they can be stored in the refrigerator for 3 to 4 days or up to 3 to 4 months in the freezer.

Using this broth in other recipes: Because of the rich flavor of this bone broth, it's best used in recipes where you want a pork or bacon flavor. It's great as a base for potato soups which will be topped with bacon or when making rice that will be later used to make pork fried rice.

Bits & Bobs Bone Broth

When you're cleaning out your refrigerator or freezer and find various bits and bobs of bones, meat scraps, and vegetables coming close to their prime, it's the perfect time to make this bone broth. And by all means you can mix and match any bones you want. Beef and chicken work together exceptionally well.

PREP TIME: **1 HOUR 30 MINUTES**
COOK TIME: **12 HOURS**
TOTAL TIME: **13 HOURS 30 MINUTES**
YIELD: **APPROXIMATELY 1 GALLON (3.75ML)**

INGREDIENTS

6lb (2.75kg) assorted meat
  scraps and bones
  (see **Cook's Notes**)

1 cup red vermouth
  (see **Cook's Notes**)

9 cups packed vegetable
  scraps (see **Cook's Notes**)

2 bay leaves

10 black peppercorns

Enough water to cover the
  ingredients

1   Follow the **Bone Broth Master Recipe** (p. 44) to
    prepare this bone broth.

········· COOK'S NOTES ·········

Choosing meat scraps and bones: This can include leftover pieces of assorted cooked or raw meats, meaty bones or marrow bones from ruminant animals, and poultry carcasses, as well as poultry feet, necks, and backs.

Using alcohol: You can use other fortified wines, such as Madeira, Marsala, or port, in place of the red vermouth. If you don't want to use alcohol, you can substitute ¼ cup apple cider vinegar or 2 tablespoons lemon juice.

Choosing vegetable scraps: These can include onion skins; carrot tops, tips, and shavings; and the base of celery stalks. If you do not have vegetable scraps, you can add three medium yellow onions with skins on that have been quartered; three unpeeled carrots, roughly chopped; and three stalks of celery, roughly chopped.

Reusing the bones: If any bones contain undissolved cartilage, wrap them well and refrigerate for 3 to 4 days or freeze for 3 to 4 months and then reuse them to make another batch.

Thyroid-Loving Fish Bone Broth

This bone broth is rich in thyroid-loving iodine and can be ready in a little over 45 minutes. It's wonderful as a base for fish bisques, soups, and stews or as a substitute for clam broth when making homemade clam chowder.

PREP TIME: **5 MINUTES**
COOK TIME: **45 MINUTES**
TOTAL TIME: **50 MINUTES**
YIELD: **3–4 QUARTS (2.85–3.75L)**

INGREDIENTS

5lb (2.25kg) mild whitefish bones (with heads and tails)

1 tbsp clarified butter, ghee, or olive oil

2 medium yellow onions, quartered with skins on

2 carrots, unpeeled and roughly chopped

2 stalks celery, with leaves and roughly chopped

1 bay leaf

1 tsp whole black peppercorns

½ cup white vermouth (see **Cook's Notes**)

1 cup hot water (plus extra to cover the bones)

1 Rinse the fish bones very well to remove any slime. Cut out and discard the gills. Set the bones aside.

2 Add the butter, ghee, or olive oil to a large stockpot over medium heat. Once sizzling, add the onions, carrots, and celery. Sauté approximately 5 minutes. Turn the heat down to low.

3 Add the fish bones on top of the vegetables and then add the white vermouth along with the bay leaf, peppercorns, and 1 cup hot water.

4 Cover the stockpot and allow bones to "sweat" for approximately 15 minutes.

5 After 15 minutes, remove the lid and add enough additional hot water to cover the bones. (Be sure to use water that has been brought to a simmer in a tea kettle or in a saucepan on the stovetop.)

6 Increase the heat to medium. Bring to just a simmer and then turn the heat back down to low. Continue simmering, uncovered, for 30 minutes.

7 After 30 minutes, turn off the heat and allow the bone broth to cool slightly before removing any solids with a slotted spoon.

8 Once the solids have been removed, line a colander with cheesecloth or a flour-sack towel that has been moistened with water, rung out, and place over a deep pot. Ladle the bone broth from the stockpot to the lined colander. (The broth will drain through the lined colander and into the pot.)

9 Transfer the strained bone broth to one or more airtight containers that can be refrigerated or frozen.

10 For best quality, the bone broth will stay fresh in the refrigerator for 3 to 4 days. If frozen, the bone broth generally remains fresh for approximately 4 to 6 months, but for best quality it should be used within 2 to 3 months.

········· COOK'S NOTES ·········

Using alcohol: If you prefer not to use alcohol, you can substitute 1 tablespoon apple cider vinegar or 1 teaspoon of lemon juice.

Why is the simmer time so short? Fish bone broth is basically a fish stock and does not require a long simmer as it may develop an off-putting flavor. When mild whitefish bones are used, there will be very little fish fat, if any, on the top of fish bone broth. Any fat you do see will mostly be the fat you used to sauté the vegetables.

Why you should avoid using higher-fat fish: You want to avoid making fish bone broth with the carcass of higher-fat fish, such as salmon, because there is a chance that the omega-3 oils in fatty fish will become rancid during simmering and develop an off flavor.

Can you use vegetable scraps in place of fresh vegetables? Fish bone broth is best made with fresh vegetables as opposed to vegetable scraps.

Cheap & Cheerful Bone Broth

If rising prices for chicken are making it difficult for you to make chicken bone broth, this recipe uses inexpensive chicken parts to make some of the most gelatin-rich bone broth you'll ever taste, and you'll be able to make it for around two dollars.

PREP TIME: **1 HOUR 30 MINUTES**
COOK TIME: **6 HOURS**
TOTAL TIME: **7 HOURS 30 MINUTES**
YIELD: **APPROXIMATELY 1 GALLON (3.75ML)**

INGREDIENTS

6–8 raw chicken feet

6–8 raw chicken necks (see **Cook's Notes**)

¼ cup apple cider vinegar or 2 tbsp lemon juice

9 cups packed vegetable scraps
  (see **Cook's Notes**)

2 bay leaves

10 whole black peppercorns

Enough water to cover ingredients

1   Follow the **Bone Broth Master Recipe** (p. 44) to prepare this bone broth.

········· COOK'S NOTES ·········

Using chicken necks: Alternatively, you can use 4–6 chicken backs or a combination of necks and backs.

Using vegetable scraps: This can include onion skins; carrot tops, tips, and shavings; and the base of celery stalks. If you do not have vegetable scraps, you can add three medium yellow onions, quartered with skins on; three unpeeled carrots, roughly chopped; and three stalks of celery, roughly chopped.

Reusing the parts: Chicken feet, necks, or backs may still contain some undissolved cartilage after you make the broth. If so, they can be wrapped well and refrigerated for 3 to 4 days or frozen for 3 to 4 months and then reused to make another batch.

Turkey Bone Broth

When Thanksgiving or Christmas rolls around and you find yourself with a turkey carcass and some scraps, it's time to make Turkey Bone Broth. This bone broth makes a perfect base for soups that use up leftover turkey when friends and family want a change of pace from turkey sandwiches.

PREP TIME: **1 HOUR 30 MINUTES**
COOK TIME: **6 HOURS**
TOTAL TIME: **7 HOURS 30 MINUTES**
YIELD: **APPROXIMATELY 1 GALLON (3.75ML)**

INGREDIENTS

1 roast turkey carcass and scraps, including skin

Roast turkey pan drippings (if available)

1 cup white vermouth, ¼ cup apple cider vinegar, or 2 tablespoons lemon juice

3 medium yellow onions, quartered with skins on

3 celery stalks with leaves, roughly chopped

3 carrots, unpeeled and roughly chopped

2 bay leaves

10 black peppercorns

Enough water to cover the ingredients

1   Follow the **Bone Broth Master Recipe** (p. 44) to prepare this bone broth.

Clean-Out-the-Crisper Bone Broth Soup

Developing the good habit of never wasting food can begin with the simple task of cleaning out your refrigerator once per week and then using what you find to make a simple meal. One of the best places to find a few hidden treasures that might be a bit past their prime is the crisper in your fridge. Those veggies, along with some bone broth as the base, will make a delicious and nutritious meal.

PREP TIME: **5 MINUTES**
COOK TIME: **15 MINUTES**
TOTAL TIME: **20 MINUTES**
YIELD: **4–6 SERVINGS**

INGREDIENTS

1 tbsp butter

1 tbsp olive oil

1 medium yellow onion, diced

1 tsp fine ground sea salt

$\frac{1}{2}$ tsp freshly ground black pepper

$\frac{1}{8}$ tsp red pepper flakes (optional)

4 cups assorted raw vegetables, chopped into 1-inch (2.5cm) pieces (see **Cook's Notes**)

1–2 cups shredded, cooked chicken or meat of any variety

8 cups chicken bone broth or beef bone broth

2 cups cooked beans, grains, or pasta (optional) (see **Cook's Notes**)

1 Add the butter and olive oil to a large soup pot over medium heat.

2 Once the butter has melted, add the onion. Sauté until it's translucent, but not browned.

3 Add the salt, black pepper, and red pepper (if using). Stir well.

4 Add the chopped vegetables, stir well and then sauté for 1 minute.

5 Add the shredded chicken or meat, stir well and then add the bone broth.

6 Bring to a boil and then turn the heat down to medium. Cover and allow the soup to simmer for 15 minutes.

7 After 15 minutes, add the warmed cooked beans, grains, or pasta (if using) to the pot and stir. (See **Cook's Notes.**) Taste and season with additional salt, if needed.

8 Ladle the soup into bowls and serve.

COOK'S NOTES

Choosing raw vegetables: A variety of chopped vegetables might include carrots, celery, lettuce, and sweet bell peppers, as well as cruciferous vegetables, such as broccoli and cauliflower. You can also use chopped, precooked vegetables, but you'll want to reduce the cooking time to a point where everything is simply warmed through.

When do you add the pasta or grains? If you want to add grains or pasta to this soup, I recommend adding them in individual portions, unless the entire batch of soup will be eaten in one sitting. This will help prevent the grain or pasta from becoming too mushy by absorbing the bone broth. You can add warm cooked grains or pasta to the individual serving bowls and then ladle the soup over it.

Chapter Three
THE SKINNY ON FATS

GETTING STARTED WITH RENDERING FATS

One of the most nutrient-dense foods you can stock in your traditional foods pantry is real animal fat. It's also one of the easiest traditional foods to make; you only need to do a little chopping, and the stovetop, oven, or slow cooker does the rest. The animal fats we'll be focusing in this chapter are leaf lard, beef tallow, and schmaltz. These nutrient-dense fats are loaded with vitamins and minerals, including A, D, E, K_2, thiamin, niacin, riboflavin, selenium, iron, phosphorus, and potassium.

Beef Tallow

When rendered from the fat of cows that have been raised on pasture, tallow is exceptionally rich in conjugated linoleic acid (CLA), which is a natural anti-inflammatory. Tallow has a very high smoke point, allowing it to be heated to approximately 400°F (204°C). (If the term *smoke point* is new to you, it means the point to which a cooking fat can be heated before it begins to smoke. We want to know this temperature because we do not want to heat fats past their smoke point. If we do, we damage the fats. And consuming damaged fats is bad for our health.) Tallow is an all-purpose fat that is widely used in the traditional foods kitchen and especially for panfrying and deep-frying. This is definitely a fat that our ancestors relied on. And don't worry if the beef fat you render to make tallow is not from grass-fed cows, it still contains CLA; it's just not as concentrated.

In order to be called *tallow*, it needs to be rendered from a specific type of beef fat called *suet*. Beef suet is found around the kidneys of the cow, and it renders into an almost odorless fat that ranges in color from white to pale yellow. (The variation in color depends on the breed of the cow, as well as its diet.) Tallow has a very high melting point, meaning that it stays quite solid at room temperature. This is why it's a wonderful choice for making savory pie crusts that rely on the fat staying cool and solid before being put into a hot oven. Once in the oven, the fat melts, forming little air pockets that create a light and flaky crust.

If you can't find suet to render, don't despair. You can use any type of beef fat you trim off other cuts of meat, but you'll only be able to make rendered beef fat, as opposed to actual tallow. (The rendering process is the same.) The only real differences are that rendered beef fat has a mild beef aroma, is slightly softer at room temperature, and has a shorter shelf life than tallow.

Leaf Lard

Leaf lard is rendered from what is known as *leaf fat* in a pig. Leaf fat surrounds the pig's kidneys and is prized by chefs, and especially bakers. It is pure white once rendered and has no pork aroma. But don't worry if you can't find leaf fat. Any pork fat, but preferably from the back of the pig, can be rendered in the same way; it will just have a bit more of a pork aroma. If you render fat from a fat other than leaf fat, it is just regular lard.

Compared to tallow, regular lard (often just referred to as *lard*) and leaf lard both have a smoke point of approximately 370°F (188°C). This makes them well suited for pan sautéing. As with tallow, both types of lard have a relatively high melting point, making them especially nice for baking. If you have never baked with either type of lard, you are in for a treat! Regular lard works exceptionally well when baking with chocolate, since the mild pork aroma and flavor is overshadowed by the chocolate. Regular lard also makes a tender and flavorful savory pie crust. The mild pork flavor will blend with anything savory added to it. For more versatility in baking, leaf lard is the baker's choice. It can be used in any type of baked good, including sweet pie crusts. And what a pie crust it will make! A mixture of butter and leaf lard will give you both a flavorful and a flaky pie crust that will be destined to win a blue ribbon at any country fair or simply lots of praise from family and friends.

Schmaltz

Schmaltz has a smoke point of 375°F (191°C) which, like lard, makes it a wonderful option for pan sautéing. It's exceptionally tasty when used to make scrambled eggs or when panfrying cubed potatoes. It's a quintessential ingredient when making chopped chicken livers, and it is used in numerous other traditional Eastern European Jewish recipes. Using schmaltz when caramelizing onions or roasting root vegetables will add a scrumptious flavor to both. Schmaltz is delicious spread on toast in place of butter. It has a rich flavor and creamy mouthfeel not unlike butter, but it also has the added benefit of a mild chicken flavor.

Schmaltz can also be used to replace butter or lard in quick breads. It works especially well when making a Southern cornbread. And try adding in the *gribenes* instead of lard cracklings to your batter for a tasty treat. Since schmaltz has a lower melting point than tallow or lard (or even butter), it's best not used for pie crusts or pastries that require the fat to stay cool and firm.

FREQUENTLY ASKED QUESTIONS

Where can you source animal fats?

First, check with your butcher. If they don't have these fats readily available, they often are willing to order them for you. You can also talk with farmers and ranchers at your local farmers' market to see if they sell these types of fats. (I have found that many of them do.) And of course, like pretty much everything today, both suet and leaf fat can be ordered online.

When should you render animal fats?

The best time to render fats is when the weather becomes cooler, so you will have a good supply of cooking fats to last you through the fall and winter, when traditional diets tend to rely more heavily on rendered animal fats for cooking. This is the process our ancestors followed.

Can you use a slow cooker?

Yes, you can render both suet and leaf fat in a slow cooker. However, you need to be careful when doing so. You need to keep your slow cooker on its lowest setting and keep an eye on it. Don't let it burn. When using a slow cooker, many home cooks will add some water when rendering these fats to avoid burning them. But I do not recommend adding water when rendering animals fats. For this reason, I do not recommend using a slow cooker.

Can you eat the cracklings?

Ahh ... the cracklings! As suet, leaf fat, and chicken fat and skin render, they create tasty little bits of solid material that are left over after the rendering is complete. The cracklings from both the rendered leaf fat and the chicken fat and skin are delicious to snack on, as they are quite crisp. Suet cracklings are also tasty, just slightly less crisp. But if you have a sweet dog—as I do—you will find that your pup will gobble up those tender tallow cracklings in a second!

Should you add water?

When you add water to fats that are being rendered, the added water may not evaporate. Any water that remains in the fat will only shorten its shelf life. When rendered properly at home, both tallow and lard are very shelf stable because the rendering process removes any moisture and other impurities in the fat. And unlike in a factory, the home cook might not be able to tell if that extra added water has completely evaporated. Through the natural process of slowly rendering animal fat, and allowing the cracklings to crisp, you'll get a good indication that all the moisture has evaporated. With the added water, the cracklings still might crisp, but you can't guarantee that the added water has completely evaporated. And continuing with the process might cause the cracklings to over crisp, burn, and give the rendered fat an off flavor.

Rendering Pork Leaf Fat to Make Leaf Lard

Leaf lard is one of the best fats available for baking, especially when it's used to create flaky, tender pie crusts. Once pork leaf fat is rendered, it will not have any lingering pork flavor. For this reason, leaf lard is sought after by pastry chefs all over the world. Fortunately, you can make it quite easily right in your home kitchen!

PREP TIME: **15 MINUTES**
COOK TIME: **5–6 HOURS**
YIELD: **APPROXIMATELY 4 PINTS (1.90L)**

INGREDIENTS

5lb (2.27kg) pork leaf fat, cut into 1-inch (2.5cm) cubes

⋯⋯⋯ COOK'S NOTES ⋯⋯⋯

What if you can't find leaf fat? If you can't find pork leaf fat, you can use 5 pounds (2.27kg) of pork back fat instead.

How long does leaf lard stay fresh? One jar can be kept at room temperature and will stay fresh for up to 6 months. The remaining jars should be refrigerated or frozen to extend their shelf lives. Leaf lard will stay fresh in the refrigerator for up to 1 year and up to 2 years in the freezer.

Can beef suet be rendered using this method? You can use this same method to render beef suet and make tallow.

---

1 Preheat the oven to 200°F (93°C).

2 Place the pork leaf fat in a large unlined metal colander or large mesh strainer, both with a 9-inch to 10-inch (23cm to 25.5cm) opening.

3 Place the colander or mesh strainer over a large stockpot, preferably a tall 10-quart (9.46L) stockpot. (Using a tall stockpot is important because you don't want the colander or strainer to touch the rendered leaf lard as it drips into the stockpot.)

4 Place the stockpot with the colander or mesh strainer filled with the pork leaf fat into the oven and on the lowest rack.

5 Allow the pork leaf fat to render for 1 hour. At 1 hour, use pot holders to carefully lift the colander or mesh strainer while still keeping it over the stockpot. You should see that the leaf lard is dripping into the stockpot.

6 Carefully lower the colander or mesh strainer back on top of the stockpot and close the oven door. Raise the oven temperature to 225°F (107°C) and allow the pork leaf fat to render for approximately 5 to 6 hours.

7 Periodically check the rendering fat. If at any time the fat appears to be bubbling or boiling, reduce the oven temperature to 200°F (93°C).

8 After approximately 5 hours, open the oven door and look at what remains in the colander or mesh strainer. These are pork cracklings. They will not render into leaf lard. If they appear golden brown and crisp, you have successfully rendered all the lard from your pork leaf fat. If they are not quite crisp yet, close the oven door and continue to allow the leaf fat to render. Continue to periodically check on the rendering fat. Although it should be completely rendered within 6 hours, every oven is different, so it might take longer.

9 Once the pork cracklings are crisp and all the leaf fat is rendered, use pot holders to carefully transfer the stockpot with the colander or mesh strainer to a heatproof surface.

10 Transfer the cracklings from the colander or mesh strainer to a plate lined with a paper towel and allow them to cool slightly. (These are best enjoyed when freshly made, as they will become soggy if refrigerated.)

11 Line a mesh strainer with a dry flour-sack towel or cheesecloth and then place the strainer over a heatproof bowl. Using pot holders, grasp the stockpot by its handles and pour the rendered leaf lard through the strainer.

12 Using a ladle, transfer the strained warm leaf lard into clean heatproof pint-size glass jars.

13 Allow the warm leaf lard to cool to room temperature and then place a lid on each jar.

Rendering Suet to Make Tallow

Tallow is one of the best fats for deep-frying. As you render the suet, there will be a beef-like aroma that will fill your kitchen, but the final product will basically be tasteless and odorless, which makes it perfect for deep-frying pretty much any food. And trust me, once you experience the delightful crunch associated with deep-frying in tallow, it will be hard to go back to frying with any other fat.

PREP TIME: **15 MINUTES**
COOK TIME: **5–6 HOURS**
YIELD: **APPROXIMATELY 2 QUARTS (1.89L)**

INGREDIENTS

5lb (2.27kg) beef suet, cut into 1-inch (2.5cm) cubes

1 Preheat the oven to 225°F (107°C).

2 Place the suet in a Dutch oven or other heavy-bottomed pot. Place the pot on the middle rack of the preheated oven.

3 After 1 hour, stir the rendering fat. Continue checking and stirring the rendering fat periodically. If at any time the tallow appears to be bubbling or boiling, reduce the oven temperature to 200°F (93°C). (Small bubbles on the surface are an indication that moisture is evaporating.)

4 If at any time during your periodic checks, the cracklings (the small crisp-looking bits) have turned a golden brown and sunk to the bottom of the pot, use a slotted spoon to remove them to a paper towel–lined plate. (You do not want the cracklings to burn.)

5 After 5 to 6 hours, the fat should be rendered into tallow. You will know that the suet has completely rendered into tallow when there is a predominantly yellow liquid in the pot, all the golden brown cracklings have sunk to the bottom of the pot, and no small bubbles are coming up to the surface of the tallow. Although it should be completely rendered within 6 hours, every oven is different, so it might take longer.

6 Remove the pot from the oven and place it on a heatproof surface. Using a slotted spoon, remove any cracklings that remain in the tallow.

7 Line a fine-mesh strainer with a dry flour-sack towel or cheesecloth and then place it over a heatproof bowl. Carefully pour the tallow through the strainer and into the bowl.

8 Decant the tallow into clean heatproof glass containers fitted with airtight lids. Allow the tallow to cool completely before sealing. (You can use glass jars, but because tallow is so hard at room temperature, you might find shallow glass containers to be a better choice.)

······················· COOK'S NOTES ·······················

What if you can't find suet? If you can't find beef suet, you can use 5lb (2.27kg) of beef fat trimmings.

Do not use high heat! Do not be tempted to raise the oven temperature to speed up the process. It can take anywhere from 5 to 6 hours to render 5 pounds of suet. You can cover your pot if you wish, as this will help the fat to start melting in the first hour or so, but be sure to remove the lid after the first hour to allow any moisture to easily evaporate.

How long will the tallow stay fresh? You can leave one container of tallow at room temperature to use for cooking. It should remain fresh, unrefrigerated, for approximately 1 year. For long-term storage, you can refrigerate or freeze the remaining containers of tallow. If refrigerated, the shelf life of tallow will be extended to at least 18 months. If frozen, the shelf life of tallow will be extended to at least 2 to 3 years.

Rendering Chicken Fat to Make Schmaltz

If you enjoy chopped chicken livers or other Eastern European dishes, you'll want to make sure you have schmaltz on hand. But you are not limited to using schmaltz for those types of recipes. If you find duck fat, or the especially elusive goose fat, difficult to come by, schmaltz is the next best thing. So whenever you see a recipe recommending that you fry potatoes in goose fat, just use your schmaltz. You'll love the taste!

PREP TIME: **10 MINUTES**
COOK TIME: **30 MINUTES**
YIELD: **APPROXIMATELY 8 TABLESPOONS**

INGREDIENTS

2 cups chicken fat and chicken skin, chopped into ½-inch (1.25cm) pieces

1 tsp salt

½ tsp ground black pepper

1 medium yellow onion, peeled and sliced (optional)

1. Add the chopped chicken fat, chicken skin, salt, and pepper to a medium bowl. Toss to coat.

2. Place a nonstick skillet or well-seasoned cast-iron skillet over medium-low heat.

3. Add the seasoned chicken fat and skin to the skillet. Cover and allow the chicken fat and skin to begin to render.

4. After 15 to 20 minutes, remove the lid and increase the heat to medium. Add the onion slices (if using) and stir well.

5. Allow the chicken fat and skin to render for another 15 to 20 minutes, stirring occasionally. (Watch closely and do not allow the mixture to burn.)

6. After approximately 15 minutes, the chicken fat should be dissolved and the chicken skin should be a deep golden brown and very crispy. Turn off the burner and transfer the skillet to a heatproof surface.

7. Place a mesh strainer over a heatproof bowl. Slowly pour the liquid from the skillet into the strainer to catch any of the crispy chicken skin bits. (You can line the mesh strainer with a flour-sack towel or cheesecloth, but I have not found it to be necessary.)

8. Transfer the crispy bits to a paper towel–lined plate to cool. Decant the liquid into a heatproof jar with an airtight lid. (The rich golden color liquid in the jar is your schmaltz or rendered chicken fat.) Transfer the cooled crispy bits to a container with a lid.

··· COOK'S NOTES ···

What are gribenes? The bits of fried chicken skin are known as *gribenes*. They are quite tasty and can be used in place of croutons to top salads or other dishes where you are looking for a delicious crunch. Sprinkled with a little salt, you will find that gribenes may just replace potato chips as a favorite snack!

How do you store the schmaltz? Both the schmaltz and gribenes must be stored in the refrigerator. The schmaltz will stay fresh in the refrigerator for approximately 1 week. The gribenes should also be consumed within 1 week. Schmaltz can also be stored in the freezer and will stay fresh for up to 6 months.

Chapter Four
THE HOMEMADE DAIRY

GETTING STARTED WITH HOMEMADE DAIRY

Making an assortment of homemade dairy-based foods is a skill every modern pioneer should learn. Traditionally prepared homemade dairy actually requires little time on your part, no special equipment, and only a short list of ingredients that includes nothing more than milk, cream, and salt. You'll be amazed at how easy it is to make homemade dairy products.

And as far as culturing dairy goes, you are in luck if you have a warm home or live in a warm climate. Unlike vegetable ferments, dairy ferments love to be cultured where it is warm and cozy! So spring and summer are perfect times to get started with cultured dairy. The warmer months are an ideal time to start making homemade dairy items, especially if you can find milk from cows that have been grazing on lush, nutrient-rich pasture. Cows generally calve and produce more milk during the spring and less milk during colder months. So if you want to follow the seasonal rhythms of our ancestors, enjoy fresh and cultured milk during the warmer seasons.

Different Types of Milk

There are so many homemade dairy-based foods you can make by simply starting with just a gallon of milk. The term *milk* can be a broad one, but the recipes in this chapter are made only with cow's milk. There are different varieties of cow's milk, but for simplicity's sake, you'll want to only buy full-fat whole milk. Why? The homemade dairy-based foods you'll make from whole milk will be much better tasting, but more importantly, much more nutritious than anything made from nonfat or lowfat milks. Whole milk contains a host of vitamins and minerals including Vitamin A, B12, calcium, choline, magnesium, phosphorus, potassium, selenium, and zinc. (Milk may also contain Vitamin D if it has been fortified.)

Earlier, we discussed the benefits of conjugated linoleic acid (CLA) in tallow, and all whole milk contains CLA too. And milk from cows that have been raised on pasture will have the highest percentage of CLA. In addition to providing anti-inflammatory properties, preliminary animal studies have shown that this nutrient may have cancer-fighting properties and also help with weight loss! Even if the milk you buy is not from grass-fed cows, it will still contain some CLA. But the better quality of milk you can buy, the more CLA it will contain.

Whole Milk

Generally speaking, milk is sold as low-temp pasteurized, pasteurized, or ultra-pasteurized. All these milks are heated to specific high temperatures and then quickly cooled. The only differences are the temperatures at which the milks are heated, and the length of time they are kept at those temperatures

before being cooled. Ultra-pasteurized milk will last longer than low-temp pasteurized or pasteurized milk, but that is actually not a good thing. Remember that you want to consume foods and beverages that are in their most natural states and are as fresh as possible or have been properly prepared through culturing or fermentation.

Unfortunately, during the pasteurization process, regardless of the temperature, vital enzymes and good bacteria are destroyed. The higher the temperature at which milk is pasteurized, the greater the number of nutrients that are destroyed. The pasteurization process can make milk difficult for many people to digest because the enzymes that naturally occur in milk—and also aid in proper digestion and assimilation of nutrients—are destroyed during the pasteurization process. So the lower the temperature that milk has been pasteurized at, the better.

When buying whole milk, you'll want to determine whether or not it has been homogenized. (This should be clearly marked on the carton.) Homogenization is a process that blasts the milk fat globules (the cream) to make them permanently blend with the milk so that the cream does not rise to the top, as it would in fresh milk that's been taken straight from the cow. This process may cause the milk fat to react differently in the body, but what is immediately more noticeable when comparing the taste and texture of homogenized milk to unhomogenized milk is the mouthfeel. Some people may find that unhomogenized milk has a slightly sweeter flavor. When the cream is combined with the milk by shaking the two together, the cream creates a smooth, silky texture in the milk that can be lost when the cream's fat globules are broken apart through homogenization. Homogenization may make drinking milk easier because you do not have to shake your milk bottle first to disperse the cream throughout the milk, but this is not a natural process. You want to find milk that has not been homogenized.

In summary, focus on finding whole milk that is low-temp pasteurized and not homogenized. And if the milk is from grass-fed cows, all the better! If all you can find at your local grocery store is homogenized, ultra-pasteurized milk from feed-lot cows, don't lose heart. Just focus on finding whole milk and we'll go from there. We can work at re-establishing some of what has been lost through the pasteurization and homogenization processes by properly preparing various forms of cultured dairy.

Raw Milk

I did want to share a bit of information with you about raw milk. Raw milk is teaming with probiotics, which are beneficial lactic acid bacteria that nourish our digestive systems. Drinking raw milk, or culturing it in a way that does not destroy that beneficial bacteria, is the most nutritious way to consume it. And raw milk is one of the easiest foods to culture. Raw milk has neither been pasteurized or homogenized; it's straight from the cow and is rich in beneficial bacteria and enzymes! In this chapter, I share one recipe that exclusively uses raw milk. But don't worry. All of the remaining recipes use pasteurized or ultra-pasteurized milk or cream since they are the most readily available for most home cooks.

Whether you have access to raw milk will depend on where you live. If you are blessed with your own dairy cow, you are all set. If not, a quick internet search should tell you if raw milk is available for purchase for human consumption in your area. Today, most states allow consumers to purchase raw milk either directly at the dairy farm or the farmers' market. Some states allow its sale at the grocery store. So if you have raw milk available to you, great! If not, don't worry. As I shared above, there is a lot you can do to return some of the nutrition to milk that has been destroyed through the pasteurization and homogenization processes. Keep in mind that even if you have access to raw milk, but you do not feel comfortable purchasing it—let alone drinking it—I understand completely.

(Note that the U.S. Food and Drug Administration warns that pregnant women, nursing mothers, individuals with weakened immune systems, children, teenagers, and older adults should never drink raw milk.)

Making Cultured Dairy

It's so easy to culture dairy, but why do we want to do it? When we do not have access to raw milk, we want to try to improve the nutritional profile of the milk we are able to buy as much as possible. And that's where culturing comes in. If we are starting with any level of pasteurized milk and cream, we can restore some of the nutrition that has been lost through the pasteurization process by turning that dairy into yogurt, cultured butter, real buttermilk, or a homemade version of cream cheese, as well as a delicious cultured effervescent beverage called *kefir*.

There are differences as to how certain dairy items are made, whether you are starting with raw milk or pasteurized milk. Culturing dairy, for the most part, is easier when you start with raw milk. If you are using raw milk, there is generally only one step you have to take: you leave it on the counter to culture!

> ### NONDAIRY MILKS
>
> Yes, you can make nut milks and various grain milks, and in the chapter on soaking and sprouting grains I will share with you how to make Traditional Fermented Oat Milk. The key word in that recipe title is "traditional." Many of the milk alternatives sold at the grocery store today are not properly prepared and are actually a hindrance to our health.

When culturing pasteurized milk, you'll need to give your milk a little boost, in addition to leaving it out to culture, which means it's a two-step process. By culturing pasteurized dairy, we create a food that is now rich in probiotics (good or beneficial bacteria), including certain strains of bacterial enzymes. These bacteria and enzymes support a healthy digestive system to help our bodies better digest the lactose that is present in milk. Since lactose can be difficult for many people to digest, and especially so as we age, culturing dairy helps us enjoy these foods and assimilate their nutrients.

But the benefits go far beyond being able to simply better digest lactose. When dairy is cultured and then consumed by us, it boosts our immune systems because our healthy digestive systems are better able to absorb the vitamins and minerals from all the foods we eat. This all boils down to what scientists tell us: the stronger our immune systems, the healthier we are. So the more good bacteria we can introduce into our digestive systems, the healthier we will be overall.

In addition to learning how to culture dairy, it's important to learn how to make some basic dairy-based ingredients for our traditional foods kitchens. In the recipes that follow, I'll show you how easy it is to make clarified butter, ghee, and brown butter. You can make these with your homemade butter or butter you purchase at the grocery store. Clarified butter and ghee are butters that have had the milk solids removed, which raises their smoke points and makes them ideal for sautéing. Plus, they add a wonderful level of flavor, as well as nutrition, to any meal since they are more concentrated than regular butter. Browned butter contains milk solids, but it will take your quick breads and muffins to a whole new level. It works especially well with the rich flavors that whole sugars, like unrefined whole cane sugar and coconut sugar, bring to baked goods.

As traditional home cooks, we also want to make sure we have at least one good stovetop cheese recipe in our repertoire. Stovetop cheeses are the types of cheeses that have been made for years in traditional foods kitchens and are often referred to as *farmer's cheese* (or *farmer's pot cheese*). These stovetop cheeses are easy to make because they require no rennet (an enzyme that causes the coagulation of the proteins in milk). One of the easiest stovetop cheeses to make is cottage cheese, so that is what I share in this chapter. Once you make your own cottage cheese, it will be difficult to ever buy the store-bought version again! You'll create a nice curd, but better yet, you control how much cream and salt you add to it. This provides you with flexibility when choosing how you want to use your homemade cottage cheese—whether you eat it right out the bowl or add it to a recipe.

A Note about Whey

In many cases, when making homemade dairy you will also create a by-product called *whey*. There are three types of whey: sweet whey, acid whey, and cultured whey. Sweet whey is a by-product of cheesemaking that involves the use of rennet. We won't be making any cheeses using rennet, as that is a more advanced process. However, we will be making a stovetop cheese in which the by-product will be acid whey. We will also be making cultured whey, which is a by-product of straining cultured dairy products, including clabber, yogurt, and kefir.

Although acid whey has its uses, cultured whey is the real prize! Whey from cultured dairy is very nutritious and full of gut-loving probiotics. You can drink cultured whey straight, add it to a smoothie, or mix it with sparkling water and pour over ice for a refreshing beverage. You can also combine cultured whey with the water in which grains are soaked or add it to the brine used to ferment vegetables. You can even use it to feed your sourdough starter.

Cultured whey from any type of cultured dairy is best stored in a clean glass jar with a lid. This type of whey will stay fresh in your refrigerator for approximately 2 weeks. You can also freeze it for up to 2 months in a freezerproof container. The beneficial bacteria will become dormant, but once it is defrosted, it can be used in the same way as fresh whey. (As with freezing any liquid, remember to leave at least 1 inch [2.5cm] headspace when filling a freezerproof jar or container to allow for expansion once frozen.)

Although technically not whey, real cultured buttermilk, which is a by-product of making cultured butter, is very similar to cultured whey and can be used in similar ways. However, I would not use it for vegetable ferments since it can thicken over time and impart an unusual cloudiness to ferments that exceeds the natural cloudiness caused by the fermentation process. Cultured buttermilk is best stored in a clean glass jar with a lid. It should stay fresh for approximately 2 weeks in the coldest part of your refrigerator (this is usually on the lowest shelf in the back of the refrigerator but never in the refrigerator door). It can also be frozen for up to 2 months.

A Note about Freshness

When it comes to making any homemade food, how long it can stay fresh is not as predictable as it is with store-bought foods that contain preservatives. Most cultured dairy will stay fresh anywhere from 1 to 2 weeks, but sometimes it can stay fresh longer when wrapped well or stored in an airtight container. The one exception is acid whey, which can usually stay fresh for much longer.

In the recipes that follow, I have shared approximate timeframes for how long each homemade dairy item will stay fresh at room temperature, in the refrigerator, or in the freezer. However, keep in mind that these timeframes can be somewhat subjective. Always trust your eyes and nose. If at any time your homemade dairy develops mold or takes on a foul (as opposed to a sour or yeasty) aroma, discard it.

Homemade Yogurt

If you've never made homemade yogurt, you are in for a treat! It has a smooth, silky quality, with a pleasantly tart flavor, making it great to eat plain or sweetened with a bit of homemade jam or puréed fruit. A dollop of homemade yogurt is also tasty on top of granola or sweet fresh fruit that is in season.

PREP TIME: **15 MINUTES**
CULTURING TIME: **8–12 HOURS**
TOTAL TIME: **8–12 HOURS PLUS 15 MINUTES**
YIELD: **APPROXIMATELY 1 QUART (946ML)**

INGREDIENTS

1 quart (946ml) whole milk (low-temp pasteurized or pasteurized and homogenized or nonhomogenized) (see **Cook's Notes**)

¼ cup plain whole milk yogurt with live cultures

········· COOK'S NOTES ·········

Can you use ultra-pasteurized milk? You can! And you do not have to heat it to 180°F (82°C). You simply need to warm it to 110°F (43°C) or until it feels like warm bath water and then proceed with the recipe.

Why do you need to heat pasteurized milk to 180°F (82°C)? Although pasteurized milk has been heated to destroy some of the enzymes and good bacteria in the milk, there isn't always consistency as to what temperature is used when pasteurizing milk. When making yogurt, you actually want to destroy most of the enzymes and good bacteria in your pasteurized milk so that they do not compete with the new bacteria culture you are introducing to the milk to make the yogurt.

---

1 Cover a rimmed baking sheet with a dish towel and then place a large bowl on the covered baking sheet. (This bowl can be made of tempered glass, stainless steel, ceramic, earthenware, or stoneware, but do not use a plastic bowl.) Set aside.

2 Pour the milk into a medium saucepan. Over medium heat, bring the milk to a simmer, stirring continually to ensure that the milk does not burn on the bottom of the pan. You want to heat the milk to 180°F (82°C). (A candy thermometer is useful to determine this temperature, but if you do not have a candy thermometer, heat the milk to the point where you see bubbles forming around the circumference of the saucepan and steam rising from the milk.) (See **Cook's Notes**.)

3 Place a medium bowl inside the larger bowl. Make sure the medium bowl is large enough to hold 4 cups of milk. (Do not use a plastic bowl.) Pour the warmed milk into the medium bowl and then add the yogurt. Whisk until the yogurt is completely incorporated.

4 Boil some water in a tea kettle. Once it comes to a boil, allow it to cool for a minute or two and then pour it into the space between the two bowls until it comes to a point just below the lip of the medium bowl.

5 If the bowls have lids, put the lid on the medium bowl and then put the lid on the large bowl. If your bowls do not have lids, you can cover them individually with plastic wrap. Cover the bowls with two dish towels or one large towel and let them stand in a warm place, undisturbed, for 8 hours. (A cold oven that has the light on or a pilot light is an ideal place.) Your goal is to try to maintain a steady temperature of 110°F (43°C).

6 After 8 hours, check the yogurt. It should appear slightly thickened and have a somewhat sour aroma. I recommend tasting it at this point. If you find the flavor pleasantly tart, then it's ready. If not, re-cover it and let it continue to culture for up to 4 more hours. The longer you allow it to culture, the tangier it will become. When the yogurt reaches a consistency and taste that you like, you can keep it in the bowl or transfer it to individual serving jars and refrigerate it. It will stay fresh for approximately 1 to 2 weeks.

Mock Cream Cheese

This mock cream cheese has a wonderfully smooth consistency that's perfect for making dips and spreads. It also works great in casseroles or cheesecake recipes calling for cream cheese. This form of homemade cream cheese has a texture almost identical to store-bought cream cheese, but I prefer this version because it's made in a different way than store-bought cream cheese. This mock cream cheese will be much better than anything you can buy at the store because your version will be rich in probiotics!

PREP TIME: **5 MINUTES**
DRAINING TIME: **24 HOURS**
FIRMING TIME: **2–5 DAYS**
TOTAL TIME: **APPROXIMATELY 3–6 DAYS**
YIELD: **APPROXIMATELY 12–16 OUNCES (340–454G)**

INGREDIENTS

32oz (907g) plain whole milk yogurt with live cultures (homemade or store-bought)

½ tsp fine ground sea salt (optional)

1 Line a mesh strainer with a flour-sack towel or cheesecloth. Place the strainer over a large, deep bowl.

2 Pour the yogurt into the strainer. Transfer the yogurt to the refrigerator to drain for 24 hours.

3 After the yogurt has drained for 24 hours, remove the yogurt from the refrigerator. (The yellowish liquid that accumulates in the bowl is cultured whey. Transfer this to a lidded jar and refrigerate for up to 2 to 3 weeks.) (See **Cook's Notes**.)

4 Add the sea salt (if using) to the strained yogurt and stir to combine. Taste and then add more salt in small amounts, if desired, until the taste is to your liking.

5 Transfer the strained yogurt to a small rectangular container lined with a piece of flour-sack towel or cheesecloth that is large enough to hang over the sides of the container. The container should be small enough to hold all the yogurt with no space left in the container. It should fit snugly into the container.

6 Once the strained yogurt is spread out evenly in the lined container, fold the lining hanging down the sides of the container over the top of the yogurt cream cheese and then cover the container with a tight-fitting lid.

7 After 2 days, check the cream cheese to see if the texture is firm. If so, you can unmold it from the flour-sack towel or cheesecloth and store it in the refrigerator.

8 If you prefer a firmer texture, rewrap the cream cheese in a fresh layer of flour-sack towel or cheesecloth and then put it back in the fridge for up to 3 more days.

9 Store the finished mock cream cheese in a container with a tight-fitting lid. Refrigerate for approximately 1 to 2 weeks.

.... COOK'S NOTES ....

How can you extend the life of the cream cheese? If you wrap the finished cream cheese in parchment paper or wax paper before placing it into a storage container, it will extend its freshness.

Can you heat the cream cheese? Yes, but keep in mind that once you heat this cream cheese, the beneficial bacteria will die off and it will no longer offer any probiotic benefit.

Storing the whey: You can store the whey in your refrigerator for approximately 2 weeks. The whey should smell a bit sour; if it takes on a foul or strong odor or it becomes discolored, discard it. You can freeze this type of whey for approximately 2 months in a freezerproof container. As with freezing any liquid, remember to leave 1 inch (2.5cm) headspace to allow for expansion. The beneficial bacteria will become dormant, but once defrosted, it can be used in the same way as fresh whey.

Clabbered Raw Milk

When left at room temperature, raw milk will ferment naturally. The result of this natural fermentation or natural souring is called *clabber*. When you allow raw milk to clabber, it creates a cultured dairy that is thinner than yogurt and more similar to kefir. And like kefir, if you leave raw milk to ferment for an extended period of time, it will separate into curds and whey, specifically known as *cultured whey*.

For the traditional home cook, one of the best things about raw milk is that it doesn't go bad, it just clabbers. (This is in contrast to pasteurized milk, which spoils because the beneficial bacteria have been destroyed through pasteurization.) This is why our ancestors, who lacked refrigeration, drank lots of clabber! You might find that clabbering milk will become your favorite way to culture raw milk.

TOTAL TIME: **1–5 DAYS**
YIELD: **APPROXIMATELY 1 QUART (946ML)**

INGREDIENTS

1 quart (946ml) whole raw milk

MAKING CLABBER

1 Pour the raw milk into a clean jar and put the lid on loosely.

2 Place the jar in area where it will be undisturbed and out of direct sunlight. Allow the milk to clabber at room temperature (65°F–85°F/18°C–29°C). (The warmer the room, the better.)

3 Within a few days, the raw milk will clabber, which will look like a thickened milk with bubbles in it. (Exactly how long this process takes will depend on the temperature, as well as how much beneficial bacteria is in the raw milk.)

4 At this point, you can enjoy your clabber by mixing the clabbered milk and cream together and drinking it like kefir, adding it to smoothies, or using it in place of yogurt to top granola or fresh fruit. (Clabber in any form does not need to be refrigerated, but it should be consumed within a few days or refrigerated. It should stay fresh in your refrigerator for 1 to 2 weeks.)

MAKING CURDS & WHEY

If you allow your clabber to continue fermenting, it will eventually separate into curds and whey, with the curds looking very much like globules of yogurt floating in liquid. This liquid is the cultured whey. You can spoon off the clabbered curds and enjoy it as you would yogurt. Or you can mix the whey back into the clabbered curds, which will create a drinkable clabber similar to the original, but it will have a tangier flavor and be lower in lactose (milk sugar). The whey should be stored in a clean jar with a lid. It can also be kept at room temperature, but like the clabber, it is best used within a few days. Otherwise, it should be refrigerated or frozen.

MAKING CLABBER CHEESE

Another option is to pour the clabber through a mesh strainer that has been lined with a flour-sack towel or cheesecloth and placed over a bowl. The whey will drain through and you will be left with the clabber curds, which will look like yogurt. You can let the curds continue to drain at room temperature until they reach the firmness that you like. The end result is called *clabber cheese*.

Milk Kefir

Milk kefir is loaded with an array of beneficial probiotics that our digestive systems love. But the best thing about kefir is its delicious fizz and tangy flavor. You can drink it as is or sweeten it with any natural whole sweetener like honey or maple syrup. It's also great served over granola or to soak muesli. You can flavor kefir by adding puréed fruit mixed into a first or second ferment to create a drinkable fruit smoothie.

PREP TIME: **1 MINUTE**
FERMENTATION TIME: **12–36 HOURS**
TOTAL TIME: **APPROXIMATELY 12–36 HOURS**
YIELD: **2 SERVINGS**

INGREDIENTS

2 cups pasteurized whole milk
  (any level of pasteurization is okay)
1 tbsp fresh or rehydrated kefir grains

FIRST FERMENT

1 Combine the milk and the kefir grains in a medium jar. Stir gently and then place a lid loosely on the jar.

2 Place the jar in a location that is out of direct sunlight and between 65°F to 85°F (18°C to 29°C). Leave it undisturbed for 12 hours.

3 After 12 hours, check the kefir to see if it has thickened. If it has thickened, taste it. If the taste is to your liking, place a small mesh strainer over a clean glass jar and strain the milk kefir into the jar, using the strainer to catch the grains. (When making kefir, the milk may separate into curds and whey, but that's normal. After straining, you can mix it all together again.)

4 If you prefer a more acidic flavor, place the lid back on the jar and allow to ferment for another 12 to 24 hours, checking the kefir every 12 hours, until the flavor is to your liking. Strain as instructed.

5 You can drink the milk kefir right away or refrigerate it to enjoy cold. Milk kefir can be refrigerated in a glass jar with a lid for approximately 1 to 2 weeks.

COOK'S NOTES

Using, storing, and drying kefir grains: This recipe requires a special ingredient most likely not available at your grocery store. If you decide you want to culture your milk to make kefir, you will need kefir grains. These grains look like small pieces of cauliflower, but they are actually a symbiotic culture of bacteria and yeast that create billions of microorganisms you can use to culture milk into this delightfully tangy and effervescent beverage. As the grains multiply, share them with friends or eat them. They are rich in probiotics.

To store the grains when not in use, you can refrigerate the grains in some milk in a glass jar with a tight-fitting lid for up to 3 weeks. You can also dehydrate the grains and store them in the freezer. To do this, rinse them in filtered, chlorine-free water and then dehydrate them in an electric dehydrator set at a temperature no higher than 85°F (29°C). Alternatively, lay the grains on a clean, dry surface and allow them to air dry. (This may take as long as 5 days.) Once the grains are dry, toss them with a bit of powdered milk and store them in a freezerproof bag.

Making a second ferment from the first ferment: Rather than drinking the first ferment, you can use the strained kefir to make a second ferment. This second ferment will be made without the kefir grains and will further reduce the amount of lactose in the kefir. (The second ferment does not need to be strained.)

Clarified Butter, Ghee, and Brown Butter

It's amazing what you can do if you have some butter in your refrigerator! You can make two types of cooking oil: clarified butter and ghee. Both oils have a higher smoke point (485°F [252°C]) than butter, making them perfect for high-temperature sautéing, oven roasting, and even deep-frying! Plus, both oils are shelf stable, which means they don't require refrigeration. You can also change the flavor of basic butter by making brown butter. Brown butter will lend a whole new layer of flavor to anything you use it in—from baked goods to sautéed potatoes. And it can be substituted one to one in any recipe where butter is called for.

COOK TIME: **10–20 MINUTES**
TOTAL TIME: **10–20 MINUTES**
YIELD: **APPROXIMATELY 1 ¾ CUPS**

INGREDIENTS

1lb (454g) or 4 sticks or 2 cups unsalted butter (preferably uncultured), cut into 1-inch (2.5cm) pieces (The amount of butter specified represents making one type of butter.)

CLARIFIED BUTTER

1 Place the butter in a medium saucepan over low heat. Allow the butter to melt very slowly. (Do not rush this process. It may take up to 10 minutes.)

2 Once the butter has completely melted, you will notice a white foam or film forming on the surface of the butter. Use a spoon to remove this as best as you can. Once you have removed all the foam, you should be able to see that the white milk solids have dropped to the bottom of the pan.

3 Using a ladle or large spoon, gently scoop out the clarified butter, leaving the milk solids behind. Transfer the clarified butter to a clean glass jar.

4 Once you have removed as much of the clarified butter as possible, line a mesh strainer with a flour-sack towel or cheesecloth and pour the remaining clarified butter through the lined strainer and into the jar. (This will remove all the milk solids from the remaining clarified butter.)

5 Allow to cool completely and then put a lid on the jar. Store at room temperature for up to 6 months.

GHEE

1 Place the butter in a saucepan over low heat. (If possible, use a saucepan that has a light-colored interior so you can monitor the browning of the milk solids. You do not want the milk solids to burn!)

2 Allow the butter to melt very slowly. (Do not rush this process. It may take up to 10 minutes.)

3 When the foam rises to the top of the ghee, just allow the ghee to continue to simmer. After a few minutes, the foam should sink back down to the bottom of the pan. The foam and other milk solids should all be at the bottom of the saucepan. Allow the ghee to continue simmering until the milk solids turn golden brown. (Keep a close eye on this, as you do not want the milk

solids to burn.) Once the milk solids have turned a golden brown, use a ladle or large spoon to gently scoop out the ghee, leaving the milk solids behind. Transfer the ghee to a clean glass jar.

4 Once you have removed as much of the ghee as possible with the ladle or spoon, line a mesh strainer with a flour-sack towel or cheesecloth and pour the remaining ghee through the lined strainer and into the jar. (This will remove the remaining milk solids from the ghee.)

5 Allow the ghee to cool completely and then put a lid on the jar. Store at room temperature and out of direct sunlight for 3 to 4 months or refrigerate for up to 1 year.

BROWN BUTTER

1 Place the butter in a saucepan over low heat. (If possible, use a saucepan that has a light-colored interior so you can monitor the browning process.)

2 Stir the butter continuously as it is melting. Once the butter has completely melted, adjust the heat to medium. The butter should begin to foam and sizzle. (Brown butter can burn easily, so never leave it unattended, and be sure to stir it continuously as it browns.)

3 Continue stirring for about 5 to 10 minutes or until the foam and milk solids have dropped to the bottom of the pan and have turned a deep golden brown, and the browned butter has also turned a deep golden brown. (Make sure the milk solids do not burn.) Immediately turn off the heat and remove the saucepan from the stovetop.

4 Carefully pour the browned butter, along with the browned milk solids, into a clean heatproof jar. (For brown butter, you do not want to strain out the milk solids. They contribute to the intense flavor.)

5 Once the brown butter has cooled, put a lid on the jar and tighten. Store in the refrigerator for up to 2 weeks.

Cultured Cream

As with butter, heavy cream, sometimes referred to as *heavy whipping cream,* is another workhorse in the traditional foods kitchen. But it's even better once it's cultured, creating a cream that is rich in probiotics. And culturing cream couldn't be easier. It's delightful swirled into soups or poured over fresh berries or a bread pudding just out of the oven. And you can use it as a base for making creamy salad dressings. Most importantly, it's the pivotal ingredient for making cultured butter. Whatever way you use this cream, you will be giving your digestive system a probiotic boost!

CULTURING TIME: **UP TO 8 HOURS**
TOTAL TIME: **APPROXIMATELY 8 HOURS**
YIELD: **APPROXIMATELY 32FL OZ (946ML)**

INGREDIENTS

32fl oz (946ml) pasteurized or raw heavy whipping cream with at least 36% fat

1 tbsp cultured buttermilk (store-bought or homemade) or strained plain milk kefir (no grains)

1   If using pasteurized whipping cream, pour the cream into a clean quart-size jar and add 1 tablespoon of the cultured buttermilk or kefir. Mix well with a large clean spoon and then cover the jar loosely with a lid or a clean cloth secured with a rubber band or piece of twine. (If using raw whipping cream, simply pour the cream into the jar and then cover the jar as instructed.)

2   Place the jar in a location that is out of direct sunlight and between 65°F to 85°F (18°C to 29°C).

3   Taste the cream with a clean spoon every few hours until the cream reaches a level of tanginess that you like. (Use a clean spoon each time.) Allow the cream to culture for up to 8 hours, but no longer. (You want the cream to remain pourable and not become firm.)

4   Once the cultured cream reaches the flavor you like, tighten a lid on the jar. This cream is best used after being refrigerated for 24 hours and will stay fresh in the refrigerator for 1 to 2 weeks.

COOK'S NOTES

What to look for when purchasing whipping cream: Use only heavy whipping cream for this recipe. Do not use table cream, light cream, or heavy cream that is not labeled heavy whipping cream. Try to find a brand that does not contain stabilizers or other ingredients, including cellulose gum, carrageenan, diglycerides or mono-diglycerides, or polysorbate 80. These can interfere with the culturing process.

What if whey forms on your cultured cream? As your cream cultures, a small amount of liquid may form on top of the cream. This liquid is cultured whey. This can happen if the cream was cultured too quickly in an exceptionally warm environment. Simply mix the whey back into the cream and refrigerate it.

What if the cream separates into solids (curds) and whey? If the cream separates into curds and whey, the cream has overcultured. If this happens, do not attempt to use it to make cultured butter, but do not discard it. The curds and whey can be mixed back together and you will have something more similar to a crème fraîche.

Cultured Butter and Cultured Buttermilk

If you've not had cultured butter, you're in for a treat! It has a delightful tang that makes it the ideal spread on toasted homemade sourdough bread. It's also perfect melted over vegetables, atop a baked potato, or melted over a perfectly cooked steak. Since this butter is cultured and teaming with beneficial bacteria, it's best not to use it in cooked recipes, as the cooking process would destroy its benefits. The bonus in this recipe is that you also make cultured buttermilk!

TOTAL TIME: **6–11 MINUTES**
YIELD: **APPROXIMATELY 1LB (454G)**

INGREDIENTS

32fl oz (946ml) cultured cream that is cool but not cold (it should be approximately 50°F–60°F (10°C–16°C)

½ tsp fine ground sea salt (optional)

1. Pour the cultured cream into a medium bowl or the bowl of a stand mixer.

2. Using an electric handheld whisk or stand mixer with the whisk attachment (often referred to as a *balloon whisk*), whip the cream until butter forms and a pale milky white liquid is left in the bottom of the bowl. (This white liquid is real cultured buttermilk and can be used just like store-bought buttermilk.) Transfer the buttermilk to a resealable glass jar and set it aside.

3. Line a colander or mesh strainer with a flour-sack towel or cheesecloth and place the lined strainer over a bowl. Transfer the butter into the lined mesh strainer. Pull the corners of the cloth together and squeeze out as much additional buttermilk as possible from the butter. Add the additional buttermilk to the resealable glass jar and place it in the fridge.

4. Transfer the butter from the flour-sack towel or cheesecloth to a clean bowl and cover it with cold water that is filtered and chlorine-free.

5. Press the butter with a spatula to release any bits of remaining buttermilk. (The water will become cloudy.) Pour off the water and repeat the process until the water remains clear and no more buttermilk can be pressed out of the butter.

6. Drain off the water from the bowl, but keep the butter in the bowl. Press the butter with the spatula to release any water that still remains from the rinsing process. (You can also use a flour-sack towel to press and dry the butter.)

7. Once there is no more water on the butter, add the salt (if using) and use the spatula to work it into the butter.

8. Transfer the butter to a surface covered with wax paper, parchment paper, or plastic wrap. Form the butter into a log or rectangular shape. Wrap the butter well or put it in a butter dish and refrigerate. The butter should remain fresh for approximately 2 weeks.

> ········· COOK'S NOTES ·········
>
> ***Why the cream needs to be cool and not cold:*** To have success making butter, whether cultured or not, it is very important that you start with cool cream and not very cold cream. If you do not have a thermometer to check the temperature, you are simply looking for the container holding the cream to feel pleasantly cool to the touch—like cool tap water. If you start with very cold cream, the butter might not form.
>
> ***Storing and using cultured buttermilk:*** The buttermilk should stay fresh for approximately 2 weeks in the coldest part of your refrigerator (usually on the lowest shelf in the back and never in the refrigerator door). It can also be frozen for up to 2 months. Over time, the buttermilk might thicken a bit to resemble store-bought buttermilk, but it can be used in any recipe calling for store-bought buttermilk. Cultured buttermilk is rich in probiotics, so you can drink it for a beneficial bacteria boost!

Easy Stovetop Cottage Cheese

There are a number of ways to make homemade cottage cheese, and the way outlined in this recipe is by far the easiest! It's an excellent go-to ingredient whenever you have a recipe calling for some sort of stovetop or farmer's cheese. It's also a great substitution in recipes calling for cream cheese, mascarpone, Neufchâtel, ricotta, or sour cream. And it's high in protein, so it can be added to smoothies in place of expensive protein powders.

COOK TIME: **20–25 MINUTES**
RESTING TIME: **30 MINUTES**
STRAINING TIME: **10 MINUTES**
TOTAL TIME: **APPROXIMATELY 1 HOUR**
YIELD: **APPROXIMATELY 3 CUPS**

INGREDIENTS

1 gallon (3.75L) pasteurized whole milk

¼ cup 5% white distilled vinegar (alternatively, fresh or bottled lemon juice can be substituted, but it will impart a mild lemon flavor)

¼ cup heavy cream (optional)

Fine ground sea salt, to taste (optional)

1. Add the milk to a large pot over medium heat. Warm the milk, stirring frequently, until it reaches approximately 120°F (49°C) on a food-safe thermometer, like a candy thermometer. (This may take 20 to 25 minutes.) Alternatively, use a clean spoon to remove a bit of the warm milk from the pot and use your finger to touch the milk in the spoon. It should feel comfortably warm to the touch, like a warm bath. (Do not return this milk to the pot.) Don't worry if the milk is warmed to slightly under or over 120°F (49°C), all that will happen is that you will have a slight variation in the texture of the final product.

2. Once the milk reaches the desired temperature, remove the pot from the heat to a heatproof surface and then gently pour in the vinegar. Stir for a minute or two to ensure the vinegar is well distributed throughout the milk. Cover the pot and set it aside to rest for 30 minutes.

3. After 30 minutes, the milk should have curdled significantly and the liquid surrounding the curds should be a pale yellow. If the liquid still looks a white milk color, add an additional ¼ cup of vinegar and stir gently. More curds should form fairly quickly and the liquid should turn a pale yellow. Sometimes this can take a few extra minutes, but you do not need to re-cover the pot.

4. Line a colander or mesh strainer with a flour-sack towel or cheesecloth and then place it over a bowl. Pour the contents of the pot into the lined colander. The yellow liquid, which is acid whey, will strain through, and you should be left with curds in the towel or cheesecloth. Allow the curds to strain for approximately 10 minutes or until very little whey is dripping into the bowl.

5. You should now have approximately 3 cups of cottage cheese that has the appearance of dry curds. Add the heavy cream (if using) to the curds and then add sea salt to taste (if using) to give the curds a taste and texture more similar to store-bought cottage cheese.

6. Transfer the cottage cheese to a container with a tight-fitting lid. It should stay fresh in the refrigerator for approximately 1 to 2 weeks.

> ···················· COOK'S NOTES ····················
>
> *Using this cottage cheese in recipes:* If you use this cottage cheese to replace cream cheese, Neufchâtel, marscapone, ricotta, or sour cream in a recipe, run it through a blender or food processor first to create a creamy texture. If you want to use this cottage cheese in place of marscapone in a recipe, do not add salt to it.
>
> *Can you use raw milk in this recipe?* I specify using pasteurized milk in this recipe since we are heating it. I would reserve raw milk, if available, for drinking or where it will not be heated beyond 110°F (43°C).

Chapter Five
PICKLING AND FERMENTING

GETTING STARTED WITH PICKLING AND FERMENTING

Pickling and fermenting are easy and tasty ways to preserve fruits and vegetables in the same way our ancestors did. Although they are quite different in their preparation, both pickling and fermenting have places in the traditional foods kitchen. They prevent waste through the preservation of a variety of foods and help with digestion, especially when served with cooked foods.

What Is Pickling?

Pickling is the simple process of pouring a hot brine over fresh produce and then giving it a bit of time to pickle. This brine can be as simple as a mix of vinegar, salt, and water or you can enhance it with a bit of sugar, herbs, and spices. Vegetables are the most commonly pickled produce. The pickling process preserves the vegetables so that they can be enjoyed when their fresh counterparts are not available. In addition, pickled vegetables are often high in fiber, which serves as a prebiotic. This type of fiber feeds the probiotics—the good or beneficial bacteria—in our digestive systems.

If you are new to preserving fresh produce, pickling is a great place to start. It's basically foolproof. It also allows you the luxury of being able to home can your produce, which you will learn more about in the chapter on water bath canning.

Even though pickled vegetables are not rich in gut-loving probiotics, there is a little trick you can employ to add in some good bacteria. In a way, I like to think of this as the busy home cook's quick and easy mock fermentation. After placing your fresh produce in a jar, only fill the jar three-quarters of the way with hot brine. Allow the brine to cool, then top the jar with raw apple cider vinegar (homemade or store-bought). Raw apple cider vinegar contains the "mother." This "mother" is rich in the probiotic acetic acid bacteria. This type of bacteria differs from the lactobacillus bacteria commonly found in naturally fermented foods, but it is still rich in probiotics.

What Is Fermenting?

Fermenting, specifically, lacto-fermentation, is a type of fermentation to preserve food that uses lactic acid–producing bacteria called *Lactobacillus*, which are naturally occurring on fresh produce. These lactobacillus bacteria convert the naturally occurring sugars in vegetables and fruits into lactic acid. This is the same lactobacillus that assists in the fermentation process and is present in fermented dairy, such as yogurt, and in sourdough starter. These bacteria also live in our digestive tracts. Because the bacteria reside on the fresh produce being fermented, they do not need the help of naturally occurring yeasts and bacteria in the air. Since no air is required to ferment fresh produce, it is referred to as an *anaerobic* (without oxygen) fermentation.

The process of lacto-fermentation involves submerging fresh produce under a saltwater brine and then leaving it at room temperature for a specified time. During this time, the naturally occurring bacteria on the produce begin the process of lacto-fermentation. Lacto-fermentation not only preserves the fresh produce, it actually makes the produce more nutritious than when it was raw! Lacto-fermentation creates a probiotic-rich food and preserves the live enzymes present in raw food to make it easier for our bodies to absorb the available nutrients. Lacto-fermentation may also increase certain vitamins in the food being fermented. This keeps our digestive systems healthy and boosts our immunity too, because the more good bacteria we have in our digestive tracts, the better we can absorb the nutrients from our food, and in turn, the healthier we are overall.

In addition to discussing the good bacteria present in ferments, I want to take a moment to focus on the live enzymes. Raw foods, also sometimes referred to as *living foods*, contain live enzymes. During the lacto-fermentation process, these enzymes break down the nutrients contained in the fresh produce into more easily digestible particles. The more we make our food digestible, the easier it is for our bodies to absorb the nutrients it contains.

A great deal of scientific research has been devoted to the study of fermented foods. These types of foods have been eaten by basically every traditional culture throughout history. Lacto-fermentation was a way traditional cultures were able to preserve food long before the invention of refrigeration or home canning. But even though we have these modern conveniences available to us today, we want to be sure to include a variety of fermented foods in our diets since they contributed to the good health of generations before us and now can serve to keep us healthy as well!

Sauerkraut Makes the Best Sandwich!

When I was growing up, my mother often pickled vegetables. It was a great way to make use of various scraps she had around the kitchen by turning them into a crunchy pickle. As a child, my favorites were always those she pickled in a sweet-and-sour brine. Don't get me wrong, pickled vegetables that often carried the "dill" moniker weren't bad and are some of my favorites today, but I think every child loves that hint of sweetness when encouraged to eat their vegetables!

We had ferments bubbling away in our kitchen. Most of the time it was sauerkraut, an Italian vegetable mix, or something called *mostarda*, which is a fermented fruit and mustard combination often served with cooked meats. My mom is of Northern Italian heritage, so it wasn't as though sauerkraut was a familiar food to her. My father was of

Irish heritage, and sauerkraut wasn't exactly an Irish food either. But as a boy, my dad grew up in Jersey City, where he worked in a little food market that had a German bakery next door. Mrs. Linda, as my dad called her, made the best rye bread he had ever had. Plus, she always had a crock of sauerkraut bubbling in the back room for putting between two pieces of that heavenly rye bread. At the end of a long workday, Mr. MacGillacuddy, who ran the little market, would give my dad a thick slice of liverwurst wrapped in butcher paper. Heading over to Mrs. Linda's with wrapped liverwurst in hand, my dad would offer to help sweep the floor and do other odd clean-up jobs around the bakery.

Once my dad was finished with his chores, Mrs. Linda would give him two thick slices of rye bread and a heaping helping of sauerkraut. My dad would then make what he fondly remembered as the best sandwich ever. He would sit on the curb outside the bakery and enjoy every last bit of it! The sauerkraut, he would tell me, was what made the sandwich so delicious.

Since fermenting was a skill familiar to my mom, it was easy for her to make the transition from fermenting Italian veggies to fermenting cabbage. She was so happy to make foods my dad enjoyed, and she soon discovered that she loved homemade sauerkraut too. She even turned red cabbage into a sweet fermented sauerkraut, my favorite, often served with pork chops slow simmered in apple juice.

Lacto-fermentation—Patience Coupled with a Little Bit of Trial and Error

Lacto-fermentation takes a bit more skill than pickling. Although it's not difficult, you must be patient and be prepared for a bit of trial and error. The secret to a successful fresh produce ferment, such as with vegetables, comes down to temperature. Ferments don't like to be too hot or too cold.

Our ancestors generally started their ferments at the end of the harvest season. The fall season would be approaching, and temperatures would be cooling off a bit from the heat of the summer. There are differences of opinions as to the optimal temperature for fermentation, in this case lacto-fermentation, but it is often recommended that a successful fresh produce ferment will occur somewhere between 68°F and 72°F (20°C and 22°C). But you can still successfully ferment as low as 60°F (16°C) and as high as 75°F (24°C). Some sources might even say you can ferment at a temperature as high as 80°F (27°C). (From personal experience, I have found that to be a bit too high.)

Keeping the Bad Bacteria at Bay, While the Good Can Proliferate

Ferments generally do not like to be rushed. When the temperature climbs, the fermentation process can speed up, creating a ferment that has a mushy texture and possibly a slimy texture too! There is also the challenge of keeping bad bacteria and molds at bay while giving the good bacteria a chance to gain a strong foothold in the ferment. That's why the right temperature is so important. At the optimal temperature, the good bacteria will take over to create lactic acid, which is a natural preservative that will make it considerably more difficult for spoilage to occur. With the right conditions, the ferment creates an environment that is no longer hospitable to the bad bacteria.

The good news is that once you locate the best place in your home for fermenting vegetables at the right temperature, you will be well on your way to success. That was certainly my biggest challenge when I started fermenting in our home. In central Texas, even in the fall season, temperatures can still run high, topping out in the 90s. And running the air conditioning to get my western exposure kitchen down to 72°F (22°C) was not an option. Can you imagine my electric bill?!

Finding the Sweet Spot for Ferments

Even though we have an old home that is probably not the best insulated, we have a bedroom closet on the northern side of the house (read: no direct, unrelenting sun exposure) with no windows. And how convenient that this closet has shelves. Maybe they were intended for shoes, but I saw them as a staging area for my vegetable ferments.

God bless my husband. He has lived through many an interesting traditional foods adventure with me. I have often told him to look away and not concern himself with my kitchen alchemy. He's usually happy to make an about-face from the kitchen and oblige. But bubbling ferments in our bedroom closet were something that he simply couldn't avoid. Those, along with the vinegar "mother" in the laundry room, were both believed by my husband and son to one day assuredly escape and take over the house like the Blob from the old 1958 movie!

I tell you this, a bit tongue in cheek, to show you that you never know where you might find that sweet spot in your home where your ferments do the best. Oh, and a word to the wise: always remember to put your jar of ferments in a bowl. This bowl will save the day if your ferment bubbles out and over the jar lid. There will be no necessary clean-up of sticky shelves, brine-soaked carpet, or salt-stained shoes. Trust me, I speak from experience! Just use a bowl and everything else will stay clean and dry.

Fermentation of any kind all boils down to a bit of trial and error. But you will discover that perfect fermentation sweet spot quickly when it comes to lacto-fermentation, because if you don't start to see some bubbling in your jar within a day or two, it's time to continue your search.

Remember to use your kitchen journal to record the time period, location, temperature, food item, and success (or mishaps) of your fermentation attempts. Looking through the past ferment records in your journal will help you understand where your ferments thrive and where they may encounter challenges the next time you try another fermentation.

And speaking of bubbles, what exactly are they and why do we want to see them? There are a lot of reactions going on in your fermentation jar, and the most important one is when the good bacteria are hard at work creating lactic acid. This reaction creates gas, which causes the visible bubbles you will observe throughout the jar after a few days of room-temperature fermentation. Seeing bubbles in a ferment is a sign that the lacto-fermentation process is off to a great start.

Start with Lacto-fermenting Vegetables

For the home cook, it's easiest to ferment vegetables. You can ferment fruits, but it requires a watchful eye to avoid creating alcohol, if that is not your intent. Remember, wine is a ferment!

When I was new to fermenting fruit many years ago, I once gave my father some fermented raisins. I had read in an alternative health magazine that they were supposed to help ease arthritis pain in the hands, which he had. After about a month, I asked my dad how the raisins were working. He responded that he didn't know about the raisins, but the alcohol they were preserved in was working great! It's for this reason that as a beginner, it's best to start with vegetable fermentation first and then master the art of fruit fermentation later.

The Benefit of Tannins

When fresh produce is properly fermented, it will have a delightfully tangy taste with a sour but pleasant aroma. It will also be crisp. However, sometimes maintaining the crispness of certain fermented produce can use a little help. Enter tannins.

Tannins are astringent compounds commonly found in a wide variety of foods, including grape leaves and grape skins. But for the home cook attempting lacto-fermentation, one of the easiest ways to incorporate tannins into your ferment is with tea leaves or bay leaves. And as to the tea leaves, it doesn't matter whether they are black or green tea leaves or caffeinated or decaf tea leaves. None of that matters. We are after the tannins that are present in all varieties of tea. (However, don't use herbal tea.)

It may sound odd to place a tea bag into a jar of fresh produce ready for fermentation, but you will not notice it's in there. Instead, you will note how nice and crisp your ferments are. Now keep in mind that not all lacto-fermented fresh produce benefits from tannins. Some—such as sauerkraut, which is best as it softens over time—do just fine without them. However, carrots and cucumbers are best fermented with tannins to help keep them crisp.

What About the Water?

As with salt, you want to keep the water you use when fermenting as pure as possible. This means you want to use water that is free of chlorine or chemicals related to chlorine, such as chloramines. These chemicals sanitize drinking water, but they can also interfere with the lacto-fermentation process. Plus, you'll want to filter out other impurities that are in tap water that might interfere with the fermentation process. So using bottled water, spring water, or water run through a home filtration device will often yield the best results.

But do not stress over this. If the only option you have is chlorinated tap water, you can pour it into a pitcher and leave it out on the counter overnight. This will help some of the chlorine to dissipate, and you can then use this water for the lacto-fermentation process. If you find that your ferments are unsuccessful when following this step, consider buying bottled water or using a home water-filtration device.

The Reassurance Offered by pH Strips

When you first start lacto-fermenting, you might wonder when your ferment is ready. I always recommend, especially for the beginner, that you do not keep your ferment at room temperature for more than 14 days. At this point, the lacto-fermenation process should be in full swing, and chances are your ferment has a pleasant sour taste and has still retained its crunch.

But how do you know for sure that your ferment is ready? First, the slightly sour but pleasant aroma is one indication. Taste is another. The ferment should be tangy, similar to a pickled vegetable, but less vinegary. But even with these two tests, you might still wonder if your ferment is ready. And many home cooks who are new to lacto-fermenation may also wonder if it is safe to eat.

Enter pH strips. pH measures the acid or alkaline level of a liquid. When it comes to lacto-ferments, you want them to be acidic. This acidity keeps bad bacteria at bay and makes your ferment safe to eat. With this in mind, if you test the brine of your ferment before refrigerating it, you are looking for a pH of 4.6 or lower. pH strips are easy to find at most drug stores or online and are reasonably priced. So when you first start making lacto-ferments, be sure to have some pH strips on hand. They will provide you with the assurance that you are doing everything correctly.

Refrigerating Your Ferment

Refrigerating your ferment when the pH is 4.6 or lower will allow it to maintain its pleasant flavor and texture. And when looking for the best place in your fridge for your ferment, the top shelf or the door shelves are your best bets. Ferments are happy when stored for the long term at a temperature of around 40°F (4°C). This slows the fermentation process considerably, maintaining the quality of your ferment for as long as possible. The top shelf of your refrigerator or the door are usually the warmest spots compared to the rest of the fridge, which generally is closer to 38°F (3°C). It's important to note that vegetable ferments of any kind cannot be stored at room temperature.

Keep in mind that even though the ferment has been refrigerated, the lacto-fermentation process will continue, just at a much slower rate. Over time, the fermented produce will soften and is best consumed within 6 months of being refrigerated. However, the fermentation is best consumed at its peak within 4 months of being refrigerated for the optimum flavor and texture.

A World of Possibilities

As you begin to pickle and ferment fresh produce, you will discover what you like best. Although I share some of my favorites in the recipes that follow, start to experiment once you hone your skills. There is a world of pickled and lacto-fermented foods that awaits you! Experiment with different levels of sweetness, as well as a variety of herbs and spices. You really can't go wrong. And remember: always save a bit of your brine from your latest ferment. You can always add a bit of that brine to a new ferment to help jump-start the process and ensure success.

Choosing Fermentation Vessels for Vegetable Ferments

When it comes to creating a successful vegetable lacto-fermentation, water, salt, and temperature all play essential roles. But the vessel you choose for your fermentation can also affect your success. Does that mean you need to purchase expensive equipment to start fermenting? Definitely not! But you do want to make sure that whatever vessel you do choose will keep your ferments completely submerged under the brine.

When you culture dairy or make a sourdough starter, you don't need to worry about protecting them from air because they are aerobic ferments, so they are happy to be exposed to air.

However, when it comes to vegetable ferments, air—and specifically oxygen—is the enemy. So to be successful with an anaerobic fermentation (without oxygen), you must keep air away from your ferment. One of the most affordable options when choosing an anaerobic fermentation vessel is a wide-mouth 32-ounce (.95L) or 64-ounce (1.90L) glass jar with a screw-on lid. The lid may not be perfectly airtight, but that's okay because you'll use another smaller jar to submerge your ferment under the brine and keep it away from air.

A wide-mouth glass jar has an opening (between 3 and 4 inches [7.60cm and 10.15cm]) that allows you to easily place the smaller regular-mouth glass jar (preferably 4 ounces [118ml], often referred to as a *canning jelly jar*, and with an opening under 3 inches [7.60cm]) into the larger jar and on top of your ferment before you screw on the lid. This small jar will be your homemade version of a glass fermentation weight. You will have created the perfect fermentation vessel and will be using one of my favorite ways to ferment vegetables.

Having larger and smaller glass jars is the ideal place to start when you are new to ferments because there is very little expense associated with creating this type of fermentation system. Chances are, the jars you use for fermentations will most likely be jars you are already using as food storage containers or as part of your existing home-canning equipment.

As you become more experienced with fermentation, you may find that you would like to upgrade your supplies to include vessels specifically made for ferments. There are a whole host of modern options, including special jars, weights, airlock lids, and carbon dioxide–release valves. However, if you want to feel like a true modern pioneer in the kitchen, then be on the hunt for a food-safe crock that is usually ceramic or stoneware. You can often find these crocks at country stores or thrift stores. And today, they are even sold online. Although many people will use these types of crocks for home decorations, they are actually made for fermentation.

When purchased new, these fermentation crocks often come with a two-piece set of heavy ceramic or glass food-grade weights to help keep your ferments submerged under the brine. Along with the weights, most complete crock sets will also include a stoneware, ceramic, or wood lid to keep pests at bay. If you happen to find a food-safe crock in used condition that is without the added equipment, don't worry; the weights and lids are available for sale online or often can be found at local hardware stores.

A WORD ON SALT

The process of lacto-fermenting fresh produce generally needs salt. But how do you know how much salt? Yes, you can get involved in mathematical calculations using a scale, but I think that's a bit overkill. And to be honest with you, I never want to tell anyone they have to buy a scale. It just goes against my inner modern pioneer! Do we really think traditional cultures were measuring salt so precisely? I don't think so.

I suspect that our ancestors put their fresh produce in layers in a crock, alternating with a handful of salt, to submerge everything under a brine. They then waited until it reached a consistency and taste they were happy with. That's certainly what I saw my mother do. And as modern pioneers in the kitchen, we can do the same thing!

There are various recommendations about how much salt to use when fermenting, so that you have enough to keep bad bacteria at bay but not so much that you kill your good bacteria. Generally, if you start with about 3 pounds (1.35kg) of fresh produce, specifically fresh vegetables, you can use somewhere between 2 round tablespoons of coarse salt or 1½ level tablespoons of fine ground salt.

I recommend using sea salt or any salt that simply lists the word *salt* as the only ingredient, such as canning and pickling salt. You do not want to use iodized salt or any salt containing chemicals such as anticaking agents. All of these additional ingredients might interfere with the lacto-fermentation process. And since ferments can be, as I often say, persnickety, we want to start with the best ingredients possible to ensure we achieve the best possible outcome.

Initially, your completed ferment may taste a bit salty, but once you refrigerate it, it will begin to mellow. The vegetables will absorb more of the brine and become tastier, while the brine will become less salty.

Pickled Vegetables

When you don't have the time to wait for a ferment, a pickle can be your answer. You can pickle pretty much any vegetable, including vegetable scraps, for a tasty treat. And a pickle can be ready generally within 24 hours, hence the often-named *quick pickle*.

Some of my favorite fresh produce to pickle includes peeled beets, carrots, cauliflower, celery, green tomatoes, corn, cucumbers, peeled ginger, okra, sliced red onions, parsnips, peppers (both sweet and spicy), and radishes.

PREP TIME: **5 MINUTES**
COOK TIME: **1 MINUTE**
TOTAL TIME: **6 MINUTES**
YIELD: **4–8 SERVINGS (DEPENDING ON THE VEGETABLE BEING PICKLED)**

INGREDIENTS

1lb (454g) or enough to fill a quart-size jar of vegetables or vegetable scraps, cut into bite-size pieces

1 tbsp fresh herbs (optional) (see **Cook's Notes**)

1 cup tap water

1 cup white vinegar (see **Cook's Notes**)

1 tbsp canning and pickling salt

2 tbsp white sugar or whole sweetener (optional) (see **Cook's Notes**)

1 tbsp Pickling Spice Mix (optional) (see **Cook's Notes**)

1 tsp red pepper flakes (also labeled "crushed red pepper") (optional)

1. Add the bite-size vegetables or scraps to a clean and warm quart-size jar (or 2 pint-size jars). If you are using fresh herbs, also add these to the jar. Pack everything tightly up to the rim of the jar(s).

2. Add the water, vinegar, and salt to a nonreactive saucepan (stainless steel or ceramic). If using, also add the sweetener and pickling spices. For a spicy kick, add the red pepper flakes. Bring the mixture to a boil over high heat.

3. Once the mixture comes to a boil, turn the heat off, remove the saucepan from the stovetop, and place it on a heatproof surface. (This mixture is your pickling brine.)

4. Ladle the warm pickling brine over the vegetables in the jar(s). Make sure to fill the jar with the pickling brine up to the rim of the jar so that all the vegetables or scraps are submerged under the brine.

5. Allow the jar(s) to cool to room temperature, about 1 hour. Once cooled, place the lid(s) on the jar(s) and refrigerate.

6. Quick pickles are best enjoyed after being refrigerated for 24 hours and will stay fresh and crisp in the refrigerator for approximately 2 months. After 2 months, they may begin to lose their crisp texture.

.... COOK'S NOTES ....

What fresh herbs can use you use? If you decide to add fresh herbs, options that work well include bay leaves, chives, dill, oregano, and thyme. Rosemary should be used only in small quantities, as it can be overpowering and create a soapy flavor.

Making a tangier pickle: For a tangier pickle, increase the ratio of water and vinegar to 1 part water to 2 parts vinegar.

Choosing a sweetener: If you decide to make a sweetened brine, you can use white sugar. If you prefer to avoid white sugar, other options include whole sweeteners (ones in which the nutrients have been left intact, such as unrefined whole cane sugar, maple sugar, maple syrup, date sugar, or date syrup). Do not use honey, since is generally recommended that it should not be heated, and I do not recommend using molasses, because the flavor is too strong.

Pickling Spice Mix recipe: Pickling spice can be purchased premixed in most spice aisles or home-canning aisles at the grocery store and is labeled as such. It generally includes a mix of (but is not limited to) allspice, bay leaves, cardamom, cinnamon, cloves, coriander, ginger, mustard seeds, and peppercorns. If you do not have pickling spice on hand, you can make your own by combining the following in a quart-size jar with a tight-fitting lid:

1 cup yellow mustard seeds
½ cup allspice berries
½ cup dill seed
½ cup celery seed
¼ cup whole cloves
¼ cup caraway seeds
1 cinnamon stick, broken into pieces
2–3 bay leaves, crumbled
½ tsp dried ground ginger

Sauerkraut

Homemade sauerkraut is a wonderful nutrient-rich food that is slightly tangy and a touch effervescent. It makes the perfect accompaniment to any meal because it's high in probiotics, as well as enzymes, both of which aid the digestive tract by improving gut health and assisting with digestion, allowing our bodies to better absorb nutrients from the food we eat.

PREP TIME: **15 MINUTES**
FERMENTATION TIME: **7–14 DAYS**
TOTAL TIME: **7–14 DAYS PLUS 15 MINUTES**
YIELD: **4–6 SERVINGS**

EQUIPMENT

Stand blender

Large stainless steel bowl (avoid using glass or pottery to prevent shattering)

Kraut pounder, manual potato masher, or wooden spoon

2 wide-mouth quart-size glass jars with lids

2 small glass jars that are no larger than a 4-ounce canning jelly jar and can fit into the opening of the half-gallon–size jar (If you use 2 quart-size jars, you will need 2 small glass jars.)

2 bowls large enough to hold the large jars

pH strips (for checking the acidity)

INGREDIENTS

1 large head green cabbage (about 3lb [1.35kg])

2 rounded tbsp coarse ground sea salt or 1½ tbsp fine ground sea salt

1 medium green apple, quartered, cored, and roughly chopped

Enough filtered, chlorine-free water to cover the vegetables

PREP INSTRUCTIONS

1   Remove a few outer leaves of the cabbage and reserve. Cut the head of cabbage in half and then cut out and reserve the cores. Slice each half into thin strips.

2   Place the shredded cabbage and salt in a large metal bowl. Pound with a kraut pounder (or other utensil) for approximately 5 minutes or until the cabbage begins to release some of its juices.

3   Add the chopped apple to a blender. Coarsely chop the cores of the cabbage and add to the blender. Add enough filtered water to cover the ingredients. Blend to make a slurry.

4   Add the apple-cabbage slurry to the bowl with the cabbage. Mix well.

5   Place all the apple-cabbage mixture into the jars. (The entire cabbage mixture should be used. There should be nothing remaining in the bowl.)

6   Firmly press the mixture down into the jars using the kraut pounder or a wooden spoon. Compact the cabbage mixture as tightly as possible.

7   Fold the reserved cabbage leaves and place them into the jars and on top of the shredded cabbage mixture.

8   Place the small glass jars (jelly jars) into the larger jars and on top of the folded cabbage leaves. (The smaller jars will work as weights to hold the entire mixture under the liquid.)

9   If needed, add additional filtered water to ensure that all the cabbage mixture is completely submerged under the liquid, but still allowing for approximately 1 inch (2.5cm) of headspace from the neck of the jar to the very top rim of the jar. (The liquid should reach only to the beginning of the neck of the jars.)

10 Place the lids on the jars and tighten gently. (You do not have to use brute force!)

11 Place the jars into the bowls so they are sitting securely. (The bowls will catch any liquids that might escape from the tops of the jars as the cabbage mixture ferments.)

FERMENTATION INSTRUCTIONS

1   Place the jars in an undisturbed place with an ideal average room temperature range somewhere between 68°F and 72°F (20°C and 22°C). The jars should also be out of direct sunlight, as ferments do not like temperature fluctuations.

2   After a few days, you should see bubbles forming in the jars. Recheck the jars daily and loosen and then retighten the lids to release some of the carbon dioxide. (This will help keep your jars from breaking.)

3   After seven days, remove the lids on the jars and smell the ferments. They should begin to take on a bit of a sour but pleasant aroma—somewhat like a mild vinegar. At this point, check the pH of the sauerkraut by using a clean spoon to remove some of the liquid from the jars. Place the liquid in a small glass and insert the pH strip into the liquid.

4   Quickly remove the pH strip from the liquid, and measure the level of acidity against the colored chart provided with the strips. If the pH is 4.6 or lower, it has successfully fermented and is safe to taste. If you like the taste, refrigerate it. It's now ready to enjoy.

5   If you are not satisfied with the taste of the sauerkraut or if the pH is still above 4.6, you can allow it to continue fermenting for up to 14 days at room temperature before refrigerating. (See **Cook's Notes.**) The refrigerated sauerkraut is best consumed within 4 to 6 months.

······· **COOK'S NOTES** ·······

Can you omit the green apple? You can omit the green apple, but it is an insurance policy to guarantee a successful ferment. The natural fruit sugar is gobbled up by any yeast that may be present and then primarily consumed by the good bacteria. This helps to jump-start the fermentation process and minimize the possibility of bad bacteria or molds taking over.

Can you use a red apple? Yes, you can use a red apple in this recipe, but if you leave the skin on you may see red flecks in your sauerkraut. However, this can be easily resolved by peeling the apple.

When should you discard the ferment? If the pH for the sauerkraut still does not measure 4.6 or lower on the fourteenth day of your ferment, you should discard your ferment, and try it again under different conditions. For example, the location where your ferment was resting may not have been in the proper temperature range. If you leave your ferment out at room temperature for too long, the texture will decline, your ferment will become mushy and slimy, and mold may develop.

Can you drink the kraut juice? For an added gut health benefit, drink some of the kraut juice, which is the liquid that accumulates in the jar. The juice is teeming with good bacteria!

Reserving the juice as a starter: Always reserve at least 1 tablespoon or up to ¼ cup of the kraut juice to use as a starter for making your next ferment. Just add it to the jar with the vegetables you plan to ferment.

Always-Crisp Fermented Dill Pickle Spears

Making crisp lacto-fermented pickles is easy and considerably less expensive than buying them from high-end grocery stores. This probiotic-rich food is perfect for good gut health, and best of all, by adding a regular black tea bag to the brine, these will never become mushy! And the tea will not impart any noticeable flavor.

PREP TIME: **5 MINUTES**
FERMENTATION TIME:
 APPROXIMATELY 7 DAYS
TOTAL TIME: **APPROXIMATELY 7 DAYS PLUS 5 MINUTES**
YIELD: **16 PICKLE SPEARS**

EQUIPMENT

1 wide-mouth quart-size glass jar with lid (A wide-mouth jar has an opening that is approximately 3⅓ inches [8.5cm] across or larger.)

1 small glass jar that is no larger than a 4-ounce canning jelly jar and can fit into the opening of the quart-size jar

1 bowl large enough to hold the quart-size jar

pH strips (for checking the acidity)

INGREDIENTS

1 black tea bag (optional)
 (see **Cook's Notes**)

4 pickling cucumbers (such as Kirby)

1 tbsp pickling spice (or any combination of spices you prefer)

4 sprigs fresh dill (optional)

1½ level tbsp coarse ground sea salt or 2¼ level tsp fine ground sea salt

Enough filtered, chlorine-free water to cover the cucumbers

Chapter Five
PICKLING AND FERMENTING

1. Place the tea bag (if using) and pickling spices into the bottom of the quart-size jar.

2. Slice the blossom end from each cucumber. The slice should be very thin, about $\frac{1}{16}$ inch. (The blossom end is the side that was not attached to the plant. This end contains enzymes that can make your cucumbers mushy.) Quarter each cucumber lengthwise into spears.

3. Pack the cucumber spears tightly into the jar. (If using the dill, alternate placing the spears into the jar with placing the dill sprigs into the jar.)

4. Sprinkle the sea salt into the jar and on top of the cucumbers.

5. Pour enough water into the jar to cover the cucumbers completely. Place the jelly jar on top of the cucumbers.

6. Place a lid on the quart-size jar and tighten. Place the jar into the bowl. (The bowl will catch any liquid that might escape from the top of the jar as the cucumbers go through the fermentation process.)

7. Place the jar in a room-temperature area that averages between 68°F and 72°F (20°C and 22°C) and is out of direct sunlight. (Cucumbers ferment best in a cooler rather than a warmer environment.)

8. By the second day of fermentation, you may begin to see bubbles developing in the jar. From this point forward, release the lid daily and then retighten. (This will release some of the carbon dioxide and prevent the jar from breaking.)

9. After a few days, you will notice that the brine might become quite cloudy. This is a normal part of the fermentation process. At this point, remove the jelly jar and use a clean spoon to remove some of the brine and test the acidity level using a pH strip. A successful ferment will have a pH of 4.6 or lower. If the pH is at the correct level, use a clean fork to remove one of the pickle spears and transfer it to a clean plate. Either cut into the spear or taste it. If the texture is to your liking, put a lid on the jar and refrigerate your cucumbers. If the cucumbers have not reached a correct pH level or a satisfactory texture, continue to allow them to ferment.

10. By the seventh day, once again use a spoon to remove some of the brine and then test the acidity level using a pH strip. If the pickles have a pH of 4.6 or lower, remove the jelly jar, put a lid on the jar, and refrigerate your cucumbers. If the pickles still have not reached the proper pH level, it's best to discard the ferment and start over. Refrigerated, lacto-fermented pickles will stay fresh for approximately 4 to 6 months.

········· COOK'S NOTES ·········

What if the pickles taste too salty? After 7 days of fermentation, the cucumbers, which will be lacto-fermented, will taste salty. Over the next few weeks during refrigeration, the pickles will absorb more of the brine, increasing their flavor, and the brine, which clings to the pickles, will become less salty.

Why not add the salt directly into the brine? You will notice that I have you toss the salt into the jar and right on top of the cucumbers. Some online recipes may call for mixing your salt and water brine separately and then pouring this brine into the jar. The problem with this method is that you may not need all the brine to fill the jar, resulting in some of the brine being left behind and you losing some of the salt. Putting the salt straight into the jar guarantees that all the salt you need will be going into the jar, providing you with the best possible outcome for a successful ferment.

Other flavoring options: If desired, you can use 2 green tea bags or 3 to 4 dried or fresh bay leaves in place of the black tea bag. If you are using bay leaves, insert the leaves down the sides of the jar to be parallel with the cucumber spears.

Sweet & Sour Fermented Red Cabbage

Traditional sauerkraut made with green cabbage is delicious with its tangy crunch. However, sweetened, fermented red cabbage is exceptionally scrumptious, simply eaten by the bowlful or served along with a traditional German-inspired meal that might include boiled bratwurst or schnitzel.

PREP TIME: **15 MINUTES**
FERMENTATION TIME: **7–14 DAYS**
TOTAL TIME: **7–14 DAYS PLUS 15 MINUTES**
YIELD: **4–6 SERVINGS**

EQUIPMENT

Stand blender

Large stainless steel bowl (avoid using glass or pottery, which can shatter)

Kraut pounder, manual potato masher, or wooden spoon

2 wide-mouth quart-size glass jars with lids

2 small glass jars that are no larger than a 4-ounce canning jelly jar and can fit into the opening of the half-gallon–size jar. (If you use 2 quart-size jars, you will need 2 small glass jars.)

2 bowls large enough to hold the large jars

pH strips (for checking the acidity)

INGREDIENTS

1 large head red cabbage (about 3lb [1.36kg])

2 rounded tbsp coarse ground sea salt or 1½ level tbsp fine ground sea salt

1 green apple, quartered, cored, and roughly chopped

Enough filtered, chlorine-free water to cover the cabbage

¼ cup maple syrup or raw honey

PREP INSTRUCTIONS

1   Remove a few outer leaves of the head of cabbage and reserve. Cut the head of cabbage in half and then cut out and reserve the cores. Slice each half into thin strips.

2   Place the shredded cabbage and salt in a large nonreactive metal bowl. Pound with a kraut pounder (or other utensil) for approximately 5 minutes or until the cabbage begins to release some of its juices.

3   Add the chopped apple to a blender. Coarsely chop the cores of the cabbage and add to the blender. Add enough filtered water to cover the ingredients. Blend to make a slurry.

4   Add the apple-cabbage slurry to the bowl with the shredded cabbage. Mix well.

5   Place all the apple-cabbage mixture into the jars. (The entire cabbage mixture should be used. There should be nothing remaining in the bowl.)

6   Firmly press the mixture down into the jars using the kraut pounder or a wooden spoon to compact the mixture as tightly as possible.

7   Fold the reserved cabbage leaves and place them into the jars and on top of the shredded cabbage mixture.

8   Place the small glass jars (jelly jars) into the larger jars and on top of the folded cabbage leaves. (The smaller jars will work as weights to hold the entire mixture under the liquid.)

9   If needed, add additional filtered water to ensure that all the cabbage mixture is completely submerged under the liquid, while still allowing for approximately 1 inch (2.5cm) of headspace from the neck of the jar to the very top rim of the jar. (The liquid should reach only to the beginning of the neck of the jars.)

10 Place the lids on the jars and tighten gently. (You do not have to use brute force!)

11 Place the jars into the bowls so they are sitting securely. (The bowls will catch any liquids that might escape from the tops of the jars as the cabbage mixture ferments.)

FERMENTATION INSTRUCTIONS

1   Place the bowls in an undisturbed location with an ideal average room temperature range somewhere between 68°F and 72°F (20°C and 22°C) and out of direct sunlight.

2 After a few days, the red cabbage should begin fermenting and you should see bubbles forming in the jars. Recheck the jars every day and release some of the carbon dioxide by loosening and then retightening the lids.

3 After 7 days, remove the lids on the jars and smell the ferment. It should begin to take on a bit of a sour but pleasant aroma—somewhat like a mild vinegar. At this point, check the pH. Use a clean spoon to remove some of the liquid from the jars. Place the liquid in a small glass and insert the pH strip into the liquid. Quickly remove the pH strip from the liquid and measure the level of acidity against the colored chart provided with the strips. If the pH is 4.6 or lower, it has successfully fermented and is safe to taste. (Note that when fermenting red cabbage, the color of the brine may interfere with being able to see an exact pH, but you should be able to at least determine a range. If you are unable to determine a range, use the nose-and-eye test to examine the red cabbage. If there is a foul odor or any sign of mold, discard it and start over.)

4 If you are not satisfied with the texture of the red cabbage, or if the pH still appears to be above 4.6, you can allow the red cabbage to continue fermenting at room temperature for up to 7 more days before refrigerating. (See **Cook's Notes**.)

5 When the cabbage has reached the proper pH level, transfer the cabbage to a bowl. Add the maple syrup or honey, then stir to combine. Taste and add more, if desired, until the sweetness level pleases your palate. (I have generally found that ¼ cup of sweetener is sufficient.) (See **Cook's Notes**.)

6 Return the sweetened cabbage to the jar, place the lid on the jar, and tighten. Transfer the cabbage to the refrigerator. Store at approximately 40°F (5°C) on the top shelf or the door of your refrigerator. (Fermented red cabbage cannot be stored at room temperature.) The red cabbage is best consumed within 4 to 6 months.

······················· COOK'S NOTES ·······················

When should you discard the ferment? If the pH for the cabbage still does not measure 4.6 or lower on the fourteenth day of your ferment, you should discard the ferment. If you leave your ferment out at room temperature for too long, the texture will decline, your ferment will become mushy and slimy, and mold may develop.

Why do you not sweeten the cabbage at the start of the fermentation process? The reason is twofold. First, the sweetness associated with the maple syrup or honey might speed up the fermentation process while it is at room temperature, creating an overly softened and less palatable cabbage. And second, whenever we mix a sweetener with a ferment, there is always the possibility of creating alcohol. (I suspect most people are not interested in making—or drinking—cabbage wine!) When we sweeten the red cabbage at the end of the fermentation process, we immediately transfer the ferment to the refrigerator. Refrigeration slows down the fermentation process considerably, so there is significantly less chance of the red cabbage ferment creating an alcohol brine.

Fermented Giardiniera

Giardiniera is a tasty, probiotic-rich Italian relish that's perfect for topping sandwiches, salads, and more! It's especially nice served alongside grilled meats, chicken, or fish.

PREP TIME: **15 MINUTES**
FERMENTATION TIME: **3–14 DAYS**
TOTAL TIME: **3–14 DAYS PLUS 15 MINUTES**
YIELD: **APPROXIMATELY 24 SERVINGS**

EQUIPMENT

1 wide-mouth half-gallon–size glass jar with lid (A jar is considered to have a wide mouth when the opening is approximately 3⅓ inches [8.5cm] across or larger.)

Kraut pounder (optional)

1 small glass jar that is no larger than a 4-ounce canning jelly jar and is small enough to fit into opening of the half-gallon–size jar

1 bowl large enough to hold the half-gallon–size jar

pH strips (for checking the acidity)

INGREDIENTS

1 head cauliflower, cut into bite-size florets

6 carrots, peeled and sliced into ¼-inch rounds

1 red bell pepper, sliced into 2-inch (5cm) strips

1 yellow onion, peeled and sliced into 2-inch (5cm) strips

2 jalapeño peppers, sliced into rings with membrane and seeds removed (optional)

4–5 dried or fresh bay leaves

2 rounded tbsp coarse ground sea salt or 1½ level tsp fine ground sea salt

Enough filtered, chlorine-free water to cover the vegetables

1. Begin filling the half-gallon–size jar with the cauliflower, carrots, red bell peppers, onions, and jalapeños (if using), while periodically sprinkling the salt into the jar. Continue alternating adding the vegetables, onions, jalapeños and salt until you reach the neck of the jar. Insert the bay leaves down along the sides of the jar.

2. Using a clean hand or the kraut pounder, compact the mix as tightly as possible.

3. Add just enough water to cover the vegetables, but do not fill the jar to the rim. (You need to leave room to accommodate the jelly jar and also not have the brine spill out and over the jar.)

4. Place the small jelly jar on top of the vegetables and then put a lid on the jar. Place the jar into the bowl.

5. Place the bowl in a room-temperature area that averages between 68°F and 72°F (20°C and 22°C) and is out of direct sunlight.

6. By the second day of fermentation, you may begin to see bubbles developing in the jar. From this point forward, loosen the lid daily and then retighten. (This will release some of the carbon dioxide and prevent the jar from breaking.)

7. After 3 days, you will notice that the brine might become slightly cloudy. This is a normal part of the fermentation process. Remove the jelly jar and use a clean spoon to remove some of the brine and test the acidity level using a pH strip. A successful ferment will have a pH of 4.6 or lower. If the pH is at the correct level, use a clean fork to remove a piece of the cauliflower and transfer it to a clean plate. Cut into the cauliflower. If the texture is to your liking, put a lid on the jar, and refrigerate your giardiniera. If the giardiniera has not reached a correct pH level or a satisfactory texture, continue to allow it to ferment.

8. At 7 days, once again remove some of the brine to test the acidity level. If the pH strip registers 4.6 or lower, remove the jelly jar, put the lid on the larger jar, and refrigerate. If the pH still doesn't reach 4.6 or lower, you may continue to ferment the giardiniera for up to 7 more days. (See **Cook's Notes.**) The giardiniera will stay fresh in the refrigerator for approximately 4 to 6 months.

When should you discard the ferment? If the giardiniera does not have a pH of 4.6 or lower after 7 days, the conditions may not be suitable for the ferment to thrive. However, if there's no sign of mold or foul smells, you can try leaving the giardiniera out at room temperature for up to 7 more days. Continue checking the pH of the giardiniera during this time to see if it reaches 4.6 or lower. If the pH still does not measure 4.6 or lower by the fourteenth day, you should discard the giardiniera. If you leave the giardiniera out for too long, the texture will decline, your ferment will become mushy and slimy, and mold may develop.

Other flavoring options: If desired, you can use 1 black tea bag or 2 green tea bags in place of the bay leaves. For this ferment, I find that bay leaves work exceptionally well at retaining the crispness of the vegetables, while also adding a lovely flavor. If you prefer to use tea leaves in place of bay leaves, place the tea bag(s) in the bottom of the jar before adding the vegetables.

Spicy Fermented Ginger Carrot Coins

Pickled carrots of any shape or size are always a welcome treat, but how about taking them one step further and fermenting them? You will improve their nutritional profile over pickled carrots. You'll also treat yourself to a delightful new flavor that still has a bit of that pickled tang but is not as tart as traditional vinegar-pickled vegetables.

PREP TIME: **5 MINUTES**
FERMENTATION TIME: **7–14 DAYS**
TOTAL TIME: **7–14 DAYS PLUS 5 MINUTES**
YIELD: **4–6 SERVINGS**

EQUIPMENT

1 wide-mouth quart-size glass jar with lid

Kraut pounder (optional)

1 small glass jar that is no larger than a 4-ounce canning jelly jar and can fit into the opening of the quart-size jar

1 bowl large enough to hold the quart-size jar

pH strips (for checking the acidity)

INGREDIENTS

Black tea bag (optional) (see **Cook's Notes**)

4–5 carrots or enough to fill a quart-size jar once peeled and sliced into ¼-inch (.65cm) disks

1-inch (1.25cm) piece fresh ginger, peeled and finely grated

1½ level tbsp coarse ground sea salt or 2¼ level tsp of fine ground sea salt

Enough filtered, chlorine-free water to cover the vegetables

1 If using a tea bag, place it in the bottom of the quart-size jar.

2 Peel the carrots and then slice them into ¼-inch (.65cm) disks. Add the disks to the jar as you slice them, while periodically sprinkling in some of the grated ginger and sea salt. Continue alternating adding the carrots, ginger, and salt to the jar until you reach the neck of the jar.

3 Using a clean hand or a kraut pounder, compact the carrots as tightly as possible by pressing down on them.

4 Add just enough water to cover the carrots, but do not fill the jar to the rim. (You need to leave room to accommodate the jelly jar and not have the brine spill out and over the jar.) Place the jelly jar on top of the carrots and press the jelly jar down firmly. Place a lid on the larger jar and then tighten. Place the jar into the bowl.

5 Place the bowl in a room-temperature area that averages between 68°F and 72°F (20°C and 22°C) and is out of direct sunlight.

6 By the second day of fermentation, you may begin to see bubbles developing in the jar. From this point forward, release the lid daily and then retighten. (This will release some of the carbon dioxide gas that is produced by the fermentation process and prevent the jar from breaking.)

7 After a few days, you will notice that the brine might become quite cloudy. This is a normal part of the fermentation process. Remove the jelly jar and use a clean spoon to remove some of the brine and test the acidity level using a pH strip. A successful ferment will have a pH of 4.6 or lower. If the pH is at the correct level, use a clean fork to remove a carrot coin and transfer it to a clean plate. Cut into the carrot. If the texture is to your liking, put a lid on the jar, and refrigerate your fermented carrots. If the carrots have not reached a correct pH level or a satisfactory texture, continue to allow them to ferment.

8 By the seventh day, once again remove some of the brine and test the acidity level. (See **Cook's Notes.**) If the pH is 4.6 or lower, remove the jelly jar, put a lid on the jar, and refrigerate the carrots.

(Carrots are rich in natural sugars, which contribute to a relatively quick fermentation, so you need to check the texture and the pH level regularly to make sure you are on the right track.) Lacto-fermented carrots will stay fresh in the refrigerator for approximately 4 to 6 months.

9 If the carrots do not have a pH of 4.6 or lower, you may continue to ferment them for up to seven more days. (See **Cook's Notes.**)

····················· COOK'S NOTES ·····················

For a less spicy ferment: If you wish for a ferment with a little less bite, you can leave out the ginger.

Substitutes for black tea bags in the ferment: If desired, you can use 2 green tea bags or 3 to 4 dried or fresh bay leaves in place of the black tea bag. If you are using bay leaves, insert the leaves down the sides of the jar to be parallel with the sides of the jar.

What if the carrots taste too salty? After 7 days of fermentation, the carrots, which by now should be lacto-fermented, will taste salty. This salty flavor is coming from the brine that is clinging to the carrots. Over the next few weeks during refrigeration, the carrots will absorb more of the brine, increasing their flavor and making the brine, which clings to the carrots, less salty.

When should you discard the ferment? If the carrots do not have a pH of 4.6 or lower after 7 days, the conditions may not be suitable for the ferment to thrive. If there's no sign of mold or foul smells, you can try leaving the carrot ferment out at room temperature for up to 7 more days. If your pH still does not measure 4.6 or lower on the fourteenth day of your ferment, you should discard your ferment and try again. If you leave your ferment out for too long, especially when it comes to carrots, the texture will decline, your ferment will become mushy, and mold may develop. One of the biggest problems facing an all carrot ferment is the possibility of them becoming very slimy—and highly unappetizing!

Making carrot sticks or grated carrots: Carrots of all shapes and sizes make great ferments. In place of making carrot coins, you can also make carrot sticks or grated carrots. The recipe is exactly the same. The only thing that changes is how you prepare the carrots, whether it be coins, sticks, or grated. Fermented carrots sticks are a great addition to a school lunch box. And fermented grated carrots make a refreshing side dish when served in a similar fashion to sauerkraut.

Mostarda di Frutta Fermentada (Fermented Fruit and Mustard Chutney)

If you are new to traditional foods, *Mostarda di Frutta* might not be something you've heard of. But I am confident you will find it to be not only a unique form of mustard, but an exceptionally tasty Northern Italian alternative to British chutneys. Mostarda is commonly served during the colder months alongside heavier meals, including cooked meats.

PREP TIME: **15 MINUTES**
FERMENTATION TIME: **2–4 DAYS**
TOTAL TIME: **2–4 DAYS PLUS 15 MINUTES**
YIELD: **APPROXIMATELY 12 SERVINGS**

EQUIPMENT

1 wide-mouth quart-size glass jar with lid

Kraut pounder (optional)

1 bowl large enough to hold the jar

INGREDIENTS

1 cup small unsweetened dried fruit, such as currants, raisins, cranberries, or cherries (not treated with any type of oil)

1 cup unsulphured dried apricots, cut into bite-size pieces (alternatively, unsulphured prunes may be used)

1 small green or firm apple, peeled, cored, and cut into bite-size pieces

1 small firm Anjou (green) pear, peeled, cored, and cut into bite-size pieces

1 small yellow onion, peeled and diced

1-inch (2.5cm) piece fresh ginger, peeled and grated

1 tbsp mustard seeds

2 tbsp dry mustard

1½ level tbsp coarse sea salt or 2¼ level tsp fine ground sea salt

Enough filtered, chlorine-free water to cover the fruit

¼ cup raw honey, plus more to taste

Raw apple cider vinegar, as needed (optional)

1. Begin adding all the ingredients (except the water, honey, and apple cider vinegar) to the jar, alternating between the dried and fresh fruit, onion, grated ginger, mustard seeds, dry mustard, and salt. Use a kraut pounder or clean hand to compress the mixture tightly into the jar.

2. Cover the contents of the jar with enough water to come within 1-inch (2.5cm) of the rim of the jar. Place the lid on the jar and tighten. Place the jar into the bowl.

3. Place the bowl in a room-temperature area that averages between 68°F and 72°F (20°C and 22°C) and is out of direct sunlight.

4. For each day after day 1, remove the lid from the jar, stir the mostarda, and then return the lid and retighten. (If the mostarda is difficult to stir because the fruit has absorbed all the water, add a bit more filtered water and then stir.)

5. After 2 days, but no more than 4 days, check the pH. Remove some of the mostarda brine to a glass and press the pH strip into it. If the mostarda has reached a pH level of 4.6 or lower, top off the jar with the honey and stir well. (If the mostarda has thickened considerably, transfer it to a bowl, mix it with the honey, and then return the mixture to the jar.) Add the lid and tighten. Transfer to the refrigerator to cool for 24 hours and allow the flavors to meld. You can now serve the mostarda.

6. If after 4 days, the mostarda has not reached a pH of 4.6, but you see no sign of mold on the fruit and there is no foul odor emanating from the jar, pour 1 tablespoon of raw apple cider vinegar into the jar, stir, and then check the pH again. Continue adding the vinegar, 1 tablespoon at a time and then stirring, until the mostarda reaches the correct pH. (See **Cook's Notes**.) Once the mostarda reaches the proper pH level, add the honey, stir, and then transfer to the refrigerator to cool for 24 hours before serving.

7 Mostarda is best consumed within 1 month. After that time, the fruit may become overly softened, and with this particular fruit-based ferment, the flavor may begin to become quite sharp. (When you first taste the mostarda, it may be slightly effervescent. This is normal and it will only last for a day or two. The mostarda will have a strong mustard flavor tempered by a bit of sweetness from the dried fruit and honey.)

········· **COOK'S NOTES** ·········

Why do you use apple cider vinegar in this ferment?
The apple cider vinegar will not hurt the lacto-fermentation process and will help lower the pH. And since this is a short ferment, we want to ensure the mostarda doesn't turn into alcohol by fermenting it too long before getting it into the fridge.

You may also be wondering why we haven't used apple cider vinegar in other ferments.
We don't do this with other lacto-ferments because we want the natural lactic acid to ferment the fresh produce, instead of us forcing a lower pH with vinegar at the beginning of the fermentation process, thereby creating a pickle. In other ferments, we are working with vegetables and not fruit. Vegetables ferment slower than fruits, so we can give them the time they need to begin the fermentation process. Fruit, however, ferments very quickly, so we have to catch it before it turns into alcohol.

Your mostarda will hopefully contain some lactic acid after the short 2 to 4-day ferment. Also, by using the raw apple cider vinegar, we are introducing acetic acid, which will lower the pH and help maintain the freshness of the mostarda while also adding a bit of additional good bacteria.

Chapter Six
THE HOME BAKER

GETTING STARTED WITH HOME BAKING

For me, it is impossible to think of any sweeter smell than the aroma wafting from a kitchen where bread is being baked. Any bread. It can be a quick bread, yeast-risen bread, or sourdough bread. It doesn't matter. There is nothing like home-baked bread.

I have such wonderful memories surrounding home-baked goods. My mom was a fantastic baker. As a child, I looked in awe at how she seemed to effortlessly mix a few ingredients to create a variety of home-baked goodies. The best treat came when she put a little white pinafore apron on me and appointed me as her official kitchen assistant. When I went on to have a son, he became my official kitchen assistant, albeit not in the white pinafore apron! When my dad's workplace celebrated different holidays, they would hold their festivities right in the office, potluck style. Everyone would bring something to share. And when the event was being coordinated, my dad's coworkers always requested my mom's many delicious baked goods. She was always willing to please, so she would load up my dad with a shopping bag full of beautifully wrapped quick breads and a large round sourdough bread (usually called a *boule*). If it was a really special holiday, she would go all out and send him with homemade sourdough dinner rolls and a baked ham. The combination made some of the best sandwiches!

Years later, when I was working in the Washington D.C. area, I would pick my mom up at the airport and bring her back to my workplace. She always had two suitcases packed: one with her clothes and, I kid you not, the other with homemade quick breads, a boule, dinner rolls, and, yes, a baked ham. My coworkers were in awe and said she was welcome at the office anytime!

Begin to Build Your Skills

Becoming a home baker opens a new world of skills and recipes. You will develop skills that give you the ability to make, enjoy, and share a lifetime of delicious baked goods. You'll begin your journey by making the following recipes that help you build your baking skills:

- A traditional quick bread
- An easy no-knead sandwich bread
- Sourdough starter
- A no-knead sourdough boule

As we begin this journey together, we'll start with an easy-yet-traditional quick bread. This is an excellent introduction to home baking because you will freeform this quick bread into a round rather than pouring it into a loaf pan. (Knowing how to form dough into a ball will help you when making a sourdough boule!) Next, we'll move on to making an easy no-knead sandwich bread. And just like the skill you learned from working with a quick bread dough, you'll learn additional techniques by working with a bread dough risen with packaged yeast. You'll learn how to recognize what a no-knead dough looks like and how to work with greased hands instead of floured hands when handling the dough. Your expanding skill set will prepare you for when you need to use wet hands when working with sourdough.

Once you learn how simple it is to make sandwich bread, you will never look at the bread aisle at your grocery store in the same way. Rather than buying sandwich bread that is packaged in a plastic sleeve, you'll have the knowledge needed to easily make your own bread—white or wheat—using the ingredients you want.

At this point, you'll move on to learning how to create a sourdough starter in preparation for making a sourdough boule. Thanks to your experience making a quick bread, you'll already know how to hand shape a shaggy dough into some semblance of order. (If the term *shaggy* is new to you, it means that the dough should be well mixed with all the flour moistened but look lumpy, not smooth, and it should be somewhat sticky.)

When you make your first sourdough boule, you will be amazed at how simple it is to create a round loaf of crusty bread in your own kitchen. And it will be time for a big congratulations on becoming a modern pioneer baker!

Limiting Whole Grain Flour

If you are new to working with whole grains, you will be relieved to learn that you never have to make a bread that is comprised of 100% whole grains. Breads made exclusively with whole grain flours can be dense and often difficult to digest. And it doesn't matter if you are baking with modern-day whole wheat flour or one of the ancient whole grain flours, such as spelt or einkorn.

When whole grain is ground into flour, this flour contains three parts: the bran (fiber), the germ (protein and fat), and the endosperm (protein and starch). When all three parts are left intact, you have whole grain flour. And when the bran and germ are sifted away, only the endosperm is left behind. This is what we consider flour, as in the white or plain flour that's often sold as all-purpose flour or bread flour. (Bread flour is ground from a wheat that contains slightly more protein, making it better for bread baking.)

Throughout history, bakers often sifted out some of the bran and the germ from their flour that had been freshly stone-ground milled. I imagine that through trial and error they discovered if they did this bit of sifting, their bread would turn out lighter, and maybe they also realized it was easier for their digestive systems to handle.

In the recipes that follow, whenever we are baking with whole grains, I recommend that you sift out a bit of the bran and germ if you are home milling your flour. Don't worry. This is not an exact science. You'll just take about a cup or two of your freshly milled flour and sift it using a mesh strainer or flour sifter, leaving some of the bran and germ behind. You'll then add the sifted flour back in with your freshly ground whole grain flour. If you are using flour that you purchased from the grocery store, I recommend that you use part whole grain flour and part all-purpose flour or bread flour, the latter two being free of bran and germ. This will come as close as possible to mimicking the texture of breads baked by our ancestors.

The Oregon Trail Pioneer Brown Bread recipe in this chapter uses a mix of whole wheat flour and bread flour to help re-create the unrefined flours known as *shorts* or *middlings* that were commonly used by the pioneers. These were not 100% whole grain flours, but they weren't thoroughly sifted either. Both contained a mixture, in varying degrees, of bran, germ, and endosperm.

If you're concerned about losing the nutrition that whole grain brings, don't worry. It's okay to sift the bran and germ out of some of your flour and cut your whole grain flour with all-purpose or bread flour. You are still getting plenty of good nutrition from the whole grains that are included in the bread. Your quick bread and breads made with packaged yeast never have to be 100% whole grain. And as a matter of fact, you don't want them to be! Whole grains contain phytic acid, which can make it difficult to digest the whole grains and, thereby, difficult to absorb the nutrients. It can also strip additional nutrients from your body. So unless you are working with whole grain dough that has been soaked, sprouted, or soured, you want to limit how much whole grain flour you add to your bread baking repertoire. (Note, however, there is an upside to phytic acid, which we'll discuss in the sourdough section.)

Advancing to Sourdough Baking

After learning how to make an easy quick bread and a basic sandwich bread, we'll make a sourdough starter. It is much easier to make a sourdough starter than you may have been led to believe. And no matter what goes wrong, I promise you it is almost impossible to kill a starter once it gets going.

The most important thing to keep in mind when learning how to make a sourdough starter and then baking sourdough bread is that we are home bakers. I can't stress the word *home* enough! We are not professional bakers. Nothing needs to be perfect or 100% predictable. When you go to a bakery, you expect that the bread you bought last week will be as close to identical as the bread you buy this week. Such exactness is not required of the home baker.

Now, don't get me wrong. This doesn't mean that your sourdough bread isn't going to be great. It will be! Your home-baked bread will be delicious, and everyone will rally around your kitchen when the aroma of home-baked bread begins to waft through your home. But does that mean it needs to be the most perfect loaf of bread that has ever been baked? No, of course not. It just needs to be good enough. And good enough is *great* when it comes to home baking.

If you have been dissatisfied in the past with your foray into bread baking because it seemed so complex and complicated only to produce poor results, let me reassure you that things are about to change. I am not going to overcomplicate this. You might hear that baking is a science—an exact science. I couldn't disagree more! Starters do not need to be precisely measured when feeding, and nothing needs to be weighed—not the starter, water, or the flour. I promise I will never tell you that you need a scale.

I have a whole host of tips and tricks for making what I like to call a "foolproof" sourdough starter. And once you get that wild yeast bubbling and growing, I'll show you how easy it is to make sourdough bread. And yes, it will be a no-knead bread! As a matter of fact, pretty much every bread in this chapter will be no-knead. It just makes kitchen life so much easier when you let water and time do the kneading for you!

No-Knead Bread Throughout the Centuries

You may recall that back in 2006, no-knead bread made a splash on the baking scene thanks to a newspaper article highlighting an easy technique for making artisan-quality bread. Although not a true sourdough bread, this modern no-knead bread used only a ¼ teaspoon of packaged yeast and a long, slow rise. All of a sudden, this bread was heralded as, and forgive the pun, the best thing since sliced bread!

But did you know that no-knead bread is actually nothing new? Even in the 1940s, Pillsbury Mills was touting a 25¢ pamphlet titled, "Bake the No-Knead Way—Ann Pillsbury's Amazing Discovery." Now keep in mind, Ann

Pillsbury was a fictional character, just like Betty Crocker, but both were beloved by home cooks who were ready to embrace what Ann was teaching.

So how did Ann make this amazing discovery? I'm not exactly sure, but I will share that back in the 1700s—1739 to be exact, when Eliza Smith was sharing her recipes in a cookbook titled *The Compleat Housewife* (that's not a typo, but the accurate spelling for "complete" in 1739). In her recipe for French bread, when describing how to handle the dough, Eliza tells us:

... a peck of fine flour ... a little salt ... a pint of ale yeast ... stir it about with your hand, but be sure you don't knead them ...

Apparently, Eliza had made her own amazing discovery. But Eliza didn't have modern-day commercially packaged yeast, so what did she do? Well, maybe her recipe discovery went back to the Middle Ages, and possibly well before, when French bakers were making sourdough bread (Eliza's French bread, perhaps) that most likely was never kneaded.

Instead of kneading the dough, the sourdough starter did all the work during a slow rise, in the same way Eliza's pint of ale yeast, otherwise known as the *wild yeast barm*, rose her bread with a slow rise and no kneading. So like Eliza and the French bakers before her, we, too, are going to be traditional bakers by embracing our sourdough starter and the no-knead way of making bread.

MAKING QUICK BREADS
(THE EASIEST BREADS TO MAKE)

When first learning how to bake, the easiest breads to start with are quick breads. These types of breads require no yeast, no kneading, and no rise time. Instead, you simply mix the ingredients and then freeform them into a round loaf or pour the mixture into a baking pan. Within an hour or so of popping it in the oven, you have bread! It can be sweet or savory, but either way, quick breads are always a welcome treat at any meal. They also make a great snack or accompaniment at tea time.

If you have ever made a quick bread but were disappointed with the dense results, there is a reason. Quick breads do not like to be overmixed. Instead, you should gently mix your ingredients just until all the flour is moistened and then put your mixing spoon down and step away from the bowl! Overmixing creates a dense texture that many new bakers experience with quick breads. But if you use a very light hand, you will be rewarded with a light, airy bread.

Quick bread batters also offer the option of turning them into muffins, as opposed to a round, like a soda bread, or a loaf, like banana bread. You can divide the batter into a muffin tin, pop the tin in the oven, and adjust the baking time. Sweet muffins are common, but you can also make savory muffins which, to me, are the quick and easy way to make a stand-in for biscuits.

A Rising Agent Time Line

As pioneers first ventured along the Oregon Trail in the early days, baking powder and baking soda were not yet invented. Although most pioneers carried their sourdough starter with them, sometimes they did not have the luxury of time (traveling in a covered wagon) to allow their bread dough to rise undisturbed. But without baking powder or baking soda, what were their options if they wanted to make a quick bread? Enter *pearl ash*.

Pearl ash is a substance obtained from wood ash. It may sound odd to us today that something made from wood ash was used to rise bread, but it was commonly used long before the pioneer days. Pearl ash is highly alkaline, and when mixed with some type of acid, such as clabbered milk, the mixture creates gasses that make quick breads rise.

Eventually, pearl ash was replaced with what was called *saleratus*, which we know today as baking soda. Eventually, baking powder was invented, giving home cooks and those on wagon train trails easy options for reliable ingredients for baking. As modern pioneers in the kitchen, it's nice to know that we can make quick breads like the early pioneers, but we have the luxury of using baking soda or baking powder instead of wood ash!

NO NEED TO KNEAD
(THE EASY WAY TO MAKE YEAST BREADS)

When we think about making homemade bread with yeast, many of us focus on all the kneading that is going to be involved, and it suddenly becomes an unattractive project. But as we discussed at the beginning of this chapter, we really don't have to knead dough in order to make a great loaf of homemade bread.

Amazingly, if you don't mind working with a bit of wet and sticky dough, often referred to as a *shaggy dough*, you will be rewarded with a bread that has a soft and airy internal texture—or *crumb*—as it is often referred to. Shaggy doughs can initially be off-putting because they may stick to your hands, and as a result, you may be tempted to add more flour. But don't do it! And you might be thinking that surely a dough like this can't rise, but you'll be pleasantly surprised.

There are some secrets to working with no-knead bread dough. The first is to make sure you add enough water or other liquid to your flour. Next, you'll only want to handle the dough when your hands are well greased or wet. This will ensure that the dough will not stick to your hands. You will be so surprised to see how easy it is to handle a sticky dough when your hands are well greased or wet.

You may have heard of baking terms like the "windowpane test" or the "poke test," but you don't need either when making this bread. Generally, the windowpane test stretches kneaded dough to see if you can get it thin enough to look through it, hence the name *windowpane*. And once you can look through it, it's kneaded enough. But what about the poke test? This one can really confuse the new home baker. With the poke test, you poke the dough with your finger after your dough has risen for a certain period of time. If the dough stays indented, it's probably ready to go into the oven. However, some bakers say this may indicate that the dough has over-risen. Conversely, if the dough springs back quickly, it has probably not risen enough. But what if the dough looks like it may be staying indented, but maybe it's beginning to slowly spring back? All I can say is ... oh dear!

Determining if the dough is not springing back, if it's springing back quickly, or if it's springing back slowly can often stump the new baker. In the sandwich bread recipe that follows, we're not going to worry about using the poke test. And in the later sourdough recipes that follow, you can try the poke test if you want, but do not stress over it too much! Whether your dough didn't quite rise enough or it rose a bit too much, it doesn't really matter. There may be slight differences in the final bread one way or the other, but no one will notice. All they will see is that you made homemade bread!

Oregon Trail Pioneer Brown Bread

Brown bread was a quick bread recipe brought along the Oregon Trail by Irish immigrants traveling west from the New England area of the United States. So if you want to get a taste of what the pioneers ate along the trail, this quick bread is for you. It's also a great place to start learning how to bake bread since this is about the simplest bread to make. And as to taste, if you are familiar with Irish soda bread, you will find this similar but with a richer flavor imparted by the addition of molasses.

PREP TIME: **15 MINUTES**
BAKE TIME: **45–55 MINUTES**
TOTAL TIME: **60–70 MINUTES**
YIELD: **1 ROUND LOAF**

INGREDIENTS

2½ cups unbleached bread flour

2 cups whole wheat flour

1 tsp baking soda

1 tsp fine ground sea salt

1¾ cups clabbered milk (or buttermilk)

1 large egg

¼ cup molasses (or maple syrup)

4 tbsp cold butter, cubed (plus more to grease the skillet)

1 cup dried currants (or any small dried fruit, such as raisins)

1 Place the oven rack in the middle position. Preheat the oven to 375°F (190°C).

2 Coat a 10-inch cast-iron skillet with butter. (Alternatively, you can line it with a round of parchment paper.)

3 In a large bowl, whisk together the bread flour, wheat flour, baking soda, and sea salt.

4 In a separate bowl, whisk together the clabbered milk, egg, and molasses. Set aside.

5 Work the cubed butter into the flour mixture, rubbing it between your hands so that when you squeeze the flour-butter mixture, it stays together like wet sand but easily breaks apart when touched. Add the currants and toss to combine.

6 Make a well in the center of the flour-butter mixture. Pour the clabbered milk, egg, and molasses mixture into the well.

7 Form your fingers into a claw and gently mix in the liquid until the dough comes together into a lumpy ball. (The dough should be somewhat sticky to the touch.) If it appears dry, you can add additional buttermilk, 1 tablespoon at a time, and mix until the dough reaches the correct consistency. (Be careful not to overmix!)

8 Transfer the dough to a floured work surface and lightly dust the top of the dough. Next, slightly flatten the dough and fold it in half about five times, rotating the dough a quarter turn and then flattening it after each fold.

9 Once the dough holds together, encircle the dough with your cupped hands and form it into a ball by rotating the dough clockwise, gently tucking the dough edges in and under the center of the dough.

10 Transfer the dough ball to the prepared cast-iron skillet. Lightly dust the top of the dough with flour and then use the palm of your hand to flatten the dough ball slightly.

11 Using a very sharp knife, cut a cross, about a ½ inch (1.25cm) deep, across the top of the bread. (Tradition holds that by carving a cross into the dough, you are blessing it.)

12 Using the tip of the knife, make a small piercing in the center of each quadrant of the bread. (Legend states that you must release the fairies from the dough if you want your bread to rise!)

13 Bake the bread for about 45 to 55 minutes or until it is a rich golden brown and appears to be baked through. If you are unsure, use a pot holder to remove the skillet from the oven and place it on a heatproof surface. Using the pot holder, lift the bread and tap the bottom. It should sound hollow. If it sounds more like a thud, return it to the oven. (If the bread is browning too quickly but has not yet finished baking, you can tent it with foil.)

14 Remove the skillet from the oven and place it on a heatproof surface. Remove the bread from the skillet and place it on a cooling rack. If you prefer a soft crust instead of a crisp crust, cover the bread with a clean tea towel as it is cooling. (This will help keep the crust of the brown bread soft.)

15 After allowing the bread to cool for about 10 to 15 minutes, you can slice it while it is still warm (but not hot) using a serrated knife. Slices of Pioneer Brown Bread are best served warm and slathered with butter.

16 Pioneer Brown Bread is best eaten the day it is baked. However, it can be stored in the refrigerator, well wrapped, for 3 to 4 days. It can also be stored in the freezer, well wrapped, for 2 to 3 months. It's best enjoyed toasted if not eaten freshly baked.

Super Soft No-Knead White Sandwich Bread

Most people love a good slice of soft white sandwich bread that is commonly sold in a plastic sleeve at the grocery store. But you can make this bread very easily at home. And it will be better than anything you can buy at the store. Plus, you can control exactly what goes into this bread and what doesn't—like dough conditioners and preservatives.

The technique used in making this bread is based on the early nineteenth century recipe known as *batter bread*. As the name implies, this bread is made from a dough that is simply mixed together, as you would a batter. And there is certainly no need to knead a batter! The first batter bread recipe appeared in the cookbook titled *The Virginia Housewife* by Mary Randolph, originally published in 1824. Batter breads became a regular staple in the southern part of the United States and were often made with the common Southern pantry staple—cornmeal. But over the years, housewives in other regions of the United States adapted the batter bread recipe to be made with any type of flour to create a simple no-knead bread.

PREP TIME: **5 MINUTES**
RISE TIME: **2 HOURS 10 MINUTES**
BAKE TIME: **40 MINUTES**
TOTAL TIME: **APPROXIMATELY 3 HOURS**
YIELD: **2 LOAVES**

INGREDIENTS

6 cups unbleached all-purpose flour

1 tbsp fine ground sea salt

1 tbsp white sugar

1 (.25oz/7g) package or 2¼ tsp instant yeast

3 cups warm tap water (similar to bath water)

3 tbsp unsalted butter, melted and divided

2½ tsp unsalted butter, softened

1 Whisk together the flour, sea salt, sugar, and yeast in a large bowl.

2 Add the warm water and 2 tablespoons melted butter to the bowl with the flour mixture.

3 Mix all ingredients until they come together to form a shaggy dough.

4 Cover the bowl with plastic wrap, and transfer it to a warm place to rise for approximately 1½ hours or until it appears to have doubled in size. (See **Cook's Notes**.) After 1½ hours of rise time, the dough should have doubled in size and should have a puffy appearance, like a pillow with a slightly domed top. (Don't stress over trying to be exact, just eyeball it.)

5 After the rise time is complete, rub ½ teaspoon of the softened butter between the palms of your hands. Use your greased hands to deflate the dough by pressing down on it. Divide the dough into two equal portions.

6 Using the remaining 2 teaspoons of softened butter, grease two 9-inch x 5-inch (23cm x 12.75cm) loaf pans. Transfer equal portions of the dough into each buttered loaf pan. Even out the dough, pushing it into the corners of the pans using well-greased hands. (The dough will be very sticky.)

7 Place the loaf pans, uncovered, in a warm area and allow the dough to rise for approximately 40 minutes or until it is level with the rims of the loaf pans. (Do not let the dough rise past the rims of the pans, and do not let it form domes in the middle. This will affect the interior texture of the baked bread causing it to be slightly dense and less fluffy.) This rise can take less than 40 minutes in a very warm kitchen, so keep an eye on them.

8 As the dough begins to rise to about three quarters of the way up the sides of the pans, preheat the oven to 375°F (190°C) with the oven rack in the middle position.

9 Place the loaf pans on the middle rack in the oven. Bake for approximately 40 minutes or until the top crusts are golden brown.

10 Using pot holders, remove the loaf pans from the oven and place the pans on a cooling rack. Immediately brush each top crust with the remaining 1 tablespoon of melted butter. (If you prefer a crisp top crust, do not brush the tops of the loaves of bread with the melted butter.) Remove the loaves from the pans and transfer to a cooling rack.

11 Allow the bread to cool completely before slicing. When ready to slice, use a serrated knife.

12 Store at room temperature in a bread box or cloth bag. It will stay fresh for 2 to 3 days. You can also store it well wrapped (such as in plastic wrap and then placed into a plastic storage bag) in the refrigerator for up to 1 week or in the freezer for 2 to 3 months. Defrost unwrapped bread at room temperature.

······················ **COOK'S NOTES** ······················

Finding a warm place for the rising: A warm place in your kitchen can be in an oven that is turned off but has an electric light or pilot light on, on top of a refrigerator, or in a microwave oven that is off. Even a kitchen counter in a warm kitchen is an ideal place to let the dough rise. Just make sure that wherever you rise your dough, that you keep it away from drafts.

Whole wheat variation: To make a whole wheat version of this bread, substitute 2 cups of whole wheat flour in place of 2 cups of all-purpose flour. As to the water, the general rule is that for each cup of whole wheat flour used to replace the all-purpose flour, you will need an additional 2 teaspoons of liquid. For example, when substituting 2 cups of whole wheat flour for 2 cups of all-purpose flour, you will need an additional 4 teaspoons of water for a total of 3 cups and 4 teaspoons of water. If your dough seems dry after adding this additional water, continue adding 1 teaspoon of water at a time and mix until the dough comes together in the correct shaggy consistency.

Accounting for differences in ovens: Every oven is different, and whole wheat flour can often brown more quickly than all-purpose flour. If you are making this bread for the first time, check it in your oven at 25 minutes to ensure it is not overbrowning. If it is overbrowning but is not yet fully baked (when you tap the top, it does not sound hollow), tent or loosely cover the loaf pans with aluminum foil and allow the bread to continue baking for an additional 5 to 10 minutes.

WHAT'S SO SPECIAL ABOUT SOURDOUGH BREAD?

At its very basic level, sourdough bread is simply a naturally leavened bread. However, instead of using commercially packaged dry yeast to leaven (rise), sourdough bread relies on a starter made of water and flour. And the flour—any flour—is the key ingredient.

In place of commercially packaged yeast, a sourdough starter, and the bread dough that is eventually made with it, uses the wild yeast and lactic acid bacteria (beneficial *Lactobacillus*) that are naturally occurring in flour to slowly rise dough. When the bread is allowed to rise slowly in this way—using wild yeasts and beneficial bacteria—several important chemical reactions take place that improve the overall quality of the bread. These chemical reactions include the work of live enzymes, which make the bread easier to digest. When we can better digest our food, we are more readily able to absorb the nutrients that contribute to improved health and give a boost to our immune systems.

Making sourdough starter and baking sourdough bread has been gaining in popularity for a while, but the interest in this bread has exploded over the last few years. Home cooks have strived to become more self-sufficient in their kitchens so they do not have to rely on packaged yeast from the grocery store. And although it might seem like a fad, making bread in this fashion has been around for a long time. Archeologists haven't pinpointed the exact date when sourdough bread first appeared, but it is believed to have been around for at least 5,000 years! And it's a way of making bread that traditional cultures have relied on ever since.

Natural yeast—or wild yeast—is everywhere. All we need to do is harness its power by creating a hospitable environment to attract it. This ideal environment is a mixture of water and flour. Wild yeast in the air will find your mixture, deposit itself down into it, and start to proliferate. Along with lactic acid bacteria (mostly *Lactobacillus*), which are naturally occurring in flour, these two entities will create a bubbling colony that together will help rise bread dough.

You might recall our discussion about lactic acid bacteria in the chapter on fermentation. They are the same beneficial bacteria in flour that is also on vegetables and fruits. And it is lactic acid bacteria that give sourdough its distinct sour taste. Just as with the fermentation of fresh produce, once the lactic acid bacteria get a strong hold on the fermentation process by gobbling up the naturally occurring starch in flour, they will proliferate and make the environment inhospitable to bad bacteria and molds. This chemical reaction keeps your sourdough starter fresh and able to sit out on your counter—just as long as you regularly feed that good bacteria! But more on that later.

Something that is especially interesting about sourdough bread is that lactic acid bacteria change the actual composition of the bread dough, specifically the starch. This chemical change makes our bodies absorb the starch in sourdough bread at a slower rate, as opposed to the starch in nonsourdough breads.

The glycemic index measures the process of absorbing starches (and sugars) in our food. And on this index, sourdough bread has a lower rating than many other breads. This is a good attribute because when our bodies can absorb food at a slower rate, our blood insulin levels are unlikely to spike. And when we can keep our insulin levels in check, we are less likely to develop diseases that affect our kidneys, nerves, eyes, and heart.

In addition to being lower on the glycemic index, sourdough bread is also considered to be lower in gluten. Now keep in mind that sourdough bread is not a gluten-free food. However, during the fermentation process, the lactic acid bacteria break down the gluten in bread dough, making the resulting bread baked with this dough easier to digest. So if you have found commercially risen bread difficult to digest at times, you might discover sourdough to be a good option.

But what about the nutritional profile of sourdough bread? When we bake sourdough bread, the yeasts and the lactic acid bacteria are killed by the high temperature of the oven, but that's okay. They have both done their work already by rising the dough, lowering the glycemic index rating, and breaking down the gluten in flour, whether it's all-purpose flour, bread flour, or whole grain flour. If your sourdough bread is made from whole grain flour, you get the added benefit of being able to better absorb the nutrients the whole grains have to offer, thanks to the enzymatic action mentioned earlier.

The first recipe for sourdough bread I share uses bread flour in which the bran and germ have been sifted out. Bread flour works very well when used to make bread that is risen with commercially packaged yeast or a sourdough starter. As the name implies, it is specifically milled for making bread. It has a higher protein content than all-purpose flour, which assists in providing a good rise to bread by creating more gluten.

Later recipes in this chapter include sourdough breads made with whole grains. The nutritional profile of whole grain sourdough bread is excellent. In addition, the minerals from the whole grain flours are readily available and absorbable by our digestive tracts thanks to the slow fermentation souring process and also to the deactivation of some of the phytic acid. We'll discuss phytic acid, and its counterpart, phytase, in detail when we make our whole grain sourdough breads.

SOURDOUGH STARTER—TIPS FOR SUCCESS

Before you make sourdough bread, you need a sourdough starter. If you have ever attempted to make a sourdough starter and failed or you have never tried to make one because it seemed too hard, I will show you how easy it is to do.

If you have found recipes for making a sourdough starter overwhelming because there was a lot of talk about weighing ingredients on a scale and measuring everything in grams, I have good news for you: as I shared previously, we are not professional bakers; we are home bakers. And unless you are planning on opening a bakery or

selling your bread at the farmers' market, you do not need a scale and you do not need to measure your ingredients in grams.

Your sourdough starter is going to be bubbling before you know it, and your sourdough bread is going to bake up great! Will each loaf be a bit different than the last? Of course. This is home baking. But that's okay! Each loaf will still be delicious, and the whole process will be simple for you. You will be delighted to find yourself getting into a simple, manageable kitchen rhythm when it comes to baking sourdough bread on a regular basis.

What Are the Best Ingredients for Making a Sourdough Starter?

When preparing to make a sourdough starter, the first task is to decide which type of flour to use. Keep in mind that any time you use whole grain flour to make your starter, you'll want to make sure that the flour is fresh. Whole grain flours can go rancid easily because the bran and germ contain oils. These oils go rancid over time and taint the whole grain flour. Generally, whole grain flours will stay fresh for 6 months to 1 year. You can check the "best by" date on the packaging, but you can usually tell if they are fresh by smelling them. Whole grain flours that have gone rancid will have an off-putting, sour smell.

If it is available to you, the best flour to make your starter is whole grain rye flour, preferably freshly ground rye flour. Rye flour works so well at creating a successful sourdough starter because it is rich in *amylase*, an enzyme that is a protein which successfully breaks down carbohydrates, as well as other nutrients and microbes. These elements quickly convert sugars in the rye to create a successful fermentation, and that's exactly what you want. Once a successful fermentation starts, it's difficult to stop it. As the yeasts and good bacteria develop a strong hold in the flour, there is little, if any, chance of mold or bad bacteria taking over. A successful starter establishes an inhospitable environment for spoilage.

Don't worry if you can't find rye flour. There are many flours you can use to make a sourdough starter. I only mention using rye flour because it is very easy to get a starter going with it. And that quick success is usually a boost of confidence to the new home baker. If rye flour is not available to you, your next best option is whole wheat flour. You can use any modern-day whole wheat flour or any of the ancient whole grain ancestors of whole wheat, including whole grain spelt or einkorn flour. Whole wheat flour is available at most grocery stores, so it makes a convenient option for kicking off your sourdough starter. Just make sure the whole wheat flour you use is fresh and within its "best by" date.

The last two options are a bread flour or an all-purpose flour. Bread flour is preferred and should be readily available at most stores. Keep in mind, when shopping for either bread flour or all-purpose flour, both should be unbleached. Organic flour is a plus too. When making a starter with unbleached all-purpose flour, you can use the basic all-purpose flour sold at most grocery stores, but you can also use the all-purpose versions of spelt flour or einkorn flour available at specialty grocery stores or online.

Once you decide on the flour you will be using to make your sourdough starter, the only other ingredient you will need is water. As with all fermentations, it's best to use filtered, chlorine-free water, such as spring water or bottled water. Chlorine and other impurities can interfere with the fermentation process. If the only water available to you is chlorinated tap water, pour some into a pitcher and leave it out overnight. Some of the chlorine will dissipate and you can then use this water to create and feed your starter.

Making Your Sourdough Starter

Once you have your flour and water ready, all you need to do is mix equal amounts of flour and water together in a jar, cover the jar loosely with a clean cloth, place the jar in a room temperature area between 68°F and 72°F (20°C and 22°C) and then wait.

Over the course of a few days, you will feed your new starter with more flour and water to encourage the fermentation process to begin. The flour contains natural yeasts and good bacteria that, when combined with water, kick off the fermentation process as the yeasts and bacteria gobble up the starch in the flour. The next thing you know, they are releasing gasses that make your starter all bubbly and ready to rise dough! Once this happens, you will have an active sourdough starter and can try your hand at making sourdough bread.

I can imagine that you might think I am making this sound all too easy, especially if you have failed at making a sourdough starter in the past. But chances are you did not fail. Sometimes it can take more than a few days for the fermentation process to start. Since there can be a lag when you spot a few bubbles forming, you may have thought you failed and thrown out your starter. But maybe all your starter needed was a little extra food, a slightly warmer environment, and a little more time, along with a healthy dose of patience on your part.

Feeding Your Starter

Once your starter gets going, you need to feed it by removing some of the starter.

This removed starter is called *sourdough discard*. Do not throw it out; put it in a clean jar and refrigerate it. Once the sourdough discard is removed, feed your remaining starter with some new flour and water. You are never wedded to always using the same flour to feed your starter that you originally used to make your starter. You can introduce a different type of flour to feed your starter, but it's best to do this little by little, adding small amounts of the new flour in relation to the original flour so that your starter gets used to its new food. But this transition generally goes very smoothly, and your starter will simply be happy that it is being fed!

If you bake regularly and want to leave your starter on the counter, you'll need to feed it every 12 hours—discarding some of the starter and adding that discard to your previous sourdough discards jar in the refrigerator. Next, you'll feed your remaining starter with equal parts flour and water. If you do not bake regularly, you can put a lid on your starter jar and refrigerate it. You will still want to feed your refrigerated starter weekly.

Using Yeast Water to Feed Your Starter

You can use yeast water in place of plain water to feed your starter. Yeast water provides wild yeast to help jump-start the process. To make yeast water, first add a half cup of sulfur dioxide–free raisins, sliced dates, or quartered figs to a quart-size jar, along with 1½ tablespoons of white sugar and 1 teaspoon of fine ground sea salt. Next, fill the jar with nonchlorinated water, put a lid on the jar, and shake it well until the sugar and salt are dissolved. Place the jar in an undisturbed area at room temperature and out of direct sunlight. Shake the jar twice daily, preferably once in the morning and once in the evening. (Be sure to loosen and then retighten the lid before shaking the jar. This process will release some of the buildup of carbon dioxide gas in the bottle or jar and prevent breakage.) Once the fruit floats to the top of the jar, strain the fruit and transfer the liquid to a clean bottle. This is your yeast water. Use this water to feed your starter in place of plain water. You can refrigerate yeast water for up to 2 months. Before making new yeast water, be sure to retain at least 1 tablespoon or up to ¼ cup of your original yeast water to jump-start your new batch of yeast water.

Saving and Using Sourdough Discard

As mentioned above, when you are feeding your new sourdough starter or maintaining a mature one, you will be removing some of the existing starter in your jar before adding new flour and water. You will need to remove some of your starter daily if you leave it on your counter or weekly if you refrigerate it. Although you can throw out the starter you remove (the sourdough discard), you do not want to toss it out. It's a traditional foods cook's best friend.

The sourdough discard you save will stay fresh in your fridge for 1 to 2 weeks. You can even freeze it and it could last indefinitely, but it's probably best used within 1 year. As you will learn in some

of the following recipes, you can use sourdough discard to make a whole host of baked goods. It's terrific for making biscuits, crackers, flatbreads, casserole toppings, pancakes, and more! You will love all the options that sourdough discard provides.

And when you use your discard, you will truly be a modern pioneer in the kitchen, following in the footsteps of generations of pioneers before us who never wasted anything—including their discard. When we think of the pioneers, we often think of biscuits. Well, guess what? Original biscuits were regularly made with sourdough discard!

Baking with Your Sourdough Starter

Once your starter is bubbling, it's ready to bake with, but remember that your starter is new. Some people may call this a "young" starter, but they really mean a new starter. The terms *young* and *new* can be confusing, and I will explain why.

Keep in mind that a new starter may not perform as well as a more mature starter. Over time, the more you use and feed your starter, the stronger it will become, as the wild yeasts multiply more and more—all that beautiful wild yeast that will rise your bread. So go easy on yourself as you begin to bake bread with a new starter. As your starter matures, your sourdough bread will rise to new heights!

As you get ready to bake sourdough bread, make sure that your sourdough starter has been fed and is at its peak, so you can use it to rise bread. Determining this peak can be tricky for new home bakers, but I will make this as easy for you as possible.

When you feed your starter, you will notice that it will start to rise after some time and may begin looking as though it is getting close to doubling in height. Generally, this is referred to as a *young starter* (regardless of whether it is a "new" or "mature" starter). Your starter will eventually rise to where it crowns, or rounds out, on top. This means that your starter has peaked and is ready for you to bake with.

But if you are ready to bake bread before your sourdough starter peaks, that's okay. As long as your starter has risen to a point where it has approximately doubled in height, it's ready to be used for baking. And if you are new to sourdough bread, baking with a sourdough starter at this stage will create a less sour sourdough bread.

If the crown has deflated a bit, you can still use your starter for baking. The only real difference you will notice is a slightly lower rise in your bread and a bit more sour flavor. But personally, I have never found the difference in the rise or the flavor to be significant. The only people who would probably notice that your starter was not at its perfect peak will be professional bakers. Everyone else will say with a big smile, you baked bread for me!

The only time you will want to hold off on using your sourdough starter is if you forgot to feed it and it is completely deflated and hungry. In this case, just go ahead and feed your starter and wait until it's bubbly and ready to be used.

Determining If Your Starter Is Ready to Use

When making a sourdough starter and using it to make sourdough bread, you don't want to get wrapped up in trying to bake with the perfect starter. If you try to perfectly time your starter at its peak, you might find yourself overwhelmed, wondering when you will be able to bake bread and whether the timing will work into your schedule. So let me share a tip. When you get ready to bake bread, feed your starter and then use that starter 12 hours later to bake sourdough bread. Chances are in the average kitchen that ranges in temperature somewhere between 68°F and 72°F (20°C and 22°C), your fed starter is going to peak at around 12 hours after being fed.

Can your starter peak earlier or later? Yes, but as long as it looks light, airy, and bubbly, you can use it for baking. When you use a starter that hasn't quite peaked or has already peaked and has only slightly begun to deflate, it will still rise your bread. Will there be a bit of variation in the rise? Yes, but as a new baker, I do not want you to focus too much on this. Instead, start baking with your starter on a schedule you can live with. The more you bake, the more experience you will develop. Over time you will be able to fine tune your baking schedule. For now, just focus on feeding your starter every 12 hours and honing your sourdough bread–baking skills. Before you know it, you'll be turning out incredible loaves of home-baked bread!

If your starter has doubled in height or has developed a rounded top, it's ready to bake with. But how long does this take to happen? It depends on the temperature in your kitchen. If you have a warm kitchen, it might peak within 4 hours after you feed your starter. If your kitchen is cool, it might take a bit longer. This is not an exact science. However, I want to make this really easy for you, so just focus on using your starter 12 hours after feeding it.

You may have heard bakers mention something called the *float test*. To perform the float test, you take a bit of your starter and drop it into a glass of water. If it floats, it's ready to bake with; if it sinks, it's not ready. But there is a problem with this test. Just like other bread tests—the windowpane test and the poke test—sometimes these tests can be challenging for new home bakers. If you deflate your bit of sourdough starter (which can be easy to do) before dropping it into a glass of water, it may not float. Because of this, the float test is not an accurate way to determine if your starter is ready, so I don't recommend using it.

How to Maintain Your Starter If You Don't Bake Regularly

Don't worry if you can't bake sourdough bread regularly. Your sourdough is happy to sleep in your refrigerator as long as you feed it a little flour every week to keep it

happy and well fed. However, if feeding your starter every week is too much responsibility, you can easily dehydrate and reconstitute it whenever you are ready to make sourdough bread. (See chapter 12 *Preserving Foods by Drying* for instructions on how to dry and rehydrate your starter.)

Having dehydrated starter in your pantry is like having your own stash of packaged yeast—it's just wild packaged yeast! And to keep this supply of wild yeast on hand, you don't need a dehydrator. You don't even have to turn on your oven. Once you have a successful sourdough starter, simply spread your starter out on a parchment paper–lined baking sheet and let it dry at room temperature. Once dry, break the starter into pieces or pulverize it in a blender and store it away in a container with an airtight lid. Even if you have an active starter going that you use frequently, having a dehydrated starter backup is an excellent insurance policy in case anything happens to your regular starter.

To rehydrate your dehydrated starter, simply take the broken pieces or pulverized pieces and place them in a jar. Cover them with room-temperature water and stir to create a mixture that resembles pancake batter. Cover the jar loosely and place it in a warm area. Feed your starter every day, removing some discard and then adding equal parts water and flour to the jar. Within a few days, the starter should be bubbling and doubling in size after being fed. It will then be ready to bake with.

How to Make a 100% Hydration Sourdough Starter

This recipe makes a 100% hydration sourdough starter, which means it is made up of equal amounts of flour and water. This type of starter is the most versatile for the new sourdough home baker. You can use it to easily transform commercial yeast-based bread recipes into sourdough recipes because one cup of a 100% hydration starter is approximately equivalent to one (.25oz/7g) package of commercially packaged yeast. Once you create your sourdough starter, a whole new world of baking will be opened up to you. You will never have to worry about buying commercially packaged yeast ever again. Instead, you will catch your own wild yeast and rise dough in the same way our ancestors did.

PREP TIME: **APPROXIMATELY 15–30 MINUTES**
RESTING TIME: **APPROXIMATELY 4–10 DAYS**
TOTAL TIME: **APPROXIMATELY 4–10 DAYS**
  PLUS 30 MINUTES
YIELD: **APPROXIMATELY 1½–2 CUPS**

INGREDIENTS

Rye flour (preferably freshly milled) (see **Cook's Notes**)

Filtered chlorine-free water (room temperature)
  (see **Cook's Notes**)

1   Day 1 (morning): Using a teaspoon, spoon the flour into a ½ cup measuring cup. Do not compact the flour, just gently spoon it into the measuring cup. (Each time you measure the flour for this recipe, you will measure it this way. When filled, it will weigh approximately the same as a ½ cup of water.)

2   Transfer the flour from the measuring cup to a wide-mouth jar large enough to hold approximately 1 quart of liquid.

3   Add a ½ cup of water to the jar with the flour and then stir well with a spoon to make a slurry. If the mixture is the least bit dry, add additional water 1 tablespoon at a time until the consistency is correct. (Your starter-in-the-making should have the consistency of pancake batter. As you go forward with the steps that follow, your starter should always have the consistency of pancake batter, so be sure to add additional water as needed.)

4   Cover the jar loosely with a clean cloth or paper towel, secure it with a rubber band, and place it on a plate or in a bowl. Set it aside to rest for 12 hours in an undisturbed room temperature location that is between 68°F and 72°F (20°C and 22°C) and out of direct sunlight.

5   Day 1 (evening): Add a ½ cup of flour and a ½ cup of water to the jar. Stir well with a spoon to make a slurry. Allow your starter to rest for 12 hours.

6   Day 2 (morning): Add an additional ½ cup of flour and ½ cup of water to the jar. Stir well with a spoon to make a slurry. Re-cover the jar and set your starter aside to rest for an additional 12 hours.

7   Day 2 (evening): Remove approximately half of the starter-in-the-making (eyeball it). This is the first time you will be removing some of the starter from the jar. What you're removing is the discard, but do not discard it. Instead, add it to a separate clean jar, put a lid on the jar, and refrigerate it for later use. Once you have removed the discard, add another ½ cup of flour and ½ cup of water to the mixture. Stir to incorporate the ingredients and make a slurry. Once again, cover the jar, return it to its warm place, and allow it to rest for another 12 hours.

8   Day 3 (and beyond): Repeat the process of removing half the starter and then feeding the remaining starter with another ½ cup of flour and ½ cup of water every 12 hours until the starter becomes bubbly and frothy. Generally, this process can take as little as 4 to 5 days or as long as 10 days or even more, depending on the temperature in your kitchen. Be patient and persevere. As long as no mold has developed, you are doing great!

9   Once the starter is bubbly and frothy, you can use it for baking sourdough bread.

······················ COOK'S NOTES ······················

Choosing and using flour for your starter: You'll need ½ cup of flour to create your sourdough starter at the beginning. This recipe does not specify the total amount of flour you'll need to make this sourdough starter at the end of this process since that will depend on how fast or slow your starter gets bubbling and how often you decide to feed it. If you can't find rye flour, whole wheat flour is your second best option, with bread flour and all-purpose flour your less optimal choices. You can use any of these flours individually or mix them together. Even though, technically, I say that this starter contains equal amounts of flour and water, you do not need a scale to measure either ingredient. For example, I will show you in this recipe specifically how to measure 1 cup of flour so as to come as close as possible in weight to 1 cup of water. And that's close enough. It does not need to be exact. Amazingly, sourdough starters are very forgiving of inaccuracies!

Choosing and using water for your starter: Try to use water that is filtered and chlorine-free when making your starter. Chlorine and other chemicals used to sanitize water can interfere with the sourdough fermentation process, just as they do with the fermentation of fresh produce. Bottled or spring water are both great options. However, if all you have available is chlorinated tap water, fill a pitcher with the water and allow it to air out overnight to help dissipate some of the chlorine. The next day you can use this water to make your starter.

MAKING SOURDOUGH STARTER—FREQUENTLY ASKED QUESTIONS

What if your starter never bubbles?

If you can't get your starter bubbling, don't worry, and don't throw it out! There are several steps you can take to improve your outcome. Note that not every sourdough baker will agree with what I am sharing here, but there are so many ways to make a sourdough starter and I want you to have these resources in your sourdough repertoire. I am a firm believer that sometimes the home baker needs a little help to get past a few obstacles that might keep you from advancing to making sourdough bread. So never feel you need to be a purist when making a starter. As home bakers, taking a few shortcuts is okay when we run into setbacks. If you are having trouble getting your sourdough starter going, try one or all of these tips (in no particular order):

- Move your starter to a warmer location.

- Feed your starter every 8 hours instead of every 12 hours.

- If you are using all-purpose or bread flour, try switching to whole wheat or rye flour.

- If you have a successful ferment such as sauerkraut or another vegetable ferment; fermented dairy, such as yogurt or milk kefir; a ginger bug; or some

kvass, you can add a tablespoon of liquid from any of these ferments to your starter to help jump-start the fermentation process. This minor addition will not flavor the starter.

- Add a teaspoon of white sugar to your starter and stir well.

- In place of water, use yeast water or what I like to call "fortified water." This is water in which potatoes or pasta have been boiled. Just cool the water to room temperature first. It's rich in starch that your yeast and good bacteria will gobble up. If you don't boil potatoes or pasta, you can keep a supply of instant potatoes on hand. All you need to do is add about a teaspoon or two to the water that you use to feed your starter to help give it a boost.

- You can buy a small amount of premade starter (or ask a friend for some). Then all you have to do is maintain it.

Can you use prepackaged yeast to kick-start the fermentation process?

You can use a little bit of what most bakers will consider a cheat, but I don't feel that way about it at all. If you simply can't get your starter to bubble, add a pinch (about ⅛ teaspoon) of commercially packaged yeast to your sourdough starter, stir well, and feed your starter every 8 hours. This should definitely jump-start your starter. And don't trouble yourself about this little "cheat" at all! Over time, your starter will take on lots of wild yeasts and be as wild as any other starter. Once your starter is thriving, you can return to feeding it every 12 hours.

Why does the sourdough starter smell like nail polish remover?

If your starter starts to smell like nail polish remover (acetone) or strong vinegar, don't worry. Nothing is wrong with your starter. Your kitchen environment and the seasons are always changing and so is your starter. Sometimes certain good bacteria in your starter become stronger, especially when you feed them whole grain flour or more flour than water. When this happens, the yeast will take a bit of a back seat and becomes weaker.

A sourdough starter contains wild yeast and good bacteria acids. The yeast rises the dough, and the bacteria give it that sour taste in the form of lactic acid and acetic acid. However, there are times when acetic acid can become quite strong and overpower the yeast and lactic acid. When this happens, the acetic acid can give your starter that strong nail polish remover or vinegar aroma. If you use your starter at this point to make bread, the bread will be very sour. Some bakers really like this flavor. However, if you are

new to sourdough, you might want to encourage the yeast to become stronger. Instead of baking with this sour starter, you can encourage the wild yeast to overtake the acetic acid. Sometimes a few 8-hour feedings with lots of water and all-purpose flour or bread flour will make a nice loose starter that can turn things around. But that may not be enough. You can try placing your starter in the refrigerator. Wild yeast can tolerate the cold better than the acetic acid bacteria. Once refrigerated, the yeast will be able to proliferate while the growth of the acetic acid will slow down. When you take this action, you need to continue feeding your starter daily so that your wild yeast has plenty to eat. You do not want your starter to go to sleep! Your wild yeast will be hungry. After about a week of being refrigerated and fed daily, preferably every 8 hours, your sourdough starter should smell nice and yeasty again. Then, you can remove it from the refrigerator and return it to room temperature.

What is that brown liquid on top of the sourdough starter?

If you decide to refrigerate your starter, you might see a brown liquid form as a top layer above the starter. This liquid is called *hooch*. It indicates that your starter is very hungry, so be sure to feed it. As to the liquid, you have two options: you can stir it back into your starter to make a very tangy starter, or you can pour it off. Either action is acceptable.

Beginner's No-Knead Sourdough Boule

If the word *boule* is new to you, it refers to a round loaf of crusty bread. You often see these lovely breads at bakeries or specialty markets, and they are also becoming more common in the bakery departments of large grocery stores. They are a delight to eat, but they are even better when you learn how to make your own, especially when they are sourdough!

This boule recipe is the best bread to start with if you have never made sourdough bread. However, once you have made your first loaf, I am confident this will become your favorite go-to sourdough recipe. It makes a superb sourdough boule, with a crusty exterior and soft crumb, making this bread perfect for toasting or for using for sandwiches.

PREP TIME (SOURDOUGH STARTER): **12 HOURS**
PREP TIME (DOUGH): **1 HOUR 35 MINUTES**
FERMENTATION TIME: **12 HOURS**
RISE TIME: **1–2 HOURS**
BAKE TIME: **35–45 MINUTES**
TOTAL TIME: **APPROXIMATELY 28–29 HOURS**
YIELD: **1 SOURDOUGH BOULE**

EQUIPMENT

5–6 quart Dutch oven with a heatproof knob (usually stainless steel) that is safe to 500°F (260°C). (Alternatively, a parchment lined baking sheet can be used. However, the rise might be less.)

INGREDIENTS

3 cups unbleached bread flour

1½ tsp fine ground sea salt

½–1 tsp diastatic malt powder (optional) (see **Cook's Notes**)

1¼–1½ cups filtered, chlorine-free water (room temperature)

1 cup active sourdough starter

1 tbsp olive oil, divided

PREPARING THE SOURDOUGH STARTER

If you kept your starter at room temperature:
At 12 hours before you plan to make the bread, feed your starter with equal parts flour and water. Leave it at room temperature. Note that your starter may peak earlier than 12 hours. Depending on the temperature in your kitchen, a starter can peak anywhere from as soon as 4 hours to as late as 12 hours. However, in a kitchen that ranges between 68°F to 72°F (20°C to 22°C), a starter may generally peak closer to 10 to 12 hours. But I do not want you to worry about this. As long as your starter looks bubbly, which in most cases it should at the 12-hour mark, you can use it to prepare your dough. If your starter is completely deflated, and possibly even liquid has pooled on top, it clearly peaked very quickly. Therefore, before you use your starter for baking, you will want to feed it one more time and keep an eye on it. If you find it peaks within 4 hours, go ahead and bake with it.

If you refrigerated your starter: You will want to return your starter to room temperature and feed it equal parts flour and water. Allow sufficient time—at least 24 to 48 hours—to wake up your refrigerated starter, as it may require two feedings before it becomes bubbly and ready for baking. You may even want to consider feeding your starter every 8 hours instead of every 12 hours.

FERMENTATION STAGE

1   In a medium bowl, mix together the flour, salt, and ½ teaspoon of diastatic malt powder (if using). Whisk until combined.

2   In a separate medium bowl, whisk together 1¼ cups of water and the sourdough starter until the starter has fully dissolved in the water.

3   Make a well in the flour and pour in the liquid. Using a wet hand, mix everything together until you have a shaggy ball of dough. If not, add water, 1 tablespoon at a time, and mix until it reaches the correct consistency.

4   Cover the bowl with a dish towel and allow the dough to rest for 20 minutes. After 20 minutes, remove the towel. Using a wet hand, firmly grab the dough from the underside and pull it up and over itself. (This is called the *stretch-and-fold method*.) Rotate the bowl a quarter turn and repeat. Rotate the bowl a quarter turn 3 more times, repeating the stretch-and-fold method with each quarter-turn rotation. This completed process is called a *set*. Repeat this set 4 more times at 15-minute intervals (covering the bowl after each set) for a total of 5 sets.

5   Rub a ½ teaspoon of the olive oil over the top of the dough, flip it over and rub the remaining ½ teaspoon over the bottom. Flip the dough so that it is right side up to ensure it is completely covered with the olive oil. Cover the bowl with a flour-dusted towel or plastic wrap.

6   Place the bowl in a room temperature location that is between 68°F and 72°F (20°C and 22°C) and out of direct sunlight. Allow the dough to rest for 12 hours. Alternatively, if you think you will not be ready to bake bread in 12 hours, you will still place the bowl in a room-temperature location that is between 68°F and 72°F (20°C and 22°C) and out of direct sunlight. (See **Cook's Notes**.) Allow the dough to rest for 1 hour and then cover the bowl with a lid or plastic wrap and place it in the refrigerator for 18 to 24 hours. Use the dough within 24 hours for the best rise. If you leave the dough in the refrigerator past 24 hours, it is best used to make a flatbread, as it will not have any significant rise.

7   Once the fermentation stage is complete, the dough should appear to have doubled in size and have a domed top, almost with the appearance of a pillow. Place a piece of parchment paper on a baking sheet, flour it lightly, and set it aside.

RISING STAGE

1 Lightly dust a flat work surface with flour. Using a plastic bench scraper, spatula, or wet hands, remove the dough from the bowl and transfer it to your work surface. Flatten the dough using wet hands. (If the dough is exceptionally sticky, you can lightly flour your hands or the top of the dough and then flatten it. But try to avoid adding too much flour.)

2 Fold the flattened dough into thirds, as you would a letter. Fold over each end, meeting in the middle on top of the dough. Flip the dough over and use cupped hands to encircle the dough and work it into the shape of a ball, rotating the dough clockwise and tucking the dough edges in and under the center of the dough. This will create a seam on the bottom of the dough and tension on top of the dough.

3 Once you've shaped the dough into a ball, place it on the flour-dusted parchment paper, seam side down. Lightly dust the dough ball with flour and cover it loosely with a flour-dusted towel.

4 Place the baking sheet with the covered dough in a room-temperature location that is between 68°F and 72°F (20°C and 22°C) and out of direct sunlight. (See **Cook's Notes.**) Allow the dough to rise for 1 to 2 hours. (This is not an exact science. You are simply looking for a dough that appears to have almost doubled in size. If your kitchen is cooler, this will take closer to 2 hours. If your kitchen is warmer, this will take closer to 1 hour. If you are using dough that you had previously refrigerated, this rise time will take longer.)

5 If you feel compelled to use the poke test after 1 hour, poke the dough with your finger, inserting it into the dough no farther than past the first joint and then quickly pulling back your finger. If the dough appears to stay indented or seems to be springing back very slowly, the dough has sufficiently risen and is ready to bake. If it springs back right away, give the dough another 15 minutes or so to rise.

6 While the dough is rising, preheat the oven to 500°F (260°C) and place a round Dutch oven, with the lid on, on the middle rack of the oven. You want the oven to be very hot, so begin this preheating process about 30 to 45 minutes before you think the bread will go into the oven. (See **Cook's Notes.**)

BAKING STAGE

1 Once the dough has risen, use a sharp knife to score the bread. (You can also use a lame, which looks like a short stick with a razor blade attached.) If you are a beginning baker, I recommend you just make a simple cross on top of the bread. This scoring will allow steam to escape from the bread and prevent it from cracking in an uneven pattern. (With future loaves, you can experiment with various patterns.)

2 When the bread is ready to go into the oven, use pot holders to carefully remove the Dutch oven from the oven and then place it on a heatproof surface. Next, remove the lid from the Dutch oven, facing it away from you as you do so to prevent the burst of heat from coming toward you. Place the lid on a heatproof surface.

3 Using the parchment paper to lift the dough, carefully place it into the Dutch oven. Next, carefully tuck in the parchment paper so it doesn't stick out of the Dutch oven. Using pot holders, put the lid back onto the Dutch oven and return it to the middle rack of the oven. Close the oven door, lower the temperature to 475°F (246°C), and bake the bread for 30 minutes.

4 After 30 minutes, use pot holders to carefully remove the Dutch oven from the oven and place it on a heatproof surface. Remove the lid from the Dutch oven, again facing it away from you as you do so to prevent the steam from coming toward you, and place the lid on a heatproof surface.

5 Using a pot holder, slip the parchment paper out from underneath the bread, return the Dutch oven with the bread uncovered to the center rack of the oven. Continue baking for approximately 5 to 15 minutes more or until the bread is a golden brown. (Watch the bread closely at this stage, as you do not want it to burn on top.)

6 Once the bread is finished baking, transfer the Dutch oven to a heatproof surface, use pot holders to lift the bread out of the Dutch oven, and transfer it to a cooling rack. Tap on the bottom of the bread, it should sound hollow. If it does not sound hollow, place the bread back into the Dutch oven, return the Dutch oven, uncovered, to the center rack of the oven, and continue baking at 475°F (246°C) for approximately 5 minutes more. (You can tent the bread with foil to prevent it from overbrowning.)

7 Allow the bread to cool thoroughly (if you can!) before slicing it with a serrated knife. This bread will stay fresh at room temperature in a bread box or bag for 4 to 5 days. Well wrapped, it will stay fresh in the refrigerator for an additional 2 to 3 days, but it may begin to become stale. (Generally, sourdough bread is best not refrigerated.) If well wrapped and frozen, this bread can maintain freshness for about 3 months. Defrost, uncovered, at room temperature.

COOK'S NOTES

What is diastatic malt powder? Diastatic malt powder, also known as barley malt flour, is whole grain barley that has been soaked, sprouted, dried, and ground into flour, specifically sprouted flour. The powder contributes to several actions when added to flour, but it mainly helps create a successful oven spring (a burst of rising when the dough goes into a hot oven), which contributes to a strong rise.

Most organic flours do not contain diastatic malt powder, so if you use organic flour, it can be helpful to add this ingredient to your mix when baking bread. The general rule is to add ½ to 1 teaspoon of diastatic malt powder for every 3 cups of flour used. But never overdo it; a little goes a long way. Too much will turn your bread into a gummy mush! So start with a ½ teaspoon, and if you are pleased with the rise of your bread, great! If not, you can try increasing the amount used, up to 1 teaspoon, on your next batch of dough.

You can usually find diastatic malt powder at specialty markets and often in the baking aisle at most large grocery stores.

What is the ideal room temperature for fermenting and rising? I like to have both the fermentation stage and the rising stage for my sourdough at room temperature 68°F to 72°F (20°C to 22°C). This temperature doesn't rush the fermentation and allows for a nice flavor development. Of course, you can allow your sourdough to rise in a warmer area for a faster rise, but for the fermentation stage, stick with room temperature or cooler.

Compensating for differences in ovens: If you are completely new to baking bread in a Dutch oven, note that every oven is different both in size and how it maintains temperature. Your first loaf of bread will require a bit of experimentation as you get to know your oven. I have a very small oven, so I have found that I have to place my oven rack in the middle position; otherwise, my bread will darken too much on the bottom. However, if you have a large oven, you might need to place your oven rack in the lower third position so that your bread browns sufficiently on the bottom and bakes evenly. If your first loaf of bread overbrowns on the bottom, go easy on yourself. You are learning! Chances are it will simply lean on the darker side and not be burnt.

How will your first sourdough bread turn out? Your bread, especially if you have a relatively new starter, may not look like what you have seen at a bakery. That's okay! Chances are that the bread's interior will have fewer holes and a softer crumb than professionally baked sourdough breads. It may also have a milder flavor. In many ways, if you are new to sourdough bread, this may be a good feature as you give your palate time to adjust slowly to the texture and flavor of sourdough bread.

Trust me: the longer you maintain your sourdough starter and the more you practice baking sourdough bread, the more you will be amazed at the results you can achieve. Hang in there, and remember that we are home bakers. Most people who you bake bread for, including yourself, will be delighted simply by the heavenly aroma of bread baking in your oven and the scrumptious taste of homemade bread slathered with cultured butter!

No-Knead Sourdough Spelt Boule or Einkorn Boule

Spelt makes a great-tasting bread with a sweet, nutty flavor. It's one of my favorite ancient whole grains to bake with because it is high in fiber, zinc, iron, and a host of other vitamins and minerals. I also love baking with einkorn; it has a wonderfully unique flavor, almost like toasted nuts. You'll want to incorporate both ancient grains into your traditional foods pantry. They're delicious! Einkorn is exceptionally rich in carotenoids, especially the antioxidant lutein, which may contribute to protecting our eyes from damaging ultraviolet rays. And thanks to these carotenoids, einkorn flour has a rich yellow color that creates a beautiful hue to any bread baked with it.

From a nutritional standpoint, both ancient grains are high in protein. But interestingly, the protein present in spelt and einkorn creates less gluten formation and a weaker gluten formation than created by modern-day wheat. This weaker gluten formation breaks down easier during the sourdough fermentation process, making the sourdough bread made from these ancient whole grains easier to digest. (But keep in mind, none of the ancient whole grains that are ancestors of wheat are gluten-free.)

PREP TIME (SOURDOUGH STARTER): **12 HOURS**
PREP TIME (DOUGH): **1 HOUR 35 MINUTES**
FERMENTATION TIME: **12 HOURS**
RISE TIME: **APPROXIMATELY 1–2 HOURS**
BAKE TIME: **45 MINUTES**
TOTAL TIME: **APPROXIMATELY 28–29 HOURS**
YIELD: **1 SPELT SOURDOUGH BOULE OR 1 EINKORN SOURDOUGH BOULE**

EQUIPMENT

5–6 quart Dutch oven with a heatproof knob (usually stainless steel) that is safe to 500°F (260°C). (Alternatively, a parchment-lined baking sheet can be used. However, the rise might be less.)

INGREDIENTS

2 cups whole grain spelt flour or whole grain einkorn flour

1 cup unbleached bread flour

½–1 tsp diastatic malt powder (optional) (see **Cook's Notes**)

4½ tsp vital wheat gluten (optional) (see **Cook's Notes**)

1½ tsp fine ground sea salt

1 cup filtered, chlorine-free water (room temperature)

¼ cup maple syrup

1 cup active sourdough starter

1 tbsp olive oil

PREPARING THE SOURDOUGH STARTER

If you kept your starter at room temperature: At 12 hours before you plan to make the bread, feed your starter with equal parts flour and water. Leave it at room temperature. Note that your starter may peak earlier than 12 hours. Depending on the temperature in your kitchen, a starter can peak anywhere from as soon as 4 hours to as late as 12 hours. However, in a kitchen that ranges between 68°F to 72°F (20°C to 22°C), a starter may generally peak closer to 10 to 12 hours. But I do not want you to worry about this. As long as your starter looks bubbly, which in most cases it should at the 12-hour mark, you can use it to prepare your dough. If your starter is completely deflated, and possibly liquid has pooled on top, it clearly peaked very quickly. Therefore, before you use your starter for baking, you will want to feed it one more time and keep an eye on it. If you find it peaks within 4 hours, go ahead and bake with it.

If you refrigerated your starter: You will want to return your starter to room temperature and feed it equal parts flour and water. Allow sufficient time—at least 24 to 48 hours—to wake up your refrigerated starter, as it may require two feedings before it becomes bubbly and ready for baking. You may even want to consider feeding your starter every 8 hours instead of every 12 hours.

FERMENTATION INSTRUCTIONS

1   Whisk together the spelt or einkorn flour, bread flour, salt, ½ teaspoon diastatic malt powder (if using), and vital wheat gluten (if using) in a medium bowl. Set aside.

2   Mix the water and maple syrup together in a bowl or large measuring cup. Once the maple syrup is dissolved, add the active sourdough starter and mix well to combine.

3   Make a well in the flour and pour in the liquid. Using a wet hand, mix everything together until you have a shaggy ball of dough. If not, add water, 1 tablespoon at a time, and mix until it reaches the correct consistency.

4   Cover the bowl with a dish towel and allow the dough to rest for 20 minutes. After 20 minutes, remove the towel. Using a wet hand, firmly grab the dough from the underside and pull it up and over itself. (This is called the *stretch-and-fold method*.) Rotate the bowl a quarter turn and repeat. Rotate the bowl a quarter turn 3 more times, repeating the stretch-and-fold method with each quarter-turn rotation. This completed process is called a

set. Repeat this set 4 more times at 15-minute intervals (covering the bowl after each set) for a total of 5 sets.

5   Rub a ½ tablespoon of the olive oil over the top of the dough, flip it over and rub the remaining ½ tablespoon over the bottom. Flip the dough back so that it is right side up to ensure it is completely covered with the olive oil.

6   Lightly cover the bowl with a flour-dusted towel or plastic wrap.

7   Place the bowl in a room temperature location that is between 68°F and 72°F (20°C and 22°C) and out of direct sunlight. Allow the dough to rest for 12 hours. Alternatively, if you think you will not be ready to bake bread in 12 hours, you will still place the bowl in a room-temperature location that is between 68°F and 72°F (20°C and 22°C) and out of direct sunlight. (See **Cook's Notes.**) Allow the dough to rest for 1 hour and then cover the bowl with a lid or plastic wrap and place it in the refrigerator for 18 to 24 hours. Use the dough within 24 hours for the best rise. If you leave the dough in the refrigerator past 24 hours, it is best used to make a flatbread, as it will not have any significant rise.

8   Once the fermentation stage is complete, the dough should appear to have doubled in size and have a domed top, almost with the appearance of a pillow. Place a piece of parchment paper on a baking sheet, flour it lightly, and set it aside.

RISING STAGE

1   Lightly dust a flat work surface with flour. Using a plastic bench scraper, spatula, or wet hands, remove the dough from the bowl and transfer it to your work surface. Flatten the dough using wet hands. (If the dough is exceptionally sticky, you can lightly flour your hands or the top of the dough and then flatten it. But try to avoid adding too much flour.)

2   Fold the flattened dough into thirds, as you would a letter. Fold over each end of the dough, meeting in the middle on top of the dough. Flip the dough over and use cupped hands to encircle the dough and work it into the shape of a ball, rotating the dough clockwise and tucking the dough edges in

and under the center of the dough. This will create a seam on the bottom of the dough and tension on top of the dough.

3   Once you have shaped the dough into a ball, place it on the flour-dusted parchment paper, seam side down.

4   Lightly dust the dough ball with flour and cover it loosely with a flour-dusted towel.

5   Place the baking sheet with the covered dough in a room-temperature location that is between 68°F and 72°F (20°C and 22°C) and out of direct sunlight. (See **Cook's Notes.**) Allow the dough to rise for 1 to 2 hours. (This is not an exact science. You are simply looking for a dough that appears to have almost doubled in size. If your kitchen is cooler, this will take closer to 2 hours. If your kitchen is warmer, this will take closer to 1 hour. If you are using dough that you had previously refrigerated, this rise time will take longer.)

6   If you feel compelled to use the poke test after 1 hour, poke the dough with your finger, inserting it into the dough no farther than past the first joint and then quickly pulling back your finger. If the dough appears to stay indented or seems to be springing back very slowly, the dough has sufficiently risen and is ready to bake. If it springs back right away, give the dough another 15 minutes or so to rise.

7   While the dough is rising, preheat the oven to 500°F (260°C) and place a round Dutch oven, with the lid on, on the middle rack of the oven. You want the oven to be very hot, so begin this preheating process about 30 to 45 minutes before you think the bread will go into the oven. (See **Cook's Notes.**)

BAKING STAGE

1   Once the dough has risen, use a sharp knife to score the bread. You can also use a lame, which looks like a short stick with a razor blade attached. (See **Cook's Notes** for tips on scoring these boules.)

2   When the bread is ready to go into the oven, use pot holders to carefully remove the Dutch oven

from the oven and then place it on a heatproof surface. Next, remove the lid from the Dutch oven, facing it away from you as you do so to prevent the burst of heat from coming toward you. Place the lid on a heatproof surface.

3 Using the parchment paper to lift the dough, carefully place it into the Dutch oven. Next, carefully tuck in the parchment paper so it doesn't stick out of the Dutch oven. Using pot holders, put the lid back onto the Dutch oven and return it to the middle rack of the oven. Close the oven door, lower the temperature to 475°F (246°C), and bake the bread for 30 minutes.

4 After 30 minutes, use pot holders to carefully remove the Dutch oven from the oven and place it on a heatproof surface. Remove the lid from the Dutch oven, again facing it away from you as you do so to prevent the steam from coming toward you, and place the lid on a heatproof surface.

5 Using a pot holder, slip the parchment paper out from underneath the bread, return the Dutch oven with the bread uncovered to the center rack of the oven. Continue baking for approximately 5 to 15 minutes more or until the bread is a golden brown. (Watch the bread closely at this stage, as you do not want it to burn on top.)

6 Once the bread is finished baking, transfer the Dutch oven to a heatproof surface, use pot holders to lift the bread out of the Dutch oven, and transfer it to a cooling rack. Tap on the bottom of the bread, it should sound hollow. If it does not sound hollow, place the bread back into the Dutch oven, return the Dutch oven, uncovered, to the center rack of the oven, and continue baking at 475°F (246°C) for approximately 5 minutes more. (You can tent the bread with foil to prevent it from overbrowning.)

7 Allow the bread to cool thoroughly (if you can!) before slicing it with a serrated knife. This bread will stay fresh at room temperature in a bread box or bag for 4 to 5 days. Well wrapped, it will stay fresh in the refrigerator for an additional 2 to 3 days, but it may begin to become stale. (Generally, sourdough bread is best not refrigerated.) If well wrapped and frozen, this bread can maintain freshness for about 3 months. Defrost, uncovered, at room temperature.

COOK'S NOTES

Why add diastatic malt powder and vital wheat gluten? When baking bread using whole grain flours that are either low in gluten or have a weak gluten structure, consider adding diastatic malt powder or vital wheat gluten to your flour. Although spelt and einkorn are both delicious and nutritious ancient whole grains to use when making sourdough bread, these ancient whole grains have a weaker gluten structure, which is a drawback. This more fragile gluten structure can create a weaker rise in your baked bread. However, to compensate for this weaker structure, we first add bread flour to help increase the gluten, by also adding diastatic malt powder and vital wheat gluten, we can further help bring structure and a better rise to the dough. Diastatic malt powder and vital wheat gluten can be used together or individually, but provide the best results when used together.

Baker's tip for the spelt boule: The gluten structure in your spelt dough is weak, which can affect the rise of the dough. So when scoring your dough, resist making large cuts across the top of the dough ball, which may travel down the sides of the dough. Instead, make a small cross on the top. This is sufficient to allow the steam to release, but it will not interfere with the rising of the dough.

Baker's tip for the einkorn boule: The gluten structure in einkorn dough is the weakest among ancient wheats, so resist scoring the dough with large, long, or decorative cuts. Instead, make the traditional einkorn score: four small cuts at the very top of the dough ball that create a square. This will allow the steam to escape, but will not interfere with the rising of the dough.

Baker's tip for a less-sour sourdough bread: If after you make your first sourdough bread, you find that the taste is too sour, you can add a ½ teaspoon of baking soda to the recipe the next time you make it. The baking soda is kneaded into the dough as you are shaping it into a boule right before the rise time. This technique can also be used with any baked sourdough discard recipe.

Cast-Iron Griddle Sourdough English Muffins

English muffins are probably one of my favorite ways to enjoy bread. And these American muffins, as the British sometimes call them, are no exception. That's right! The British don't call them English muffins. Instead, the British were introduced to these muffins when they were imported from the United States. But the British can still take all the credit for these tasty muffins because the baker, Samuel Bath Thomas, was originally from England and living in New York City where he was baking and selling his toaster crumpets. (I think we need to give the Brits credit for this one!)

PREP TIME (SOURDOUGH STARTER): **12 HOURS**
PREP TIME (DOUGH): **1 HOUR 35 MINUTES**
FERMENTATION TIME: **12–18 HOURS**
RISE TIME: **1 HOUR**
COOK TIME: **8–12 MINUTES**
TOTAL TIME: **APPROXIMATELY 26–32 HOURS**
YIELD: **10–12 ENGLISH MUFFINS**

EQUIPMENT

3-inch (7.5cm) biscuit cutter

INGREDIENTS

2 cups unbleached bread flour

1 cup whole wheat flour

1 tsp fine ground sea salt

1–1¼ cups whole milk

1 tbsp maple syrup

1 cup active sourdough starter

1 tbsp olive oil

¼ cup cornmeal

PREPARING THE SOURDOUGH STARTER

1   Prepare your sourdough starter per the instructions in the **Beginner's No-Knead Sourdough Boule** recipe (p. 132).

FERMENTATION INSTRUCTIONS

1   When the starter is ready, whisk together the bread flour, whole wheat flour, and sea salt in a large bowl. Set aside.

2   In a medium bowl, whisk together 1 cup of milk and the maple syrup. Once the maple syrup is fully incorporated, add the sourdough starter and whisk.

3   Make a well in the flour mixture. Pour in the milk mixture and mix to form a shaggy dough. (If the dough is dry, add additional milk, 1 tablespoon at a time, and mix until the dough reaches the proper consistency.)

4   Cover the bowl with a towel and allow the dough to rest for 20 minutes. After 20 minutes, remove the towel. Using a wet hand, firmly grab the dough from the underside and pull it up and over itself. (This is called the *stretch-and-fold method*.) Rotate the bowl a quarter turn and repeat. Rotate the bowl a quarter turn 3 more times, repeating the stretch-and-fold method with each quarter-turn rotation. This completed process is called a *set*. Repeat this set 4 more times at 15 minute intervals (covering the bowl after each set) for a total of 5 sets.

5   Drizzle a ½ tablespoon of the olive oil on top of the dough, flip it over in the bowl, and then drizzle the remaining ½ tablespoon of olive oil over the rest of the dough. Flip the dough back right side up, ensuring all the dough is coated with the olive oil.

6   Cover the bowl with a lid or plastic wrap and place it in a room-temperature location between 68°F and 72°F (20°C and 22°C) and out of direct sunlight. Allow the dough to rest for 12 to 18 hours. Alternatively, if you think you will not be ready to bake the muffins in 12 to 18 hours, you will still place the bowl in a room temperature location that is between

68°F and 72°F (20°C and 22°C) and out of direct sunlight. Allow the dough to rest for 1 hour and then place the covered bowl in the refrigerator for 18 to 24 hours. (This will create even more nooks and crannies in the muffins.) Once the fermentation stage is complete, the dough should appear to have approximately doubled in size and have domed on top.

RISING INSTRUCTIONS

1 Line a baking sheet with parchment paper and dust it with cornmeal. Set aside.

2 Lightly dust a flat work surface with flour. Using a plastic bench scrape or a spatula, remove the dough from the bowl and transfer it to the work surface. Flour the top of the dough and then flatten it with your hand so that the dough is approximately 1 inch (2.5cm) thick.

3 Using the biscuit cutter, cut out one round, place it on the baking sheet, and sprinkle the top with cornmeal. Continue cutting out rounds until all you have left are dough scraps. As you cut each round, put it on the baking sheet and sprinkle it with cornmeal.

4 Pull all the scraps together into a ball and reflatten it to 1 inch (2.5cm) thick. Continue to cut out as many rounds as possible until you have no scraps left. As you cut each round, put it on the baking sheet and sprinkle it with cornmeal.

5 Cover all the English muffins with a towel and allow them to rise at room temperature between 68°F and 72°F (20°C and 22°C) for 1 hour and out of direct sunlight. (This may take longer if you are working with dough that has been refrigerated.)

COOKING INSTRUCTIONS

1 On the stovetop, preheat a well-seasoned cast-iron griddle or skillet or a nonstick skillet over low heat. Place 4 English muffins into the skillet and cover. Cook for 4 minutes and then check the underside. If they have not browned, let them cook for another minute or two until they are golden brown. (Watch them carefully. They can burn easily.)

2 Once the underside of each English muffin is golden brown, flip it over. After all the muffins are flipped, put the lid back on the skillet, and allow the other sides to cook until they are golden brown, approximately 4 to 6 minutes. Once the English muffins are golden brown on both sides, transfer them to a cooling rack and continue to cook the remaining English muffins.

3 Allow the English muffins to cool completely, then use a fork to split them in half. Toast the English muffins before serving.

4 These English muffins are best stored at room temperature in an airtight container for up to 4 days. After that, it's best to fork split any leftovers, wrap each half individually in plastic wrap, and store them in a freezerproof container for 2 to 3 months.

······· COOK'S NOTES ·······

Substituting whole grain spelt or einkorn flour for whole wheat flour: You can substitute whole grain spelt or einkorn flour for whole wheat flour in any of the sourdough or sourdough discard recipes calling for whole wheat flour. If you do so, you may need to adjust the liquid. In this recipe, if you substitute spelt or einkorn flour for the whole wheat flour, reduce the milk to ¼ cup. If all the flour does not appear to be dampened when mixing in the milk and the sourdough starter, add extra milk, 1 tablespoon at a time, and mix until you achieve the desired results.

Cast-Iron Skillet Sourdough Discard Biscuits

As you create and maintain your sourdough starter and make sourdough bread, you will begin accumulating sourdough starter discard. This is the perfect time to try your hand at making sourdough biscuits. These biscuits are light and fluffy with a delightful sourdough tang. And baking up these biscuits in a cast-iron skillet will have you embracing your pioneer spirit!

PREP TIME: **15 MINUTES**
COOK TIME: **APPROXIMATELY 15 MINUTES**
TOTAL TIME: **APPROXIMATELY 30 MINUTES**
YIELD: **10–12 BISCUITS**

EQUIPMENT
Large box grater
Rolling pin
2½-inch (6.35cm) biscuit cutter

INGREDIENTS
1 tsp butter for greasing pan
1½ cups unbleached all-purpose flour (preferably organic)
½ cup whole wheat flour (see **Cook's Notes**)
2 tsp unrefined whole cane sugar
2 tsp baking powder
1 tsp fine ground sea salt
½ tsp baking soda
8 tbsp unsalted butter, frozen
½ cup buttermilk (homemade or store-bought)
1 cup 100% hydration sourdough starter discard

1 Preheat the oven to 450°F (232°C).

2 Grease a 10-inch (25.5cm) cast-iron skillet with butter or line it with a round of parchment paper. (Alternatively, you can line a baking sheet with parchment paper.)

3 In a large bowl, combine the all-purpose flour, whole wheat flour, unrefined whole cane sugar, baking powder, salt, and baking soda. Mix well.

4 Grate the frozen butter with the large holes of a box grater. Transfer the grated butter to the bowl with the flour. Mix gently to coat the butter with the flour.

5 Make a well in the flour-butter mixture. In a separate bowl or large measuring cup, mix the buttermilk and the sourdough discard. Pour the mixture into the well in the flour.

6 Using a wooden spoon, stir the mixture just until the dry ingredients are dampened with the liquid, but do not overmix.

7 Transfer the dough to a lightly floured work surface and lightly dust your hands with flour. Work the dough gently until it comes together by folding it in half and then flattening it slightly after each fold.

8 Once the dough stays together, use a rolling pin dusted with flour to roll out the dough into a rectangle that is approximately 1 inch (2.5cm) thick. Dust the biscuit cutter in flour and then cut out as many biscuits as possible. (You will likely be able to cut out approximately 8 to 10 biscuits.) Do not twist the cutter, simply press down and then pull up. You can use a different-size biscuit cutter to cut out the biscuits, but you will have a different number of biscuits. Smaller biscuits will need a minute or two less to cook, while larger biscuits will need a minute or two more to cook.) Reroll the scraps and cut out 2 more biscuits.

9 Place the biscuits into the prepared skillet (or onto the baking sheet). Bake for 15 to 16 minutes or until golden brown.

10 Remove the skillet (or baking sheet) from the oven and place it on a heatproof surface. Transfer the biscuits to a cooling rack. Allow them to cool for a few minutes and then enjoy them while they are warm. These biscuits are best enjoyed the day they are made.

> ········· **COOK'S NOTES** ·········
>
> ***Substituting whole grain spelt or einkorn flour for whole wheat flour:*** You can substitute whole grain spelt or einkorn flour for whole wheat flour in any of the sourdough discard recipes calling for whole wheat flour. If you do so, you may need to adjust the liquid. In this recipe, if you substitute spelt or einkorn flour for the whole wheat flour, reduce the buttermilk to 6 tablespoons. If the flour does not appear to be dampened when mixing in the buttermilk and the sourdough starter, add in extra buttermilk, 1 tablespoon at a time, and mix until the desired results are achieved.

Slice-and-Bake Cheesy Sourdough Discard Crackers

This is one of the easiest sourdough crackers you will ever make using your sourdough discard. If you don't like to waste anything, including your discard, this recipe is for you! These are melt-in-your-mouth tender crackers that you can customize to meet any taste. Here I share how to make a cheese cracker with an herb variation, but don't stop there. You can experiment with a variety of flavors to make this recipe your own.

PREP TIME: **15 MINUTES**
CHILLING TIME: **1 HOUR**
COOK TIME: **14–16 MINUTES**
TOTAL TIME: **1 HOUR 30 MINUTES**
YIELD: **APPROXIMATELY 20 CRACKERS**

INGREDIENTS

1¼ cups whole wheat flour (see **Cook's Notes**)

1 tsp fine ground salt

½ tsp dry mustard powder (Alternatively, you can use prepared mustard, but increase it to 1 teaspoon and mix it with the cream.)

2 tbsp cold butter, cubed, plus extra to grease the baking sheet

1 cup shredded hard cheese (cheddar, Gruyère, or Parmesan)

¼–⅓ cup cream

½ cup 100% hydration sourdough starter discard

Flaky sea salt (optional)

1. Whisk together the flour, salt, and dry mustard in a large bowl.

2. Using your hands, work the cold butter into the flour mixture until it reaches a crumblike texture. Mix in the shredded cheese until well coated with the flour mixture.

3. In a medium bowl, mix together ¼ cup of cream and the sourdough starter discard.

4. Make a well in the flour mixture and pour in the cream-discard mixture. Mix until the dough easily forms a ball and holds together very well. If the dough is dry and does not hold together, add additional cream, 1 tablespoon at a time, and mix. If the dough appears too sticky and won't be easily rolled into a log, add additional flour, 1 tablespoon at a time, and mix well.

5. On a floured work surface, roll the dough into a log approximately 2 inches (5cm) in diameter. Wrap the log well in plastic wrap and place it in the freezer for 1 hour. (See **Cook's Notes**.)

6. While the dough log is chilling, preheat the oven to 350°F (177°C). Line a baking sheet with parchment paper or grease it lightly with butter.

7. Remove the dough log from the freezer and unwrap. On a flat surface, use a sharp knife to slice the dough into ¼-inch (0.65cm) rounds and place the rounds on the prepared baking sheet about 1 inch (2.5cm) apart. Sprinkle each round with the flaky sea salt (if using).

8. Place the baking sheet on the middle rack in the preheated oven. Bake for approximately 14 to 16 minutes, rotating the baking sheet halfway through the baking time to ensure even baking.

9. Bake until the edges of the crackers turn a golden brown. Remove them from the oven and transfer from the baking sheet to a cooling rack. Allow to cool completely.

10. Store the crackers in an airtight container to help maintain their crispness in the pantry. The stored crackers will stay fresh for at least 2 weeks.

COOK'S NOTES

Substituting spelt or einkorn flour: You can substitute spelt or einkorn flour in place of the whole wheat flour when making these crackers. The liquid in this recipe is limited, so you will not need to reduce it; instead, add additional flour until you reach the desired consistency.

Freezing the dough: If you are not planning on baking the crackers immediately after the freeze time, you can store the cracker dough logs in the freezer for 2 to 3 months if they're wrapped well.

Making whole grain herb crackers: To turn these cheese crackers into herb crackers, omit the cheese and the dry mustard. Instead, add 2 tablespoons of unrefined whole cane sugar and 1 tablespoon of your favorite dried herbs to the flour. I like to use a blend of Italian herbs, including basil and oregano. Follow the same directions for making the cheese crackers into a log for easy slice-and-bake crackers.

Making whole grain dried fruit and nut crackers: To turn these cheese crackers into dried fruit and nut crackers, omit the cheese and the dry mustard. Instead, add a ½ teaspoon of cinnamon, a ½ cup of small dried fruit (I like to use currants), and a ½ cup of chopped nuts, any variety, to the flour. Follow the same directions for making the cheese crackers into a log for easy slice-and-bake crackers.

No-Knead Sourdough Rye Bread with Caraway Seeds

Here is an easy recipe for how to make rye bread. Yes, you can leave out the seeds, but I highly recommend you try it with them once. They add a special flavor that can't be beat.

This bread is baked in a traditional loaf pan, making it a wonderful slicing bread for sandwiches. Try it spread with liverwurst and home-fermented sauerkraut for a nutrient-dense treat that was my dad's favorite. Or for a unique but tasty sandwich, try sardines smothered with pickled red onions on toasted and buttered rye bread. Just scrumptious!

PREP TIME (SOURDOUGH STARTER): **12 HOURS**
PREP TIME (DOUGH): **1 HOUR 35 MINUTES**
FERMENTATION TIME: **12 HOURS**
RISE TIME: **1–3 HOURS**
BAKE TIME: **40–45 MINUTES**
TOTAL TIME: **APPROXIMATELY 40 HOURS**
YIELD: **1 LOAF**

INGREDIENTS

1 cup whole grain rye flour

1 tsp fine ground sea salt

1½ tsp caraway seeds

½ tsp diastatic malt powder (optional) (see **Cook's Notes**)

4½ tsp vital wheat gluten (optional) (see **Cook's Notes**)

¾–1¼ cup filtered chlorine-free water (room temperature)

1 tbsp molasses

1 cup 100% Hydration Sourdough Starter

1½–2 cups unbleached bread flour (preferably organic)

1 tbsp olive oil

1 tsp unsalted butter

PREPARING THE SOURDOUGH STARTER

1   Prepare your sourdough starter per the instructions in the **Beginner's No-Knead Sourdough Boule** recipe (p. 132).

FERMENTATION INSTRUCTIONS

1   When the starter is ready, whisk together the rye flour, sea salt, caraway seeds, and diastatic malt powder (if using), and the vital wheat gluten (if using) in a large bowl. Set aside.

2   Whisk together ¾ cup water, molasses, and the sourdough starter in a medium bowl or large measuring cup. Add this to the rye flour mixture and mix well using a wooden spoon.

3   Add 1½ cups of the bread flour to the rye flour mixture and mix well with a wooden spoon or a wet hand until all the flour is moistened. (If your dough has a shaggy consistency, do not add any more flour. If your dough has an overly wet consistency after adding the 1½ cups of bread flour, add more bread flour, 1 tablespoon at a time, and mix until the mixture reaches a shaggy consistency.)

4   Cover the bowl with a towel and allow the dough to rest for 20 minutes. After 20 minutes, remove the towel. Using a wet hand, firmly grab the dough from the underside and pull it up and over itself. (This is called the *stretch-and-fold method*.) Rotate the bowl a quarter turn and repeat. Rotate the bowl a quarter turn 3 more times, repeating the stretch-and-fold method with each quarter-turn rotation. This completed process is called a *set*. Repeat this set 4 more times at 15 minute intervals (covering the bowl after each set) for a total of 5 sets.

5   Rub some of the olive oil over the top of the dough. Flip the dough over and rub the remaining olive oil over the bottom of the dough. Flip the dough so it is right side up, ensuring the entire surface is coated with the oil. Loosely cover with plastic wrap.

6   Place the bowl in a room-temperature location that is between 68°F and 72°F (20°C and 22°C) and out of direct sunlight. Allow the dough to rest for 12 hours. Alternatively, if you will not be ready to bake in 12 hours, you will still place the bowl in a room-temperature location that is between 68°F and 72°F (20°C and 22°C) and out of direct sunlight. Allow the dough to rest for 1 hour and then cover the bowl with a lid or plastic wrap and place it in the refrigerator for 18 hours, but no longer than 24 hours before baking. Once the fermentation is complete, the dough should appear to have doubled in size and have a domed top.

RISING INSTRUCTIONS

1   Grease an 8-inch x 4-inch (20cm x 10cm) loaf pan with butter. Set aside.

2   Lightly dust a flat work surface with flour. Using a plastic bench scraper, spatula, or wet hands, remove the dough from the bowl and transfer it to the work surface. Using wet hands, flatten the dough into a rectangle that is approximately 8 inches x 10 inches (20.5cm x 25.5cm).

3   Roll the dough into a log, and press lightly on the seam to seal it. Flip it over so the seam side is down. Tuck under each end of the dough log and then place it seam side down into the prepared loaf pan.

4   Place the loaf pan in a room temperature location that is between 68°F and 72°F (20°C and 22°C) and out of direct sunlight. Cover the pan loosely with a tea towel that has been dusted with flour. Allow the dough to rise for 1 to 2 hours or until it is three quarters of the way to the rim of the loaf pan.

BAKING INSTRUCTIONS

1   Once the dough has risen to three quarters of the way to the rim of the pan, preheat the oven to 450°F (232°C). As the oven is preheating, allow the dough to continue rising until it reaches the rim of the pan and has slightly domed in the middle. (See **Cook's Notes**.) Once the dough has finished rising, transfer the loaf pan to the middle rack of the preheated oven and lower the temperature to 400°F (204°C). Bake for approximately 40 to 45 minutes or until the top is golden brown and the bread begins to pull away from the sides of the pan.

2   Using pot holders, remove the loaf pan from the oven, invert the pan, remove the bread, and transfer the loaf, right side up, to a cooling rack. Allow to cool completely before slicing using a serrated knife.

3   This rye bread will stay fresh at room temperature in a bread box or bread bag for 4 to 5 days. Well wrapped, it will stay fresh in the refrigerator for an additional 2 to 3 days, but may begin to become stale. (Generally, sourdough bread is best not refrigerated.) If well wrapped and frozen, this bread can maintain freshness for about 3 months. Defrost, uncovered, at room temperature.

············· **COOK'S NOTES** ·············

What is the proper rising time for the dough? How long the dough needs to rise is not an exact science. You are simply looking for a dough that appears to have risen to fill the loaf pan to the rim and slightly domed in the middle past the rim of the pan. Just eyeball it. If your kitchen is cooler, this will take closer to 2 hours; if your kitchen is warmer, this will take closer to 1 hour. If you are using dough that you had previously refrigerated, this rise time will take longer, possibly closer to 3 hours.

Why use diastatic malt powder or vital wheat gluten? When it comes to baking with whole grain flours, sometimes they can benefit from a little help. Although diastatic malt powder and vital wheat gluten play slightly different roles, they both contribute to creating a better whole grain bread. They are, in essence, dough boosters. Diastatic malt powder helps improve the rise of the dough as well as create a nice interior texture; however, its best quality is that it creates a beautiful golden brown crust on the bread. Vital wheat gluten is a protein that gives whole grain flours the boost they need to help dough made with them rise to their maximum height to create a bread that will more resemble one made with all-purpose or bread flour. These two boosters can be used individually but to create a really great loaf of whole grain bread, they work very well when used together.

Sourdough Discard Flapjacks and Waffles

The word *flapjack* originated in England and referred to a type of flat oat cake that looked somewhat like a modern-day granola bar. In the United States, *flapjack* takes on a bit of a different meaning and has become a regional colloquialism—specifically in the southern United States—to mean *pancakes*. Whatever you call them, when they are made with sourdough starter discard, they are light, fluffy, and delicious!

These easy and tasty pancakes are made with discarded sourdough starter. If you feel like waffles instead of flapjacks, just bring out your waffle maker and use the same batter to make a crispy treat. You'll never throw out your sourdough starter discard again!

PREP TIME: **5 MINUTES**
COOK TIME: **15–30 MINUTES**
TOTAL TIME: **20–35 MINUTES**
YIELD: **APPROXIMATELY 8–10 PANCAKES**

INGREDIENTS

2 cups 100% hydration sourdough starter discard

2 tbsp unsalted butter, melted and cooled

2 tbsp maple syrup

2 large eggs

½ tsp fine ground sea salt

¼ cup to ½ cup all-purpose flour (if needed)

½ tsp baking soda

1 tsp baking powder

2–3 tbsp unsalted butter, for greasing the skillet or griddle

Additional butter and maple syrup, for serving

1. Place the sourdough starter in a large bowl and add the melted butter. Mix well.

2. Add the maple syrup, eggs, and salt to the sourdough mixture. Mix well. If the mixture appears very loose, add flour, up to ½ cup, until it reaches the consistency of pancake batter.

3. Add the baking soda and baking powder to the sourdough mixture and mix gently to incorporate. (The mixture may bubble up slightly. This is normal.)

4. In a well-seasoned cast-iron (or nonstick) skillet or griddle, melt 1 tablespoon of butter over medium heat and then ladle approximately ¼ cup of the batter into the skillet or onto the griddle for each pancake.

5. Allow each pancake to cook for approximately 2 to 3 minutes or until bubbles appear on the surface. Flip the pancakes and cook for an additional 30 seconds to 1 minute.

6. Transfer the cooked pancakes to an ovenproof plate. To keep the cooked pancakes warm, place the plate in an oven preheated to 200°F (93°C). (Alternatively, cover the cooked pancakes with a clean kitchen towel.)

7. Continue cooking the pancakes, adding more butter to the frying pan as needed. Once all the pancakes are cooked, serve them immediately with a pat of butter and a drizzle of warm maple syrup over the top.

8. Well-wrapped pancakes can be stored in the refrigerator for 2 to 3 days and up to 3 months in the freezer. To rewarm pancakes, place them on a baking sheet lined with aluminum foil or parchment paper. (Alternatively, you can place the pancakes on a nonstick baking sheet.) Wrap the baking sheet tightly with aluminum foil so the pancakes are completely covered. Place in a preheated 350°F (177°C) oven for 5 to 10 minutes or until the pancakes are heated through.

Sourdough Discard Crisp Flatbread

This is one of my favorite ways to use up sourdough discard. You can serve these flatbreads right out of the oven or use them as a base for any topping, including turning them into flatbread pizzas.

PREP TIME: **5 MINUTES**
COOK TIME: **20 MINUTES**
TOTAL TIME: **25 MINUTES**
YIELD: **APPROXIMATELY 4 ROUND FLATBREADS**

INGREDIENTS

2 cups sourdough starter discard

1 tsp garlic powder, onion powder, or chili powder (any variety)

1–2 tsp dried herbs (divided) (see **Cook's Notes**)

1 tsp crushed or ground spices (see **Cook's Notes**)

½ tsp fine ground sea salt

¼–½ cup all-purpose flour (if needed)

¼ cup olive oil

1 tsp flaked sea salt (optional)

1 Preheat the oven to 425°F (218°C) and set the oven rack to the lowest position.

2 Line a baking sheet with parchment paper. Set aside.

3 Mix together the sourdough discard; garlic, onion, or chili powder; 1 teaspoon dried herbs; spices; and sea salt in a large bowl. (This is your flatbread batter.) If your batter appears very loose, add up to ½ cup of flour. It should still be pourable but not runny.

4 Using a ladle, scoop the batter out onto the prepared baking sheet, forming 4 rounds. Drizzle the rounds with olive oil. If desired, sprinkle the batter with the flaked sea salt or the remaining 1 teaspoon of dried herbs, or both.

5 Place the baking sheet on the lower rack of the oven. Bake for approximately 20 minutes or until the flatbreads appear golden and are beginning to gently brown around the edges.

6 Remove the baking sheet to a heatproof surface. Allow the flatbreads to cool for a few minutes and then serve whole or sliced. (They will be quite crisp and can be easily sliced with a pizza cutter or sharp knife.) These flatbreads are best eaten the day they are made.

···················· COOK'S NOTES ····················

My favorite flatbread seasoning combinations: My favorite combinations include Italian seasoning with garlic powder, herbes de Provence with onion powder, Mexican oregano with crushed cumin seeds and coriander seeds, and ancho chili powder or chipotle chili powder.

Making sweet flatbreads: To make sweet flatbreads, omit the savory powders, herbs, and spices, decrease the salt to a ½ teaspoon, and add a combination of ½ teaspoon ground cinnamon, ¼ teaspoon ground cloves, and ¼ teaspoon ground allspice to the sourdough discard. In place of the olive oil, drizzle a ¼ cup melted butter over the top of the flatbreads, and if desired, sprinkle them with a ¼ teaspoon of cinnamon mixed with a teaspoon of sugar (white sugar or a Demerara or Turbinado sugar work best for this, as unrefined whole cane sugar may burn).

Chapter Seven
SOAKING AND SPROUTING

GETTING STARTED WITH SOAKING AND SPROUTING

You may be familiar with the practice of soaking dried beans, but did you know you can sprout beans, lentils, and grains too? This might be new to you, and 25 years ago, it was new to me too! But as I've discovered, sprouted beans, lentils, and grains can actually be something to eat and easily digest at the same time.

Soaking and Sprouting Beans and Lentils

Soaking beans is a common method for making them easier to cook. It also helps make them more digestible. Beans and lentils contain phytic acid; therefore, it's best if some of the phytic acid is neutralized so that we can absorb the nutrients that beans have to offer. We also want to neutralize some of that phytic acid so it doesn't strip vitamins and minerals from our bodies.

We're not going to be able to neutralize all the phytic acid through soaking, but that's okay, since phytic acid also has a good side. It serves as an antioxidant to protect our cells from free radicals, which are molecules that may play a role in creating disease. So the fact that some of our foods contain phytic acid is good, because we can learn from traditional cultures how to properly prepare beans and lentils by soaking them.

Now, let's go one step further by not only soaking beans but sprouting them too! Why do we want to take this extra step?

Scientific studies have found that when we sprout beans, we alter their structure in a way that increases their vitamins, minerals, and essential amino acids. And the good news is that this step takes very little effort on our part—the beans do all the work. And the same is true of lentils. As with beans, the lentils do all the work and sprout quite easily, also improving their nutritional profile.

Soaking Whole Grains

Whole grains are nutritious and rich in B vitamins and fiber. They also contain a whole host of minerals, including calcium, iron, phosphorus, potassium, and zinc. But for all the good they contain, there are drawbacks to consuming whole grains in their natural state because they also contain phytic acid, like beans and lentils do.

Traditional cultures have fermented grains for centuries by soaking them. Once the grains were soaked, and thereby soured or fermented, they were turned into various types of porridges or baked into slowly risen breads that we commonly call "sourdough" today. Traditional cultures also ate grain that had not been soaked and soured by fermentation. But they only ate grain in this unfermented way at certain times of the year. For example, unleavened bread is bread that has not been fermented through soaking and souring and was generally eaten by early civilizations only in the spring. This is fascinating because phytic acid has what is known as a *chelating effect*. The process of chelation is believed to be responsible for removing toxins and heavy metals from our bodies. So by eating unleavened bread, maybe our ancestors were engaging in a springtime detox! Our ancestors ate soaked and soured grains for three seasons and limited unfermented grains to the spring. Nowadays, we are eating unfermented grains all year long and stripping our bodies of the nutrients we need for healthy digestive systems and overall good health. At the very least, most of the year we need to return to soaking our grains, such as when making oatmeal or other grain-based porridges, and when baking sourdough breads.

Today, modern societies often appear to be plagued with various types of digestive disorders. Why has this become so commonplace? Depending on your age, you might have been raised on a fairly basic diet of real foods: foods that were homemade and prepared in more traditional ways than how food is prepared today. And certainly, packaged and fast foods were not as prevalent as they are now. But what does all of this have to do with grains? A lot has to do with the fact that we have moved away from eating real foods, and in doing so, have weakened our digestive health. As a result, we are less able to digest our foods properly and absorb the nutrients we

need for good health. And when it comes to grains, we are usually eating a lot of packaged grain-based foods that have not been properly prepared by soaking and souring. Plus, we are eating these types of grains throughout the year.

If we understand the benefits of soaking, do we need to take this soaking and souring process one step further and sprout grain? Although the evidence as to whether our ancestors intentionally sprouted grain is not firmly established, it might be something that we, in modern society, may need to do.

Sprouting Whole Grain

When baking, we often turn to whole grain flours for better nutrition, but before using these flours, we also need to deactivate some of the phytic acid, since the grain's bran and germ are present in the flour. This means that if you make quick breads or breads risen with commercially packaged yeast, you will benefit from soaking and sprouting the whole grains you use and then grinding the soaked, sprouted, and dried whole grain into flour. (Note that you don't need to go through the sprouting process for whole grain breads you make with a sourdough starter. The long sourdough fermentation process deactivates some of the antinutrients contained in the grains.)

Making and Baking with Sprouted Flour

Making sprouted flour is relatively easy since the grain does most of the work. Yes, you will need some way to grind your sprouted grain into flour, but once you invest in a grain mill—preferably a stone grinding mill—you can transform your sprouted and dried grain into sprouted flour. (And chances are your grain mill will last you a lifetime, so you won't need to buy another one after your initial investment.) Plus, you can use your mill to grind all your grain, not just your sprouted grain. Your grain mill will be a welcome addition as you progress along your journey to creating a traditional foods kitchen. Sprouting and grinding your own flour will give you a supply of sprouted flour for baking yeast-risen breads or quick breads that will turn out great, with a light and airy texture.

If you don't want to invest in a grain mill, you can use certain high-speed blenders to grind whole grain, but you may need a specific container approved by the manufacturer for doing this. If you go the blender route, let me share a tip: freeze your grain, whether regular or sprouted, before you grind it. This will help prevent it from overheating and damaging any of the oils that are contained in whole grain.

If you would prefer not to have to soak, sprout, dry, and grind your own whole grain to make sprouted flour, you can also purchase it. It is available at most specialty grocery stores and also online.

The packaging will indicate that the grain from which the flour has been milled was sprouted. Look for labeling such as "sprouted spelt flour."

You can also consider sprouting any whole grains used for making cereal. At the very least, any grains you consume as a cereal should be soaked, but taking the time to also sprout those grains will further enhance their digestibility and allow for better nutrient absorption by the digestive system.

Is it the end of the world if you don't soak, sour, and sprout grain? No. If you have an otherwise healthy diet, one in which you are consuming real foods that are properly prepared, and grains are not a large part of your diet, the occasional slice of a packaged yeast-risen whole grain bread made from unsprouted flour is fine. And so is a slice of cake or a muffin. But if you enjoy these types of packaged yeast-risen breads or quick breads on a regular basis, you should consider making them with sprouted flour, particularly if you are not using a sourdough starter or soaking your flour first.

Soaking and Sprouting Nuts and Seeds

When it comes to nuts and seeds, I soak and dry them, but I generally don't sprout them. Nuts and seeds are high in unsaturated fats, so I like to limit the time I keep them at room temperature and exposed to air and light to avoid making the fat contained in them rancid.

Sprouting seeds and eating sprouts raw are common practices. However, they can also be a breeding ground for *E. coli* and salmonella bacteria that can make you ill. The United States Department of Agriculture always recommends that sprouts be cooked to avoid foodborne illness. To kill *E. coli* and salmonella that may develop during the sprouting process of nuts and seeds, you will need to heat them to 165°F (74°C) for 1 hour. However, this high temperature will also deactivate the enzymes contained within them that are beneficial to our digestive systems. Plus, the unsaturated fatty acids in nuts and seeds are more susceptible to rancidity when exposed to heat. And the last thing we want to eat are rancid fats! Avoiding exposing nuts and seeds to air, light, and heat is in our best interest from a nutritional standpoint. Instead, stick with simply soaking and then drying them at a low temperature.

A Bowl, a Colander, or a Jar? Which is Best for Sprouting?

When you begin to soak and sprout beans, lentils, or whole grains in the recipes that follow, you will learn that often all you need is a bowl of water to jump-start the process. However, sometimes you need to take things one step further and transfer what you are soaking to a colander. Why do I recommend using a colander and not a jar?

You will often see the process of sprouting beans, lentils, or whole grains being done in a jar. Sometimes, it's a simple quart-size jar tipped on its side, and other times, it's a jar specifically made for sprouting with a special lid that makes rinsing and draining your sprouting foods an easy task.

I'm not a fan of the jar method because, all too often, I have found that what I am trying to sprout in a jar begins to develop mold! You have to keep in mind that sprouting creates a damp environment, and where there is dampness, it's easy for mold to take a foothold. Yes, you should change the water in the jar and rinse the sprouts regularly, but sometimes mold can still take over, especially if you live in a damp or humid climate or are experiencing a lot of rainy weather.

Through a lot of trial and error, I have discovered that sprouting beans, lentils, or whole grains in a colander is an almost foolproof way of creating a perfectly sprouted end product with no sign of mold. So if you have struggled with trying to sprout beans, lentils, or whole grains in the hopes of continuing to cook them—or in the case of the lentils and grains, drying them and turning them into sprouted flour—try the colander method. You will be quite pleased to learn how easy and successful sprouting can be!

How to Soak, Brine, and Cook Dry Beans for Use in Any Recipe

Giving dried beans a long soak will help to deactivate the compounds that would otherwise make them difficult to digest. Plus, salt brining the beans gives them a pleasant flavor, and it will not cause them to toughen during the simmering process. Once cooked, these beans become a convenient food that you can use in any recipe, including adding on top of salads, in soups and stews, served as a side dish, or turned into a tasty dip. These beans will become a flavorful staple in your four-corners traditional foods pantry!

SOAK TIME: **12 TO 24 HOURS**
COOK TIME: **45 MINUTES TO 2 HOURS 30 MINUTES**
TOTAL TIME: **APPROXIMATELY 13–26 HOURS**
YIELD: **APPROXIMATELY 6 CUPS**

INGREDIENTS

1lb (454g) dried beans (approximately 2 cups), any variety (see **Cook's Notes**)

8–12 quarts (7.50L–11.35L) of room-temperature tap water, divided

2–4 tbsp fine ground sea salt, divided, plus 1 tsp (optional)

1–2 bay leaves (optional)

1 tsp dried herbs, such as parsley, thyme, rosemary, or a combination (optional)

1 tsp ground spice, such as crushed red pepper, cumin, coriander, or a combination (optional)

1   Rinse the beans well in a colander or strainer. Sort to remove any discolored beans, as well as any small stones or pebbles. Set aside.

2   Add 4 quarts (3.75L) of fresh water to a large stockpot and then add 2 tablespoons of salt. Stir well to dissolve the salt.

3   Transfer the beans from the colander to the stockpot. (Add additional water if needed to ensure the water is at least 3 to 4 inches [7.5 to 10cm] above the beans.) Cover the stockpot.

4   Soak the beans for 12 hours, either at room temperature or in the refrigerator.

5   After 12 hours, remove any beans that have floated to the top of the water. Drain the beans from the stockpot into the colander. (At this point, you can rinse the beans and proceed to cooking. However, to further improve the digestibility of the beans, follow the next steps to continue soaking the beans.)

6   To continue soaking the beans, refill the stockpot with 4 quarts (3.75L) of water and 2 more tablespoons of sea salt. Stir to dissolve the salt and then transfer the beans from the colander back to the stockpot. Soak the beans for an additional 12 hours.

7   After 12 hours, drain the beans in the colander and rinse thoroughly. Transfer the beans from the colander back into the stockpot and fill the pot with 4 quarts (3.75L) of fresh water. (Add additional water if needed to ensure the water is at least 3 to 4 inches [7.5 to 10cm] above the beans.)

8   Place the stockpot on the stove and bring the water to a boil over high heat. Skim off any foam that rises to the top and then turn the heat down to a medium simmer. (See **Cook's Notes** for the instructions on how to cook kidney beans.)

9   During the simmering time, check the beans occasionally to see if you need to add more water so that the beans are always submerged under the water. Depending on the variety of the bean, the simmering time will range from 45 minutes to 2½ hours. (See **Cook's Notes**.)

10 Once the beans are tender, remove the stockpot from the heat. If desired, add 1 teaspoon of salt to the cooking water with the beans and then stir to dissolve the salt. Additionally, you can add the bay leaves, dried herbs, and spices (if using). Allow the beans to sit in the seasoned water for approximately 5 minutes.

11 Drain the beans and remove the bay leaves. The beans are now ready to eat or can be transferred to an airtight container and set aside to cool. Refrigerate for up to 3 to 4 days. These beans may also be frozen, in a freezerproof container for 2 to 3 months.

COOK'S NOTES

Important! Kidney beans must be boiled!
If you're cooking kidney beans, you'll need to bring the beans up to a boil. Boil for 5 minutes on high and then reduce heat to a simmer and continue cooking until tender. Kidney beans contain phytohemagglutinin, a lectin which must be destroyed by boiling. If this compound is not destroyed, kidney beans can cause severe digestive upset.

Cooking times for beans: The cooking time for beans depends on the type of bean, presoaking time, and age of the beans. Based on all three factors, the cooking time will vary. Some beans may finish cooking after being simmered for 45 minutes or less, while others may take as long as 2 hours or longer. Any type of bean is finished cooking once they are tender and have a creamy texture. I recommend you start checking on your simmering beans at the 30-minute mark and then every 15 minutes thereafter.

Adding salt during cooking: I recommend brining the beans but avoiding adding salt during the cooking stage, as it can extend the cooking time and cause the beans to be tough. However, adding salt, herbs, and spices off the heat, after the beans have been cooked, and allowing the beans to absorb some of those additions for 5 minutes will make the beans exceptionally flavorful.

Using flavor additions: When cooking beans, you can include additions, such as a ham bone or onions, during the simmering time if you want those flavors in your beans.

How to Sprout Beans, Lentils, and Whole Grains

Soaking and sprouting beans, lentils, and whole grains can improve their digestibility, thereby improving their nutritional value. The technique for the soaking and sprouting process can vary based on the season. For example, nothing more than an overnight soak might be sufficient in warmer months to encourage the sprouting process. But in the cooler months, it might take a two-step process and a few days longer as outlined in the recipe. Either way, you will be rewarded with a highly digestible food that is perfect for anyone who may have struggled with eating these foods in the past.

You can sprout pretty much any variety of beans and lentils. As to whole grains, some of your best grains to sprout include einkorn, rye, spelt, and wheat berries. However, you may not be able to sprout oat groats because they are usually heat treated before being sold to the public.

SOAK TIME: **12 HOURS**
SPROUTING TIME: **12 HOURS TO 4 DAYS (OR MORE)**
TOTAL TIME: **1–4 DAYS (OR MORE)**
YIELD: **APPROXIMATELY 2–3 CUPS**

INGREDIENTS

2 cups dry beans, lentils, or whole grains

Filtered, chlorine-free water, for soaking

Tap water, for rinsing

1 Place the beans, lentils, or whole grains in a large bowl. Pour enough chlorine-free water into the bowl to cover the contents. Allow the contents to soak in the water for 12 hours at room temperature.

2 In the warmer months, the beans, lentils, or whole grains should begin to show sprouts within 12 hours while in the water. If not, transfer them to a colander and place the colander over a bowl.

Using a clean hand, toss them around in the colander and rinse them under running tap water while in the colander twice per day. They should begin to sprout within 24 hours. During cooler months, if the beans, lentils, or grains are newly purchased and they have not sprouted within 12 hours, transfer them to a colander and place the colander over a bowl. Using a clean hand, toss them around in the colander and rinse them under running tap water while in the colander twice per day. They should sprout within 4 days or slightly longer if they are older.

3 Once the beans, lentils, or whole grains have sprouted, they are ready to be cooked. (See **Cook's Notes.**) Once cooked, they can be enjoyed as a side dish, added to soups or stews, or used in any recipe calling for cooked beans, lentils, or whole grains.

····················· COOK'S NOTES ·····················

Avoiding foodborne illnesses: To avoid foodborne illness, the United States Food and Drug Administration recommends that sprouts always be cooked to kill any *E coli* or salmonella bacteria that may have developed during the sprouting process. So I follow their guidelines and always cook sprouted beans, lentils, and grains. I also cook them immediately after sprouting. I do not store them in the refrigerator or freezer unless they have been cooked first.

Cooking and brining sprouted beans: Once you have sprouted beans, they are ready to cook according to the times stated on their original package directions. The sprouted beans do not require any additional soaking time prior to cooking. However, you may want to give them a second soak overnight in a salty brine and then rinse them well before cooking. The salty brine will impart a nice flavor and will not prevent the beans from softening as they cook.

Cooking sprouted lentils and sprouted whole grains: Sprouted lentils and sprouted whole grains generally have shorter cooking times as compared to their nonsprouted counterparts. Simply add 2 parts water to 1 part sprouted lentils or sprouted whole grains in a saucepan. Bring the mixture up to a boil on the stovetop and then turn the heat down to low. Put the lid on the saucepan. The simmering time for sprouted lentils and whole grains can vary. The time can range from approximately 5 to 15 minutes for sprouted lentils and 15 to 45 minutes for sprouted whole grains or until all the water is absorbed and the lentils or whole grains are tender.

How to Soak and Dry Nuts for Better Digestion

Just as with soaking beans, soaking nuts will make them easier to digest, and our bodies will be better able to absorb the nutrients they offer. Generally, this process is best completed using a dehydrator that will maintain vital enzymes in the nuts by keeping them from overheating. You can use this technique with any type of nut. You can also soak and dry seeds, such as pumpkin, sesame, and sunflower seeds.

SOAK TIME: **8 TO 12 HOURS**
DRYING TIME: **APPROXIMATELY 24 HOURS**
TOTAL TIME: **32–36 HOURS**
YIELD: **APPROXIMATELY 24 1/4-CUP SERVINGS**

EQUIPMENT
Electric food dehydrator

INGREDIENTS
1 ½ lb (680g) raw nuts
 (see **Cook's Notes**)

2 tbsp coarse ground sea salt or
 1 tbsp fine ground sea salt

1 tsp fine ground sea salt (optional)

Filtered, chlorine-free water (for soaking)

1 Place the nuts in a large bowl. Sprinkle 2 tablespoons of coarse ground sea salt or 1 tablespoon of fine ground sea salt over the nuts.

2 Cover the nuts with enough water that they are completely submerged. Cover the bowl loosely with a towel or plastic wrap and allow the nuts to soak at room temperature for 8 to 12 hours.

3 After soaking, drain the nuts in a colander and then rinse well.

4 Using a dehydrator, spread the nuts onto dehydrator trays lined with nonstick dehydrator sheets (such as silicone sheets or parchment paper cut to size) or onto solid dehydrator trays (such as those used to make fruit leathers). Sprinkle the nuts lightly with an additional 1 teaspoon fine ground sea salt (if using) if you want more highly salted nuts. (This will be in addition to the salt they've absorbed from the soak.)

5 Place the dehydrator trays into the dehydrator and set the temperature to 100°F (38°C). Allow the nuts to dry for approximately 24 hours. (You can begin checking them at the 12-hour mark. When you check them, stir them around a bit to help with even drying.) Nuts in the dehydrator are dry when they are crisp. (See **Cook's Notes**.)

6 Once dry and cooled, store the nuts in an airtight container. They will stay fresh for 6 months in the refrigerator and up to 1 year if stored in the freezer.

······················· COOK'S NOTES ·······················

What type of nuts can be soaked and dried? Both tree nuts and peanuts (a legume) can be soaked and dried with this recipe. Common tree nuts include almonds, Brazil nuts, cashews, hazelnuts, pecans, pistachios, and walnuts.

How long does it take to dry nuts and seeds? The drying time for making these nuts will vary depending on the type of nut you use; 24 hours of drying time in the dehydrator is the general rule. If you are not sure the nuts are completely dry, leave them to dry for another hour or so. You can also soak and dry seeds in the same way. Larger seeds, like pumpkin seeds, may average a drying time of approximately 24 hours in a dehydrator, while smaller seeds, like sunflower seeds or sesame seeds, will most likely take less time. Once dry, you should store them in the refrigerator or freezer.

Can nuts and seeds be dried in the oven? Generally, nuts and seeds are best dried in a low-temperature dehydrator to protect the vital enzymes they contain. However, if you do not have a dehydrator, you can dry nuts and seeds in the oven. You will want to place the nuts or seeds on a parchment-lined baking sheet. Next, set the oven to its lowest possible bake setting and place the baking sheet on the middle rack of the oven. The nuts and seeds should be dry within approximately 12 hours. Periodically check on them and move them around on the baking sheet. Some of their enzymes will be destroyed but they do still contain some nutrition, will be easier to digest, and will have a nice crisp texture to them.

How to Make Sprouted Flour with Lentils or Whole Grains

Once you learn how to soak and sprout lentils and whole grains, it's easy to move on to making homemade sprouted flour. Sprouted flour creates tender baked goods that are easily digestible. Plus, you don't need to soak or sour this flour, and you can immediately use it to make quick breads or breads that are risen with packaged yeast.

PREP TIME: **5 MINUTES**
DRYING TIME: **8–14 HOURS**
TOTAL TIME: **8–14 HOURS PLUS 5 MINUTES**
YIELD: **2–3 CUPS**

EQUIPMENT

Grain mill or specialty blender with grain grinding container

INGREDIENTS

2 cups recently sprouted lentils or whole grains (see **Cook's Notes**)

1 Spread the sprouted lentils or sprouted grains on parchment-lined baking sheets. Dry in a cool oven set to 165°F (74°C). (If your oven's lowest temperature setting is between 170°F and 200°F [77°C and 93°C], that's fine too.) Dry for approximately 8 to 12 hours.

2 Halfway through the drying time, stir the lentils or grains to assist with even drying.

3 After 8 to 12 hours, feel the grains between your fingers. If they feel very dry and crisp, they are dry. If you are not sure, continue to dry them for 1 to 2 hours longer.

4 Once the sprouted lentils or sprouted grains are dry, you will need to run them through a grain mill to turn them into flour. (Alternatively, you can use a specialty blender fitted with a manufacturer-approved grain grinding container.)

5 Sprouted flours are best stored in the freezer in an airtight container and will stay fresh for up to 1 year.

COOK'S NOTES

Why are breads made with sprouted flours susceptible to mold? Sprouted flour breads are more quickly susceptible to the development of mold if stored at room temperature because they contain no preservatives. And unlike the natural protections against spoilage afforded breads made using the sourdough process, whole grain sprouted breads made with commercially packaged yeast do not have the same protections. So always refrigerate or freeze your whole grain sprouted breads.

Are good enzymes affected by the drying process? Yes, the enzymes in the sprouted lentils and sprouted grains will be deactivated when dried at temperatures above 100°F (38°C), but that's okay. First, keep in mind that you will be using these flours for baking at much higher temperatures, so the enzymes would be deactivated at that stage. Second, sprouts are susceptible to developing both *E. coli* and salmonella bacteria, which can cause foodborne illness, so they need to be dried at higher temperatures to ensure these bacteria are destroyed. So, I prefer to thoroughly dry the sprouted lentils and sprouted whole grains to ensure that the sprouted flour made from these ingredients will not contain any unwanted bacteria and will be ready to store safely.

Why are we not making sprouted bean flour? As a general rule, I do not recommend making flour from beans, whether sprouted or not. You should cook beans for the best digestion, so you would need to soak and sprout beans first, then dry them, then cook them, and then dry them again before you could grind them into flour. This seems like a lot of work, especially since most sprouted flour bread recipes often only call for a tablespoon or two of sprouted bean flour. So to make life easy, it's best to skip the process of making sprouted bean flour and instead focus on making sprouted flours made from grains and lentils, which can be used in larger quantities. If you decide to grind raw beans into flour, you are leaving all the antinutrients (phytic acid and more) intact. Plus, uncooked beans, and the flour ground from them, will most likely be hard to digest. And the whole point of making breads from sprouted flour is to improve their digestibility!

How to Make Soaked Oat Groats and Traditional Fermented Oat "Milk"

If the term *oat groat* is new to you, it means the whole grain of oat, similar to other whole grains like wheat berries. Using oat groats to make a creamy soaked oatmeal and traditional oat milk is nutritious and affordable. Of the three types of traditional oats you can purchase—flaked or old-fashioned rolled oats, steel-cut oats, and oat groats—the oat groats will be your best buy per ounce. They also stay the freshest the longest.

This recipe creates two products: a creamy soaked oatmeal porridge and an oat beverage that's loosely based on the old traditional Scottish recipe for *swats*. Originally, this recipe would make a type of oatmeal with two by-products known as *sowans* or *sowens* (pronounced soo-an) and swats. The main ingredient to make these three items was called *sids*. These sids were a combination of the husk from the oat and bits of the oat kernel.

We'll be soaking the oat groats in water for about 8 to 12 hours. (This spread in the soaking time allows for flexibility in the home cook's schedule.) This short soak is a form of fermentation which will help to deactivate some of the phytic acid contained in the oats. If we fermented the oat groats longer, strained them out, and did a second longer ferment with the liquid, we would create the creamy sediment that the Scots called *sowans*, which would sink to the bottom of the liquid. But don't feel bad about missing out on this. When separated from the swats, sowans is a very unusual creamlike substance that many modern-day palates are not accustomed to consuming. However, I would hate to see it go to waste, so instead, we'll keep it in the liquid (or short-cut swats) that we'll call "oat milk."

Although this is technically not the long version of traditionally made oat milk, as it is only inspired by the original recipe, it is more traditional than modern-day oat milk which is not fermented. And I think you will be in for a treat! If you have tried making modern-day oat milk in the past to only create a slimy mess, you will be delighted at the clean, smooth texture of this refreshing quick ferment oat milk. The secret is using oat groats instead of old-fashioned rolled oats, and the difference it makes is amazing!

SOAK TIME: **8–12 HOURS**
DRAINING TIME FOR OAT MILK: **5 MINUTES**
COOK TIME FOR SOAKED OAT GROATS: **20 MINUTES**
TOTAL TIME: **8–12 HOURS PLUS 35 MINUTES**
YIELD: **2–3 CUPS OF FERMENTED OAT MILK AND 4 SERVINGS OF OAT GROAT PORRIDGE (OATMEAL)**

INGREDIENTS

1 cup oat groats (see **Cook's Notes**)

¼ tsp fine ground sea salt

Filtered chlorine-free water, room temperature

2 tbsp raw honey or maple syrup (optional) (see **Cook's Notes**)

1 tsp vanilla extract (optional)

4 tsp unsalted butter (optional)

1 tsp ground cinnamon (optional)

2–3 cups tap water

1   Place the oat groats and sea salt into a quart-size jar.

2   Fill the jar with enough filtered chlorine-free water to fill the jar to the lower part of the neck. Using a wooden spoon, stir the mixture to help dissolve the salt.

3   Place the lid on the jar and tighten it. Place the jar in a room temperature location that is between 68°F and 72°F (20°C and 22°C) and out of direct sunlight for 8 to 12 hours.

4   After 8 to 12 hours, empty the contents of the jar into a blender. (For a creamier oat milk, do not add any additional water. For a more fluid oat milk, add 1 additional cup of chlorine-free water to the blender.)

5   Begin blending the mixture on a low speed so that it doesn't rise up quickly and leak through the lid. Slowly increase the speed, but don't blend the mixture for any longer than 30 seconds. (I like to blend this mixture in 10-second intervals, stopping the blender and checking on the

consistency of the oat groats.) If you are using a high-speed blender, only blend for 10 seconds. The oat groats should appear broken into pieces, like steel-cut oats, and sink to the bottom of the blender. This is exactly what you are looking for. Do not blend the mixture any further. Only blend for a few more seconds if the oat groats have not broken into pieces.

6   Place a flour-sack towel or cheesecloth over a large bowl. Using one hand to hold the cloth in place, use the other hand to pour the pureéd oats from the blender and into the cloth.

7   Gather up the ends of the flour-sack towel or cheesecloth and gently lift the ends, forming the oats contained within into a loose ball. (As you do this, the oat milk will drain down into the bowl.) Once the oats are formed into a ball, press the ball very gently to try and release more liquid, but do not squeeze it tightly. Squeezing it too tightly can leach out too much starch, which can contribute to a slimy oat milk.

8   If you want a sweetened oat milk, add the honey or maple syrup (if using) and the vanilla extract (if using). Use a whisk to mix in these additional ingredients or return the oat milk to the blender and mix everything together for a few seconds.

9   Transfer the oat milk to a bottle with a cap and refrigerate. (Before using the oat milk, always shake the bottle.) The oat milk will stay fresh, refrigerated, for approximately 5 days.

10 Transfer the oats from the flour-sack towel or cheesecloth into a saucepan and spread them out with a wooden spoon or spatula. Add 2 to 3 cups of tap water to the saucepan, making sure the oat groats are covered by 1 inch (2.5cm) of water.

11 Place the saucepan on the stovetop, bring the mixture to a boil on high heat and then immediately turn the heat down to the lowest setting and cover the saucepan. Periodically check on the oats and stir. Cook the oats until tender and the water is absorbed to create a creamy porridge, about 20 minutes.

12 Once the oat groats are cooked, remove the saucepan from the heat and add the butter and cinnamon (if using). Stir until the butter is melted and serve. You've now created your second product: soaked oatmeal porridge.

13 Refrigerate the porridge in an airtight container for up to 4 days. To reheat, place in a saucepan with a small amount of water and warm gently over low heat.

COOK'S NOTES

Where can you find oat groats? Oat groats are becoming more common, especially in the bulk bin area of large grocery stores. If you can't find them, you can substitute steel-cut oats. The results will not be as perfect as if you had started with oat groats. However, the oat milk will be considerably better than anything made with old-fashioned rolled oats.

Sweetening fermented oat milk: If you're new to fermented beverages, fermented oat milk may be a new taste for you. It has a different flavor from the oat milk you may buy at the grocery store. It also tastes different from homemade oat milk made with old-fashioned rolled oats. To create a pleasant flavor, I highly recommend sweetening this oat milk, preferably with raw honey, and adding in vanilla extract. If you are familiar with horchata, the Mexican soaked-rice beverage, you might find this fermented oat milk tastes similar. If you discover you like a sweetened oat milk, raw honey is the perfect addition since it contains the enzyme amylase, which can help prevent oat milk from becoming slimy.

Using a blender: Although I blend my soaked oat groats in a standard blender and have not encountered any problems, you may want to check with your blender's manufacturer. Their specifications will help you determine if you can blend soaked grain in your blender or if you need an alternative grain blending container.

Sprouted-Flour Sandwich Bread

Once you start making sprouted flour, it's easy to make sprouted-flour bread because these breads use packaged yeast, so they rise and bake up quite quickly compared to a sourdough. Even though these breads are not sourdough, they are still highly digestible. This bread is exceptionally easy to make because it is based on the batter bread technique.

PREP TIME: **5 MINUTES**
RISE TIME: **APPROXIMATELY 2 HOURS 10 MINUTES**
BAKE TIME: **APPROXIMATELY 45–55 MINUTES**
TOTAL TIME: **APPROXIMATELY 3 HOURS**
YIELD: **1 LOAF**

INGREDIENTS

¼ cup butter, melted and cooled, plus additional to grease the loaf pan and your hands

2½ cups sprouted spelt flour (see **Cook's Notes**)

½ cup sprouted lentil flour

1 (2.5oz/7g) package or 2¼ tsp instant yeast

¾ tsp fine ground sea salt

½ tsp barley malt flour (optional)

1½ cups whole milk

2 tbsp maple syrup

1   Grease a 9-inch x 5-inch (23cm x 13cm) loaf pan with butter. Set aside.

2   In a large bowl, whisk together the spelt flour, lentil flour, yeast, sea salt, and barley malt powder (if using). Set aside.

3   In a medium bowl or large measuring cup, whisk together the milk, maple syrup, and butter.

4   Make a well in the flour and then pour in the liquid.

5   Using a wet hand, mix the flour and liquid together until it comes together to form a shaggy dough. Cover the bowl with plastic wrap and place it in a warm spot. Allow the dough to rise until it has approximately doubled in bulk, about 1½ hours.

6   Punch down the risen dough and place it in the prepared loaf pan. Using greased hands, flatten the dough gently so that it fills each corner of the pan.

7   Place the loaf pan, uncovered, in a warm area and allow it to rise for approximately 40 minutes or until the dough is even with the rim of the loaf pan. (Do not let the dough rise past the rim of the pan, and do not let it form a dome in the middle. In a very warm kitchen, this rise can take less than 40 minutes, so keep an eye on it.) When the dough reaches a point about three quarters of the way up the sides of the pan, preheat the oven to 375°F (191°C) with the oven rack in the middle position.

8   When the dough has risen to the rim of the loaf pan, transfer the pan to the oven and bake for about 45 to 55 minutes or until the top is golden brown.

9   Using pot holders, remove the loaf pan from the oven and place the pan on a cooling rack. Flip the pan over to remove the bread from the pan and place the bread onto the cooling rack.

10 Allow the bread to cool completely before slicing. (When ready to slice, use a serrated knife.) Store, well wrapped, in the refrigerator for up to 1 week or in the freezer for 2 to 3 months. Defrost the unwrapped bread at room temperature. (Do not store this bread at room temperature because it will be susceptible to the development of mold.)

······················· COOK'S NOTES ·······················

Substituting other whole grain sprouted flours: This recipe uses whole grain sprouted spelt flour, but you can substitute other whole grain sprouted flours. Whole wheat sprouted flour can be used 1:1 in place of the spelt flour. However, you will need additional milk to moisten the whole wheat flour completely. Add 1 tablespoon of milk at a time until you reach the desired consistency. If you decide to use whole grain sprouted einkorn or sprouted rye flour for some of the sprouted spelt flour, they are best mixed 1:1 with sprouted spelt flour or sprouted whole wheat flour to assist with the rise. For example, if you use 1 cup of sprouted einkorn flour to substitute 1 cup of sprouted spelt flour, you will also add the remaining 1½ cups of sprouted spelt flour for this recipe. As to the sprouted lentil flour, you can substitute sprouted millet flour for the lentil flour or use a mix of millet and lentil flours.

Cast-Iron Skillet Sweet Sprouted Spelt Cornbread

Skillet sweet sprouted spelt may be a tongue twister, but this tender buttermilk cornbread has a crisp, crunchy crust thanks to being baked in a cast-iron skillet with a generous amount of whole sweetener. And the sprouted spelt flour adds an extra dose of nutritional goodness that is highly digestible.

PREP TIME: **15 MINUTES**
BAKE TIME: **20–25 MINUTES**
TOTAL TIME: **35 MINUTES**
YIELD: **8 SERVINGS**

EQUIPMENT
10- to 12-inch cast-iron skillet

INGREDIENTS
2 tbsp butter (for greasing the cast-iron skillet)

1¼ cups stone-ground cornmeal

¾ cup whole grain sprouted spelt flour

1 cup unrefined whole cane sugar

2 tsp baking powder

½ tsp baking soda

½ tsp fine ground sea salt

1 stick butter, melted and cooled

2 large eggs

1½ cups buttermilk (homemade or store-bought)

1 Preheat the oven to 425°F (218°C).

2 Place 2 tablespoons of butter in the cast-iron skillet. Set aside.

3 Combine the cornmeal, spelt flour, unrefined whole cane sugar, baking powder, baking soda, and sea salt in a large bowl. Stir to combine.

4 In a large measuring cup, whisk together the cooled melted butter, eggs, and buttermilk.

5 Make a well in the center of the dry ingredients and then add the wet ingredients. Stir together until the dry ingredients are just moistened. (Do not overmix.)

6 Place the cast-iron skillet in the preheated oven. Allow the butter to melt and then use a pot holder to carefully remove the skillet from the oven. Scrape the batter into the skillet and swirl it around to spread it evenly.

7 Return the skillet to the oven and bake until the top of the cornbread is golden and a toothpick inserted into the center comes out clean, about 20 to 25 minutes, depending on the size of the skillet used.

8 Transfer the skillet to a heatproof surface and allow the cornbread to cool for 10 minutes. Slice and serve warm.

9 Store, well wrapped, in the refrigerator for up to 1 week or in the freezer for up to 2 to 3 months. Defrost, unwrapped, at room temperature. (Do not store this cornbread at room temperature because it will be susceptible to the development of mold.)

··· COOK'S NOTES ···

Why is there so much sweetener in this recipe? Yes, 1 cup of sweetener is correct in this recipe. I know it may seem like a lot, and you can cut it back to half a cup if you want, but I highly recommend you try it this way first. Although a sweetener, the unrefined whole cane sugar contains more nutrients than white sugar because the molasses is still present. Unrefined whole cane sugar brings a certain overall crispness to the top of the cornbread, making it a luscious treat unlike any cornbread you have ever had. You can even serve this cornbread as a dessert topped with fresh whipped cream and a few sliced strawberries as a more nutritious twist on strawberry shortcake.

Sprouted Spelt and Oats Breakfast Bread

Since this bread is made using only nonperishable ingredients, it's the perfect bread to make when you want to use up ingredients in your working pantry or extended pantry. It couldn't be easier to make! If you enjoyed making and eating the Super Soft No-Knead White Sandwich Bread and the Sprouted-Flour Sandwich Bread, you will also like this bread as it is a batter bread. And thanks to the soaked oats, this is a moist bread that refrigerates beautifully without drying out. Plus, it has a light and airy crumb, similar to an English toasting bread, making it ideal when toasted and slathered with butter and jam for the perfect breakfast!

PREP TIME: **8–12 HOURS**
RISE TIME: **APPROXIMATELY 2 HOURS 10 MINUTES**
BAKE TIME: **45–55 MINUTES**
TOTAL TIME: **APPROXIMATELY 11–15 HOURS**
YIELD: **2 LOAVES**

INGREDIENTS

2 cups old-fashioned rolled oats

2 cups hot water

¼ cup whole liquid sweetener (see **Cook's Notes**)

1 tbsp fine ground sea salt

2 tbsp ghee, plus more for greasing your hands and the loaf pans

2 cups sprouted spelt flour

2 cups bread flour

1 (.25oz/7g) package or 2¼ tsp instant yeast

½ tsp diastatic malt powder (optional)

1½–2 cups warm water

1. Put the oats in a large mixing bowl. Pour the hot water into the bowl and mix well. Cover the bowl with plastic wrap and refrigerate, allowing the oats to soak for 8 to 12 hours.

2. After the oats have soaked, add the sweetener, sea salt, and ghee to the bowl. Mix well.

3. In a second large bowl, whisk together the spelt flour, bread flour, yeast, and diastatic malt powder (if using).

4. Add the cooled oat mixture to the second large bowl with the flour and the add 1½ cups of warm water. Using a wooden spoon, mix until all the flour is moistened. The dough should be shaggy. If it is dry, add additional water, 1 tablespoon at a time, and mix.

5. Cover the bowl with plastic wrap and transfer it to a warm place to rise for approximately 1½ hours or until it appears to have doubled in bulk.

6. Generously grease two 9-inch x 5-inch (33cm x 22cm) loaf pans with ghee.

7. Once the first rise time is complete, use greased hands to deflate the dough by pressing down on it. Divide the dough into two equal portions. Transfer equal portions of the dough into each buttered loaf pan.

8. Using well-greased hands, even out the dough into the corners of the pans. (The dough will be very sticky.)

9. Preheat the oven to 375°F (191°C) with the oven rack in the middle position.

10. Place the loaf pans, uncovered, in a warm place and allow to rise for approximately 30 to 40 minutes until the dough is even with the rim of the loaf pan. (Do not let the dough rise past the rim of the pan and form a dome. In a very warm kitchen, this rise can take no longer than 30 minutes, so keep an eye on them.)

11. Place the loaf pans on the middle rack in the oven and allow the dough to bake for approximately 45 to 55 minutes or until the top crusts are golden brown.

12. Using pot holders, remove the loaf pans from the oven and flip the loaves out onto a cooling rack.

13. Allow the bread to cool completely before slicing. (When ready to slice, a serrated knife works best.)

14. Store, well wrapped, in the refrigerator for up to 1 week or in the freezer for up to 2 to 3 months. Defrost, unwrapped, at room temperature. (Do not store this bread at room temperature because it will be susceptible to the development of mold.)

.... COOK'S NOTES ....

Sweetener options: There is a lot of flexibility regarding the whole sweetener you use in this recipe. Each will add a slightly different flavor to the bread, and I recommend that you experiment with any of the following: coconut syrup, date syrup, maple syrup, or molasses. My favorite choice is typically maple syrup.

Why you may want to use diastatic malt in this recipe: As I shared in The Home Baker chapter, diastatic malt powder, also known as *barley malt flour*, is whole grain barley that has been soaked, sprouted, dried, and then ground into flour, specifically sprouted flour. The powder contributes to several actions when baking with an ancient grain like spelt, which is both lower in gluten and has a weaker gluten structure than modern day whole wheat flour. This is also the case when baking with oats, which are naturally gluten-free. Adding diastatic malt powder to this bread dough will help create a successful oven spring (a burst of rising when the dough goes into a hot oven) as well as contribute to a nice browning of the exterior of the baked bread. But don't over do it! When it comes to diastatic malt powder, a little goes a long way. More is not better and will actually create a gummy texture to the crumb (the interior) of the bread.

Are all oats naturally gluten-free? Although this bread is made with oats, it also includes both spelt flour and bread flour, neither of which are gluten-free. But as to the oats, yes, oats are naturally gluten free. However, in the factories in which the oats are processed, the oats may be contaminated by other grains that are not gluten-free. If you must only consume gluten-free foods, make sure that the packaging indicates that the oats are in fact guaranteed to be gluten-free.

Chapter Eight
CONDIMENTS AND FLAVOR BOOSTERS

GETTING STARTED WITH CONDIMENTS AND FLAVOR BOOSTERS

If you have been working your way through this book, beginning with chapter 1, you deserve a round of applause. You have learned how to make bone broth, render fats, culture dairy, ferment fresh produce, and even bake homemade sourdough bread! These are the major skills that will help you on your journey to create a real traditional foods kitchen.

But now it's time to move on to learning what I like to think of as the accompaniments to a traditional foods kitchen: those things that are, in essence, the icing on the cake! They may be minor skills compared to what you have learned so far, but they are essential skills that every traditional foods home cook should know.

In this chapter, these essential skills include learning how to make homemade ketchup, mustard, salsa, seasonings, salad dressings, and more. Can you buy most of these things? Certainly, but when you make these foods homemade, you save money and also control the ingredients. There are no preservatives, chemicals, artificial sweeteners, or highly processed oils anywhere in sight in these recipes.

Just the Right Seasoning

When my son, Ben, was a little boy, he loved to pull out all the different herbs and spices I had stored in my pantry. He would mix a bunch of them together to make his own house seasoning blend and then use that blend to top crackers that he would serve as an appetizer to my husband and me. Keep in mind that he was just a little guy at the time and didn't know what a particular herb or spice was. All that mattered was that he was mixing up a great combination that he was pleased and proud to serve to his parents.

Well, my husband and I found ourselves enjoying crackers covered in a variety of chili powders and just a few mild herbs. Between gulps of water, we praised our adorable son for his creativity. He is, after all, a born and bred Texan to whom it made complete sense that any seasoning mix should surely contain a lot of red powder! (In this chapter, I share a recipe for our house seasoning that you'll enjoy. It's a bit milder than the one my son created all those years ago, but if you like spicy things, be sure to add a bit more of that red powder than is called for in the recipe. Ben would be proud!)

Making Fermented Condiments without Air

Some of the condiments in this chapter are fermented, but I think you might find a few of these a bit simpler to make than those covered in the chapter on pickling and fermenting. Yes, there will certainly be the traditional anaerobic (without air) ferments, but some will only need to stay on your counter for a few days to kick off the lacto-fermentation process.

You'll tuck these short-term ferments into the refrigerator where the fermentation process slows down considerably, so there is little to no chance of developing mold or bad bacteria that could lead to rancidity. This is important when making homemade fermented condiments, like mustard, ketchup, and salsa, that are thick and don't require a salty brine.

Making Fermented Condiments with Air

In addition to traditional anaerobic ferments, I introduce something new here: aerobic (with air) ferments. Making raw homemade apple cider vinegar is known as aerobic fermentation because good bacteria in the air brings about its fermentation, specifically a bacteria called *Acetobacter*, which creates acetic acid. (You may recall learning about this bacteria in The Home Baker chapter.) Thanks to this bacteria, making vinegar—pretty much any vinegar—is very easy. You basically leave the liquid exposed to air, and the *Acetobacter* does the rest of the work. Next thing you know, you have vinegar!

Have you ever opened a bottle of wine and not finished it, only to find that a few weeks later it has taken on a very sharp, almost vinegar flavor? Yes, you guessed it! It's turning into vinegar. The same process happens with apple cider. When you have fresh-pressed raw apple cider and leave it exposed to air for a period of time, it turns into raw apple cider vinegar. However, I always find this process for making apple cider vinegar a waste of perfectly good fresh apple cider! So

instead I show you how to take apple scraps and turn them into a raw apple cider vinegar. Is it 100 percent the real thing? No, but I think it's better. Save your freshly pressed apple cider to drink and use your apple scraps, either from making apple cider or any other type of apple recipe, and instead use those scraps to make vinegar. These types of recipes truly go to the heart of not only creating a traditional foods kitchen but a no-waste one as well!

The Shelf Lives of Homemade Condiments

The condiments you buy at the store typically contain preservatives, enabling you to keep them on your pantry shelf or in your fridge for extended periods of time. Conversely, homemade condiments do not have the same added preservatives, so they generally do not have the same shelf lives. As with so many homemade foods, it can be difficult to predict precisely how long they will stay fresh. But thanks to the fermentation process, we can extend the shelf lives of our fermented homemade condiments, as opposed to unfermented homemade condiments. The fermentation process also helps to preserve our homemade foods in place of added preservatives.

How long are all these homemade condiments going to last? Well, it not only depends on the fermentation process, it also depends on what we are fermenting. For example, you can think of homemade vinegar as a forever food; you can store it at room temperature, and thanks to the vinegar's high acidic level, it's been my experience that you don't have to worry about vinegar going bad.

For the anaerobically fermented condiments in your fridge, the general rule is that most should be consumed within 4 to 6 months. But I would add that they will be at their peak within the first 3 months, and you should use them up at that point. So when making fermented condiments, think about how you generally use their unfermented store-bought counterparts and how long it takes you to consume them. Then base the amount you make homemade on that estimate.

Note that if you ever notice mold or smell a foul odor in any of your homemade condiments, you should immediately discard them and start the recipe anew. Your homemade condiment may have gone past its shelf life.

What About Homemade Mayonnaise?

Years ago, a friend shared with me that whenever her husband would ask her where the jar of homemade mayonnaise was, she would respond by putting the food processor on the counter. He would look at that piece of kitchen equipment, shrug, and say, "I think mustard will be fine." So many of us feel this way when we hear someone tell us that we should make mayonnaise homemade. We might be able to look past the blender stick, food processor, or regular blender we'll use to make it. But what's more bothersome is that it will probably only stay fresh in the fridge for a few days.

When we look at the ingredients of most mayonnaise sold today at the grocery store, the main ingredient is usually soybean oil. We can't trace this highly processed oil back to its use by traditional cultures, so it's not something we want in our traditional foods kitchens. Yes, gourmet mayos contain better oils, but they are usually costly. The good news is that making homemade mayonnaise isn't that difficult. And although we don't need to worry about fermenting it, our mayonnaise will still have a good shelf life once we refrigerate it because we'll be adding in some cultured whey or brine from a previous successful ferment. These liquids are loaded with good bacteria, which will help to keep your mayonnaise fresh in the fridge for longer than just a few days.

Never Buy Another Vegetable Bouillon Cube Again!

Vegetable bouillon cubes make life easier when you want to add a flavor boost to soups and stews. The drawback is that, like so many commercially prepared foods, store-bought bouillon cubes contain a list of ingredients that aren't welcome in a traditional foods kitchen. I can say with 100 percent certainty that my great grandmother never used modified palm oil, monosodium glutamate, autolyzed yeast extract, or disodium inosinate when making homemade vegetable bouillon!

Instead of unfamiliar ingredients, your homemade vegetable bouillon will contain vegetables and salt. That's it! And thanks to the salt, which is a natural preservative, your homemade bouillon will have a long shelf life in the refrigerator. But it's great to store in the freezer too. All you have to do is put it in a freezerproof container and scoop out however much you need when you're cooking. Again, thanks to the salt, the mixture never freezes solid!

But better yet, it's easy to dehydrate your vegetable bouillon if you would prefer a powdered mixture that is shelf stable. And you don't need any special equipment to do this. An oven on a low setting is all you need.

A Cozy Kitchen and the Lure of Everything Homemade

About a year ago, someone told me they were amazed to learn that you can make your own ketchup. They thought it was a special process that could only be done in a factory. I know some people might wonder if that person has ever cooked before, but I never think that. Understandably, many people may not realize that most things sold at a grocery store can be homemade.

It's not unusual when children are asked where milk comes from, they will respond in unison, "The grocery store!" And they usually follow up their response with a quizzical look implying that they are confused that you didn't know this basic fact. As a society, many of us have come to rely heavily on our local markets, not realizing that we often just have to shop the perimeter of the store for the unprocessed real food. We don't have to rely on all the packaged or prepared foods sold in the interior aisles except to search out dried and canned foods with simple ingredients. As we spend more time in our store's perimeter and in our own kitchens, more of us will realize where our food really comes from and how to properly prepare it in the most wholesome and nutritious way.

Making homemade condiments might seem like small side recipes, but these little things add up to creating the foods and meals that nourish our bodies well beyond what we can buy in a store. We can see this even when it comes to something as simple as ketchup! Instead of serving a sugar-laden, overly processed tomato product, you'll enjoy a fermented ketchup made from tomatoes (even homegrown tomatoes, maybe, in time) that are teeming with gut-loving good bacteria.

For homemade sandwiches, nothing creates a cozier kitchen than a sliced loaf of sourdough bread, an assortment of lettuces, and some meats and cheeses brought to the table alongside petite serving spoons and charming little containers of homemade ketchup, mustard, and mayonnaise.

Dinner might be simple sandwiches, but no one at the table will be disappointed. Everyone will be well nourished and satisfied, something that doesn't often happen when eating the empty calories associated with processed foods—what are often thought of as junk food or convenience foods. You might be full after eating a bag of packaged snack food, but you are hardly well nourished. And in many cases, the antinutrients in processed foods might actually be stripping your body of vitamins, minerals, and good bacteria!

Raw Apple Cider Vinegar

You can make real homemade apple cider vinegar from fresh pressed apple cider, but why waste perfectly good cider? Instead, with just apple scraps or a few apples getting a little close to their prime, you can make a simple *fruit scrap* vinegar without having to use fresh-pressed apple cider. Your final product, a homemade apple cider vinegar, will be indistinguishable from the real thing, and you will be well on your way to creating a no-waste kitchen.

PREP TIME: **5 MINUTES**
PASSIVE TIME: **30 DAYS**
TOTAL TIME: **APPROXIMATELY 30 DAYS**
SERVINGS: **APPROXIMATELY 1½ QUARTS (1.40L)**

EQUIPMENT

1 half-gallon–size glass jar

Thin clean cloth or coffee filter

Rubber band or kitchen twine

Flour-sack towel or cheesecloth

Bowl large enough to hold the glass jar

32-ounce (946ml) glass bottle with tight-fitting cap

Colander

pH strips

INGREDIENTS

Peels and cores or cut up apples (any variety), with seeds removed, sufficient to fill the half-gallon jar ¾ full

¼ cup white sugar (optional)

Filtered, chlorine-free water (room temperature)

1   Fill the jar with the apples, apple scraps, or a combination of the two. If you use apples or scraps from tart or mildly tart apples, such as Granny Smith or other varieties, pour the sugar into the jar.

2   Fill the jar with enough water to cover the apples, but leave at least 2 to 3 inches (5 to 7.5cm) of headspace from the rim of the jar.

3   Cover the top of the jar with a piece of thin, clean cloth, such as a single layer of flour-sack towel or a paper coffee filter. Secure with a rubber band or a piece of kitchen twine. Put the jar into the bowl.

4   Place the jar in a room-temperature area that is between 68°F and 72°F (20°C and 22°C) and out of direct sunlight.

5   Each day, for 30 days, remove the fabric or coffee filter and stir the vinegar in the morning and again in the evening. (The handle of a wooden spoon or a wooden chopstick works best.) Put the fabric or coffee filter back on the jar and secure it with the rubber band. You will notice that the vinegar in the making will initially smell like apples, then it will begin to bubble and smell like beer or alcohol. Eventually, the mixture will become cloudy, there may no longer be any bubbling, and it will start to take on a more vinegary aroma. These are all indications that you are on the right track.

6   If you have not used any sugar in this process and notice that you do not see any bubbles developing in the jar by the second day, add ¼ cup of sugar to the jar and stir well.

7   During the 30 days of the vinegar-making process, if the apples float to the top and there's a lot of water underneath, that's okay. Continue to stir the vinegar and, over time, the apples will eventually lose their buoyancy and solid consistency as they ferment.

8   After 30 days, use a clean utensil to remove a small amount of the liquid from the jar and then use a pH strip to check the acidity level. It should be from 3.0 to 3.5 or lower. If so, you have successfully made raw vinegar. (See **Cook's Notes**.)

9   Place a colander or mesh strainer lined with a flour-sack towel or cheesecloth over a bowl. Pour the contents of the jar into the lined colander or mesh strainer to strain out the apple scraps. Pour the vinegar collected in the bowl into the glass bottle and seal with the cap. Store at room temperature, preferably in a pantry and out of direct sunlight.

COOK'S NOTES

What if my vinegar's pH is not as low as 3.0 to 3.5? Generally, apple cider vinegar has a slightly higher pH than other vinegars (which might have a pH as low as 2.0) because it contains more alkaline nutrients than other vinegars. If you were to test the pH of a store-bought apple cider vinegar, it might register around 3.0 or a bit higher. Your homemade vinegar's pH needs to be below 4.6. A pH between 3.0 and 3.5 is ideal for a tangy vinegar. If, after 30 days, your homemade vinegar does not register a pH of 3.0 to 3.5, but it is 4.6 or lower and has a vinegar aroma, taste it to see if it has a strong vinegar flavor. If so, you can decant it. If not, allow it to ferment longer until the taste becomes stronger.

What is that jelly-like substance forming on top of my vinegar? You may notice a jelly-like substance forming on top of the liquid in your jar. Don't worry! This substance is your vinegar's "mother." It's a culture of cellulose and acetic acid bacteria. Having a mother is a good sign of a healthy vinegar. When you decant your vinegar, you will want to remove the visible mother. Even though you are removing this gelatinous mass, there is still plenty of mother—or good bacteria—in your newly made vinegar.

Oh no! Your vinegar has developed mold on top! Now what? During the vinegar-making process, various substances might develop in your jar and on top of the liquid. Before you discard your vinegar, you'll want to first determine if it's actually mold. If it's white and weblike—almost like a spider web—you might actually have kahm yeast. This substance is a bit of a pest, but it's not harmful. You can use a clean spoon to remove as much of the yeast as possible and then give the vinegar-in-the-making a good stir. The kahm yeast may or may not return. If it returns, just scoop it out again and proceed as usual. Eventually, once you decant your vinegar, it will give up and go away. If it's mold, however, it likely will be fuzzy in appearance and might take on different colored hues. Some sources recommend just scooping off the mold and giving the vinegar-in-the-making a good stir. I am not comfortable with this option. When it comes to food safety, I believe it is better to err on the side of caution and just discard the contents completely.

Can I use my homemade apple cider vinegar for home canning? No, never use homemade vinegar of any kind for home canning! Although you may be able to use pH strips to validate the acidity level of your homemade vinegar, there is always room for error. Home canning requires precise ingredients, so the National Center for Home Food Preservation recommends using store-bought vinegar in canning recipes. This guarantees the exact level of acidity called for in the canning recipe and meets food safety guidelines.

Nutrient-Rich House Seasoning

This all-purpose recipe makes a flavorful, nutrient-rich seasoning mix you can use to improve the flavor of any savory dish. It's loaded with all sorts of herbs and spices that contribute to good health. That's what's wonderful about herbs and spices: you can use them for culinary purposes, but they also have medicinal purposes, including their ability to fend off illness and disease.

PREP TIME: **5 MINUTES**
TOTAL TIME: **5 MINUTES**
YIELD: **APPROXIMATELY 1½ CUPS**

INGREDIENTS

1 cup fine ground sea salt

2½ tbsp sweet paprika

1 tbsp ground black pepper

1 tbsp onion powder

2 tsp dried dulse powder, preferably organic (see **Cook's Notes**)

1 tsp dried basil

1 tsp chili powder (I like to substitute powdered ancho or chipotle pepper too.)

1 tsp dried chives

1 tsp dried dill

1 tsp dried oregano

1 tsp dried thyme

½ tsp dried rosemary

½ tsp dried sage

½–1 tsp garlic powder (optional)

1 Combine all the ingredients plus ½ teaspoon of the garlic powder (if using) in a blender or spice grinder. Pulse until the ingredients form a fine powder and are incorporated completely.

2 Taste and add another ½ teaspoon garlic powder if you desire a stronger garlic taste. (The garlic powder can be omitted completely if you don't prefer the taste of garlic.)

3 Transfer the mixture to a jar with a tight-fitting lid. This seasoning can be used in place of salt in any recipe in which you want a boost of flavor and nutrition. The seasoning mix will stay fresh for in your pantry for approximately 1 year. (When seasoning dishes, start by adding a ½ teaspoon of the mix to the dish and then increase the amount to suit your taste.)

COOK'S NOTES

What is dulse? Dulse is a red seaweed rich in nutrients, including iodine, which nourishes your thyroid gland. It is also rich in protein, potassium, iron, and vitamin K. However, if you have medical issues with your thyroid, check with your doctor before ingesting any seaweed or seaweed powder. If you are new to the flavor of dulse, buy a small amount and taste it. If you like it, you will find it very pleasant when used in this house seasoning recipe. You can certainly try other seaweed powders, including kelp (also known as *kombu*), nori, arame, or wakame. If you can't find dulse or other seaweed in powder form, you can grind a small amount of dried whole seaweed in a spice grinder.

Can additional herbs and spices be added to this mix? Definitely. This house seasoning is simply a template to get you started. Make it your own. Leave out any herbs or spices you don't like or add more herbs and spices with the flavors and nutritional benefits you prefer. For example, ground ginger and turmeric are wonderful additions for creating a nutrient-rich and anti-inflammatory house seasoning. Simply start with a ½ teaspoon of each and increase to a strength you like.

Can more rosemary be added to this seasoning mix? When it comes to using rosemary for culinary purposes, you need to increase the amount slowly. Too much rosemary to many a palate can begin to taste like soap. So when making this seasoning mix the first time, add only the recommended amount. More can always be added to the finished product, if you wish, and mixed well to incorporate.

Herbal Salts

In addition to having a homemade house seasoning in your pantry, be sure to include some herbal salts. These types of salts not only add a delightful flavor to savory dishes like soups and stews, they are also a way to preserve herbs. Preserving herbs in salt gives you more options instead of just drying them, allowing you to enjoy their fresh flavors and nutrition throughout the winter months.

PREP TIME: **5 MINUTES**
DRYING TIME: **12 HOURS**
TOTAL TIME: **12 HOURS 5 MINUTES**
YIELD: **APPROXIMATELY 2 CUPS**

INGREDIENTS

1 cup fine ground sea salt, divided

2 cups packed fresh herbs, divided (see **Cook's Notes**)

1 tsp lemon zest (optional)

½ tsp crushed red pepper (optional)

1 Add half the amount of herbs and half the amount of salt to a food processor or blender. Pulse for 30 seconds.

2 Add the lemon zest (if using), crushed red pepper (if using), and all remaining herbs and salt, and pulse for 1 minute more. Stop after 30 seconds and scrape down the sides of the processor bowl or blender with a rubber scraper.

3 At this point, you can transfer this moist herbal salt mixture to a jar with a tight-fitting lid and store it in the refrigerator. Or you can transfer the herbal salt to a freezerproof container and store it in the freezer.

4 Alternatively, if you prefer a dry herbal salt, transfer it to a parchment-lined baking sheet and allow it to dry. You can do this in an oven with only the pilot light or electric light turned on. The drying process will take approximately 10 to 12 hours. Alternatively, you can allow the herb salt to air dry over a few days. (Periodically toss the herb salt to make sure it dries evenly.)

5 Once dried, transfer the herbal salt to a jar or crock and store it in your pantry. It is shelf stable and does not need to be refrigerated. Your herbal salt will stay fresh for at least 1 year.

·· COOK'S NOTES ··

What herbs are best for making herbal salts? You can use any herb to make an herbal salt, but remember that some herbs are stronger in taste than others. Start with smaller amounts of stronger-tasting herbs, like rosemary and thyme, when first making herbal salts and then work up to an amount that pleases your palate. If this is your first time making this recipe, start with a basic mixture of 1 cup Italian parsley (also known as *flat-leaf parsley*) and ⅓ cup each of oregano, thyme, and rosemary.

How can I add variety to my herbal salts? You can add variety to herbal salts by adding freshly grated ginger or turmeric. Also, try adding a variety of citrus zest in addition to lemon zest—other options include lime, orange, or grapefruit. Try blending sea salt with fresh mint and fresh Italian parsley (also known as *flat-leaf parsley*) for an herbal salt that is perfect for using on lamb. (This combination is a flavorful substitute for mint jelly.) For seasoning greens, such as creamed spinach, try an herbal salt combination of salt, Italian parsley, and grated nutmeg.

Can you make herbal sugars? Definitely! Simply replace the finely ground sea salt with white cane sugar or a dried whole sweetener of your choice, such as unrefined whole cane sugar, coconut sugar, or maple sugar. Herbs that are exceptionally flavorful when used to make herbal sugars are lavender and mint (especially peppermint), but you can also use dried citrus peel or dried ground spices, including allspice, anise, cinnamon, cloves, or ginger. When using dried citrus peel, pulverize a ½ cup of dried peel in a blender or spice grinder to create a fine powder, then add this powder to 1 cup of sugar. When using spices in place of herbs, add ¼ cup of the dried ground spice to 1 cup of of sugar.

Homemade Salad Dressings

These dressings are all so simple to make, and they're so much healthier than anything you'll find at the store. Refrigerated, oil-based salad dressings will stay fresh for 2 weeks, while dairy-based dressings will stay fresh for 1 week.

PREP TIME: **15 MINUTES**
TOTAL TIME: **15 MINUTES**
YIELD: **APPROXIMATELY ¾–1 CUP PER DRESSING**

··········· COOK'S NOTES ···········

Choosing sweeteners for salad dressings: For the whole sweetener called for in the House Salad Dressing recipe, you can use unrefined whole cane sugar, honey, maple sugar or syrup, coconut sugar or syrup, or date sugar or syrup.

Using alternate vinegars and juices: If you prefer to be more authentic, you can substitute the raw apple cider vinegar in the French vinaigrette with white wine vinegar or red wine vinegar or substitute balsamic vinegar in the Italian dressing recipe. You can also use fresh orange juice in place of lemon juice in either the French or Italian dressing to create a sweeter, citrus-based dressing.

Making a true emulsion: You can make any of the oil-based dressings in a bowl using a whisk or in a food processor. To do this, slowly drizzle in the olive oil to make a true emulsion while whisking or processing. (In these recipe instructions, I share the quick-and-easy way to make an oil-based dressing. If you use this method and don't make a true emulsion, be sure to shake the jar or cruet to re-emulsify the dressing before pouring it over a salad.)

HOUSE SALAD DRESSING

1 tsp fine ground sea salt

½ tsp freshly ground black pepper

1 tbsp whole sweetener, any variety (see **Cook's Notes**)

¼ cup raw apple cider vinegar or citrus juice (lemon, lime, grapefruit, or orange)

¾ cup extra virgin olive oil

1 Add salt, pepper, sweetener, and apple cider vinegar (or citrus juice) to a jar or a cruet with a tight-fitting lid. Allow the salt to dissolve.

2 Add the olive oil to the jar, put the lid back on the jar, and shake well until emulsified. (See **Cook's Notes**.)

FRENCH VINAIGRETTE

1 tsp fine ground sea salt

½ tsp freshly ground black pepper

¼ cup raw apple cider vinegar or fresh lemon juice (see **Cook's Notes**)

1 tbsp Dijon mustard

1 shallot, finely chopped (Alternatively, substitute ½ finely chopped small red onion)

¾ cup extra virgin olive oil

1 Add the salt and pepper to a jar with the apple cider vinegar (or fresh lemon juice). Allow the salt to dissolve.

2 Add the mustard and shallot to the jar, put the lid on the jar, and shake until the mustard dissolves.

3 Remove the lid, add the olive oil, put the lid back on the jar, and shake well until emulsified.

ITALIAN DRESSING

1 tsp fine ground sea salt

½ tsp freshly ground black pepper

¼ cup raw apple cider vinegar or fresh lemon juice

1 tbsp dried oregano or Italian seasoning

1 garlic clove, finely minced

¾ cup extra virgin olive oil

1 Add the salt and pepper to a jar along with the apple cider vinegar (or fresh lemon juice). Allow the salt to dissolve.

2 Add the garlic and oregano, put the lid on the jar, and shake the jar to mix the additions with the vinegar.

3 Remove the lid, add the olive oil, put the lid back on the jar, and shake well until emulsified.

THOUSAND ISLAND DRESSING

1 tsp fine ground sea salt

½ tsp freshly ground black pepper

2 tbsp raw apple cider vinegar or fresh lemon juice

¼ cup diced pickles (preferably fermented)

¼ cup ketchup (preferably fermented)

½ cup sour cream (preferably cultured)

¼ cup mayonnaise (preferably homemade)

1 tbsp honey or maple syrup

1   Add the salt and pepper to a jar along with the vinegar (or lemon juice). Allow the salt to dissolve.

2   Add the diced pickles and ketchup to the jar. Mix well using a long-handled spoon.

3   Add the sour cream, mayonnaise, and sweetener. Mix until all the ingredients are well incorporated and the dressing takes on a light pink hue.

BLUE CHEESE DRESSING

½ tsp fine ground sea salt

¼ tsp freshly ground black pepper

1 tbsp raw apple cider vinegar or fresh lemon juice

¼ cup sour cream (preferably cultured)

¼ cup mayonnaise (preferably homemade)

¼ cup blue cheese, crumbled (I use a basic American blue)

1–2 tbsp milk or buttermilk (optional)

1   Add the salt and pepper to a jar and add the vinegar (or lime juice). Allow the salt to dissolve.

2   Add sour cream, mayonnaise, and blue cheese to the jar and mix well using a long-handled spoon.

3   If you want a thinner consistency, add the milk or buttermilk, 1 tablespoon at a time, and mix well.

GREEN GODDESS DRESSING

1 tsp fine ground sea salt

½ tsp freshly ground black pepper

1 tsp Dijon mustard

1 clove fresh garlic, crushed

1 tbsp raw apple cider vinegar or fresh lemon juice

1 bunch fresh parsley, stems removed

1 scallion (green onion), roughly chopped

1 tsp dried tarragon or 1 tbsp fresh, finely chopped

½ cup mayonnaise (preferably homemade)

½ cup sour cream (preferably cultured)

1 tsp anchovy paste or 1 whole anchovy (optional)

1   Add the salt, pepper, mustard, garlic, and vinegar (or lemon juice) to a food processor or blender. Process for a few seconds to chop the garlic.

2   Add the parsley and scallion. Process until finely chopped.

3   Add the tarragon, mayonnaise, sour cream, and anchovy paste (if using). Process for 1 minute or until the dressing is smooth and turns a light green color.

RANCH DRESSING

1 tsp fine ground sea salt

½ tsp freshly ground black pepper

2 tsp raw apple cider vinegar or fresh lemon juice

1 tsp dried parsley or 1 tbsp fresh, finely chopped

1 tsp dried chives or 1 tbsp fresh, finely chopped

1 tsp dried dill or 1 tbsp fresh, finely chopped

1 clove fresh garlic, minced

½ cup sour cream (preferably cultured)

¼ cup mayonnaise (preferably homemade)

½ cup buttermilk (homemade or store-bought)

1   Add the salt, pepper, and vinegar (or lemon juice) to a jar. Allow the salt to dissolve.

2   Add all remaining ingredients to the jar and then mix well using a long-handled spoon.

Fermented Mustards

Homemade lacto-fermented mustards are so easy and inexpensive to make, plus they are more desirable than their store-bought counterparts because they are rich in good bacteria. With the following recipe, you'll learn how to make a basic yellow mustard and also a stone-ground mustard. Making the stone-ground mustard variation of the basic yellow mustard is easy. Just know that your homemade version may look different than the store-bought version, but it will be tastier!

PREP TIME: **5 MINUTES**
FERMENTATION TIME: **2–3 DAYS**
TOTAL TIME: **2–3 DAYS PLUS 5 MINUTES**
YIELD: **APPROXIMATELY 1 CUP OF EACH VARIETY**

INGREDIENTS

Fermented Yellow Mustard

¾ cup filtered chlorine-free water (room temperature)

¼ cup cultured whey or brine from a previous ferment

1 cup yellow dry mustard

1 tsp fine ground sea salt

½ tsp ground turmeric

⅛ tsp paprika

1–2 tbsp raw apple cider vinegar (optional)

Fermented Stone-Ground Mustard

¼ cup brown mustard seeds

1 cup filtered, chlorine-free water (room temperature)

½ cup previously prepared fermented yellow mustard

1–2 tbsp raw apple cider vinegar (optional)

FERMENTED YELLOW MUSTARD

1   Combine the ingredients in a pint-size jar. Mix well using a long-handled spoon and then put a lid on the jar and tighten.

2   Place the jar in a room-temperature area that is between 68°F and 72°F (20°C and 22°C) and out of direct sunlight.

3   After 2 days, loosen the jar lid to let out any gas that may have developed. (You will not see any bubbling, as you would with a ferment in brine, but you may see some fizzing or foam appearing on top. This is normal.) At this point, the mustard is ready. (If you prefer to let your mustard ferment slightly longer, you can leave it at room temperature for one more day.)

4   If the consistency is too thick for your liking, you can thin it by adding the raw apple cider vinegar, 1 tablespoon at a time, and then stirring to combine. If the mustard needs additional thinning after using both tablespoons of the vinegar, add filtered water in small amounts until the desired consistency is reached.

5   Place the lid on the jar and refrigerate. Fermented yellow mustard can stay fresh for 4 to 6 months, but it's at its peak within 3 months.

FERMENTED STONE-GROUND MUSTARD

1   Soak the mustard seeds in the water overnight.

2   Drain the mustard seeds and then crush them using a mortar and pestle. (Alternatively, you can use a spice grinder—just a few pulses will be needed. Or place the seeds in a plastic bag and gently pound with the flat side of a meat pounder.)

3   Combine the ground seeds and fermented yellow mustard in a jar. Mix well and then thin with the raw apple cider vinegar, if desired.

4   Place the lid on the jar and refrigerate. Fermented stone-ground mustard can stay fresh for 4 to 6 months, but it's at its peak within 3 months.

Olive Oil & Egg Mayonnaise

This fast and easy homemade mayonnaise is delicious and nutritious, thanks to the olive oil and probiotic-rich whey. Olive oil causes the homemade mayonnaise to congeal firmer than the store-bought version, but the taste is unbeatable.

PREP TIME: **2 MINUTES**
TOTAL TIME: **2 MINUTES**
YIELD: **APPROXIMATELY 1¼ CUPS**

EQUIPMENT

Quart-size jar with a tight-fitting lid
Immersion stick blender

INGREDIENTS

1 large egg or 2 small eggs, room temperature between 68°F and 72°F (20°C and 22°C) (see **Cook's Notes**)
1 tbsp raw apple cider vinegar or fresh lemon juice
1 tsp yellow mustard (preferably fermented)
1 tsp fine ground sea salt
1 cup extra virgin olive oil
2 tbsp cultured whey or brine from a previous successful ferment

1 Bring a small saucepan of water to a boil over high heat.

2 Place the egg(s) on a large spoon or in a ladle and then lower them into the boiling water for 10 seconds. (This process will help clean any debris from the outside of the shell.) Remove the egg(s) from the water and place them on a clean towel to air dry.

3 Once dry, crack the egg(s) into the jar. (You can rinse the cracked eggshells and add them to a scrap bag for when you make bone broth.) Add the remaining ingredients to the jar.

4 Place an immersion blender into the jar so that the bottom of the blender is on top of the egg. Blend for 20 to 30 seconds or until the mixture begins to emulsify.

5 Once the mixture begins to emulsify, begin moving the immersion blender up and down for another 20 to 30 seconds to ensure all the oil is incorporated into the mixture. Remove the immersion blender from the jar and scrape any mayonnaise back into the jar.

6 Put the lid on the jar and refrigerate. Thanks to the added cultured whey or fermented brine, this mayonnaise should stay fresh in your refrigerator for about 1 month. (If at any time the mayo takes on an off odor, changes color, or mold forms on the top, discard it immediately.)

··· COOK'S NOTES ·································

A note about consuming raw eggs: The eggs in this recipe are raw. Please be advised that the United States Food and Drug Administration (FDA) states that certain people are at greater risk from salmonella from raw eggs, including pregnant women, children, older adults, and those with weakened immune systems. Please keep this in mind before making and consuming this recipe.

What if you don't have an immersion stick blender? If you don't have an immersion stick blender, you can use a blender or a food processor. The only difference is that you will initially add all the ingredients, except the olive oil, to whichever appliance you use. Then, with the blender or food processor running, you will slowly drizzle the olive oil into the mixture. You can also make this mayonnaise by hand by adding all the ingredients, except the olive oil, to a bowl. You'll then slowly pour the olive oil into the bowl while whisking constantly.

Does this mayonnaise taste like olive oil? Yes, but that's what makes it so delicious. If you like aioli, you will love this mayonnaise and be able to use it both as a condiment as well as on its own as a dip or a sauce much in the way you would use aioli. This does not include garlic, as with an authentic aioli, but that's what makes this mayonnaise so versatile.

Fermented Ketchup

Fermented ketchup is a probiotic-rich lacto-fermentation that is outstanding for your digestive health. Plus, it's delicious and so much richer in flavor than anything you'll ever find at the grocery store. It's easy to make and you can enjoy it in just a few days!

PREP TIME: **5 MINUTES**
FERMENTATION TIME: **2–3 DAYS**
TOTAL TIME: **2–3 DAYS PLUS 5 MINUTES**
YIELD: **APPROXIMATELY 2 CUPS**

INGREDIENTS

1½ cups tomato paste

⅛ tsp ground cloves

⅛ tsp ground cinnamon

1 tsp fine ground sea salt

¼ cup unrefined whole cane sugar

2 tbsp cultured whey or brine from a previous successful ferment

⅓ cup filtered, chlorine-free water (room temperature)

1 tbsp Worcestershire sauce

1–2 tbsp raw apple cider vinegar

1 Combine the tomato paste, cloves, cinnamon, sea salt, sweetener, cultured whey or brine, and water in a medium bowl. Mix well. (Add additional water in small amounts to thin the consistency, if needed.)

2 Transfer this mixture to a clean quart-size jar. Put a lid on the jar and place the jar in a room-temperature area that is between 68°F and 72°F (20°C and 22°C) and out of direct sunlight.

3 After 2 days, loosen the jar lid to let out any gas that may have developed. (You will not see any bubbling as you would with a ferment in brine, but you may see some fizzing or foam forming on the top. This is normal.)

4 At this point, if you see some fizzing or foam, you can choose to stop the room-temperature fermentation process and skip to step 5. (If you do not see any fizzing or foam, you can let your ketchup ferment slightly longer by leaving the jar at room temperature for one more day.)

5 After the ketchup has completed the fermentation process, remove the lid and mix in the Worcestershire sauce and 1 tablespoon of the vinegar. If the consistency is still thicker than you would prefer, add an additional tablespoon of vinegar. If you need any further thinning after that, add only water.

6 Once you've reached a satisfactory consistency, place the lid on the jar. Refrigerate for 4 to 6 months. (The ketchup will reach peak flavor within 3 months.)

COOK'S NOTES

Can you use alternate whole sweeteners in place of unrefined whole cane sugar? Yes, coconut sugar makes a flavorful substitute in this recipe. Other dried whole sweeteners can also be used, including maple sugar or date sugar, but they do impart a slightly different flavor.

Does the citric acid often found in store-bought canned tomato paste interfere with the fermentation process? No, you can use store-bought canned tomato paste or homemade tomato paste in this recipe with equal success.

If I made the cottage cheese from The Home Dairy chapter, can I use the whey from that recipe in this recipe? Unfortunately, no. The whey by-product from making stovetop cottage cheese is acidic or acid whey. It has been heated during the cooking process, so it is not cultured whey containing live bacteria.

Can you use a noncaloric sweetener in place of the unrefined whole cane sugar? Yes, there is sufficient natural sugars in the tomato paste to feed the good bacteria and assist in the fermentation process without the need for additional sugar. However, depending on what type of noncaloric sweetener you use, you will have to adjust the amount of water used to create the proper consistency for the ketchup.

Fermented Picante and Chunky Salsa

You can trace the concept of mixing tomatoes and spices to create a salsa or sauce back to ancient times. Fermented picante and chunky salsa are basically the same foods; the only difference is that one has a thin consistency and the other is chunky.

PREP TIME: **15 MINUTES**
FERMENTATION TIME: **2–3 DAYS**
TOTAL TIME: **2–3 DAYS PLUS 15 MINUTES**
YIELD: **APPROXIMATELY 1 QUART (946ML)**

EQUIPMENT

1 wide-mouth glass quart-size jar with a lid

Kraut pounder or wooden spoon

1 small glass jar that is no larger than a 4-ounce canning jelly jar and can fit into the opening of the quart-size jar

1 bowl large enough to hold the quart-size jar

INGREDIENTS

3 cups tomatoes, chopped into ½-inch (1.25cm) pieces

1 medium yellow onion, chopped into ½-inch (1.25cm) pieces

1 handful cilantro or Italian (flat-leaf) parsley, finely chopped

1 jalapeño, finely minced (remove the seeds and membrane for less heat) (see **Cook's Notes**)

Juice and zest of 1 lime

1½ level tbsp coarse ground sea salt or 2¼ level tsp fine ground sea salt

Enough filtered, chlorine-free water (room temperature) to cover the ingredients (optional)

1 Add all the ingredients to the jar. Using a wooden spoon, stir well to combine.

2 Use a kraut pounder or wooden spoon to pack down the mixture as tightly as possible. If the tomatoes do not release sufficient juice so that all the ingredients are submerged under liquid, add enough water to cover the ingredients, but leave enough head space to accommodate the small jar that will function as a weight.

3 Place the small jar on top of the mixture. Put the lid on the quart-size jar and tighten it. Place the quart-size jar in the bowl to catch any overflow. Place the jar and bowl in a room-temperature area that is between 68°F and 72°F (20°C and 22°C) and out of direct sunlight.

4 After 2 days, loosen the jar lid to let out any gas that may have developed. (You may see some bubbling, fizzing, or foam forming on the top. These are all normal signs that your ferment is doing well.) At this point, you can refrigerate your salsa, or, if you want to turn your salsa into a picante, simply whirl the salsa in the blender until it is completely puréed into a thin sauce. (See **Cook's Notes**.)

5 Refrigerated, your fermented salsa or picante can stay fresh for 4 to 6 months, but it will be at its peak flavor within 3 months.

COOK'S NOTES

Protect your hands when slicing jalapeños! Take precautions when working with jalapeños. Always wear gloves to protect your fingers from the oils that are present in the peppers.

Can the salsa be fermented longer? If you prefer to let your salsa ferment slightly longer, you can leave it at room temperature for one more day. On day three, loosen the lid, retighten it, then refrigerate.

Can you use a different pepper in place of the jalapeño? Definitely! When it comes to traditional recipes, almost every home cook has their own version. So make this picante or chunky salsa your own. You can use peppers that will increase or decrease the heat. Some peppers to try include poblano, Fresno, or Anaheim.

Fermented Hot Sauce (with a Twist)

This is the best fermented hot sauce you can make in your kitchen. And it contains a special ingredient that is unusual to add to a hot sauce—pickling spice! You will be using two types of peppers, so you will have both a red hot sauce and a green hot sauce, and each will have its own unique yet delicious flavor. And unlike most ordinary hot sauces, these are fermented just the way real hot sauces should be.

PREP TIME: **15 MINUTES**
FERMENTATION TIME: **7–14 DAYS**
TOTAL TIME: **7–14 DAYS PLUS 15 MINUTES**
YIELD: **APPROXIMATELY 8 CUPS (4 CUPS OF EACH VARIETY)**

INGREDIENTS

4 rounded tbsp coarse ground sea salt or 3 level tbsp fine ground sea salt, divided

½ cup Pickling Spice Mix recipe (p. 95), divided

Enough filtered, chlorine-free water (room temperature) to cover the peppers

½ cup cultured whey or brine from a previous successful ferment, divided

1lb (454g) Fresno peppers, stems removed, sliced in half, ribs and seeds removed (see **Cook's Notes**)

1lb (454g) jalapeños, stems removed, sliced in half, ribs and seeds removed (see **Cook's Notes**)

1 To each jar, add 2 rounded tablespoons of coarse ground sea salt or 1½ level tablespoons of fine ground sea salt, ¼ cup of pickling spice, and enough water to allow the salt to dissolve and mix with the spices. Stir to combine.

2 Once the salt has dissolved, add ¼ cup of whey or brine to each jar.

3 Add the Fresno peppers to one jar and then add the jalapeños to the other jar. Fill each jar with the water, leaving a space of 1 inch (2.5cm) from the rim of the jar. Cover each jar with a lid.

4 Set the jars aside for 7 days in a room-temperature area that is between 68°F and 72°F (20°C and 22°C) and out of direct sunlight. Burp the jars daily by removing the lids and then stirring the ferments to ensure all the peppers are submerged under the liquid. Retighten the lids.

5 On the seventh day, use two clean spoons to remove some of the brine from each jar. Place the brine in two separate small glasses and insert a pH strip into each glass. Quickly remove the pH strips from the brine and measure the level of acidity. If the pH is 4.6 or lower, it has successfully fermented and is safe to taste. If you like the taste, move on to preparing the hot sauce. If you are not satisfied with the taste or if the pH is still above 4.6, you can allow it to continue fermenting for up to 14 days at room temperature. (See **Cook's Notes**.)

6 Once the fermentation process is complete, strain the Fresno peppers out of the brine and add them to a blender. Add no more than a ¼ cup of the brine to the blender and then purée the peppers. If the consistency of the hot sauce is to your liking, pour it through a mesh strainer placed over a bowl and use a spoon to press the hot sauce down through the mesh strainer and into the bowl. Then decant the hot sauce into a glass bottle. If the consistency is not to your liking, add more brine, 1 tablespoon at a time, until you reach the desired consistency before straining and decanting.

7 Rinse the blender and repeat the process for the jalapeños.

8 The hot sauces should stay fresh in the refrigerator for approximately 4 to 6 months. Shake before using. (Do not discard the leftover brine. Decant it into a jar and save it in the refrigerator for future ferments.)

······················ COOK'S NOTES ······················

Protect your hands when slicing peppers! Take precaution when working with peppers. Always wear gloves to protect your fingers from the oils that are present in the peppers.

Checking the pH for the correct level of acidity. If the pH for the hot sauce-in-the-making does not measure 4.6 or lower on the fourteenth day of your ferment, you should discard your ferment and start over. If you leave your ferment out at room temperature for too long, the texture will decline, your ferment will become mushy and slimy, and mold may develop.

Homemade Vegetable Bouillon— Two Ways

Having homemade vegetable bouillon on hand is so helpful. You can add it to a mug of hot water for an instant cup of broth or add it to your soup or stew pot if you don't have any broth or bone broth on hand. You can also use it as a general seasoning in place of salt when making any savory dish.

PREP TIME: **15 MINUTES**
TOTAL TIME: **15 MINUTES**
(WET BOUILLON); 6–8 HOURS
(DRY BOUILLON)
YIELD: **3 CUPS**

INGREDIENTS

1 leek, rinsed and sliced (white part only) (Add the green parts to your vegetable scrap bag)

3 carrots, roughly chopped

3 stalks celery, roughly chopped

1 bunch Italian (flat-leaf) parsley (stems included), chopped

1 cup sun-dried tomatoes (not packed in oil)

2 cups fine ground sea salt

1 Add the vegetables to a food processor. Process for approximately 1 minute, scraping down the sides halfway through the processing. (The vegetables should be finely ground.)

2 Add the sea salt to the food processor with the chopped vegetables. Process for approximately 1 minute, scraping down the sides halfway through the processing. (The final product should resemble very wet sand.)

3 Transfer approximately 1 cup of the mixture to a small jar to keep in the refrigerator. Store the remaining 2 cups in a jar in the freezer. (You can transfer the frozen bouillon to the refrigerator when needed or simply use the bouillon directly from the freezer. Because of the high salt content, the bouillon will not freeze hard.)

4 If you prefer a dry, shelf-stable bouillon, spread the wet bouillon out onto a parchment-lined baking sheet and dry on the middle rack of a preheated 175°F (79°C) oven. Periodically check the vegetable bouillon as it is drying, using a wooden spoon to break up any clumps that appear damp. It will take 6 to 8 hours to dry completely. You will know the bouillon is sufficiently dry when you can no longer form clumps if you squeeze some in your fist. Instead, it should simply crumble into a fine sand, like salt.

5 Use your hands to crumble the bouillon or grind it in a spice grinder or blender for about 30 seconds or until a powder is formed. (Using a spice grinder or blender is much more efficient.)

6 Transfer the vegetable bouillon powder to a jar with a tight-fitting lid. Store in your pantry for up to 6 months.

····················· COOK'S NOTES ·····················

How to use homemade vegetable bouillon: To use, add ½ teaspoon of the wet bouillon or ¼ teaspoon of the dry bouillon to 8fl oz (237ml) hot water to make 1 cup of vegetable broth. You can also add this bouillon directly to soups and stews or use it as a substitute in any savory recipe calling for salt.

If you don't have leeks, what can you use instead? In place of leeks, you can use 1 medium yellow onion, 6 spring onions (including green tops), or 2 medium shallots.

Can other greens be substituted for the parsley? Yes, if you like cilantro you can use that in place of parsley. Alternatively, for adding a peppery bite to this bouillon, arugula makes a great option.

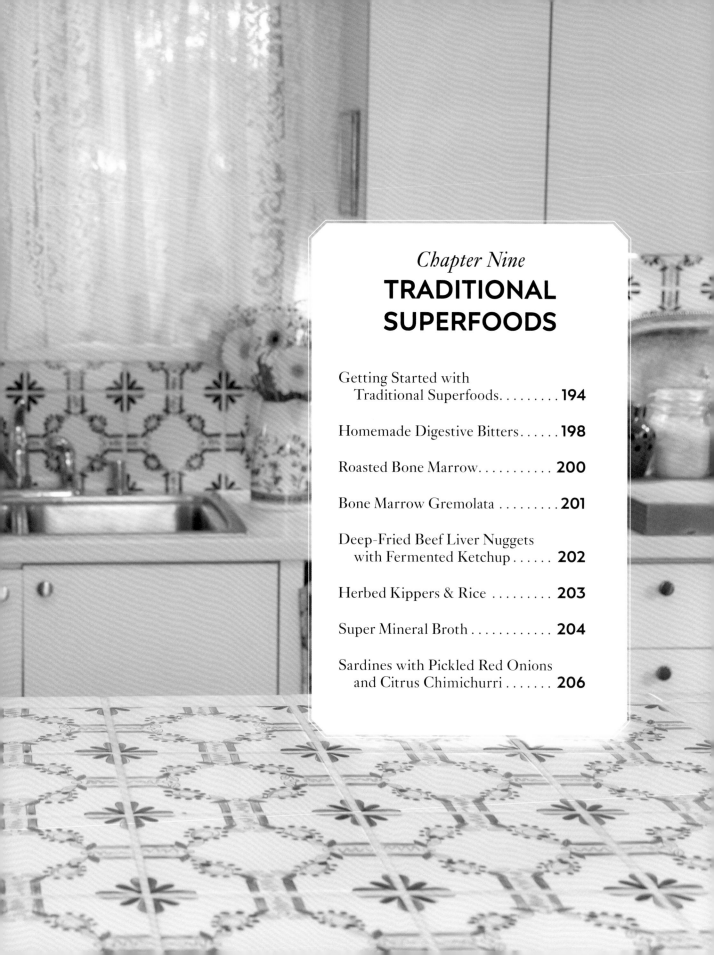

Chapter Nine

TRADITIONAL SUPERFOODS

GETTING STARTED WITH TRADITIONAL SUPERFOODS

Superfoods can mean different things to different people. Today, many people use the terms *nutrient dense* or *nutrient rich* interchangeably to describe foods high in vitamins and minerals and low in calories, such as fruits, vegetables, and bone broths. However, people may also use either term to describe foods rich in vitamins and minerals but high in calories, such as butter and bone marrow. It can all become a bit confusing!

The first category of foods are properly described as *nutrient rich,* while the second should be referred to as *nutrient dense.* Understanding the difference between these two types of foods is important because each offers a range of different vitamins and minerals to our bodies. We want to make sure that we incorporate both into our diets, just as our ancestors did, to maintain a sharp mind, muscle strength, strong bones, and overall good health.

The Nutrient-Dense Superfoods of Our Ancestors

Our ancestors may have had a completely different definition when it came to foods they thought of as being nutrient dense instead of nutrient rich. To them, real nutrient-dense superfoods were foods that were rich in vitamins and minerals and calorie dense, given their portion size or weight. These nutrient-dense foods included organ meats, fat, and bone marrow from animals, oily fish, and full-fat cultured dairy products, including cultured butter. You can look at the history of many traditional cultures and find that these foods were revered and fed generously to pregnant women and nursing mothers. Through the generations, these traditional cultures recognized that these nutrient-dense foods produced healthy children and replenished the nutritional needs of women who had given birth.

Liver on Wednesday, Fish on Friday

These nutrient-dense foods have often fallen out of favor over the years, but they are foods that our ancestors knew to include in their diets. And we should too! Maybe we need to get back to embracing the rhythm of days past when eating liver on Wednesday and fish on Friday was the norm.

As a matter of fact, in our household, we generally eat fish on Friday. I try to provide a wide variety of fish, but on many occasions, the fish I am preparing is canned fish, or what some may know as *tinned fish.* Canned fish is very affordable, yet it is a healthful option to choose when searching for foods that include omega-3 fatty acids. A wealth of scientific research surrounds this fatty acid. Scientists believe it may contribute to heart and brain health and lower inflammation in our bodies. And whenever we can reduce inflammation, that's a good thing!

My mom was fond of calling fish, including canned fish, "brain food." Even back then, scientists—and moms—knew what was good for us. I grew up eating sardines, and so did my son. My husband grew up eating tuna fish, but sardines were a relatively new food to him. He's great about trying pretty much any food, but I decided to start him out with kippers. And you might like to start there too, especially if any type of canned fish other than tuna is new to you. Kippers are smoked herring, and they are exceptionally tasty. I have yet to meet someone to who I recommend kippers who says they didn't like them, including my husband. So that is a resounding seal of approval!

The Nutrient-Rich Superfoods of Our Ancestors

Our ancestors also consumed nutrient-rich superfoods that were abundant in vitamins, and especially minerals. And yes, these foods were lower in calories than their nutrient-dense counterparts. Our ancestors usually consumed these nutrient-rich foods for their high mineral content and to aid in digestion and absorption of vitamins and minerals from the nutrient-dense foods. These types of superfoods included bitters, bone broths, and mineral broths.

Bitters are usually made from a selection of herbs and spices and are consumed in very small amounts right before a meal to help "prime the pump," so to speak, and prepare our digestive system for the food it is about to receive. But of course, you can also consume bitters after a meal when indigestion strikes!

Gelatin-rich bone broths soothe our digestive tracts and help us absorb the usable protein in our meals. They are certainly nutrient-rich superfoods. (We covered making bone broths in chapter 2.)

In this chapter, you'll learn how to make a mineral-rich broth with the nutrients our bodies need. Minerals, along with vitamins, build strong bones and teeth and keep our muscles, heart, and brain functioning properly.

You can use a wide selection of vegetables and a diverse set of herbs and spices, which is a nice feature of making mineral broth. And if at any time you have a few vegetables in your crisper that might be coming close to their prime, toss them into a stockpot with some water and turn them into a nutritious broth.

Mineral broths also make an excellent base for any soup when you want a change from bone broths. And like bone broths, mineral broths can be used in place of water when cooking grains and making sauces and gravies. If you have any vegetarians in the family, they will appreciate a gravy made with mineral broth.

The secret to making mineral broth is to use a variety of vegetables as opposed to just the carrots, celery, and onions you might use in typical vegetable broth. Now don't get me wrong. That type of vegetable broth is lovely and definitely nutritious, but when you start to add a whole host of other veggies, and maybe even a tuber or two, along with healing herbs and spices, you will have something incredibly nutritious!

Let's Talk About Cod Liver Oil

Although we won't be preparing cod livers in this chapter (I know you are wiping the sweat off your brow!), we can't talk about superfoods, whether nutrient-dense or nutrient-rich, without talking about cod livers. Depending on what part of the world you grew up in, you might have regularly enjoyed cod livers from the can. I didn't, but I was well versed in the benefits of cod liver oil.

My mom shared with me that it was common for young students to line up at school while the school nurse went down the line dispensing a spoonful of cod liver oil to each child—using the same spoon, mind you! My mom wasn't a huge fan of the taste—she described it as "fishy," but her mom told her that it was good for her, so she acquiesced and took it each day at school. Clearly, it played some sort of role in her good health since she is 98 years old!

My dad, who went to a different school than my mom, remembered the cod liver oil and same spoon adventures as well. But he would have no part of it. It's hard to say for sure, but maybe some of the cod liver oil my dad was exposed to had gone rancid and, in doing so, had passed the fishy stage and advanced to the putrid stage! I can imagine that being pretty unpleasant to stomach.

But why was there this push to get children to take cod liver oil? Cod liver oil was taken by many cultures going back to ancient times since our ancestors believed it was rich in vitamins. Cod liver oil, derived from cod livers, is rich in vitamins A and D. We need these vitamins to maintain good health, but they are often deficient in our modern-day diets. Even if we eat a traditional foods diet, we may still fall short on vitamins A and D. So enter cod liver oil. A little bit—often no more than a teaspoon taken daily—is considered by many to serve as a good source of whole food vitamins.

I don't know of any schools passing out cod liver oil today, but I started giving it to my young son when he was a toddler. I bought fresh cod liver oil and mixed it up in a bit of grapefruit juice, and he would take it right down each day. I followed it with another small cup of grapefruit juice which he would drink quickly. I called it the "chaser." Our family does not drink alcohol, but we have a good laugh about the grapefruit juice chasers to this day!

Keep in mind, like so many things in the traditional food world, cod liver oil is good when consumed in moderation. Never overdo it. Vitamins A and D are essential, but they are fat-soluble vitamins that stay in our bodies. Accumulating too much can be just as bad as having too little.

If you want to think about adding cod liver oil to your lineup of superfoods, look for one that is in its original natural state and has no added vitamins. It may be worth giving it a try and seeing if it agrees with you. If you add cod liver oil to your daily diet (and I hope you do!), stay abreast of the scientific research surrounding cod liver oil. Scientists are showing more interest in studying cod liver oil's effects on a whole host of maladies.

Kale—A Nutrient-*Dense* Superfood?

Fruits and vegetables are frequently touted as superfoods, with kale leading the pack. And kale is certainly nutrient rich when properly prepared. But is it really nutrient dense? Technically, no. Kale, along with many other leafy greens, including collards, dandelion greens, endive, spinach, and Swiss chard, is rich in nutrients and may be thought of in today's vernacular as a nutrient-dense— and more appropriately, nutrient-rich— superfood. But remember, kale, along with some of these other leafy greens, also contains pesky antinutrients including goitrogens and oxalates that can prevent our bodies from properly absorbing nutrients, as well as create problems for our kidneys and thyroid. So how do we enjoy the good side of these greens and deactivate the downside? You probably guessed it. We're going to do what our ancestors did and cook them! The next time you are tempted to put raw kale in a smoothie, think twice, and instead serve it as a cooked side dish with lunch or dinner. And make sure to put some cultured butter on it so you can better absorb all those nutrients!

Bone Marrow—The *Real* Nutrient-Dense Superfood

Consuming bone marrow was a revered practice by ancient traditional cultures. Beef bone marrow was especially prized, as it is a highly nutrient-dense food, rich in vitamins A, C, K, and the B vitamins, including riboflavin, thiamin, niacin, B6, and folate. Marrow also includes the minerals potassium, magnesium, manganese, phosphorus, calcium, iron, and copper. Bone marrow is rich in collagen and the fat-conjugated linoleic acid (CLA), which scientists believe may help to prevent the development of cancer and atherosclerosis. CLA may also help reduce body fat, improve lean body mass, improve immune function, and tamp down inflammation.

One of the best things about bone marrow is that it is very rich in collagen. Many people buy expensive collagen pills and powders, but it's completely unnecessary. Instead of wasting your money on these products, simply introduce bone marrow into your diet. Along with the regular consumption of nutrient-rich bone broth, these two superfoods will keep your skin smooth, your nails strong, and your hair thick! And remember, bone marrow and bone broth are real foods in their natural state. They have not been processed at high temperatures to be turned into powders.

If you add only one nutrient-dense food to your diet, choose bone marrow. But if you are new to traditional foods, you might find the sight of marrow bones a bit off-putting. And if you did not grow up eating bone marrow or other nutrient-dense foods, it might take your palate a few tries before it adjusts. However, you have to trust me. Try it once, and you will be hooked. I recommend spreading a bit on a toast point. Once you try it this way, you may find yourself eating it right off the spoon next time!

Homemade Digestive Bitters

When making cocktails, bitters can be used in the preparation of an aperitif or a digestif. The former is served before a meal to help us digest what we are about to eat, whereas the latter is served after dinner to help us digest what we have just eaten. Digestifs are especially welcome after eating a heavy meal. But you don't need to enjoy a cocktail to gain the benefits of improved digestion. Homemade digestive bitters are easy to make and easy to consume. It just takes a few drops to help improve your digestion. And improved digestion is always a good thing because it allows our digestive tract to better absorb the nutrients from our food.

PREP TIME: **5 MINUTES**
STEEPING TIME: **4 WEEKS**
STRAINING AND DECANTING TIME: **5 MINUTES**
TOTAL TIME: **4 WEEKS PLUS 10 MINUTES**
YIELD: **APPROXIMATELY 1 ½ CUPS**

EQUIPMENT

1 pint-size glass jar with lid

3–4 (4fl oz/120ml) dark-colored glass jars or bottles (preferably with caps that contain eyedroppers and are tight-fitting to prevent evaporation)

INGREDIENTS

3 tbsp dried angelica root

1½ tbsp dried dandelion root

1 tbsp dried ginger root

1 (3-inch/7.5cm) cinnamon stick

Whole peel and pith of 1 small lemon (preferably organic) (see **Cook's Notes**)

Whole peel and pith of 1 small orange (preferably organic)

1 tsp green cardamon pods, cracked open

½ tsp anise seeds (or 1 star anise)

½ tsp fennel seeds

½ tsp whole cloves

1 sprig of a fresh herb, such as lemon balm, lemon verbena, or rosemary

1½ cups vodka or enough to fill the jar and cover the contents

1 Combine all the ingredients, except the vodka, in the pint-size glass jar.

2 Pour the vodka into the jar, leaving approximately a 1-inch (2.5cm) headspace from the rim of the jar. Put the lid on the jar and shake it a few times.

3 Place the jar in a dark, room-temperature area, such as a pantry or cupboard.

4 For the next 4 weeks, shake the jar once daily to ensure that the ingredients are well distributed and submerged under the vodka.

5 After 4 weeks, line a colander or mesh strainer with a flour-sack towel or cheesecloth and place it over a bowl. Pour the contents of the jar through the lined colander and allow the liquid to drain into the bowl. Discard the solids.

6 Decant the strained bitters from the bowl into the small glass bottles or jars. Homemade digestive bitters generally have a shelf life, in terms of efficacy, of approximately 5 years. But technically, alcohol preparations can last much longer, thanks to the alcohol's role as a potent preservative.

········· **A WORD OF CAUTION** ·········

Keep in mind that bitters are made with herbs and spices, and although these are commonly used for culinary purposes, they also have medicinal properties. It's generally recommended that pregnant women, nursing mothers, and anyone with digestive disorders talk to their doctor before ingesting herbs and spices or digestive bitters made with them. And it's best to talk to your pediatrician before giving this or any herbal preparation to children.

········· **COOK'S NOTES** ·········

Using bitters to aid digestion. Thirty minutes before eating a meal, place ¼ teaspoon of the digestive bitters directly onto your tongue. Or you add the same amount to a ¼ cup of room-temperature water and drink it. If you develop indigestion after eating, add ¼ teaspoon of the digestive bitter to a ¼ cup of room-temperature water and drink it.

What is the pith? This recipe calls for the entire peel and pith of both a lemon and an orange. In addition to the outer zest, the peel also includes the white interior known as the *pith*. It has a bitter flavor, which helps stimulate the flow of our digestive enzymes. The pith is also loaded with nutrients, including vitamins A and C, the vitamin B family, and the mineral calcium. The pith's vitamins are worth extracting and including in digestive bitters.

What if I don't want to use any type of alcohol? If you do not want to make digestive bitters using alcohol, I recommend making a homemade hot tea using angelica root and dandelion root as your base and then adding the other herbs and spices to make a digestive tea. Teas are a delightful way to enjoy herbs and spices that aid digestion. You can enjoy your digestive tea before, with, or after your meal.

Why is there no gentian root included in this recipe? Although gentian root is commonly seen in recipes for making digestive bitters because it stimulates saliva and stomach acid production, I do not recommend including it in this recipe. You should approach this root with caution. Individuals prone to gastrointestinal irritation should avoid this root since it may introduce other digestive problems. However, if you want to use gentian root when making digestive bitters because you believe it will agree with you, add equal parts angelica root and gentian root to your recipe, up to a total of 3 teaspoons combined.

What other herbs and spices can I use when making digestive bitters? The following herbs and spices are generally associated with aiding digestion or soothing digestive upset: allspice berries, anise seeds or star anise, caraway seeds, chamomile flowers, cinnamon sticks, cloves (whole), coriander seeds, cumin seeds, fennel seeds, fenugreek seeds, ginger root, lemon balm, lemon verbena, mint, oregano, rosemary, savory, and thyme. The basic recipe for digestive bitters typically contains angelica root and dandelion root, but after those ingredients, you can try different combinations of herbs and spices to customize your digestive bitters.

Roasted Bone Marrow

Roasted bone marrow is delicious. If you like butter and steak, you will love bone marrow! It basically tastes like steak butter. As a matter of fact, its nickname is *the butter of the gods*! Your marrow recipe can be ready in as little as 15 minutes once you pop the bones in the oven. Now that's what I truly call a quick-and-easy, nutrient-dense superfood!

PREP TIME: **5 MINUTES**
COOK TIME: **15 MINUTES**
TOTAL TIME: **20 MINUTES**
YIELD: **2 SERVINGS**

INGREDIENTS

6 (1-inch/2.5cm) thin-cut beef marrow bones

6 toasted baguette slices or small triangle slices of toasted sourdough bread (often referred to as *toast points*)

Sea salt, any variety (fine, coarse, or flaked), to taste

Small handful fresh Italian (flat-leaf) parsley, chopped

1 Preheat the oven to 450°F (232°C).

2 Place the marrow bones on a baking sheet lined with parchment paper.

3 Place the bones in the preheated oven. Roast for 15 minutes or until the marrow is light brown in color.

4 Remove the baking sheet from the oven and place on a heatproof surface

5 Use a spoon to scoop the marrow out of bones. Spread the marrow over slices of toasted baguette or sourdough toast points and then sprinkle with sea salt and chopped parsley. Roasted Bone Marrow is best eaten soon after being removed from the oven.

···················· COOK'S NOTES ····················

Can you use other cuts of beef marrow bones to make this recipe? Definitely! Canoe-cut marrow bones roast beautifully, and you don't need to adjust the recipe.

Are there other toppings, in addition to salt and parsley, that you can sprinkle over the roasted bone marrow? When it comes to preparing homemade traditional foods, you have the ability to customize your ingredients, including when making roasted bone marrow. As a traditional foods cook, you want to experiment with each recipe until you make it your own. In the case of bone marrow, an alternate topping would be to take a 1/3 cup of fig jam and warm it slightly on the stovetop to liquefy it. Remove it from the heat and stir in a teaspoon of balsamic vinegar. Drizzle this mixture over the bone marrow for a sweet and salty treat! But don't stop there. Try substituting other jams or even orange marmalade in place of the fig jam. You won't be disappointed.

After you remove the marrow from the bones, do you need to discard the bones, or can you save them to use when making bone broth? By all means, save the bones. You can freeze them in a scrap bag and then add them into the acidulated water with your larger marrow bones when making beef bone broth.

Family and friends are hesitant to try bone marrow. Is there any way you can sneak it into another food? Roasted bone marrow is quite delicious by itself, but I certainly understand some people's hesitancy to try it. The easiest way to introduce bone marrow to novices is to whip it into a cream soup. All they will notice is an extra rich buttery goodness in the soup. And most likely, they will be asking you what your scrumptious secret ingredient is!

When making beef bone broth with long or medium marrow bones, the marrow slips out when you remove the bones to strain the broth. What should you do with it? You can eat the marrow from your marrow bones used to make your bone broth in the same way you would roasted bone marrow from this recipe. Alternatively, you can whip the bone marrow into your bone broth to create a cream of beef bone broth soup. It's amazing how versatile and delicious bone marrow is when you add it to other foods.

Bone Marrow Gremolata

If you are hesitant to eat plain roasted bone marrow, you will certainly enjoy it in the form of a gremolata. Typically, a gremolata is a mixture of chopped parsley, lemon zest, and garlic. However, we are going to take this one step further and increase the gremolata's nutritional profile by mixing in roasted bone marrow.

PREP TIME: **5 MINUTES**
TOTAL TIME: **5 MINUTES**
YIELD: **2 SERVINGS**

INGREDIENTS

1 medium bunch fresh Italian (flat-leaf) parsley, washed, dried, stems removed, and minced (see **Cook's Notes**)

1 medium clove garlic, peeled and minced

Zest of 1 medium lemon

½ tsp fine ground sea salt, plus more to taste

Roasted marrow from 6 thin-cut beef marrow bones

Juice from one medium lemon (optional)

1 tbsp olive oil (optional)

6 toasted baguette slices or small triangle slices of toasted sourdough bread (often referred to as *toast points*)

1 Combine the parsley, garlic, lemon zest, and sea salt in a medium bowl.

2 Mix the ingredients thoroughly to ensure that the garlic and lemon zest are well distributed throughout the parsley.

3 Use a spoon to remove the roasted marrow from the bones. Add it to the bowl. Mix well until the marrow is evenly distributed throughout the mixture.

4 Taste and add additional salt, if desired.

5 If desired, add the optional lemon juice and optional olive oil for added flavor and a smoother texture. Stir.

6 To serve, spread over slices of toasted baguette or sourdough toast points.

···················· COOK'S NOTES ····················

What to do with the parsley stems? Parsley and its stems are rich in vitamins and minerals. However, they are also high in oxalates, which might contribute to certain types of kidney stones if you are prone to this condition. However, you don't have to completely discard parsley stems. Alternatively, you can find ways to limit your use of parsley without forgoing it entirely. For example, you can separate the parsley stems from the rest of your vegetable scraps and only add them to any homemade broth you are making for the last 10 minutes of simmering time. You want to extract some of the vitamins and minerals that parsley offers, but you do not want to overdo it by leaving parsley or its stems to simmer for many hours.

Can you use something else in place of garlic when making this gremolata? Definitely! A great substitute would be 1 tablespoon of either minced onion (any variety) or minced shallot.

If you don't have parsley to make this gremolata, can you substitute something else? The nice thing about this recipe is that you can make it your own. Traditional recipes made in the comfort of your kitchen welcome substitutions. In place of the parsley, you can use basil, carrot greens, chervil, celery leaves, cilantro, or oregano. As a matter of fact, you can even use chives for a richly onion-flavored gremolata or arugula for a peppery bite. Do as traditional cultures have done for centuries and use what you have.

Can I use other types of citrus to make this gremolata? Just as with substituting the parsley, you can substitute the lemon with the juice and zest of a lime, orange, or grapefruit.

Deep-Fried Beef Liver Nuggets with Fermented Ketchup

These buttermilk battered and deep-fried beef liver nuggets are a delicious way to enjoy nutrient-dense organ meats. And by serving them with a probiotic-rich fermented ketchup, you will aid the digestion of the beef liver along with the beef tallow, in which you will be frying them. Plus, if you are feeding these to children, the bite-sized nuggets are similar in appearance to those offered by fast food chains. This can be a bit of a sneaky way to introduce this nutrient-dense food into their diet!

PREP TIME: **1 HOUR 15 MINUTES**
FRYING TIME: **APPROXIMATELY 20 MINUTES**
TOTAL TIME: **APPROXIMATELY 1 HOUR 35 MINUTES**
YIELD: **4 SERVINGS**

EQUIPMENT

4-quart cast-iron or enamel-lined Dutch oven

Deep-frying or candy thermometer

Slotted spoon or spider strainer

INGREDIENTS

1lb (450g) frozen beef liver

1 cup buttermilk

1 cup all-purpose flour

1½ tsp fine ground sea salt, divided

½ tsp ground black pepper (optional)

Approximately 4 cups beef tallow

½ cup Fermented Ketchup (p. 186)

1 Remove the frozen beef liver from the freezer and let it thaw slightly at room temperature. Once slightly thawed, it should still be firm to the touch but you should be able to slice it with a sharp serrated knife. (See **Cook's Notes**.)

2 Once the beef liver is slightly thawed, use a serrated knife to carefully cut the beef liver into 2-inch (5cm) pieces.

3 Add the buttermilk to a large bowl. Place the liver pieces into the buttermilk and soak for 1 hour.

4 While the liver pieces are soaking, combine the flour, 1 teaspoon sea salt, and black pepper (if using) in a medium bowl. Set aside.

5 Line a large baking sheet with parchment paper. Set aside.

6 After 1 hour, remove the liver pieces from the buttermilk. Working one at a time, roll the pieces in the flour mixture, dip the flour-dusted pieces back into the buttermilk, and then roll them in the flour again. Place the battered liver pieces on the prepared baking sheet.

7 Add enough tallow in the Dutch oven so that when the tallow melts, it measures at least 1 inch (2.5cm) from the bottom.

8 Using a food-safe deep-frying or candy thermometer to measure the temperature, melt the tallow to 375°F (191°C). (You will be frying the liver at approximately 350°F [177°C], but the slightly higher initial temperature will compensate for the drop in temperature when you place the liver into the melted tallow.)

9 While the tallow is melting, place a cooling rack on a second baking sheet or line a large plate with paper towels. Set aside.

10 Using a large spoon, carefully place four pieces of liver, one at a time, into the heated tallow. Fry until golden brown, about 3 to 4 minutes.

11 Using a slotted spoon or spider strainer, remove the fried livers from the Dutch oven and place them on the cooling rack to drain. Lightly season with some of the remaining sea salt. Repeat the process until all livers pieces have been fried.

12 Serve immediately with the Fermented Ketchup as a dipping sauce.

·········· COOK'S NOTES ··········

Why does the liver need to be only slightly thawed ? It's much easier to cut the liver into small pieces when it's still partially frozen. If you work with completely thawed liver, cutting the pieces will be very messy.

Herbed Kippers and Rice

This simple dish is easy to make and also affordable when budgets are tight. But you won't be scrimping on nutrition one bit. The term *kippers* generally refers to a wood-smoked oily fish known as *herring*. These fish are rich in omega-3 fatty acids, just like more expensive fish, including salmon. Scientists believe this fatty acid may help decrease heart disease and stroke, and may also reduce otherwise damaging inflammation in our bodies.

Traditional cultures consumed many nutrient-dense foods rich in omega-3 fatty acids throughout the centuries. We also want to include these tried-and-true foods in our modern diets, and kippers are a tasty way to do this! If you are familiar with kippers, you might enjoy them as I do, right out of the can or topped on a cracker. But if their taste is new to you, flavoring them with lemon, red onions, and fresh herbs makes for a real treat.

PREP TIME: **10 MINUTES**
RICE COOK TIME: **30–35 MINUTES**
TOTAL TIME: **40–45 MINUTES**
YIELD: **4 SERVINGS**

INGREDIENTS

4 cups fish or chicken bone broth (alternatively, you can substitute Super Mineral Broth [p. 204])

1 tsp fine ground sea salt

2 cups uncooked white rice

4 (3.5oz/100g) cans kipper snacks

Juice and zest of 1 medium lemon

1 small red onion, peeled and diced

Small handful of fresh herbs, chopped (see **Cook's Notes**)

4 tsp soy sauce (preferably naturally fermented)

1   Add the broth to a medium saucepan over medium-high heat. Bring the broth up to a high simmer and then add the sea salt and rice. Stir well. Return to a high simmer and then immediately turn the heat down to low and cover the saucepan. Allow the rice to cook until all the broth is absorbed, about 30 to 35 minutes.

2   Once the rice is cooked, fluff with a fork and divide evenly across 4 shallow bowls.

3   One at a time, open a can of kippers and place the contents on top of the rice in one of the bowls. Continue until all 4 cans have been opened and topped onto the rice in each bowl.

4   Sprinkle the lemon juice evenly over the kippers in each of the four bowls, followed by a pinch of the lemon zest, a sprinkle of diced onion, and a sprinkle of the herbs. Drizzle the soy sauce over the top.

> ···················· COOK'S NOTES ····················
>
> ***What are the best fresh herbs to use with kippers?*** Fresh herbs that work well when mixed with kippers are those that have a soft texture and are light and fresh tasting, like basil, chives, dill, or Italian (flat-leaf) parsley.

Super Mineral Broth

Instead of turning to a bottle of vitamins, I love the idea of using nutrient-rich vegetables to make a broth that gives my body the minerals it needs. My mom always had some sort of mineral broth like this bubbling away on her stove. She would ladle some into a teacup throughout the day to enjoy knowing that she was making good use of vegetables from her crisper—maybe even a few that were beginning to reach their prime—and nothing was going to waste.

Although I'm sharing this recipe with you, please make this broth your own. My mom's broth was different every week based on what she had on hand. So please, do the same. Use a variety of vegetables, herbs, and spices from season to season. You will discover many delightfully delicious combinations! And don't worry if you don't have the herbs and spices called for in this recipe—simply substitute others that you like and have on hand in your pantry. And all the vegetables you use to make the broth won't go to waste. This recipe includes instructions for how to purée them to make a terrific creamy soup.

PREP TIME: **15 MINUTES**
COOK TIME: **2 HOURS**
TOTAL TIME: **2 HOURS 15 MINUTES**
YIELD: **APPROXIMATELY 1 GALLON (3.75L)**

EQUIPMENT

Large stockpot

Colander or mesh strainer

Large bowl

Flour-sack towel or cheesecloth

2 half-gallon–size (1.90L) glass jars with tight-fitting lids
(you can also use smaller jars)

INGREDIENTS

2 medium yellow onions (unpeeled), roughly chopped

1 medium red onion (unpeeled), roughly chopped

6 medium carrots (unpeeled), roughly chopped

6 medium stalks celery (with leaves), roughly chopped

1 medium head romaine lettuce, roughly chopped

6 fresh Italian plum tomatoes, roughly chopped
(if out of season, use 1 [28oz/794g] can)

2 medium sweet potatoes (unpeeled), roughly chopped
(during the summer, use 4 zucchini)

2 cups mushrooms (any variety), roughly chopped

1 (6-inch/15.25cm) piece fresh ginger root, peeled
(unpeeled, if organic)

1 (6-inch/15.25cm) fresh turmeric root, peeled
(unpeeled, if organic)

2 bay leaves

Small handful of fresh thyme, stems removed

Small handful of fresh oregano, stems removed

2 tsp whole black peppercorns

1 tsp whole allspice berries

1 head garlic, unpeeled and sliced in half (optional)

Enough water (preferably filtered) to cover the ingredients

Fine ground sea salt (or Nutrient-Rich House Seasoning
[p. 178]), to taste (optional)

1 Combine all the ingredients except the water and sea salt in a large stockpot on the stovetop. Add enough water to cover the ingredients.

2 Turn the heat up to high. Bring the mixture up to a boil and then immediately turn the heat down to the lowest setting. Allow the broth to simmer, uncovered, for 2 hours.

3 After 2 hours, turn off the heat and remove the stockpot from the stovetop to a heatproof surface. Allow the broth to cool slightly. Remove any solids from the stockpot, transfer them to a large bowl, and set them aside.

4 Line a colander or mesh strainer with a flour-sack towel or cheesecloth and place it over a medium-size stockpot or a large bowl. Strain the broth through the colander or strainer.

5 Decant the broth into the jars, set aside to cool, and then place lids on the jars and refrigerate. The broth will stay fresh for 4 to 5 days in the refrigerator. For longer storage, the broth can be frozen in freezerproof containers for approximately 3 months.

6 When ready to serve, warm gently on the stovetop and then season to taste with sea salt or Nutrient-Rich House Seasoning (p. 178).

·········· COOK'S NOTES ··········

Using the remaining vegetables to make a cream soup:
Do not discard the vegetables! Since they have only been simmered for 2 hours, they may still contain some nutrition or at the very least, can be used for their fiber content and as a thickening agent. Instead, remove the bay leaves and process the remaining solids through a food mill to create a creamy mineral-rich purée. If you do not have a food mill, you can process the vegetables in a food processor or blender, but you may need to add some of the broth to create a smooth mixture. Once you have run the vegetables through the food processor or blender, work the mixture through a mesh strainer to catch and remove any remaining pieces of herbs, spices, or vegetable skins. Add this purée, 1 tablespoon at a time, to the Super Mineral Broth until you reach a creamy consistency to your liking. I recommend freezing any vegetable purée you will not be immediately using. You can freeze this purée in ice cube trays. Once frozen, transfer the cubes to a freezerproof bag or container. This purée will stay fresh in your freezer for about 2 to 3 months. Use the cubes to add to broths or soups when desiring a creamy consistency.

Sardines with Pickled Red Onions and Citrus Chimichurri

I love to eat sardines by putting them between two slices of rye bread along with some red onions to make a tasty fish sandwich. However, I grew up eating them this way, and I realize not everyone may be ready to jump in with both feet and embrace a sardine sandwich! But not to worry. Sardines prepared in the way I share in this recipe make a splendid appetizer, allowing you to enjoy the sardines in small amounts with lots of refreshing citrus and herbaceous flavors. And as with kippers, this is another excellent way to include an omega-3-rich oily fish in your diet.

PREP TIME: **30 MINUTES**
PICKLING TIME: **30 MINUTES**
TOTAL TIME: **1 HOUR**
YIELD: **4 SERVINGS**

INGREDIENTS

½ cup apple cider vinegar (does not need to be raw vinegar)

½ cup water

1 tsp fine ground sea salt

2 tbsp maple syrup

1 large red onion, peeled and minced

1 (4.4oz/125g) can sardines (packed in water or olive oil)

1 tbsp olive oil (optional)

16 thinly sliced, toasted baguette rounds or sourdough toast points

For the citrus chimichurri

½ cup olive oil

1 bunch fresh Italian (flat-leaf) parsley (including stems), washed, dried, and minced

Small handful of fresh oregano, washed, dried, stems removed, and minced

Juice and zest of 1 medium lemon

Juice and zest of 1 medium orange

1 garlic clove, peeled and minced

1 tsp fine ground sea salt

½ tsp ground black pepper

1 In a medium bowl, mix all the chimichurri ingredients together until well blended. Set aside.

2 Make a brine by adding the apple cider vinegar, water, sea salt, and maple syrup to a small saucepan. Bring to a boil over high heat.

3 Once the brine comes up to a boil, immediately turn off the heat and place the saucepan on a heatproof surface. Add the onions and stir. Allow the onions to soften in the hot brine for 30 minutes.

4 While the onions are soaking in the brine, remove the sardines from the can and place them in the middle of a medium serving dish. Flake with a fork into bite-size chunks. Drizzle the olive oil over the sardines if they were packed in water.

5 After 30 minutes, use a slotted spoon to remove half the red onions from the brine and then spoon them over the sardines.

6 Top the red onions with generous dollops of the citrus chimichurri sauce. (You can serve any extra chimichurri sauce on the side.)

7 Surround the platter of sardines with toasted sliced baguette rounds or sourdough toast points.

8 Transfer the brine with the remaining onions to a small bowl and serve alongside the sardines. To eat, place some of the sardines with the onions and chimichurri on a baguette round or toast point and then spoon a small amount of brine with the onions over the sardines.

> ·············· COOK'S NOTES ··············
>
> *What are the best sardines to use?* You can use skinless and boneless sardines, but the sardines that have the skin and bones intact are the better choice. The bones and skin are both edible and very nutritious.
>
> *Save the lemon and orange pith!* After zesting and juicing the lemon and orange, save the pith by freezing it so you can later use it to make digestive bitters.

Chapter Ten
GOOD "BUG" BEVERAGES

GETTING STARTED WITH PROBIOTIC BEVERAGES

When we hear the term good "bugs," it can be difficult to imagine what exactly they are and why we would want them in our beverages! However, these good bugs are good bacteria that are rich in gut-loving probiotics. So when we make these probiotic beverages, we introduce these good bacteria into our digestive tracts in a most delicious and readily absorbable way.

You don't need anything special to make these beverages, except for those ingredients you probably already have on hand. This is welcome news to beginners! You don't need to acquire a SCOBY (symbiotic culture of bacteria and yeast) to make any of the beverage recipes in this chapter. Chances are, if you have some water, raw apple cider vinegar, a whole sweetener, a few herbs and spices, some fresh or dried fruits, vegetables, and a handful of stale bread, you are all set.

Traditional cultures have such a wide variety of probiotic-rich beverages. They created many of their beverages based on what was available to them at the time. The beverages I share in this chapter are all traditional beverages that date back centuries, so you know that they are taste-tested and approved by our ancestors. They are also my favorites; I hope they will be yours too!

Switchels and Shrubs—Easy Beverages to Make That Do Not Require Any Fermentation

If you want to entertain the guests at your festivities with traditional beverages, switchels and shrubs are two easy beverages you can make that do not require any fermentation.

Switchel, also commonly known as "haymaker's punch," along with a whole host of nicknames including "switzel," "swizzle," "switchy," and simply "ginger water," is the original quintessential electrolyte drink. And once you learn how to make this beverage homemade, you can say goodbye to those electrolyte drinks sold at the grocery store. Unfortunately, store-bought drinks often contain a lot of artificial coloring, which is an ingredient we do not want in our traditional foods kitchens! As you may have guessed from the nickname "ginger water," that is exactly what switchel is. You can easily make switchels with water and fresh or ground ginger. And never worry about using ground ginger in place of fresh ginger because the original recipe used ground ginger (sometimes referred to as *powdered ginger*). Switchel dates back to the early days of Colonial America when ground ginger was a common spice import. Along with some raw apple cider vinegar and a whole sweetener of your choice, you will have a delightfully refreshing and restorative beverage welcome at any summer barbecue, perfect for drinking after a hot day harvesting hay ... or maybe just working in your kitchen garden!

If you have guests who don't drink alcohol, you can offer them a tasty alcohol-free mocktail called a *shrub*. This simple mixture of fresh fruit, herbs, water, and raw apple cider vinegar creates the base for many tasty beverages, including a mock mojito! And it doesn't stop there. Using endless combinations of fresh fruits and herbs, you can take the basic formula for a shrub and make it your own. You might even find that your guests request your mocktails over actual cocktails!

Since switchels and shrubs do not require any fermentation, you can prepare and serve them in minutes when you quickly need a beverage to replenish your electrolytes. Or if an unexpected but welcome guest rings the doorbell to surprise you, you can stir up a mock mojito in no time.

Thanks to the use of raw apple cider vinegar in both switchels and shrubs, you are creating probiotic-rich beverages that are good for your digestion by keeping the good bugs—the good bacteria—alive and well.

A Little Sip of History

When you first start consuming probiotic-rich beverages, switchel and shrubs are an excellent place to start. You can sweeten these mild-tasting beverages to your liking, and they are one of the best ways to begin to wean yourself off of store-bought energy drinks or even store-bought sodas. But did you know that when you are enjoying these beverages, you are truly getting a taste—or should I say a sip—of history?

Shrubs, in particular, can be traced back all the way to the fifteenth century. Initially, they were used by many people, including medical professionals of that era, for medicinal purposes. But then smugglers embraced the recipe in the late 1600s to doctor their sea water–soaked barrels of alcohol with fruit to mask the salty flavor. This alcohol-based shrub became quite popular and was sold throughout England up through the eighteenth century. Eventually, shrubs fell out of favor as new beverages became popular.

However, in the American colonies, shrubs were quite popular and continued to be so through the nineteenth century. But shrubs in America were made a bit differently than their counterparts in England. Instead of alcohol, colonists mixed vinegar with fruit and allowed the mixture to ferment at room temperature for a few days. During this fermentation, a fruity syrup would develop, which would be strained off and then sweetened. This sweet syrup could be mixed with water—or in some cases, alcohol—to make a refreshing shrub. Unfortunately, this tasty fermented syrup was quickly forgotten with the advent of refrigeration.

Enter the 21st Century and the Rebirth of the Shrub

The good news is that fruit-based syrups and shrubs have come back into fashion. Upscale bars and restaurants in the United States and England are proving to be quite avant-garde by using fruit syrup in place of bitters, to make fancy shrub cocktails. Even the health food industry wants to be part of this beverage's resurgence. They, too, are using fruit syrups to make probiotic-rich shrubs, which they call "drinking vinegars." You may have seen these drinking vinegars sold at your local grocery store or specialty market next to the bottles of various flavors of kombucha. Shrubs used in this manner may not actually contain a fermented fruit syrup as they once did, but they still have a wonderful flavor. And when it comes to adding fruit syrup to raw vinegar to make the shrub, it is the raw vinegar that provides the "good bugs" for your digestive system.

So when you start making and drinking your own shrubs right at home, you will be sipping a fascinating piece of history that includes healers, smugglers, and trendsetters from New York to London.

Creating a Ginger Bug

You can also create your own good bugs without using raw apple cider vinegar by making a ginger bug. And best of all, once you learn how to do this, you open up endless possibilities for creating a whole host of homemade flavored good-for-you sodas.

A ginger bug is a fermented form of fresh ginger and sugar. Once it's all bubbly and frothy, you can use it to make homemade ginger ale. You have never really tasted true ginger ale until you have had it homemade. So if you love the flavor of ginger, this is the perfect homemade soda for you! You can also use your ginger bug to make any flavored soda you'd like by adding the required flavorings, such as

vanilla extract for cream soda or fresh berries for a variety of sodas, including strawberry soda. You can even use a selection of herbs to make unusual yet delicious herbaceous flavored sodas.

Kvass—an Easy-to-Make Fermented Beverage

One of my favorite good bug beverages to make is kvass. I love how simple it is to make yet how nutritious it is when finished. This classic fermented beverage doesn't have exact origins, but it may have appeared in Eastern Europe over 1,000 years ago, where it is still a popular beverage today.

If you research kvass, you will often uncover many variations in recipes for this ancient drink. This is because every household over the centuries put their own twist on it based on what they had on hand. But what they all have in common is that they are naturally fermented, providing a probiotic beverage that is also effervescent.

Most commonly, you'll make kvass with stale or heavily toasted (sometimes to the point of being burnt!) dark rye bread. However, you can also make it with beets to create something exceptionally flavorful! It's hard for me to pick a favorite since they are both tasty but also quite different.

Kvass is an anaerobic fermentation, meaning without air, but I have learned from experience not to ferment it too long at room temperature. When I first attempted a rye bread kvass many years ago, I left it to ferment for probably at least 30 days. Then, when I went to taste it, I innocently poured some of it into a glass and took a big sip. Oh my! It was as strong as strong can be. I had read that kvass was commonly drunk to ward off illness and disease, especially during the winter months when colds and flu may be rampant.

After one taste of that fermented (dare I say overly fermented) rye bread kvass, I was a believer. I am not a medical authority, but from a layperson's perspective, I can't imagine any bad bacteria being able to survive the onslaught of good bacteria that tasted like the sourest beverage I had ever had. It was like drinking straight lemon juice or vinegar. After swallowing my sip down quickly, I coughed as my eyes watered. I was confident that if there were any cobwebs in my respiratory tract, they were certainly gone now. I share this with you not to scare you, but to show you how powerful fermentation can be and why I often recommend transferring your ferments to the refrigerator to slow down the fermentation process. With kvass, I have learned that it only needs a few days of fermentation time (not 30 days!) to create a sweet-and-sour beverage with a bit of effervescence that is a delight to enjoy!

Beet kvass has a very different flavor profile than rye bread kvass. Many describe it as a bit sweet, salty, sour, and earthy. And I agree. It is a little bit of this and that when you first taste it. I might add that, to me, it tastes a bit like a very tasty pickle brine. It's superb at room temperature or over ice. But it's even better when you allow it to steep in the refrigerator with some cinnamon sticks,

allspice berries, whole cloves, and maybe a few star anise added to it.

Either variety of kvass makes an excellent nonalcoholic aperitif, almost like bitters, you can serve before a heavy holiday meal to get your digestive juices flowing. You can also reserve kvass as a digestif to quaff after a rich meal. Both beet kvass and rye bread kvass make for versatile beverages and ones that you can flavor with a host of herbs and spices to create new and exciting flavors every time you enjoy them.

Better than Store-Bought Beverages

Unlike all the sodas and assorted energy drinks with ingredients that are detrimental to our health, these homemade fermented beverages are good for us, and you can enjoy them regularly. Can you drink plain water? Certainly, but something our ancestors appeared to intuitively understand was that water is better when it is fortified with some nutrition. It isn't just about quenching one's thirst but truly hydrating and nourishing our bodies.

In the following recipes, you'll learn how to make the homemade beverages our ancestors relied on to keep them healthy and hydrated. From our earlier bone broth and dairy kefir beverages, you'll be able to now make switchel, shrubs, ginger bugs, and kvass. You'll never go thirsty! And at the same time you quench your thirst, you'll also be consuming nutritious drinks that will fill your body with vitamins, minerals, and good bugs!

Haymaker's Switchel Punch

If you need a tasty, all-natural electrolyte drink that doesn't contain artificial ingredients, switchel is the beverage for you! Switchel is an eighteenth century energy drink that's perfect for enjoying after exercise or hard work. And the best thing is that it costs just pennies to make and contains no artificial colors or ingredients.

PREP TIME: **5 MINUTES**
TOTAL TIME: **5 MINUTES**
YIELD: **8 (8FL OZ/237ML) SERVINGS**

EQUIPMENT

Half-gallon jar with tight-fitting lid

INGREDIENTS

1 tbsp ground ginger (dried ginger ground
   to a fine powder)

¼ tsp fine ground sea salt

¼ cup raw apple cider vinegar
   (homemade or store-bought)

½ cup sweetener (molasses, honey, or maple syrup)

Filtered, chlorine-free water (room temperature)
   sufficient to fill a half-gallon jar

1   Add the ginger and salt to the jar. Add a small amount of water and then mix thoroughly.

2   Add the apple cider vinegar and sweetener to the jar.

3   Fill the jar with water to 1 inch (2.5cm) below the rim of the jar. Stir well, secure the lid on the jar, and transfer to the refrigerator.

4   Serve chilled or over ice. Stored in the refrigerator, switchel will retain its flavor for approximately 1 month. (Shake well before using.)

Pineapple Mojito Shrub Mocktail

Shrub is certainly a funny name for such a tasty beverage! Many recipes for making this beverage date back to seventeenth and eighteenth century England and Colonial America. Everyone can enjoy this beverage because it does not include alcohol, hence the name *mocktail*. Plus, it puts a fun spin on a modern-day drink: the mojito. This mocktail uses a simple flavor combination of pineapple, mint, and lime to create a delightfully sweet and tangy beverage that's perfect for serving at your next party. But don't stop there. You can use the basic formula in this recipe to create any flavor combination you like. All you have to do is change the type of fruit and herbs you use.

PREP TIME: **5 MINUTES**
STEEPING TIME: **30 MINUTES**
STRAINING TIME: **5 MINUTES**
TOTAL TIME: **40 MINUTES**
YIELD: **APPROXIMATELY 16 SERVINGS**

EQUIPMENT

Half-gallon jar with tight-fitting lid

Long-handled wooden spoon, kraut pounder, or muddler

Mesh strainer

Bowl or large measuring cup

INGREDIENTS

2 cups cubed pineapple (preferably fresh)

1 cup fresh mint leaves

Zest and juice of 6 limes

1 cup honey (preferably raw)

2 cups raw apple cider vinegar (homemade or store-bought)

Filtered, chlorine-free water or sparkling water, to serve

Pineapple slices (with rind), lime slices, and mint sprigs, to garnish (optional)

1 Add the pineapple cubes, mint leaves, lime juice, and lime zest to the jar. Mash well using a wooden spoon, kraut pounder, or muddler.

2 Pour the honey and vinegar into the jar, place the lid on the jar, and shake vigorously to mix well.

3 Let the mixture steep for 30 minutes at room temperature, between 68°F and 72°F (20°C and 22°C), to allow the flavors to blend and deepen.

4 After 30 minutes, strain the mixture by placing a mesh strainer over a bowl or large measuring cup. Press the mixture in the strainer until all the liquid has strained through and into the bowl or measuring cup. (If you want a completely clear mixture, you can line the mesh strainer with a flour-sack towel or cheesecloth.)

5 Rinse out the jar, transfer the liquid to the jar, secure the lid, and refrigerate it until you are ready to use. The pineapple liquid should stay fresh and at its peak flavor for about 1 week.

6 To make the mocktail, fill a large drinking glass with ice. Pour ¼ cup of the pineapple liquid into the glass and then fill the glass with enough filtered or sparkling water to reach the rim of the glass. If desired, garnish with a slice of pineapple or a lime slice and a sprig of mint.

Homemade Ginger "Bug"

A ginger bug is a fermentation starter for making homemade carbonated beverages, including ginger ale. Wild yeasts and good bacteria will populate a ginger bug, causing it to become bubbly in a way similar to a sourdough starter. You may find that if you start out this process using organic ginger, which does not have to be peeled, your mixture may become effervescent quite quickly. This is because the skin of the ginger is loaded with yeasts and bacteria that will jump-start the process.

This ginger bug is easy to make and only takes a few minutes of preparation a day over 6 days. This is a great project in which to involve children. They will have fun stirring the ginger bug and watching as it begins to bubble within a few days. Plus, learning how to make their own homemade sodas with this bug might entice them to forgo store-bought sodas that are usually loaded with high-fructose corn syrup, artificial coloring, and a host of other ingredients that no self-respecting traditional foods cook wants in their kitchen ... or their children!

PREP TIME: **15 MINUTES**
FERMENTATION TIME: **6 DAYS**
TOTAL TIME: **6 DAYS PLUS 15 MINUTES**
YIELD: **APPROXIMATELY 2 CUPS**

EQUIPMENT

1 quart-size jar with tight-fitting lid

INGREDIENTS

¼ cup plus 3 tbsp peeled and diced fresh ginger root, divided (if organic, it does not need to be peeled)
1 tbsp plus 3 tsp white cane sugar, divided (see **Cook's Notes**)
2 cups filtered chlorine-free water (room temperature)

1. **Day 1:** Place a ¼ cup of ginger in a quart-size jar, sprinkle 1 tablespoon sugar on top of the ginger, and then pour in 2 cups of water. Put a lid on the jar, tighten, and then swirl it around a few times to help the sugar to begin to dissolve. Place the jar in a room-temperature area between 68°F and 72°F (20°C and 22°C) and out of direct sunlight.

2. **Day 2:** After 24 hours, check on the ginger bug and see if bubbles are developing. If so, loosen the lid of the jar and allow the gas to be released, and then retighten the lid and set the jar aside again. If bubbles are not forming, simply leave the jar undisturbed.

3. **Day 3:** Open the jar and add 1 teaspoon sugar and 1 tablespoon ginger. Stir and then put the lid back on the jar, tighten, and set aside again.

4. **Day 4:** Open the jar and add 1 teaspoon sugar and 1 tablespoon ginger. Stir and then put the lid back on the jar, tighten, and set aside again.

5. **Day 5:** Open the jar and add 1 teaspoon sugar and 1 tablespoon ginger. Stir and then put the lid back on the jar, tighten, and set aside again.

6. **Day 6:** The ginger bug should be nice and bubbly at this point and ready to use to make homemade ginger ale. Set it aside and prepare the ginger ale mixture.

.... COOK'S NOTES ....

Using and storing the ginger bug: You now have a successful ferment that you can use to make more soda, but you can also use it to assist in the fermentation process of other ferments by adding 1 tablespoon of the strained ginger bug to a vegetable ferment or a sourdough starter that might need a jump-start. You can store the ginger bug at room temperature if you plan to make more soda, but you will need to feed it daily. If you do not use it to make soda within a few days, you will need to discard some of the ginger bug before feeding it so the jar does not become too full. You can also refrigerate your ginger bug, but you will want to feed it once weekly with 1 teaspoon of white sugar and a tablespoon of peeled and diced fresh ginger. And as with keeping it at room temperature, you will need to discard some of it so the jar does not become too full. (Don't throw out your discard. You can freeze it and use it to make tea or add it to a smoothie for a ginger kick!)

Homemade Ginger Ale

If you have never had homemade ginger ale, you are in for a real treat. The pop of ginger flavor is so much richer than any ginger ale you can buy. But this version takes things one step further because this is a naturally fermented ginger ale. Once the fermentation process of your homemade ginger bug is complete, you will use it to make this homemade ginger ale, which is a fermented probiotic-rich soda. It's excellent for good gut health and much tastier than anything you'll find at the store.

PREP TIME: **15 MINUTES**
FERMENTATION TIME: **3 DAYS**
TOTAL TIME: **3 DAYS PLUS 15 MINUTES**
YIELD: **4 (8FL OZ/237ML) SERVINGS**

EQUIPMENT

1 quart-size jar with tight-fitting lid
4 (8fl oz/237mL) bottles with screw-on caps
 (these are not airtight) (see **Cook's Notes**)
Mesh strainer
2 bowls
Flour-sack towel or cheesecloth

INGREDIENTS

½ cup peeled and diced fresh ginger root
 (if organic, it does not need to be peeled)
6 tbsp white cane sugar (see **Cook's Notes**)
4 cups filtered, chlorine-free water (room temperature)

1 Add the diced ginger and water to a saucepan. Bring it to a boil over high heat, and then turn the heat down to medium. Simmer for 10 minutes.

2 Remove the saucepan from the heat. Add the sugar and stir until it dissolves.

3 Strain the liquid from the saucepan into a bowl using a mesh strainer lined with a flour-sack towel or cheesecloth. You should have approximately 3½ cups of strained liquid. Set aside to cool to room temperature in a location that is between 68°F and 72°F (20°C and 22°C).

4 Place a mesh strainer lined with a flour-sack towel or cheesecloth over a separate bowl. Strain ½ cup of the ginger bug from its jar. (This is easiest to do if you have a 1 cup liquid measuring cup and a small mesh strainer.)

5 Once the strained liquid has cooled, add the ½ cup of ginger bug and stir well.

6 Decant the mixture into a clean quart-size jar. Make sure there is 1 inch (2.5cm) of headspace from the rim of the jar. Tighten the lid, place the jar in a bowl, and allow it to ferment at room temperature for 3 days in a location that is between 68°F and 72°F (20°C and 22°C) and out of direct sunlight.

7 By the third day, lots of bubbles should have formed in the jar. Your homemade ginger ale should now be sufficiently carbonated.

8 To serve, pour the homemade ginger ale over ice and enjoy. If you prefer to decant it, divide the ginger ale evenly between four swing-top bottles that are specifically made to hold carbonated beverages.

···················· COOK'S NOTES ····················

Decanting carbonated beverages into swing-top bottles: I generally recommend drinking homemade ginger ale the day you make it or storing it in bottles with screw-on caps that are not airtight. The carbonation will last a few days in this type of bottle. However, if you decide to decant the ginger ale into swing-top bottles to maintain its carbonation, make sure the bottles you use are specifically made for carbonated beverages. Sometimes, swing-top bottles can break under pressure, so I do not recommend using them.

Choosing whole sweeteners for making homemade fermented sodas: White cane sugar will make your ginger ale the same color as store-bought ginger ale. However, using whole sweeteners, such as unrefined whole cane sugar (with the molasses still intact), will give the ginger ale a darker color, but it produces a rich flavor (almost gingerbreadlike) and provides more nutrition.

Beet Kvass and Spiced Holiday Kvass

Beet Kvass is a delightfully tasty beverage by itself and can be used in place of vinegar to make your favorite homemade salad dressings. But we'll take Beet Kvass one step further and allow it to steep with lots of warming spices to create a beverage to enjoy by the fireplace on a cold evening or served as an aperitif before a large winter dinner or Christmastime holiday meal.

PREP TIME: **20 MINUTES**
FERMENTATION TIME: **21 DAYS**
STEEPING TIME: **1–3 MONTHS (FOR SPICED HOLIDAY KVASS)**
TOTAL TIME: **21 DAYS TO 3 MONTHS PLUS 20 MINUTES**
YIELD: **APPROXIMATELY 1 QUART (946ML)**

EQUIPMENT

1 half gallon jar with tight-fitting lid

1 (32fl oz/946ml) bottle with a screw-on cap (this is not airtight)

Mesh strainer

1 large bowl

INGREDIENTS (BEET KVASS)

4 medium beets, peeled with tops and tails removed, cut into 1-inch (2.5cm) cubes

2 rounded tbsp coarse ground sea salt or 1 ½ tbsp fine ground sea salt

Filtered chlorine-free water (room temperature)

INGREDIENTS (SPICED HOLIDAY KVASS)

4 (3-inch/7.5cm) cinnamon sticks (preferably Ceylon cinnamon)

1 tsp allspice berries

1 tsp whole cloves

2 whole star anise (optional)

BEET KVASS

1   Place the beets in the jar and then add the salt.

2   Fill the jar with water, leaving approximately 2 inches (5cm) of headspace. Put a lid on the jar and tighten it.

3   Place the jar in a bowl (to catch any spillage) in a room-temperature location that is between 68°F and 72°F (20°C and 22°C) and out of direct sunlight.

4   After 2 days, check the jar to see if bubbles are forming. (In warmer months, bubbles will appear sooner than in cooler months.) If you see bubbles, loosen the jar lid to allow some of the carbon dioxide to escape. Retighten the jar lid.

5   Continue checking the jar each day for 5 more days, loosening the jar lid each time to release the carbon dioxide and then retightening the lid. After 7 days, place the jar in the refrigerator and leave it there for 2 weeks. (During this time, the fermentation will slow down considerably, but the beets will absorb more of the kvass brine, increasing their flavor while allowing the kvass to become less salty.)

6   After the 2-week refrigeration period is complete, remove the jar from the refrigerator. Place an unlined mesh strainer over a large bowl and strain the beets from the kvass. The liquid is your plain Beet Kvass. Set the beets aside. If you do not want to make the Spiced Holiday Kvass, pour the plain Beet Kvass into the bottle, put the cap on, and refrigerate. (You can chop up the beets and add them to a salad or serve them as a side condiment similar to how you would serve sauerkraut. They are rich in probiotics and are outstanding for digestive health.)

SPICED HOLIDAY KVASS

1   To create the Spiced Holiday Kvass, pour the Beet Kvass back into the jar and add the cinnamon sticks, allspice berries, whole cloves, and star anise (if using). Put the lid back on the jar, place the kvass in the refrigerator, and allow it to steep with the spices for at least 1 month or up to 3 months.

2   After the steeping time is complete, strain out the spices, decant the kvass into a 32-ounce (946ml) bottle with a cap, and refrigerate.

Rye Bread Kvass

Rye Bread Kvass is easy to make and creates a wonderful mildly effervescent and probiotic-rich drink. It's sweet and fizzy with a bit of spice and perfect as is. If you have had store-bought rye bread kvass, you might be surprised that homemade traditional kvass does taste different. It will be quite a bit stronger and possibly not as sweet, but that's the beauty of it. It will provide you with a taste of a truly traditional beverage.

PREP TIME: **20 MINUTES**
FERMENTATION TIME: **7 DAYS**
TOTAL TIME: **7 DAYS PLUS 20 MINUTES**
YIELD: **APPROXIMATELY 1 QUART**

EQUIPMENT

1 half-gallon jar with tight-fitting lid

Mesh strainer

1 large bowl

Flour-sack towel or cheesecloth

1 (32fl oz/946ml) bottle with a screw-on cap (this is not airtight)

INGREDIENTS

5 slices stale or toasted dark rye bread, broken into pieces

2 large unpeeled apples (any variety), seeds removed and chopped

½ cup dark raisins

2 (3-inch/7.5cm) cinnamon sticks (preferably Ceylon cinnamon)

Filtered, chlorine-free water (room temperature)

1 Add the rye bread, apples, and raisins to the jar, alternating with layers of each.

2 Slide the cinnamon sticks down the sides of the jar.

3 Fill the jar with water, leaving approximately 2 inches (5cm) of headspace from the rim of the jar.

4 Put a lid on the jar and tighten it. Shake the jar vigorously.

5 Place the jar in a bowl (to catch any spillage) in a room-temperature location that is between 68°F and 72°F (20°C and 22°C) and out of direct sunlight.

6 Each day for 6 days, loosen the lid to allow any built-up carbon dioxide to escape. Retighten the lid securely and gently shake the jar back and forth a few times. Place the jar back into the bowl, and return the bowl to a room-temperature area that is between 68°F and 72°F (20°C and 22°C) and out of direct sunlight.

7 After 7 days of fermentation, place a mesh strainer over a large bowl and line the colander with a flour-sack towel or cheesecloth. Strain the kvass through the colander and into the bowl. Decant the kvass into a 32-ounce (946ml) bottle with a cap and refrigerate. (The bread-and-apple mixture will be quite mushy at this point and is best relegated to the compost pile, which will revel in all the good bacteria.)

--- COOK'S NOTES ---

How long will kvass stay fresh? Homemade kvass beverages will stay fresh in your refrigerator for at least 3 months. They will lose their fizz after a few days but will still be tasty.

Why are we not checking the pH? When making Beet Kvass, it can be challenging to check for the pH because of the deep color of the beverage. This is where you will want to use your nose and your eyes to determine if you have a successful ferment. Beet Kvass should look slightly fizzy with no mold forming on top, and it should have a somewhat sour aroma, not unlike a lemon but with earthy overtones. As to Rye Bread Kvass, you can also use your nose and your eyes to determine its success. It will also appear slightly fizzy and will have somewhat of a sweet molasses aroma. But you can also use pH strips to check the level of acidity. Kvass should have a pH between 3.0 to 4.0. If you want to go ahead and taste it, it should taste like a very mild beer, and in our case, with slight notes of cinnamon since that is the spice we added.

Chapter Eleven
PRESERVING FOODS WITH HOME CANNING

GETTING STARTED WITH HOME CANNING

In addition to making bone broth and baking sourdough bread in your oven, you'll definitely want to add home canning to your repertoire of kitchen skills. What a delight it is to open your pantry and see all those glass jars filled with brightly colored foods that you prepared and canned yourself!

Water Bath Canning and Pressure Canning

There are two types of home canning approved by the National Center for Home Food Preservation (NCHFP)—water bath canning and pressure canning. The NCHFP is located in the United States and is a publicly funded research center that focuses solely on the topic of home food preservation. They tested various methods of preserving food to select the safest techniques to prevent foodborne illness and determined that water bath canning and pressure canning are both acceptable ways to preserve food in jars that can stay fresh and is safe for human consumption.

There are two types of home canning because different types of foods need to be home canned in different ways. Water bath canning is safe for canning high-acid foods, while pressure canning is safe for canning low-acid foods. High-acid foods include chutneys, most fruits, jams and jellies, pickles, salsas, tomatoes, and more. Pressure canning is reserved for meat, chicken, fish, low-acid vegetables, and other low-acid foods.

This chapter focuses on water bath canning, which is perfect for those new to home canning. Plus, it is the easiest way to learn how to home can since you do not need a special canner like you do with pressure canning. A simple stockpot will do when it comes to water bath canning, but if you want specialized equipment, water bath canners are readily available and reasonably priced. The customized water bath canners are well worth the investment if you find that you enjoy home canning and plan on doing it regularly.

If you find you enjoy water bath canning and want to graduate to pressure canning, the NCHFP provides helpful resources to get you started with the right equipment, and they also provide detailed instructions to ensure your pressure canning is safe and successful.

Water Bath Canning Supplies

The basic supplies you will need to get started with water bath canning include:

- Water bath canner with rack or large stockpot with rack
- Various size regular-mouth canning jars with lids and bands (rings)
- Various size wide-mouth canning jars with lids and bands (rings)
- Jar lifter
- Wide-mouth funnel for fitting over regular- and wide-mouth canning jars

- Ladle, preferably with a pour spout

- Magnetized lid lifter

- Debubbler (bubble popper) or flat butter knife

- Ruler (one may be included on your debubbler)

- Cushioned drying mat or thick dish towels

- Jelly or candy thermometer

- Canning and pickling salt

- Pickle Crisp (sodium chloride), which is made specifically for canning pickles

If you decide to purchase a water bath canner, it is important to first check with the manufacturer of your stovetop to determine which type of canner you can use on your stove. Generally, electric stoves with coils and gas stoves with cast-iron grates have various canner options. But if you have a flat glass-top stove, make sure you purchase a flat-bottom water bath canner approved for a glass-top stove. Using the wrong type of water bath canner on a glass-top stove can cause severe damage to the stovetop, including cracking the glass.

The wide-mouth funnel, the magnetized lid lifter, and the debubbler are not essential, but they make your job easier. Plus, they are very inexpensive and often come in a home-canning kit. A funnel will make the job of filling the jars easier and neater. If you do not use a lid lifter, just make sure that your hands are very clean before putting a canning lid on a jar. And if you do not have a debubbler, you can use a flat butter knife. However, most debubblers also have a ruler, which makes it easy to measure the appropriate headspace. So if you do not have a debubbler, make sure you at least have a ruler on hand.

As to the salt, it is always best to use canning and pickling salt when home canning because it is specifically free of any additives. You'll want to make sure that you use salt that contains just salt. As with fermentation, additives in salt, such as anticaking agents, can interfere with the home-canning process. Since sea salts are just salt, you may wonder if you can use those for your home canning. The NCHFP recommends using canning and pickling salt and does not mention canning with sea salt, so it is best to stay within their guidelines.

Always Have Extra Canning Jars on Hand

When home canning, always make sure that you prepare one or two extra jars beyond the recipe's stated yield in case you have a bit extra when preparing a canning recipe. (With fresh foods, there's always a little variability in how the foods fill up your canning jars.) You might have a bit of extra jam, fruit, etc. If you can completely fill an extra jar to the proper headspace, you can go ahead and water bath can it. If you cannot fill a jar to the proper headspace, you will not be canning the extras. Instead, you will want to refrigerate and consume that extra portion first before opening your canned supplies.

What Is Headspace?

When you fill your canning jars with the prepared food and accompanying liquid, you will only fill them to a specific headspace, defined as the distance between the top of the contents in the jar and the rim of the jar. Different recipes call for different headspace measurements. Generally, headspace can range from ¼ inch (.65cm) to 1 inch (2.5cm).

You'll want to leave the proper headspace in your jars because the food in the jars will expand during the canning process. Different foods expand to varying degrees, so the headspace recommendations in a recipe will take the food's characteristics into consideration. If you don't leave the proper headspace, the food in the jar may bubble out during the canning process when the air in the jar is released underwater while the canner is processing the jar. Food escaping from the jar underwater will make it very difficult for the canning lid to create a secure seal.

Speaking of filling your canning jars, never worry if you run out of hot liquid or brine to fill your jars. Most likely this won't happen with the following recipes, but if it does, chances are the amount of hot liquid you need will be a small amount. All you need to do is keep a tea kettle of hot water nearby to top off that last jar that might be a bit shy of the required headspace. And if you have leftover brine, do not discard it; instead, store it in a lidded jar in your refrigerator and use it in place of vinegar when making salad dressings.

What Is Fingertip Tight?

If you are new to canning, you will need to learn how to secure the band (ring) on your canning jar before you submerge it into the water bath canner. When you place the band (ring) on the jar, turn it until you meet resistance. Once you meet this resistance, turn it a bit more to gently tighten. This is known as "fingertip tight." Do not use brute strength to tighten the band (ring)!

The only purpose of the band (ring) is to keep the lid in place during the water bath. If it is too tight, the air can't escape from the jar during the processing time. If the jar cannot release air while processing in the canner, the unescaped air may cause the food to spoil. Once the air escapes and you remove the jar from the canner, the temperature change will create a vacuum, the lid button will depress, and you'll know you have an airtight seal.

Understanding a Proper Seal

Canning lids can be a bit perplexing if you are new to home canning, but they will become your best friends. These special lids have a small, raised dome in the center of the lid. Home canners often refer to this dome as the "button." The button will be raised when you put the lid on your jar before processing it in the water bath canner.

Once the jars are processed and you remove them from the canner, the button will make a sound as the jars cool outside the canner. Home canners usually refer to this sound as the "ping." When the canning lid experiences the temperature change from the hot water bath canner to room temperature, the button depresses, making the ping sound and creating an airtight seal for your jar. It's a beautiful sound because it reassures you that your processing was most likely successful.

Sometimes the ping happens very quickly, while other times, it can take a bit longer. You can give your canning lids 24 hours to ping. After 24 hours, observe the canning lids to ensure that all the buttons are depressed. Push on each button with your finger to see if it stays depressed. You might also notice that the lid is very slightly concave. If so, the seal is successful and you can remove the band and store your jars. If the button pops up or the lid is loose on a jar, the canning was not successful for that jar. You'll want to refrigerate that jar and consume its contents first.

Preparing the Water Bath Canner and Supplies

Each time you get ready to home can, prepare your water bath canner and supplies as follows:

1   Place the water bath canner on a stovetop burner, and then place the canner rack at the bottom of the canner.

2   Inspect your canning jars to make sure there are no cracks or chips on the rims of the jars, and then place the empty jars without lids face up into the water bath canner on the rack.

3   Fill the water bath canner with water until all the jars are submerged.

4   Bring the water in your water bath canner up to a boil, then immediately turn down the heat to a low simmer and put the lid on the canner.

5   Wash the canning lids and the rings in warm soapy water. Rinse them thoroughly and allow them to air-dry on a clean dish towel. (Never put the canning lids in boiling water. It can damage the rubber seal on the lids.)

6   You can now proceed with preparing the food you will be home canning.

Using Your Water Bath Canner

Follow these general steps as you process your food for water bath canning. (The recipes in this chapter provide you with specific steps by customizing these general steps.)

1   Once you've prepared your food for canning, remove the jars, one at a time, from the water bath canner using a jar lifter and then pour the water from the jar back into the canner. (Be careful! The water will be very hot.)

2   Place the jar on a cushioned but steady surface, such as a drying mat or double layer of terry cloth dish towels (as opposed to thin tea towels).

3   Place a wide-mouth funnel on top of the jar and ladle the hot food into the hot jar, leaving the appropriate headspace as stated in the recipe.

4   Remove any air bubbles with a debubbler or flat butter knife by poking it back and forth into the filled jar. If the contents in the jar drops below the headspace, add more food or liquid to the jar.

5   Dip a paper towel or clean rag into white vinegar and then wipe the rim of the jar.

6   Use a magnetized lid lifter to place a lid on the jar rim. Secure the jar band (ring) until it's fingertip tight.

> .... CAUTION! ....
>
> If the band (ring) is too tight and the jar cannot release air during the processing time, the jar may shatter in your canner.

7   Using the jar lifter, place the jar into the canner. Make sure that you keep the jar straight as you do this. Do not tilt it to one side or the other.

8   Repeat steps 1 through 7 with each jar until all the jars are filled and in the canner.

9   After placing the filled jars in your canner, ensure that all the jars are submerged under the water by at least 1 to 2 inches (2.5 to 5 cm) above the top of the jars. If you need to add additional water to the canner, bring this additional water up to a boil first in a separate saucepan so that you do not cool off the water in the canner.

10 Turn the heat up to high and bring the water in the canner up to a rolling boil (one in which large bubbles are continually surfacing on the top of the water). Once the water reaches a rolling boil, put the lid on the canner and set your timer for the recommended water bath canning time, as stated in the recipe, for the jar size you are using, the specific food you are canning, and your altitude.

11 When the specified time for boiling the jars has been reached, turn off the heat and remove the canner lid, but leave the jars in the canner for 5 minutes.

12 After 5 minutes, use the jar lifter to lift the jars out of the canner and place them on a drying mat or a double layer of terry cloth dish towels that provide a good cushion for the jars. As you do this, be sure to lift the jars up and out of the canner in a straight fashion. (Do not tip the jars to one side or the other.) You may start to hear the jars ping as they cool and the lids seal.

13 Allow the jars to cool for 24 hours. Once cooled, remove the rings and check the seal on each jar to ensure the canning lid sealed correctly. The jar lid should be slightly concave, the previously raised button in the middle of the jar lid should now be depressed, the jar lid should be firmly attached to the rim of the jar, and nothing should appear to have leaked from the jar.

····················· IMPORTANT! ·····················

Never reuse the lids! Once you open your home canned goods, you cannot reuse the canning lids for future canning since the rubber seal on your lid may be compromised. You can reuse the bands (rings), but never the lids. Always start each new canning project with new canning lids.

The Role of Altitude

How long you process your filled canning jars depends on the altitude where you live. Altitude refers to the elevation, or how high you are above sea level. You can generally find this information online by searching for the name of your town and state, followed by the word "altitude," or you can contact your county extension service.

Knowing your altitude matters because the boiling point for water is different at different elevations. Generally, water bath processing (boiling) times are based on an elevation of 1,000 feet or lower. At this elevation, water boils at 212°F (100°C). At higher elevations, water boils at a lower temperature. For this reason, you must process your jars for a longer period of time to ensure that the food in your jars is exposed to an adequate amount of heat to destroy any bad bacteria that could lead to food spoilage and foodborne illness.

But don't worry about having to do any fancy math calculations as you progress through this chapter. In each recipe that follows, I provide the range of processing times based on varying elevations, so you'll always know how long to boil your filled jars once they are in the water bath canner.

Knowing your altitude also plays a specific role when making jams and jellies. For jams and jellies to gel once cooled, they need to reach a particular boiling point temperature. This boiling point temperature is related to altitude. (In the recipe for Low-Sugar Old-Fashioned Pioneer Berry Apple Jam, I provide the temperature you need to reach for your altitude.)

What Is the Freezer Test?

The freezer test is the best way to determine if your homemade jam will "set up" or gel when it cools down. To conduct this test, you will want to put a small clean plate in the freezer when you are making your jam. When you believe your jam is sufficiently cooked according to the recipe directions, remove the plate from the freezer, use a clean spoon to ladle some jam onto the cold plate, and then place the plate back in the freezer. After a few minutes have passed, remove the plate from the freezer and run your finger through the cold jam. If it stays parted, it has gelled and you are ready to fill your canning jars. If it seeps back together, place the plate back in the freezer, bring the jam back up to a boil, boil for a few more minutes, and then try the freezer test again.

Tips for Keeping Your Canned Goods Fresh

When you store your home-canned goods, always make sure that the bands (rings) have been removed. If a seal loosens on one of your home-canned goods while in storage, the band (ring) will cause it to reseal, but this is what is known as a *false seal.* Air has already seeped into the jar and the contents may begin to spoil.

When you open your home-canned good, nothing should spurt out from the jar, nor should there be any foul odors or signs of mold. These would all indicate that your home-canned food has spoiled and must be discarded.

Once you open your properly home-canned goods, you will need to refrigerate them. You can use the canning lid and bring back the band (ring) to keep the lid secure, or you can use plastic lids specifically made for canning jars once they are opened. These plastic lids are available in the canning section of most grocery stores and online.

Don't Get Overwhelmed, You Can Do This!

Initially, it might feel like there is a lot to learn about home canning. But once you give this a try, you will find that you develop a rhythm that will make the process rather simple. As a matter of fact, you might find yourself wanting to home can lots of foods. Seeing all those jars in your pantry can not only be delightful to look at, but it can also give you a real sense of food security.

Now that you know the basics, let's get canning! In this chapter, you'll learn how to home can jam, fruit, tomatoes, and pickles, along with some scrumptious beets and red onions. Plus, you'll learn how to make your own pectin. Now that is something every modern pioneer in the kitchen should know how to do!

Low-Sugar Old-Fashioned Pioneer Berry Apple Jam

Our ancestors made jam this way long before grocery stores sold commercial pectin. Learning how to make jam this way is an excellent skill because you never have to worry about keeping pectin on hand. Keep in mind that homemade jam made in this old-fashioned way may have a thinner consistency than you are used to from store-bought jam. However, with this recipe, we will be adding a green apple that is rich in natural pectin which will help the jam set up (gel) nicely.

This low-sugar jam allows the flavor of the berries to shine through and isn't cloyingly sweet. I promise you won't miss the sugar. And besides, I think you will feel a little bit better about making this jam, knowing that it doesn't contain 6 cups of sugar!

PREP TIME: **15 MINUTES (NOT INCLUDING THE TIME TO BRING THE WATER UP TO A BOIL)**
COOK TIME: **APPROXIMATELY 15 MINUTES**
WATER BATH PROCESSING TIME: **10–15 MINUTES**
TOTAL TIME: **APPROXIMATELY 45 MINUTES**
YIELD: **APPROXIMATELY 7 HALF-PINT JARS**

EQUIPMENT

7 half-pint (8oz) regular-mouth canning jars

7 half-pint (8oz) regular-mouth canning lids and bands

Water bath canner and supplies

Large deep pot or jam-making pot

INGREDIENTS

5 cups berries (blackberries, strawberries, raspberries, or a combination), washed and crushed

3 cups white cane sugar (Do not substitute unrefined whole cane sugar, since it might burn.)

1 medium unpeeled Granny Smith apple, cored and grated

2 tbsp bottled lemon juice (see **Cook's Notes**)

1 Place a small plate in the freezer. Prepare the water bath canner and supplies (p. 225).

2 Add the crushed berries, sugar, grated apple, and lemon juice to a large deep pot or a jam-making pot (known as a *Maslin pan*) over high heat. Bring the mixture to a full rolling boil that cannot be stirred down. Boil hard, stirring constantly, until the mixture thickens, about 15 minutes. Once the jam thickens, skim off the foam that has accumulated on the top of the jam and then turn off the heat.

3 Test the jam to determine if it has thickened to the proper consistency and will gel once canned by using a jelly or candy thermometer to see if the jam has reached the proper gelling temperature for your altitude. (See **Cook's Notes**.) Alternatively, you can use the freezer test by removing the plate from the freezer, using a clean spoon to ladle some jam onto the cold plate, and then placing the plate back in the freezer. After a few minutes have passed, remove the plate from the freezer and run your finger through the cold jam. If it stays parted, it has gelled and you are ready to fill your jars. If it seeps back together, place the plate back in the freezer, bring the jam back up to a boil and boil for a few more minutes, and then try the freezer test again.

4 Once you've determined the jam has reached the proper consistency, remove the pot from the stove and place it on a heatproof surface close to the water bath canner and supplies.

5 One at a time, remove a jar from the water bath canner using a jar lifter and pour the water from the jar back into the canner. (Be careful. The water will be very hot.)

6 Place the jar on a level surface lined with a thick dish towel and then ladle the hot jam into the hot jar, leaving a ½ inch (1.25cm) headspace. Submerge the debubbler or a flat butter knife into the jam and move it up and down to remove any air bubbles. (If the jam drops below the ¼ inch [0.65cm] headspace, add more jam to the jar.)

7 Dip a paper towel or clean rag into white vinegar and then wipe the rim of the jar.

8 Use a magnetized lid lifter to place a lid on the jar rim. Secure the jar band (ring) until it's fingertip tight (p. 224). Using the jar lifter, place the jar back into the canner.

9 Repeat until each jar is filled and placed back into the canner. Once all the jars are in the canner, make sure the tops are covered by at least 1 to 2 inches (1.25cm to 5cm) of water. (If needed, boil additional water and pour it into the canner.)

10 Bring the water in the canner up to a rolling boil. Once the water reaches a full rolling boil, put the lid on the canner and process the jars for the recommended time based on your altitude. (See **Cook's Notes**.)

11 After the specified processing time for your altitude is completed, turn off the heat and carefully remove the lid from the canner. (Open the lid away from you as there will be a significant release of steam from the canner.) Allow the jars to rest in the canner for 5 minutes.

12 After 5 minutes, remove the jars from the canner and place them on a level surface lined with a thick dish towel. (Do not tilt the jars as you remove them from the canner. Lift them straight up and out.)

13 Allow the jars to cool for 24 hours, then remove the bands. Check the lids for a proper seal by verifying that the button on the top of the lid is depressed and the lid is slightly concaved.

14 Store the jam in your pantry. Your homemade jam is now shelf stable for 12 to 18 months, depending on the canning lid manufacturer's recommendations. Once opened, your home-canned jam will need to be refrigerated. (The NCHFP advises that home-canned jams, once opened and refrigerated, will stay fresh for about 1 month. However, I have found that mine generally stay fresh for at least 3 months. But they rarely last that long!)

COOK'S NOTES

Can you use fresh lemon juice? The United States Department of Agriculture (USDA) recommends using bottled lemon juice in home canning recipes for its consistency in terms of acidity. Since there is no guarantee as to the level of acidity in the juice from a fresh lemon, it is advisable to follow the USDA guidelines.

What are the proper cooking temperatures for cooked jam to gel once cooled? Cooked jam must reach the following thermometer temperature readings based on your altitude:

- Sea level: 220°F (104°C)
- 1,000 feet: 218°F (103°C)
- 2,000 feet: 216°F (102°C)
- 3,000 feet: 214°F (101°C)
- 4,000 feet: 212°F (100°C)
- 5,000 feet: 211°F (99°C)
- 6,000 feet: 209°F (98°C)
- 7,000 feet: 207°F (97°C)
- 8,000 feet: 205°F (96°C)

(Source: *Complete Guide to Home Canning,* United States Department of Agriculture, Agriculture Information Bulletin No. 539, revised 2015.)

What are the recommended processing times for half-pint jars of jam, based on altitude?

- 0 to 1,000 feet: 5 minutes*
- 1,001 to 6,000 feet: 10 minutes
- Above 6,000 feet: 15 minutes

(Source: *Complete Guide to Home Canning,* United States Department of Agriculture, Agriculture Information Bulletin No. 539, revised 2015.)

* For jars processed under 10 minutes, it is recommended they be pre-sterilized in boiling water for 10 minutes. If your altitude is between 0 and 1,000 feet, but you would like to avoid the pre-sterilization step, simply process your jam-filled jars for 10 minutes, similar to the guidelines for 1,001 to 6,000 feet. (I am at an altitude under 1,000 feet, and I usually avoid the pre-sterilization phase and simply process my jams for 10 minutes.)

What do you do about the band (ring) if you are giving your home-canned jam as a gift? Remove the band and separately provide the band or a plastic canning jar lid for the recipient to use once the canning lid is removed and the jar is refrigerated.

Should you add vinegar to the water in the canner? Some home canners will add a bit of white vinegar to the water in their canner, believing that this will prevent a white film from developing on the canning jars during processing in areas with hard water. Although I have very hard water, I have moved away from doing this because I have found that, over time, adding vinegar to my water bath canner degrades my canning bands (rings). Instead, I simply wipe down my jars once they have cooled, and this eliminates any problem with an exterior hard water build-up.

Homemade Pectin

If we can make Berry Apple Jam without pectin, why do we need to worry about making pectin? We can always make jam without store-bought pectin, and adding a tart apple can significantly help because it is rich in natural pectin. However, an apple's not as strong as using concentrated pectin. And that is why home cooks turn to pectin, whether homemade or store-bought.

Some fruits are so low in pectin that no matter how long you cook them, they never really thicken to the gel stage. These fruits can benefit from added pectin to help with the gelling process. Apricots, different types of berries, very ripe or sweet cherries, peaches, pears, and plums can all benefit from added pectin when turning them into jam.

PREP TIME: **15 MINUTES**
COOK TIME: **1–2 HOURS**
STRAINING TIME: **12 HOURS**
REDUCING TIME: **20–30 MINUTES**
TOTAL TIME: **APPROXIMATELY 15 HOURS**
YIELD: **APPROXIMATELY 1½ CUPS**

EQUIPMENT

Large stockpot

Large bowl

Colander or large mesh strainer

Flour-sack towel or cheesecloth

Pint-size jar with tight-fitting lid

INGREDIENTS

8 cups chopped apple scraps, including peels and cores (seeds discarded) (see **Cook's Notes**)

Zest and juice of 2 large lemons (pith discarded) (see **Cook's Notes**)

Enough water to cover the apple scraps (you can use filtered water or tap water)

1   Add the apple scraps, lemon zest, and lemon juice to a large stockpot on the stovetop. Cover the contents with enough water that the apple scraps float on the surface and are no longer touching the bottom of the pot. Bring to a boil over high heat and stir.

2 Once the mixture comes to a boil, immediately reduce the heat to low. Simmer for at least 1 hour, stirring occasionally to ensure the apples don't stick to the bottom of the stockpot. (If they stick, add additional water if necessary.) Once the apple scraps soften, appear quite mushy, and darken in color (similar to applesauce), turn off the heat.

3 Line a colander (or large mesh strainer) with a flour-sack towel or cheesecloth and then place it over a large bowl.

4 Transfer the softened apple scraps to the colander and allow the liquid to drain into the bowl for 12 hours. (You can do this at room temperature, or you can place the bowl in the refrigerator. If you leave the mashed apples to drain at room temperature, cover the bowl with a flour-sack towel to prevent dust from falling into the scraps.) The liquid draining into your bowl is your unreduced homemade pectin. Do not squeeze the flour-sack towel or cheesecloth to rush the process of releasing the liquid! This will only serve to create a cloudy pectin.

5 After 12 hours, collect the liquid that has drained into the bowl and transfer it to a saucepan. Bring the pectin up to a boil over high heat and then immediately reduce the heat to low. Simmer until the contents are reduced by about half. This can take about 20 to 30 minutes, but do not rush the process. If you heat the pectin at too high a temperature for too long, it will become hard. (See **Cook's Notes**.)

6 Once the pectin has been reduced by half, use the freezer test (p. 227) to determine if the pectin is ready. If it is ready, move on to the next step. If it's not ready, allow the pectin to reduce a bit more and then try the freezer test again.

7 Once the pectin is ready and has cooled, pour it into a clean jar with a tight-fitting lid and store it in the refrigerator. It will stay fresh in the refrigerator for approximately 4 days. Alternatively, you can freeze the pectin in an ice cube tray, measuring it out into 1 tablespoon portions. Once frozen, transfer the frozen pectin cubes to a freezer-proof bag or container. When frozen, the cubes will stay fresh for approximately 6 months.

COOK'S NOTES

Making jam with homemade pectin: When you are ready to make jam, know that approximately 2 tablespoons of homemade liquid pectin are roughly equal to 4 teaspoons of commercial powdered pectin. Most packages of commercial powdered pectin contain 6 tablespoons of powdered pectin, so if the recipe calls for a full package of powdered pectin, you would use 9 tablespoons of your homemade liquid pectin. Also keep in mind that if you modify a recipe that calls for powdered pectin, the recipe will probably recommend adding the powder toward the beginning of the jam-making process. When you substitute liquid pectin, whether homemade or store-bought, you will want to add it closer to the end of the jam-making process. The jam will be brought up to a hard boil that cannot be stirred down. That's when you'll add your liquid pectin and boil the jam for 1 more minute. If the recipe calls for using liquid pectin, you can substitute your homemade liquid pectin one for one. But keep in mind that there are variations with homemade pectin, so your results might vary slightly in that your jam or jelly might be slightly looser in consistency than if you are used to using store-bought pectin, whether powdered or liquid. But generally, the results with homemade pectin should be quite satisfactory.

Collecting the best apple scraps: When making homemade pectin, the best apple scraps to use are those that come from tart green apples, such as the Granny Smith variety. If, by chance, you have a fruit called *quince* available to you, it is rich in pectin and can be used in place of apple scraps. Since quince is not eaten raw, it is an excellent choice to use for making pectin. If you do not have 8 to 9 cups of apple scraps available, freeze what you accumulate over time. Once you have a sufficient amount of scraps, you can make pectin. Frozen apple scraps work as well as fresh when making homemade pectin. You can use whole apples for this process, chopped into 1-inch (2.5cm) pieces, but I always think of this as a waste of perfectly good apples. The apple scraps are best relegated to the compost pile once you're done cooking them.

An easy way to determine how much the pectin has reduced: Submerge the handle of a wooden spoon into the pectin and lift it straight out. Tie a piece of kitchen twine on the handle of the wooden spoon halfway between the top of the spoon handle and the wet mark from the pectin. This will give you a measurement tool that you can submerge periodically into the simmering pectin to determine when the pectin has reduced by half.

Why do you discard the lemon pith? Although lemon pith (the white part under the zest) is rich in pectin, it also has a bitter taste, so it is best left out when making homemade pectin. However, do not throw it out. Instead, save it for making homemade bitters.

How to Home Can Fresh Fruit (with No Sugar)

It's easy to home can some fresh fruits without any sugar, which means you can preserve in-season fruit in its most natural state. In this recipe, I show you how to home can fresh pears, but you can also use this recipe to home can other fruits. The key to success is making sure that the fruit you are using is fresh and firm in texture. In addition to pears, other ideal fruit options for home canning are apples, apricots, nectarines, and peaches. Softer fruits, like berries, are better served by turning them into delicious jams.

PREP TIME: **1 HOUR (NOT INCLUDING THE TIME TO BRING THE WATER TO A BOIL)**
COOK TIME: **5 MINUTES**
WATER BATH PROCESSING TIME: **25–40 MINUTES**
TOTAL TIME: **APPROXIMATELY 1 HOUR 45 MINUTES**
YIELD: **APPROXIMATELY 8 QUART-SIZE JARS**

EQUIPMENT

Water bath canner and supplies
8 quart-size (32oz) wide-mouth canning jars
8 quart-size (32oz) wide-mouth canning lids and bands (rings)
Large stockpot

INGREDIENTS

About 35 ripe but firm Bartlett pears (approximately 17 to 18 pounds)
15 tbsp bottled lemon juice, divided
Tap water

1 Prepare the water bath canner and supplies (p. 225).

2 Fill a large stockpot halfway with water. (The stockpot must be large enough to hold all the pears.) Add 1 tablespoon bottled lemon juice to the water. (The lemon juice will acidulate the water and prevent the pears from browning prior to canning.) Set aside.

3 Peel the pears, remove the stems, and then slice the pears in half. Remove the core from each half. (This is easy to do with a melon baller or metal measuring spoon.) Place each half into the stockpot of acidulated water.

4 When all the pears are in the stockpot, bring the water up to a boil over high heat. Boil for 5 minutes.

5 After 5 minutes, turn off the heat, remove the stockpot from the stove, and place the stockpot on a heatproof surface close to the canner and supplies.

6 One at a time, remove a jar from the water bath canner using a jar lifter and then pour the water from the jar back into the canner. (Be careful! The water will be very hot.)

7 Place the jar on a level surface lined with a thick dish towel. Use a slotted spoon to lift the pears out of the water, fill the prepared hot canning jar with some pears, facing the pears cut-sides down into the jar. Pack the pears tightly into the jar and then add 2 tablespoons of bottled lemon juice to the jar.

8 Fill the jar with the hot acidulated water from the stockpot, leaving a ½ inch (1.25cm) headspace. Use a debubbler to release any air bubbles. Top off the jar with additional hot water, if necessary.

9 Dip a paper towel or clean rag into white vinegar and then wipe the rim of the jar.

10 Place a lid on the jar rim. Secure the jar band until it's fingertip tight (p. 224).

11 Using the jar lifter, place the jar back into the canner. Repeat with each jar until all the filled jars are placed back in the canner. If you have any extra pears, place them into the eighth jar with the water and refrigerate. (It is not necessary to add any extra bottled lemon juice to this eighth jar. Consume these pears first.)

12 Once all the jars are in the canner, make sure they are all submerged in the water by at least 1 to 2 inches (2.5 to 5cm). If needed, boil additional water and pour it into the canner.

13 Bring the water in the canner up to a rolling boil. Once the water reaches a full rolling boil, put the lid on the canner and process the jars for the recommended time based on your altitude. (See **Cook's Notes**.)

14 After the specified processing time for your altitude is complete, turn off the heat and carefully remove the lid from the canner. (Open the lid away from you as there will be a significant release of steam from the canner.) Allow the jars to rest in the canner for 5 minutes.

15 After 5 minutes, remove the jars from the canner and place them on a level surface lined with a thick dish towel. (Do not tilt the jars as you remove them from the canner. Instead, lift them straight up and out.)

16 Allow the jars to cool for 24 hours and then remove the rings. Check the lids for a proper seal by verifying that the button on the top of the lid is depressed and the lid is slightly concaved.

17 Store the home-canned pears in your pantry. Your pears are now shelf stable for 12 to 18 months, depending on the canning lid manufacturer's recommendations. Once opened, your pears will need to be refrigerated and will stay fresh for approximately 1 week.

···················· COOK'S NOTES ····················

Recommended processing times for quart-size jars of pears packed in water, based on altitude:

- 0 to 1,000 feet: 25 minutes
- 1,001 feet to 3,000 feet: 30 minutes
- 3,001 to 6,000 feet: 35 minutes
- Above 6,000 feet: 40 minutes

These processing times will also apply when water bath canning apricots, nectarines, and peaches. For apples, decrease all the processing times by 5 minutes.

(Source: *Complete Guide to Home Canning*, United States Department of Agriculture, Agriculture Information Bulletin No. 539, revised 2015.)

Do not discard the pear peels! Save the pear peels in a scrap bag in the freezer. You can add them to bone broths or vegetable broths for added nutrition. Or you can use them to make fruit scrap vinegar similar to the recipe for Raw Apple Cider Vinegar (p. 176).

How to Home Can Tomatoes

Learning how to home can tomatoes will be a boon to anyone who has a kitchen garden or finds a real bargain on a case of tomatoes at the farmer's market. Due to their higher acidity, tomatoes can be water bath canned. And with the foolproof tips and tricks I share, you'll be canning tomatoes like a pro in no time!

With this recipe, we will be canning the tomatoes whole. However, you can follow the same process if you want to home can halved tomatoes. As to tomato varieties, I have found that the best tomatoes to home can are Roma or plum tomatoes, but you can certainly experiment with other types.

PREP TIME: **60 MINUTES (NOT INCLUDING THE TIME TO BRING THE WATER TO A BOIL)**
COOK TIME: **5 MINUTES**
WATER BATH PROCESSING TIME: **45–60 MINUTES**
TOTAL TIME: **APPROXIMATELY 2 HOURS 5 MINUTES**
YIELD: **APPROXIMATELY 8 QUART-SIZE JARS**

EQUIPMENT

Large stockpot

Large bowl

Water bath canner and supplies

8 quart-size (32oz) wide-mouth canning jars

8 quart-size (32oz) wide-mouth canning lids and bands

INGREDIENTS

Tap water

About 85 Roma or plum tomatoes (approximately 21 pounds)

14 tbsp bottled lemon juice, divided

7 tsp canning and pickling salt, divided (optional) (see **Cook's Notes**)

1 Prepare the water bath canner and supplies (p. 225).

2 Place a large stockpot on the stovetop and fill it half full with water. Set the heat to medium-high and bring the water up to a soft boil.

3 While the water is coming up to a soft boil, fill a large bowl three quarters full with ice water. Set aside.

4 Once the water in the stockpot reaches a soft boil, work quickly using a slotted spoon to lower the tomatoes one at a time into the water until you have 6 to 8 tomatoes in the stockpot. Boil for 30 seconds to 1 minute or until the skins split.

5 Once the skins split, use the slotted spoon to remove the tomatoes from the boiling water and immediately plunge them into the ice water bath. Leave the tomatoes in the ice water bath for approximately 30 seconds and then remove the tomatoes from the ice water. Use a sharp paring knife to peel off the skins and cut out the stems and cores. Set the skinned tomatoes aside. Repeat the process until all the tomatoes have been processed.

6 Place all the skinned tomatoes back into the stockpot with hot water. Bring the water up to a soft boil on medium-high heat. Allow the tomatoes to gently boil for 5 minutes. (If you are working with a smaller stockpot, you will need to do this in batches.)

7 After 5 minutes, turn off the heat, remove the pot from the stove and place it on a heatproof surface close to the canner.

8 One at a time, use a jar lifter to remove a jar from the water bath and then pour the water from the jar back into the canner. (Be careful! The water will be very hot.)

9 Place the jar on a level surface lined with a thick dish towel. Use a slotted spoon to lift the tomatoes out of the water and then fill the prepared hot canning jar with tomatoes. Pack the tomatoes tightly into the jar, leaving slightly less than a ½ inch (1.25cm) headspace.

10 Add 2 tablespoons bottled lemon juice to the jar. Add 1 teaspoon canning and pickling salt to the jar (if using).

11 Fill the jar with the hot water from the stockpot which will fill in around the tomatoes. Leave a ½ inch (1.25cm) headspace when filling the jar with the hot water. Use a debubbler to release any air bubbles and then top off the jar with additional hot water, if necessary.

12 Dip a paper towel or clean rag into white vinegar and then wipe the rim of the jar.

13 Place a lid on the jar rim. Secure the jar ring until it's fingertip tight (p. 224). Using the jar lifter, place the jar back into the canner. Repeat the process with each jar until all the filled jars are placed back into the canner. (If you have any extra tomatoes, place them into the eighth jar with the water and refrigerate. It is not necessary to add any extra bottled lemon juice to this eighth jar. Consume these tomatoes first.)

14 Once all the jars are in the canner, make sure that they are all submerged under at least 1 to 2 inches (2.5 to 5cm) of water. If needed, boil additional water and pour it into the canner.

15 Bring the water in the canner up to a rolling boil. Once the water reaches a full rolling boil, put the lid on the canner and process the jars for the recommended time based on your altitude. (See **Cook's Notes**.)

16 After the specified processing time for your altitude is complete, turn off the heat and carefully remove the lid from the canner. (Open the lid away from you as there will be a significant release of steam from the canner.) Allow the jars to rest in the canner for 5 minutes.

17 After 5 minutes, remove the jars from the canner and place them on a level surface lined with a thick dish towel. (Do not tilt the jars as you remove them from the canner. Instead, lift them straight up and out.)

18 Allow the jars to cool for 24 hours and then remove the bands. Check the lids for a proper seal by verifying that the button on the top of the lid is depressed and the lid is slightly concave.

19 Store the home-canned tomatoes in your pantry. Your tomatoes are now shelf stable for 12 to 18 months, depending on the canning lid manufacturer's recommendations. Once opened, your home-canned tomatoes will need to be refrigerated and will stay fresh for approximately 1 week.

·················· COOK'S NOTES ··················

Recommended processing times for quart-size jars of tomatoes packed in water, based on altitude:

- 0 to 1,000 feet: 45 minutes
- 1,001 feet to 3,000 feet: 50 minutes
- 3,001 to 6,000 feet: 55 minutes
- Above 6,000 feet: 60 minutes

These processing times will also apply when water bath canning halved tomatoes.

(Source: *Complete Guide to Home Canning*, United States Department of Agriculture, Agriculture Information Bulletin No. 539, revised 2015.)

Always cook home-canned tomatoes! The United States Department of Agriculture recommends that water bath home-canned tomatoes always be cooked before consuming.

Should you add salt to home-canned tomatoes? This is completely optional and comes down to taste. Tomatoes can be home canned successfully with or without salt.

Do not discard the tomato skins, stems, or cores! You can dehydrate them in an oven set to its lowest setting and then pulverize them into tomato powder for use as a seasoning or making a quick tomato soup.

Bread and Butter Pickles

Just about everyone loves bread and butter pickles. They are sweet, tangy, a bit salty, and perfect for topping on hamburgers or simply served as a side dish to enjoy with any barbecued meal. But they are also ideal for topping on a salad or a sandwich.

And speaking of sandwiches, bread and butter pickle sandwiches were a favorite during the Great Depression of the 1930s. Legend holds that might be how they got their name. When money and food, especially meat, were in short supply during the Depression, pickled cucumbers were often layered between two slices of buttered bread—hence bread and butter pickles were born!

PREP TIME: **APPROXIMATELY 2 HOURS (NOT INCLUDING THE TIME TO BRING THE WATER TO A BOIL)**
COOK TIME: **1 MINUTE**
WATER BATH PROCESSING TIME: **5–15 MINUTES**
TOTAL TIME: **APPROXIMATELY 2 HOURS 20 MINUTES**
YIELD: **APPROXIMATELY 6 PINT-SIZED JARS**

EQUIPMENT

Large stockpot or saucepan

Colander

Water bath canner and supplies

6 pint-size (16oz) wide-mouth canning jars

6 pint-size (16oz) wide-mouth canning lids and bands

INGREDIENTS

Approximately 20 3-inch to 4-inch (7.50cm to 12.75cm) pickling cucumbers (about 3 pounds or 10 cups sliced)

1 medium yellow onion, peeled and thinly sliced

½ cup canning and pickling salt

3 cups white vinegar (5% acidity)

2 cups white cane sugar (see **Cook's Notes**)

2 tbsp yellow mustard seeds

2 tsp ground turmeric

2 tsp celery seeds

1 tsp ground ginger

1 tsp whole black peppercorns

1 tsp crushed red pepper (optional)

Pickle Crisp (You will need a total of five ⅛ teaspoons. This will help keep your pickles crisp during processing.)

1 Prepare the water bath canner and supplies (p. 225).

2 Place the cucumbers in a colander. Rinse under cold water, drain, and then transfer to a cutting board. Place the colander over a large bowl.

3 Remove the blossom end of each cucumber but leave the stem end intact. Cut the cucumbers crosswise into ¼-inch (0.65cm) slices and then place the slices back into the colander.

4 Add the sliced onions to the colander with the sliced cucumbers. Toss the entire mixture with the pickling salt. Allow the mixture to drain at room temperature for 1½ to 2 hours.

5 After the cucumber mixture has completed the draining process, combine the vinegar, cane sugar, mustard seeds, turmeric, celery seeds, ginger, black peppercorns, and crushed red pepper (if using) in a large nonreactive (stainless steel or enameled) saucepan or stockpot. Bring the mixture to a boil over high heat and then stir continuously until the sugar dissolves. (This liquid is the brine.)

6 Add the drained cucumbers and onions (along with any liquid that has drained into the bowl) to the saucepan or stockpot with the brine. Bring the brine back up to a boil and stir well. Once the brine comes up to a boil, turn off the heat and transfer the saucepan or stockpot to a heatproof surface close to the water canner and supplies.

7 One at a time, use a jar lifter to remove a jar from the water bath canner and then pour the water from the jar back into the canner. (Be careful! The water will be very hot.)

8 Place the jar on a level surface lined with a thick dish towel. Sprinkle ⅛ teaspoon of Pickle Crisp into the bottom of the jar.

9 Use a slotted spoon to lift the pickle slices out of the brine, fill the prepared hot canning jar with some of the pickles, and then pack the pickles tightly into the jar, leaving a ½ inch (1.25cm) headspace.

10 Fill the jar with the hot brine from the saucepan which will fill in around the cucumber slices. Leave a ½-inch headspace when filling the jar

with the hot brine. Use a debubbler to release any air bubbles and then top off the jar with additional hot brine, if necessary.

11 Dip a paper towel or clean rag into white vinegar and then wipe the rim of the jar.

12 Place a lid on the jar rim. Secure the jar ring until it's fingertip tight (p. 224). Use the jar lifter to place the jar back into the canner. Repeat the process until all the jars are filled and placed back in the canner. (If you have any extra pickles that can't fill the sixth canning jar to within a ½-inch headspace, place them into the sixth jar with the brine and refrigerate. Consume these pickles first.)

13 Once all the jars are in the canner, make sure that they are covered by at least 1 to 2 inches (2.5 to 5cm) of water. (If needed, boil additional water and pour it into the canner.)

14 Bring the water in the canner up to a rolling boil. Once the water reaches a full rolling boil, put the lid on the canner and process the jars for the recommended time based on your altitude. (See **Cook's Notes**.)

15 After the specified processing time for your altitude is complete, turn off the heat and carefully remove the lid from the canner. (Open the lid away from you as there will be a significant release of steam from the canner.) Allow the jars to rest in the canner for 5 minutes.

16 After 5 minutes, remove the jars from the canner and place them on a level surface lined with a thick dish towel. (Do not tilt the jars as you remove them from the canner. Instead, lift them straight up and out.)

17 Allow the jars to cool for 24 hours and then remove the bands. Check the lids for a proper seal by verifying that the button on the top of the lid is depressed and the lid is slightly concaved.

18 Store the home-canned bread and butter pickles in your pantry. Your pickles are now shelf stable for 12 to 18 months, depending on the canning lid manufacturer's recommendations. Once opened, your home-canned pickles will need to be refrigerated and will stay fresh for approximately 1 week.

····················· COOK'S NOTES ·····················

Reducing the sugar in this recipe: You can reduce the sugar in this recipe, but using the amount of sugar called for in the recipe will give you a flavor that's closest to the grocery store or deli bread and butter pickles.

Recommended processing times for pint-size jars of bread and butter pickles, based on altitude:

- 0 to 1,000 feet: 5 minutes*
- 1,001 to 6,000 feet: 10 minutes
- Above 6,000 feet: 15 minutes

* For jars processed under 10 minutes, it is recommended they be pre-sterilized in boiling water for 10 minutes. If your altitude is between 0 to 1,000 feet, but you would like to avoid the pre-sterilization step, simply process your bread and butter pickle–filled jars for 10 minutes, similar to the guidelines for 1,001 to 6,000 feet. (I am at an altitude under 1,000 feet, and I usually avoid the pre-sterilization phase and simply process my pickles for 10 minutes.)

(Source: *Complete Guide to Home Canning*, United States Department of Agriculture, Agriculture Information Bulletin No. 539, revised 2015.)

Pickled Red Beets and Onions

If you think you don't like beets, you just have to give these a try. My husband was definitely one of those folks who thought he didn't like beets. Now, when we get down to our last jar, he asks me when I am going to make them again! These are a bit sweet, a bit tangy, and oh so flavorful! And you will want to make sure you always have them at the ready in your pantry.

PREP TIME: **45 MINUTES (NOT INCLUDING THE TIME TO BRING THE WATER TO A BOIL)**
COOK TIME: **35–45 MINUTES**
WATER BATH PROCESSING TIME: **30–45 MINUTES**
TOTAL TIME: **APPROXIMATELY 2 HOURS 15 MINUTES**
YIELD: **APPROXIMATELY 7 PINT-SIZE JARS**

EQUIPMENT

Large stockpot

Colander

Water bath canner and supplies

7 pint-size (16oz) wide-mouth canning jars

7 pint-size (16oz) wide-mouth canning lids and bands

INGREDIENTS

Approximately 20 medium beets
  (should yield about 10 cups cubed beets)

2 large red onions, peeled and thinly sliced
  (should yield about 2 cups sliced red onions)

3 cups white vinegar (5% acidity)

1 cup tap water

1 cup white cane sugar

1 tsp whole allspice berries

1 tsp whole cloves

1 cinnamon stick

1 tbsp canning and pickling salt (optional)

1 Prepare the water bath canner and supplies (p. 225).

2 Place a large stockpot on the stovetop, fill it halfway with water, and bring it up to a boil over high heat.

3 While you are waiting for the water to boil, rinse the beets well to remove any dirt, but leave the skins on. Trim off the green tops leaving at least 2 inches (5cm) of stem. Do not remove the long tap root. (Save the greens to sauté with olive oil and enjoy as a side dish.)

4 Once the water in the stockpot is boiling, carefully lower the beets into the water and boil for approximately 20 to 30 minutes or until tender. (The variation in time will depend on the size of the beets.) Check if they are tender by inserting a knife into the flesh of the beet. The knife should insert easily. Once tender, turn off the heat.

5 Using a slotted spoon, transfer the beets to a colander in the sink and run them under cold water until they are cool enough that you can easily handle them. Once cooled, use a sharp paring knife to remove the skin and then cut off the stem and the root. Cut the beets into approximately 1-inch (2.5cm) cubes. Set aside.

6 Combine the vinegar, water, cane sugar, allspice berries, cloves, cinnamon stick, and canning and pickling salt (if using) in a large nonreactive (stainless steel or enameled) saucepan or stockpot. (If you like a sweet and salty taste, add the canning and pickling salt; if you prefer a sweeter taste, omit the salt.) Bring the mixture up to a boil over high heat. Stir continuously until the sugar dissolves, then lower the heat to medium and simmer for 15 minutes. (This liquid is the brine.)

7 After 15 minutes, use a slotted spoon or small mesh strainer to remove the spices from the brine.

8   Add the beets and the onions to the brine. Increase the heat to high and bring the brine up to a boil. Once the brine comes up to a boil, turn off the heat and transfer the saucepan to a heatproof surface close to the water bath canner and supplies.

9   One at a time, use a jar lifter to remove a jar from the water bath canner and then pour the water from the jar back into the canner. (Be careful! The water will be very hot.)

10 Place the jar on a level surface lined with a thick dish towel. Using a slotted spoon, lift some of the beets and onions out of the brine and into the prepared hot canning jar. Tightly pack them into the jar, leaving a ½ inch (1.25cm) headspace.

11 Fill the jar with the hot brine from the saucepan which will fill in around the beets and onions. Leave a ½ inch (1.25cm) headspace when filling the jar with the hot brine. Use a debubbler to release any air bubbles and then top off the jar with additional hot brine, if necessary.

12 Dip a paper towel or clean rag into white vinegar and then wipe the rim of the jar.

13 Place a lid on the jar rim. Secure the jar band until it's fingertip tight (p. 224). Use the jar lifter to place the jar back into the canner. Repeat the process until all the jars are filled and placed back in the canner.

14 If you have any extra beets and onions that can't fill the seventh canning jar to within a ½ inch (1.25cm) headspace, place them into the seventh jar with the brine and refrigerate. (Consume these beets first.)

15 Once all the jars are in the canner, make sure that they are all covered with at least 1 to 2 inches (2.5 to 5cm) of water. (If needed, boil additional water and pour it into the canner.)

16 Bring the water in the canner up to a rolling boil. Once the water reaches a full rolling boil, put the lid on the canner and process the jars for the recommended time based on your altitude. (See **Cook's Notes**.)

17 After the specified processing time for your altitude is complete, turn off the heat and carefully remove the lid from the canner. (Open the lid away from you as there will be a significant release of steam from the canner.) Allow the jars to rest in the canner for 5 minutes.

18 After 5 minutes, remove the jars from the canner and place them on a cushioned surface. (Do not tilt the jars as you remove them from the canner. Instead, lift them straight up and out.)

19 Allow the jars to cool for 24 hours and then remove the rings. Check the lids for a proper seal by verifying that the button on the top of the lid is depressed and the lid is slightly concave.

20 Store the home-canned beets in your pantry. Your beets are now shelf stable for 12 to 18 months, depending on the canning lid manufacturer's recommendations. Once opened, your home-canned beets will need to be refrigerated and will stay fresh for approximately 1 week.

···················· COOK'S NOTES ····················

Recommended processing times for pint jars of beets, based on altitude:

- 0 to 1,000 feet: 30 minutes
- 1,001 feet to 3,000 feet: 35 minutes
- 3,001 to 6,000 feet: 40 minutes
- Above 6,000 feet: 45 minutes

(Source: *Complete Guide to Home Canning*, United States Department of Agriculture, Agriculture Information Bulletin No. 539, revised 2015.)

What if you run out of brine? This should not happen, but If you find you are a few teaspoons shy of brine for your last full jar of beets and onions, mix equal parts water and vinegar in a small saucepan and bring to a boil. Add this hot liquid to top off your last full jar.

Chapter Twelve
PRESERVING FOODS BY DRYING

GETTING STARTED WITH DRYING FOODS

One of the oldest ways of preserving food is through drying, and our ancestors commonly preserved food by air-drying. As traditional home cooks in the twenty-first century, we can still air-dry our food, but we can also leverage modern technology and use ovens or electric dehydrators to do some of the job for us.

Four Methods of Drying

You can choose from four different methods to dry food. The simplest way is to use the air around us. Although air-drying is the oldest way of preserving food, it is still as useful today as it was thousands of years ago. However, there are also more efficient ways of drying food that include using an oven set to a low temperature or an electric dehydrator that uses circulating air and a low temperature to dehydrate food. The fourth way is to use a microwave, but I prefer to avoid using the microwave when I can, so the recipes in this chapter will focus on air-drying, oven-drying, and using an electric dehydrator.

Although certain recipes are best reserved for an electric dehydrator, most of the recipes in this chapter are easy to do using the air-drying method or an oven set to its lowest setting. Unfortunately, many of today's modern ovens may have a minimum temperature that is higher than previously manufactured ovens. Don't worry; you can still use ovens that have preset temperature settings between 170°F and 200°F (77°C and 93°C) to dry food. Ovens work beautifully for drying fruit, as well as certain herbs. So if you only have air and an oven with preset temperatures, you will still be able to make many of the recipes in this chapter.

When It's Best to Use a Dehydrator

When it comes to two of the recipes in this chapter that require a dehydrator, trust me, you will thank me! One involves garlic and the other onions. These are two aromatics that you do not want to dry in your oven. And even if you have a dehydrator, you will want to relocate it outdoors for these jobs. I learned this lesson the hard way!

The first time I dehydrated onions, I innocently had my dehydrator running in the laundry room. Yes, you read that correctly—the laundry room—near all the clean and neatly folded baskets of clothes. I thought I was so smart closing the laundry room door so as not to have to listen to the hum of the dehydrator all day long. Come evening, I opened the door and was assaulted with the pungent aroma of onion. It's not that onions smell bad, but they smell strong. The smell wafted out of the laundry room, permeated the rest of the house, and it lingered for weeks. Not to mention that it took several rewashings before I could get that smell out of the clothes!

The good news is that a dehydrator is a very lightweight appliance, so on good weather days it's easy to tote outside and use it to dry onions and garlic to my heart's content. And maybe this is why our ancestors were fond of tying up their onions and garlic, allowing them to dry either in the barn or outside when the weather was favorable.

Shopping for a Dehydrator

Once you start drying food for your pantry, you'll find that having dried food comes in handy. This will lead you to want to dehydrate more and more food! And if you've only been relying on air-drying or using your oven, you may want to consider buying an actual dehydrator to make dehydrating more efficient and time-saving.

The price of dehydrators varies widely. The various models provide the same dehydrating function. However, some models do the job a little better than others, hence the higher price tags. As you shop for a dehydrator, read the reviews and look for sales to find the manufacturer, model, and price you like. There is no need to buy the best model right away. Instead, work up to the higher-end models if you find yourself dehydrating food frequently. In the interim, a mid-priced model will serve you very well.

And you'll definitely want to check out thrift stores if you are in the market for a dehydrator. Often, shopping for this appliance shortly after Christmas can help you save money. Dehydrators can be popular holiday gifts, but sadly, some home cooks lose interest in them—or never even take them out of the box! So keep your eyes peeled for a used one or one that might still be brand-new the next time you are out thrifting.

Purchasing a dehydrating machine is an investment in your traditional foods kitchen and gives you the ability to dehydrate a wider range of foods. As I mentioned earlier, you can use it indoors for most of your dehydrating needs, and for more pungent foods, you can easily move your dehydrator outside on a clear day to take care of your onions and garlic.

Helpful Dehydrator Supplies

In addition to purchasing a dehydrator, you'll want to add a few helpful supplies. For drying very small items, silicone mats or large plastic discs can help keep your items contained and prevent them from slipping through the mesh drying racks. In a pinch, you can use parchment paper, but having reusable items cuts down on waste.

I also consider having a selection of various-size jars, in which to store your dehydrated foods, to be an essential part of your supplies. My favorite is a glass jar with a clamp lid lined with a gasket. You can often find these jars at thrift stores. (Don't worry if the gasket is missing. You can easily find replacements at small hardware stores and online.) And of course, you can always make your home-canning jars do double duty by using a spent (used) canning lid and band (ring) to store your dehydrated foods.

If you live in a humid climate, silica gel packs would be another useful addition to your dehydrating supplies. You can often find these packs at health food stores, sometimes at a pharmacy, and of course, online. Silica gel packs help absorb moisture and keep your foods dry when they are placed in a jar with your dehydrated foods.

Drying Sourdough Starter

A perfect candidate for air-drying is your sourdough starter. It might sound funny to think about drying a sourdough starter, but once you have a successful starter going, drying a portion of it is one of the wisest things you can do. If your starter goes bad for any reason, you can rehydrate your dried starter and have it ready and bubbling within a few days.

A fellow home baker once shared a story with me that when she was moving, she dropped the jar that held her starter. It crashed onto the kitchen floor, with the starter and glass flying everywhere. The starter was finished! But she wasn't disheartened because she knew she had previously dried and stored her starter safely in her pantry. She carefully packed up that dried starter and rehydrated it once she arrived at her new kitchen.

You never know what can happen to that sourdough starter you worked so hard to get going and now lovingly maintain. Knowing that we have an insurance policy with dried starter in our pantry provides peace of mind to all of us who love baking sourdough bread.

Drying Low-Moisture and High-Moisture Herbs

Certain herbs, like lavender and rosemary, lend themselves beautifully to air-drying since they are low-moisture herbs. And your kitchen will certainly look like a pioneer kitchen with herbs tied together and hanging from hooks or beams. However, you need to dry high-moisture herbs like basil and chives quickly to avoid the development of mold. An oven set to a low temperature or an electric dehydrator both work well when drying high-moisture herbs.

Drying Citrus

You can easily dry citrus in an oven set to its lowest temperature. Can you use an electric dehydrator for this job? Definitely, but since the oven does a superb job with this task, I like to keep my dehydrator free for other jobs where it is specifically needed. Once you start drying citrus, you will find that having what looks like stained glass gems in your pantry will be a delightful addition to your traditional foods kitchen.

You can use dried citrus in a variety of ways, and one of the simplest and most enjoyable is to place a few dehydrated lemon or orange slices into a teacup and fill the cup with boiling water. After steeping for a few minutes, you will have a tasty, caffeine-free tea that is rich in vitamin C and includes all the antioxidants in the peel. Add a drop of honey and you've made a comforting drink whenever you are fighting a cold.

The Comfort of Dried Apples

When I was growing up, my mom would dry different fall fruits in her oven. She preferred to avoid eating certain raw fruits, like apples, since she thought they might be difficult to digest. When my mom arrived home with a couple of bushels of fresh apples from the fruit stands that dotted our New York countryside, she would quickly dry the fruit, first as a space saver, and second to extend its shelf life.

Then, every morning, she would reconstitute some of those dehydrated apples on the stovetop by simmering them in water along with a cinnamon stick or two or maybe some cloves or a star anise. Once well simmered and tender, the rehydrated and now cooked fruit was ready to be used to top hot cereal. Sometimes, we just enjoyed them warm in a bowl on a chilly morning, topped with a dollop of homemade yogurt or a splash of fresh cream.

One of my favorite afternoon snacks when I got home from school was dried apples. They were sweet and chewy and as close to candy as fruit can be. And from my smart mom's perspective as a busy homemaker, they were a lot easier to make than fruit leather!

The Benefits of Dried Foods

Learning how to dry vegetables, fruits, herbs, and even your sourdough starter can be very rewarding. Filling up your pantry with these treasures is also very reassuring when you place dried foods in your pantry next to your home canned goods. Having these two streams of food—both dried and home canned—provides you with a welcome source of food security when illness strikes or when severe weather prevents you from getting to the grocery store. Most importantly, when budgets are tight, and monies may simply not be available

to stock your pantry, you can rely on your different streams of food. You'll be prepared, and your pantry will be well-stocked thanks to the time you spent drying and home-canning food.

Each type of dried food fills a different niche. Some serve as a backup if mishaps occur, such as with a lost sourdough starter. While others allow you to preserve a bountiful harvest, whether from your garden, the farmers' market, or the grocery store. Being able to preserve fresh herbs and spices, as well as vegetables and fruits, will help see you through those cooler months when fresh food may not be readily available.

Ensuring Your Food Is Sufficiently Dried

Once you think your food (fruit, herbs, etc.) is dry, put it in a storage container, but do not rush to get it into your pantry. Instead, leave the container with the dehydrated item where you can observe it out of direct sunlight for at least a few days to ensure that no condensation develops in the container. If you see moisture, this means that your item is not fully dried, and you'll want to return it to whatever original method you used to finish drying it thoroughly.

The only exception to this test is when you are drying apples or other fruit that retains pliability, such as pears. I like to keep dried fruit tender and malleable so that it is pleasant to eat. It will not be wet, but it may be moist, so I always recommend immediately storing these types of dehydrated fruit in the refrigerator.

How to Dry Fresh Herbs

Drying fresh herbs is probably one of the easiest traditional skills to learn. And once you start, you'll stop buying basic dried herbs because you will be pleasantly surprised at how green and colorful your home-dried herbs will be. Best of all, your home-dried herbs will taste more intense than anything you can purchase. Herbs are easy to grow, whether in small pots on a sunny windowsill or in your kitchen garden. And like so many things you will make in your traditional foods kitchen, there is nothing like homegrown and home dried!

PREP TIME: **15 MINUTES**
DRYING TIME: **7–14 DAYS (IF AIR-DRYING) OR 2–4 HOURS (IF USING AN OVEN OR DEHYDRATOR)**
TOTAL TIME: **VARIES**
YIELD: **VARIES**

INGREDIENTS

Fresh herbs that have been harvested before they have flowered (see **Cook's Notes**)

EQUIPMENT (AIR-DRYING)

6–8 clean, lint-free dish towels
   (such as flour-sack towels or other thin cotton towels)
Rubber bands
Paper bags

EQUIPMENT (OVEN OR ELECTRIC FOOD DEHYDRATOR)

6–8 clean, lint-free dish towels (such as flour-sack towels or other thin cotton towels)
Baking sheet (half-size sheet pan) (for the oven)
Parchment paper or silicone baking mats (for the oven)
Electric food dehydrator or oven
Silicone drying mats or parchment paper (for the dehydrator)

PREPARATION

1 On a flat surface, set out at least three large clean, lint-free dish towels, such as flour sack towels or other thin cotton towels. (You'll want to have at least three towels covered with herbs since they dry down to a much smaller amount.)

2 Gently rinse the fresh herbs under cool running water to remove any dust, dirt, or debris.

3 Gently shake off any excess water and place the herbs, well spaced, onto a clean towel. Continue this process until all the herbs are clean and drying on the towels.

4 Place additional clean, lint-free dish towels on top of the damp herbs and pat gently until the herbs are completely dry.

AIR-DRYING

1 With the herbs still on their stems, gather no more than six stems and tie the stems together with a rubber band.

2 If your kitchen is not very sunny, hang the herbs upside down in a warm, well-ventilated area that is out of direct sunlight.

3 If your kitchen is very sunny, place the tied herbs upside down in a brown paper bag and secure the bag closed with a second rubber band. Tear a few small holes in the body of the bag to allow for ventilation and then hang the bag right side up.

4 Check the herbs every few days. They are dry when they easily crumble at your touch. (This can take anywhere from 7 to 14 days.)

OVEN OR ELECTRIC FOOD DEHYDRATOR

1 If using an oven, line the baking sheet with parchment paper or a silicone baking mat. If using an electric dehydrator, line the mesh drying trays with dehydrator silicone mats or parchment paper that has been cut to fit the trays.

2 For herbs that have larger leaves, like basil, remove the leaves from the stems and place the leaves on the prepared baking sheet or drying trays. For herbs with small leaves, like thyme, leave the leaves on the stems and place them directly on the baking sheet or drying trays. (You can then remove the leaves once they are dry.)

3 If using an oven, set it to its lowest heat level and place the baking sheet on the middle rack of the oven. (You can add additional baking sheets of herbs to your oven, but you will need to rotate the baking sheets every hour.) Dry for 2 to 4 hours, checking the herbs every hour to determine if they are sufficiently dried. (The process should generally take no more than 4 hours.)

4 If using a dehydrator, you can fill as many dehydrator levels as your appliance will hold. Set the dehydrator temperature to 95°F (35°C) if you live in an arid climate, 115°F (46°C) if you live in a moderate climate, or 125°F (52°C) if you live in a very damp or humid climate. Dry for 2 to 4 hours, checking the herbs every hour to determine if they are sufficiently dried. (The process should generally take no more than 4 hours.)

5 Once the herbs are completely dry, remove the leaves from the stems if they are still on their stems. Crumble the leaves of the dried herbs and store them separately by individual herb in airtight containers in a cool dark pantry or cabinet. Most home-dried herbs will stay fresh for 1 to 2 years.

COOK'S NOTES

Choosing herbs for drying: You can air-dry low-moisture herbs, but high-moisture herbs are best dried in an oven or electric dehydrator to prevent the development of mold.

Low-moisture herbs: bay leaves, dill, lavender, marjoram, oregano, rosemary, sage, savory (summer and winter varieties), thyme.

High-moisture herbs: basil, chives, cilantro, lemon balm, mint, parsley, tarragon.

Can you dry herbs outdoors? You can dry herbs, preferably low-moisture herbs, outdoors if you have warm, dry weather and a well-ventilated area. However, keep your herbs out of direct sunlight since the sun can damage the essential oils contained in herbs, which will affect their flavor once dry.

Shelf-Stable Homemade Mirepoix

Mirepoix is a French word to describe a fresh mixture of carrots, celery, and onions cut into small pieces and used together as a base for many delicious dishes. Under normal circumstances, you would sauté this mixture in a bit of butter until all the pieces are softened and then add the rest of your ingredients to create your meal.

But what a time-saver it will be to be able to scoop out some dehydrated mirepoix and toss it into a pan in less time than it would take to remove the carrots from the refrigerator! As you prepare your dish, the dehydrated mirepoix will rehydrate, and no one will know that you didn't start your recipe with fresh aromatics.

PREP TIME: **20 MINUTES**
DRYING TIME: **10–14 HOURS**
TOTAL TIME: **10–14 HOURS PLUS 20 MINUTES**
YIELD: **12 CUPS**

EQUIPMENT
Electric food dehydrator
6 silicone drying mats or parchment paper

INGREDIENTS
8 medium carrots (similar in thickness), peeled
8 medium celery stalks, leaves removed
4 medium yellow onions, peeled

1 Line the dehydrator trays with silicone dehydrator mats or parchment paper (cut to size). Set aside.

2 Peel the carrots and onions. Set aside. (Save the peels and skins for your scrap bag.)

3 Fill a large bowl halfway with water and ice cubes. Set aside.

4 Place a large saucepan filled halfway with water over high heat. Bring the water to a boil. Blanch the whole carrots in the boiling water for 5 minutes and then turn off the heat. Remove the carrots from the water using tongs or a large slotted spoon and then submerge them in the ice water.

5 Cut the blanched carrots, peeled onions, and celery into even-size dice. (Alternatively, you can grate the carrots, celery, and onions on a box grater or use the grater attachment of a food processor.)

6 Divide the carrots between two lined dehydrator trays, divide the celery between two lined dehydrator trays, and then divide the onions between two lined dehydrator trays. (Do not mix different vegetable types on the same dehydrator tray since the vegetable types may dry at different times.)

7 Place the dehydrator trays into the dehydrator and set the temperature at 125°F (52°C). The carrots, celery, and onions (the aromatics) will need 10 to 14 hours to dry completely. (The onions will most likely take the longest time to dry.)

8 At between 5 to 7 hours of drying time, check on the aromatics and move them around on the trays.

9 Check on them at again at 10 hours. Some of the aromatics may take longer to dry. If any of the trays contain completely dry carrots, celery, or onions, remove the trays from the dehydrator. Continue to allow the remaining aromatics to dry completely.

10 To test for doneness, the carrots and celery should be quite hard and feel like small pebbles. The onions should have the appearance of paper and be pliable.

11 Once all of the aromatics are sufficiently dry, combine them in a large bowl. Toss until well combined and then transfer to an airtight jar. Store in a cool, dark pantry or cabinet. This mirepoix is best used within 1 year.

.... COOK'S NOTES ....

Rehydrating the mirepoix: To rehydrate, add the mirepoix to any recipe that includes some liquid to assist in the rehydration process. This mirepoix works best when used in soups, stews, or casseroles.

How to Dry and Revive a Thriving Sourdough Starter

Having a thriving sourdough starter is a boon to the traditional foods kitchen. Once you develop a rhythm of feeding your sourdough starter, it's fairly easy to maintain. But what if something happens to it, and it's not thriving anymore? You won't have to worry about creating a new starter from scratch if you've previously dehydrated some of your starter and stored it away in your pantry!

Did you know that gold prospectors in Alaska used their sourdough starter discard to plug up holes in their drafty cabins? Then, if anything happened to their original starter, they just chipped out some of the sourdough plugs, revived them, and returned to baking sourdough bread in no time!

PREP TIME: **APPROXIMATELY 4 HOURS**
DEHYDRATING TIME: **12–48 HOURS**
TOTAL TIME: **16–52 HOURS**
YIELD: **½ CUP–1 CUP DRIED SOURDOUGH STARTER PIECES**

EQUIPMENT

Large baking sheet

Parchment paper

INGREDIENTS

1–2 cups sourdough starter discard

2–4 cups flour (any variety)

2-4 cups filtered, chlorine-free water

Additional flour and water to reconstitute dehydrated starter

1   Line a large baking sheet with parchment paper. Set aside.

2   Feed your sourdough starter with 1 to 2 cups of flour and an equal amount of water before removing any discard.

3   Allow your sourdough starter enough time to begin to become bubbly. (This may take approximately 4 hours.)

4   Once the starter has reached this beginning bubbly stage, remove 1 to 2 cups of discard.

5   Set the discard aside, feed your original starter once again with 1 to 2 cups of flour and an equal amount of water, and then return your starter to the place where you usually store it.

6   Spread the discard as thinly as possible across the parchment paper.

7   Place the uncovered baking sheet in a well-ventilated area and allow the sourdough starter to air-dry. (This can take from 12 to 48 hours.) If you live in an exceptionally damp or humid area, you may want to place your baking sheet into your turned-off oven with a pilot light or an electric light turned on.

8   Once the sourdough starter is dry, break it into small pieces and store it in an airtight jar. (Alternatively, you can pulverize the pieces using a spice grinder.) In this form, the shelf life of your dried sourdough starter is basically unlimited, but as a safeguard, you might want to prepare a new dried sourdough starter once per year.

9   To reconstitute your dehydrated sourdough starter, add the small pieces or the ground pieces to a jar. Add 1 to 2 cups of water and mix until you have a mixture that resembles pancake batter.

10 Feed your new starter every 12 hours by first removing some discard and then adding equal amounts of flour and water. It can take 2 to 3 days to wake up your starter to a point where it is bubbly and ready to bake with.

Homemade No-Peel Garlic Powder

Garlic skins contain lots of nutrition, including vitamins A and C and antioxidants, so you don't need to peel garlic when you are planning on using it to make a homemade garlic powder. However, when it comes to garlic, this is one of the few times I will recommend that you only buy organic garlic if you do not grow your own. Look for organic garlic that has not been bleached (to improve its appearance) or sprayed with chemicals (to prevent it from sprouting). You want to use garlic that's in its most natural state.

PREP TIME: **30 MINUTES**
DRYING TIME: **8–10 HOURS**
TOTAL TIME: **8–10 HOURS PLUS 30 MINUTES**
YIELD: **1 CUP GARLIC POWDER**

EQUIPMENT

Electric food dehydrator
Silicone drying mats or parchment paper
Spice grinder

INGREDIENTS

15 medium heads (or bulbs) of garlic (preferably organic)

1 Slice off the root of each head of garlic.

2 Separate the individual garlic cloves but leave them unpeeled.

3 Smash the cloves with the flat side of a chef's knife and then give them a rough chop. (Alternatively, you can run them through a food processor using the pulse option a few times.)

4 Divide the chopped cloves among four dehydrator trays lined with silicone drying mats or parchment paper. Spread the chopped cloves as thinly as possible. Place the dehydrator trays into the dehydrator.

5 Set the dehydrator temperature to 125°F (52°C).

6 Dehydrate the garlic for approximately 8 to 10 hours or until completely dry.

7 Check the garlic halfway through the dehydrating process and stir it around on the mat to help it dry evenly.

8 Once the garlic is completely dry, it will feel crisp. If it is not crisp, continue to dehydrate it for an additional hour or longer. Once completely dry, pulverize the dehydrated garlic in batches in a spice grinder or blender.

9 Once pulverized, use a mesh strainer to sift the garlic powder into a bowl to remove any pieces of garlic skin that have not turned into a powder.

10 Store the garlic powder in a jar with an airtight lid in a cool, dark pantry or cabinet. The garlic powder will be most potent when used within 1 year.

COOK'S NOTES

Where should you use your dehydrator for drying garlic? Because garlic can have a strong smell while dehydrating, you may want to find a nice spot outdoors to use your dehydrator for this recipe. I usually store and use my dehydrator in my laundry room, but when it comes to dehydrating garlic or onions, I quickly learned to wait for a day with good weather so I could move my dehydrator to an outside patio table.

A note as to the texture of this garlic powder: This garlic powder may not pulverize as finely as store-bought garlic powder, but this process is much easier than peeling the cloves from 15 heads of garlic. Plus, the flavor will be much fresher than anything you can buy at the grocery store.

How to Dry Citrus and Citrus Peel

Having dried citrus on hand gives you lots of options in your traditional foods kitchen. For example, you can use it to make tea, decorate cakes, and add it to a charcuterie board mingled with crackers for a unique taste treat.

If you don't have fresh citrus peels in your refrigerator, you can use your dried citrus peels to make digestive bitters. Plus, if you separate the zest from the pith, you can dry the zest by itself and have the perfect ingredient for adding citrus flavor to baked goods and savory dishes.

PREP TIME: **15 MINUTES**
DRYING TIME: **4–8 HOURS**
TOTAL TIME: **4–8 HOURS PLUS 15 MINUTES**
YIELD: **80–90 DRIED ORANGE SLICES (ABOUT 7 SLICES PER ORANGE). (YIELD WILL BE LESS FOR SMALLER CITRUS, SUCH AS LEMONS AND LIMES, AND HIGHER FOR LARGER CITRUS, SUCH AS GRAPEFRUITS.)**

EQUIPMENT

3 baking sheets (half-size sheet pans) with cooling racks

Parchment paper

INGREDIENTS

12 medium oranges or other citrus fruit, including lemons, limes, or grapefruits

1 Line three baking sheets with parchment paper and then place a cooling rack on each baking sheet. Set aside.

2 Preheat the oven to 175°F (79°C).

3 Wash and dry whole unpeeled citrus and then slice thinly into even ¼-inch (0.65cm) slices. (If using grapefruits, halve or quarter each slice for smaller pieces.)

4 Place the slices on the cooling racks. Continue until the cooling racks are full.

5 Place the baking sheets into the preheated oven. After 2 hours, rotate the baking sheets to different oven racks, checking to ensure that no citrus slices are sticking to the cooling racks. If they are sticking, loosen them.

6 After 4 hours, check the citrus slices again. If the slices feel hard and the interior fruit has taken on an appearance similar to stained glass, they are most likely dry. Take one citrus slice and try to snap it in half. If it is crisp and snaps in half easily, it is dry.

7 If the citrus slices do not appear to be dry, once again rotate the baking sheets to different racks and allow the slices to dry for up to 4 more hours or until they achieve a crisp consistency.

8 Once the citrus slices are dried, remove them from the oven and set them aside to cool.

9 Once completely cooled, transfer the dried slices to an airtight container. Store them in a cool, dark pantry or cabinet. Dried citrus slices are optimal in flavor when used within 6 months.

···················· COOK'S NOTES ····················

What if the preset lowest temperature on my oven is 200°F (93°C)? If you can't set your oven to 175°F (79°C) and if the lowest setting you have is 200°F (93°C), don't worry, you can still dehydrate citrus in your oven. However, how long it takes and how long the slices will retain their color will vary, but they will still be flavorful when rehydrated. Place the baking sheets into the preheated oven. After 2 hours, rotate the baking sheets to different oven racks, checking to ensure that no citrus slices are sticking to the cooling racks. If they are sticking, loosen them. When drying citrus at 200°F (93°C), begin checking the slices for dryness at the 3-hour mark.

How to oven-dry and store citrus peel: If you want to dry and store citrus peel in addition to drying and storing sliced citrus, simply follow the steps in the main recipe. The only difference will be that thin citrus peel might dry slightly quicker than the sliced citrus whereas thick citrus peel (as from navel-type oranges) might take slightly longer to dry than the sliced citrus.

How to oven-dry and store zest: If you find you have a lot of citrus peels after making a recipe calling for peeled citrus, you can dry the zest. When making a citrus-based recipe where you will not be using the peel, finely zest the citrus peel first. The zest is easy to air-dry by spreading it out on a parchment-lined baking sheet and placing it in a warm, well-ventilated area. Periodically toss the zest with your clean hands. This method will take a few days, but it will guarantee the most intense color. (It's unlikely that mold will develop because the concentration of citrus oils in the zest serves as a deterrent.)

If you want to oven-dry the zest, place the zest on the parchment-lined baking sheet and put the baking sheet into an oven that is turned off but has a pilot light or an electric light turned on. If dried in a cold oven, the zest will dry within 12 hours. If you want to rush the process, you can dry zest in an oven set to 170°F (77°C). If your oven only goes as low as 200°F (93°C), you can still dehydrate the zest, but keep a close eye on it to ensure that it doesn't brown. The zest will be dry in 30 minutes to 1 hour. The cooler your drying temperature, the more intense your zest color will be.

Once dry, store your zest in an airtight container in a cool, dark pantry or cabinet. You can use dried zest in a variety of dishes, but you can also grind the zest into a powder and add it to salt or sugar to make citrus salts and sugars.

How to oven-dry and store pith: The pith is best dried in an oven set to a temperature between 170°F and 200°F (77°C and 93°C). Once dry, store in an airtight container in a cool, dark pantry or cabinet. Your dried pith is best reserved for when making homemade digestive bitters.

How to Dry Apple Slices

When autumn arrives and apples are plentiful, it's the perfect time to dry them in the oven. They make a tasty snack, and you can use them to make a quick apple pie without needing to slice up fresh apples. But best of all, you can thread the dried apple slices on some string to make, in essence, an apple garland. It will make you feel like you are living on a pioneer farm!

PREP TIME: **15 MINUTES**
DRYING TIME: **6 HOURS**
TOTAL TIME: **6 HOURS PLUS 15 MINUTES**
YIELD: **APPROXIMATELY 80–90 DRIED APPLE SLICES (7 SLICES PER APPLE)**

EQUIPMENT

3 large baking sheets with cooling racks

Parchment paper

2 clean, lint-free dish towels

INGREDIENTS

Enough tap water to cover the apples

½ cup apple cider vinegar

12 apples (any variety)

Ground cinnamon (optional)

1. Line three baking sheets with parchment paper and place a cooling rack on each baking sheet. Set aside.

2. Preheat the oven to 200°F (93°C).

3. Fill a large bowl with tap water and then add the vinegar. (This mixture makes a solution of acidulated water that will prevent the apples from browning.)

4. One at a time, core and then peel the apples (or leave them unpeeled). Slice into ¼-inch (0.65cm) thick slices and then place the slices into the acidulated water.

5. When all the apples are sliced, remove the apples from the water in groups and blot between the dish towels to remove any excess water.

6. Place the slices on the cooling racks. Continue until the cooling racks are full. Sprinkle the apple slices lightly with the cinnamon (if using).

7. Place the baking sheets in the preheated oven. After 3 hours, rotate the baking sheets to different oven racks, checking to ensure that no slices are sticking to the cooling racks. (If they are sticking, turn them over.)

8. After an additional hour, check the apple slices to see if they are dry by squeezing a slice between your fingers. If they are malleable but no longer releasing moisture, they are sufficiently dried. (The complete process can take up to 6 hours.) Once the slices are dried to the desired consistency, remove them from the oven and set them aside to cool.

9. Once completely cooled, transfer the apple slices to an airtight container and place them in the refrigerator. The slices have a shelf life of approximately 6 months. (See **Cook's Notes**.)

> ### COOK'S NOTES
>
> ***Making an apple string:*** You can also collect the apple slices on a string, transfer the collection to an airtight container, and store the container in the refrigerator. Presented in this way, they make a charming display on a dessert table or charcuterie platter.
>
> ***Can you store dried apples at room temperature?*** Certain dried fruits store better at room temperature than others. However, dried apples can begin to take on moisture when stored at room temperature, so that is why I recommend refrigerating them. Refrigeration will keep your dried apples the freshest the longest, as well as prevent the development of mold.

Chapter Thirteen
SWEETS AND TREATS

GETTING STARTED WITH SWEETS AND TREATS

No cookbook would be complete without a chapter sharing a few sweets and treats. Although we want to enjoy these in moderation, the good news is that most of the desserts here are made with whole sweeteners, as opposed to white sugar. And for most of the recipes, I cut back on the traditional amount of sugar—any sugar—used to make these recipes. The extra sugar is not needed, thanks to the whole grain flours I use. These flours improve the nutritional profile and lend a certain sweetness to the dough. But don't worry. Just because I cut back on the sugar and use whole grain flour doesn't mean that these baked goods are lacking in flavor. You'll find each recipe to be a tasty treat that all will enjoy.

Baking with Whole Grain Flours

If you have been experimenting with making sourdough bread using whole-grain spelt flour and have enjoyed the taste, you will be pleased to see that a number of the recipes in this chapter are made with spelt flour. It is one of my favorite ancient grains to bake with because it reacts like modern-day whole wheat flour when making cookies and cakes. But because it is an ancient grain and lower in gluten than modern-day whole wheat flour, spelt can create tender baked goods much in the way whole wheat pastry flour does. So when you stock whole grain spelt flour, you have access to a flour that can do double duty for you in recipes calling for whole wheat flour or whole wheat pastry flour.

And keep in mind, if you find yourself baking with spelt flour on a regular basis, it makes sense to start stocking the actual whole grain spelt in your pantry. When in its whole-grain form, it has a very long shelf life. You will need a grain mill to grind your whole grain, but that mill will become one of your beloved appliances if you find yourself becoming an avid home baker!

Baking with Whole Sweeteners

Depending on where you are in creating your traditional foods kitchen, you may just be starting to add whole sweeteners to your pantry. These sweeteners are more nutritious than white cane sugar because they still maintain all their nutrients. One of my favorite whole sweeteners is unrefined whole cane sugar. This is sugar cane juice that has simply been dried. All the molasses is still intact, which makes it very nutritious. If this dried sugar cane juice were processed in a way to strip out all the nutrients (and in some cases bleach it), you would have modern-day white cane sugar. So beginning to incorporate unrefined whole cane sugar into your baking will add nutrients to your baked goods, and it will also add lots of rich flavor that's perfect for some of the sweet treats I share with you here.

Other whole sweeteners include honey, maple syrup, coconut syrup, date syrup, and all their dried counterparts. Although for everyday baking, I like to use unrefined whole cane sugar; maple sugar is a real treat to use now and again. And don't forget, if you are right at the beginning of your traditional foods journey, and all you have in your pantry is white cane sugar, that's okay. Remember that this is a journey, and you will begin to incorporate whole sweeteners into your pantry little by little. The recipes I share here are flexible. You can substitute white cane sugar in any of the recipes calling for unrefined whole cane sugar.

A Perpetual Homemade Vanilla Extract Flavoring

In the first recipe in this chapter, I share an easy technique for making your own homemade vanilla extract flavoring. Many baked goods often call for this ingredient, so it's essential to have a good supply on hand. Unfortunately, as we have seen in the past, it may be hard to find vanilla extract in the store, or it can be quite expensive. But after your initial investment in the vanilla beans, you will have close to what I like to call a "perpetual vanilla extract"—perpetual in the sense that those initial vanilla beans will create a flavorful vanilla extract for years to come.

When It's Time to Fill the Cookie Jar

Every modern pioneer in the kitchen needs to have a few flavorful cookie recipes in their repertoire. The two I share in this chapter are favorites in our home. One is a simple drop cookie that is also hearty, thanks to the fact that it is chock-full of oatmeal, chocolate chips, nuts, and even shredded coconut! The second is a homemade cinnamon graham cracker. When I was a child, cinnamon graham crackers were my favorite cookies. They also became my son's favorite when he was a little boy, and they are still his favorite cookie to this day! You will be pleasantly surprised that making this type of cookie is easier than you might think. The recipe dough is very pliable and easy to roll out, so you may find yourself making these time and time again.

Tried-and-True Traditional Desserts

Some of my favorite desserts are those that date back centuries. Traditional cultures continue to enjoy these tried-and-true classics in one form or another. Each culture has some variation on these classic recipes. And each family within a culture often has some version of these recipes that is similar yet different to that of another family.

Take bread pudding, for example. Food historians believe this recipe dates back over one thousand years and may have originated in England, where housewives would soak stale bread in hot water and mix it with spices. But that said, many other countries also have their own versions of bread pudding, with equally ancient roots. In Mexico, bread pudding takes on a sweet and savory character with cheese and brown sugar. In Egypt, there are a variety of bread puddings, including one made with puff pastry. And in India, bread pudding takes on a unique flavor where the bread is mixed with saffron, rosewater, and almonds. Even within those basic recipes, many families make them their own by adding that special or secret ingredient that many a home cook tucks away in a little recipe box to be passed down to future generations. So, even though I share my family's bread pudding recipe with you, you will make it your own over time, adding a bit of this or a touch of that. Before you know it, you will have created your own family version of bread pudding that will become a treasured recipe requested time and time again by family and friends. The bread pudding recipe I share in this book uses the sourdough bread you created in earlier recipes. You may have saved various leftover sourdough bread pieces over time or have a partial boule that you can cut up to use in the bread pudding recipe.

When "Dowdy" Is a Compliment

If you have ever shied away from making an apple pie because you were worried that the crust just wouldn't turn out right, an apple pandowdy is for you! I find the dessert name so amusing because the word *dowdy* implies that this is a frumpy dessert. It's anything but! This is one of the tastiest apple pies you will ever make, thanks to the mixture of apple pie juices and a dowdy crust that together creates a caramel-like topping that can't be beat.

The term *dowdy* might give you a hint that the pie crust for this dessert requires no special skill—the more dowdy or

messy your crust, all the better. You really can't make this crust wrong, so I can say with 100 percent certainty that this is a foolproof crust for the beginner and experienced baker too! First, you'll put a messy crust on top of your pie, and then you will start dowdying your pie crust during the baking process by breaking it up with a knife and pressing it into the bubbling apple juices!

This apple pie is fun to make because who doesn't like the idea of throwing together a few ingredients and creating something that, when brought to the table, will be met with *oohs* and *ahhhs*. Like bread pudding, this old-fashioned recipe is sheer comfort food at its best, and your family will clamor for it time and time again. Plus, you don't have to limit yourself to making a pandowdy with just apples. Experiment with any fruit in season, from peaches to pears and even berries. There is no wrong way to make a delicious pandowdy.

The Art of the Cinnamon Roll

It can be tough to walk past a bakery with the smell of cinnamon wafting onto the sidewalk without popping in, especially if that cinnamon is wrapped in layers of pillowy soft dough. Yes, those are cinnamon rolls that I'm talking about, and they have to be just about everyone's favorite sweet roll!

When I was a child, my mom frequently graced our Saturday morning breakfast table with homemade cinnamon rolls. Sometimes they had a cream cheese frosting, and other times she would simply drizzle honey across the top and call them "honey buns." Those were such a sweet and sticky treat that my dad would often check the freezer come Saturday night to see if my mom had stashed away any leftovers for future breakfasts. Even partially frozen, we all agreed that they were out-of-this-world delicious!

If you have never made cinnamon rolls, I think you will be pleasantly surprised to learn that they are easier to make than they look, especially since we are going to use a sourdough starter to make the dough. The long rise will do most of the kneading for you, removing much of the work. Once your rolls are baked, you can drizzle them with honey for a unique taste, but I also share how to make a frosting using your Mock Cream Cheese (p. 74). Either way, you will not be disappointed with the taste of these cinnamon rolls. The slight tang of the sourdough makes the perfect complement to the sweet filling and topping.

The Perfect Wedding Cake

There is such a rich history surrounding the Pioneer Wedding Molasses Stack Cake, but you do not have to reserve this cake for a wedding. It's perfect for any special occasion. This humble cake is known by many names, including "Appalachian Stack Cake," "Dried Apple Stack Cake," or "Molasses Stack Cake." Given this recipe is very old, there are probably as many versions of it as there are families living in the Appalachian Mountains! But the version I like best is the one that is the simplest to make, yet also the most charming in appearance.

The origin of this cake probably dates to the late 1700s when it would be served at weddings that took place in the Appalachian Mountains. The guests would usually bring the cake layers, while the bride's family would prepare the spiced dried-apple filling. Then the cake would be assembled at the wedding. Today, when weddings can be so extravagant, there is something special about this cake that harkens back to a simpler time when wedding celebrations were more focused on beginning a simple life together that would be filled with hard work and the raising of a family, but one in which a deep and enduring love grew.

It warms my heart to think about these modest but sweet wedding-day gatherings because that is how my husband and I started out. And there must be something to say about it since we have been happily married for over 25 years now! It's probably a common expression, but the priest who married us reminded me that a wedding is a day, and a marriage is a lifetime. Wise words! So, if you long for times when life was a little less hectic and time moved at a slower pace, try to make this cake for an upcoming wedding, a wedding anniversary, or a milestone birthday. It's easier to make than cakes that need to be iced. But to anyone you serve this cake, they will undoubtedly feel very special since it clearly looks like you made it with love. And on that note, I think we need to get started making some sweets and treats for our loved ones!

"Perpetual" Vanilla Extract Flavoring

Although technically not an official factory-made vanilla extract, you'll have a hard time telling the difference between your homemade version and what is available in the spice aisle at your local grocery store. Vanilla beans stay potent for a very long time, so although I use the term "perpetual" a bit tongue in cheek, I think you will be quite pleased with how long you will be able to keep a supply of vanilla extract in your pantry humming along and providing plenty of intense vanilla flavoring for your home-baked goodies.

PREP TIME: **5 MINUTES**
STEEPING TIME: **180 DAYS**
TOTAL TIME: **APPROXIMATELY 180 DAYS**
YIELD: **APPROXIMATELY 1 QUART (946ML)**

EQUIPMENT

Clean quart-size (32oz) glass jar with a tight-fitting lid
Clean pint-size (16oz) glass bottle with a tight-fitting cap
  (for decanting)

INGREDIENTS

12 whole vanilla beans, cut in half and split lengthwise
Approximately 1 ½ quarts (946ml) vodka

> ···················· COOK'S NOTES ····················
>
> *What do I mean by a "perpetual" vanilla extract
> flavoring?* Every 6 months you'll continue the process of
> decanting half the vanilla extract into a separate bottle and
> topping off the jar containing the vanilla beans with additional
> vodka. (Vodka works best because it's clear and flavorless.)
> By following this process, your vanilla extract should continue to
> have an intense flavor for a long time. If it begins to lose its
> intensity at any time, remove the old vanilla beans from the jar
> and replace them with fresh ones. After you remove the old
> vanilla beans from the jar, allow them to dry out so you can add
> them to any whole granulated sweetener, such as unrefined
> whole cane sugar or maple sugar. The vanilla beans should
> still contain some strength to infuse the sweetener with
> a vanilla flavor.

1   Add the vanilla beans to the jar. Fill with vodka, leaving a 1-inch (2.5cm) headspace from the rim of the jar. Place the lid on the jar and tighten it.

2   Allow the beans to steep in the vodka for 6 months in a dark pantry or cabinet.

3   After 6 months, remove half of the vanilla extract and decant it into the bottle. Place the cap on the bottle and tighten it.

4   Add new vodka to the original jar containing the vanilla beans, leaving a 1-inch (2.5cm) headspace from the rim of the jar. Return the jar to the pantry or cabinet to steep for another 6 months. Repeat the decanting process every 6 months.

Whole Grain Cowboy Cookies

I can't say for certain how these cookies got their name, but legend holds that they were first made in Texas, home of many a cowboy! And since cowboys are hardworking and hungry fellas, these cookies are giant in size—just like the state of Texas! Although there are many versions of this recipe for making these scrumptious cookies, this version is made even better by the addition of a whole sweetener and whole grain spelt flour.

PREP TIME: **10 MINUTES**
BAKE TIME: **14–16 MINUTES
  (PER BAKING SHEET)**
TOTAL TIME: **APPROXIMATELY 1 HOUR**
YIELD: **APPROXIMATELY 18 COOKIES**

INGREDIENTS

1 cup butter, softened
1 ½ cups unrefined whole cane sugar
  (see **Cook's Notes**)
2 large eggs
1 tsp vanilla extract
2 cups whole grain spelt flour
1 tsp baking soda
1 tsp fine ground sea salt
½ tsp baking powder
1 tsp ground cinnamon
1 cup old-fashioned rolled oats
1 cup chocolate chips
  (bittersweet or semisweet)
1 cup raisins or other small dried fruit
1 cup chopped pecans
½ cup shredded unsweetened coconut

1 Place the oven rack in the middle part of the oven. Preheat the oven to 350°F (177°C).

2 Line a half-size baking sheet with parchment paper (or butter the baking sheet). Set aside.

3 In a large bowl, cream the butter and sugar together for 5 minutes with a handheld or stand mixer. (You can also use a wooden spoon, if you prefer.)

4 To the large bowl, add one egg at a time and incorporate fully for approximately 30 seconds.

5 Add the vanilla extract and mix to incorporate.

6 In a separate large bowl, whisk together the spelt flour, baking soda, salt, baking powder, and cinnamon.

7 Add the dry ingredients to the wet ingredients and mix until no flour is visible.

8 Add the oats and mix until they are incorporated into the batter.

9 Add the chocolate chips, raisins, pecans, and coconut. If you are using a handheld or stand mixer, switch to using a wooden spoon and mix to incorporate.

10 Using a 2-inch (5cm) ice cream scoop or a ¼-cup measuring cup, scoop out a level measure of dough and transfer it to the prepared baking sheet. Place the dough scoops at least 3 inches (7.5cm) apart. Place only 6 scoops of dough on the baking sheet.

11 Transfer the baking sheet to the preheated oven. Bake the cookies until they are golden brown around the edges but still slightly soft in the middle, about 14 to 16 minutes.

12 Remove the cookies from the oven, and set them aside to cool on the baking sheet for 5 minutes. Afterward, transfer the cookies to a cooling rack and allow them to cool completely. Repeat the process with the remaining dough.

13 Transfer the cookies to an airtight container. Kept at room temperature, they will stay fresh for 1 week.

········· COOK'S NOTES ·········

Other optional sweeteners: If unrefined whole cane sugar is not available, you can substitute maple sugar, date sugar, or coconut sugar.

Why use spelt flour? Spelt is an ancient grain that is more nutritious than modern-day whole wheat, yet spelt bakes up very similarly to whole wheat. You'll find more large grocery stores are stocking spelt flour because of its growing popularity.

Old-Fashioned Cinnamon Graham Crackers

This cookie is one of my all-time favorites, and I hope it will be yours too! These graham crackers are crisp and topped with a cinnamon sugar that is hard to resist. They are perfect for dunking into a glass of cold raw milk or using to make s'mores by a cozy campfire.

PREP TIME: **15 MINUTES**
CHILLING TIME: **1 HOUR**
BAKE TIME: **APPROXIMATELY 15 MINUTES (PER BAKING SHEET)**
TOTAL TIME: **APPROXIMATELY 1 HOUR 30 MINUTES**
YIELD: **24 GRAHAM CRACKERS**

INGREDIENTS

For the dough

2 cups graham flour or whole wheat flour, plus additional for dusting

⅓ cup unrefined whole cane sugar

1 tsp ground cinnamon

½ tsp baking powder

¼ tsp baking soda

¼ tsp fine ground sea salt

½ cup cold unsalted butter (1 stick), cut into small pieces

⅓ cup pourable honey

2 tsp vanilla extract flavoring

Approximately ¼ cup whole milk (optional)

For the graham cracker topping

1 tbsp ground cinnamon

¼ cup white cane sugar (do not use unrefined whole cane sugar, it may burn.)

1–2 tbsp whole milk (or use any leftover milk from making the graham cracker dough)

TO MAKE THE COOKIE DOUGH

1 In a medium bowl, whisk together the flour, unrefined whole cane sugar, cinnamon, baking powder, baking soda, and salt.

2 Add the cold butter. Work the ingredients with your fingertips until the mixture looks like sand. Pour in the honey and vanilla extract. Mix until the batter comes together into a ball. (If the mixture looks dry and does not come together into a ball, add the milk, 1 tablespoon at a time, until the dough reaches the proper consistency. The dough should feel malleable to the touch and not dry.)

3 Divide the dough in half and flatten it into 2 disks. Wrap both disks in plastic wrap and transfer them to the refrigerator to chill for 30 minutes.

TO PREPARE AND BAKE THE DOUGH

1 Cut 4 pieces of parchment paper to a size that will fit on a standard baking sheet (also called a half-sheet pan). Place 1 piece of the cut parchment on a flat surface. Set the other pieces of parchment aside.

2 Remove 1 cookie dough disk from the refrigerator and unwrap it.

3 Use your hands to lightly dust the parchment paper with whole wheat flour. Place the unwrapped cookie dough disk on the dusted parchment paper.

4 Using floured hands, begin patting down the dough, flattening it to the point where you can switch to using a rolling pin. Dust the top of the dough very lightly with flour, smooth the flour across the dough with your hands, and then place a second piece of parchment paper on top of the dough. Use a rolling pin to roll out the dough until it is quite thin and within about 1 inch (2.5cm) of the edge of the parchment paper.

5 Transfer the cookie dough and parchment paper pieces to the baking sheet. Transfer the dough to the refrigerator to chill for 30 minutes.

6 Continue the same process with the remaining dough disk.

7 After chilling the dough for 30 minutes, place the oven rack in the middle position and preheat the oven to 350°F (177°C).

8 Remove the first baking sheet from the refrigerator and peel off the top layer of parchment paper.

9 Using a sharp knife or pizza cutter, score the dough to create 12 even rectangle shapes.

10 Use a fork to poke small holes in the rectangles to create an even pattern. (The holes will help the crackers remain flat and bake to a crisp texture.)

11   Make the topping by mixing together the cinnamon and white cane sugar in a small bowl. Use a pastry brush or the back of a spoon to brush the rectangles with the milk and then sprinkle a small amount of the cinnamon-sugar mixture onto each rectangle.

12   Place the baking sheet into the oven. Bake the crackers for 10 to 12 minutes or until the edges begin to appear golden brown and the crackers feel somewhat firm to the touch.

13   When the graham crackers are finished baking, remove the baking sheet from the oven and place it on a heatproof surface. Using a sharp knife or pizza cutter, cut along the original score lines with a knife. (This will make it easier to break apart the crackers once they cool.) Allow the graham crackers to completely cool to room temperature on the baking sheets.

14   Remove the second baking sheet from the refrigerator and repeat the baking process.

15   Once cool, break apart the homemade graham crackers. To keep them crispy, store in an airtight container in a cool, dark pantry or cabinet. They will stay fresh for approximately 1 week.

Maple Sugar Apple Pandowdy

Apple pandowdy dates back to the eighteenth century and was one of Abigail Adams' favorite desserts. Abigail was married to John Adams, the second president of the United States, and the first First Lady to entertain in the brand new White House, where she most certainly must have served this dessert!

An apple pandowdy is easy to make, especially if you are new to making piecrust. As the name implies, the crust topping is *dowdy*, which means untidy, and that's the secret. All you do is top your apples with a lot of little pieces of piecrust. Nothing fancy! And that's what makes this crust foolproof! I use maple sugar to sweeten the apple filling, but if you want to be truly authentic, you can use molasses and be just like an early American home cook.

PREP TIME: **15 MINUTES**
CHILLING TIME: **1 HOUR 15 MINUTES**
COOK TIME: **15 MINUTES**
BAKE TIME: **30 MINUTES**
TOTAL TIME: **2 HOURS 15 MINUTES**
YIELD: **8 SERVINGS**

EQUIPMENT

10-inch (25.5cm) Cast-iron skillet or other ovenproof skillet

INGREDIENTS

For the dowdy pie dough

⅔ cup all-purpose flour

1 tsp white cane sugar

½ tsp fine ground sea salt

3 tbsp cold unsalted butter, cut into small pieces and then frozen

3 tbsp lard or leaf lard

1 tsp vanilla extract flavoring

1 tsp apple cider vinegar

1 tbsp sour cream

4–8 tsp ice-cold water

For the apple filling

6 large Granny Smith apples, peeled, cored, and cut into ½-inch (1.25cm) slices

¼ cup maple sugar (alternatively, you can use 3 tablespoons of molasses)

½ tsp ground cinnamon

¼ tsp fine ground sea salt

Juice and zest of 1 medium lemon

3 tbsp unsalted butter

¾ cup apple juice (or water)

1 tbsp cornstarch (or tapioca flour)

For the dowdy pie dough topping

½ tsp ground cinnamon

1 tbsp white cane sugar (do not use unrefined whole cane sugar, it may burn)

1 large egg, lightly beaten (this is your egg wash)

TO MAKE THE DOWDY PIE DOUGH

1 In the mixing bowl of a food processor, pulse the flour, cane sugar, and salt for a few seconds to mix. (Alternatively, you can use a pastry cutter, two knives, or two forks to blend all the ingredients together.)

2 Add the frozen butter and lard to the food processor. Pulse until the flour mixture and fat appear like small peas. (This will take about 8 pulses.)

3 Add the vanilla extract, apple cider vinegar, and sour cream to the food processor along with 4 teaspoons of the ice-cold water. Pulse until the dough comes together in clumps and all the flour has been moistened. (If the dough does not come together, add additional water, 1 teaspoon at a time, and pulse until the dough comes together.)

4 Place the dough onto a flat surface lined with plastic wrap. Pull up the four corners of the plastic wrap to surround and cover the dough. Flip the wrapped dough over and use your hands or a rolling pin to shape the dough into a 4-inch to 5-inch (10cm to 12.5cm) disk. Wrap the disk with plastic wrap and transfer to the refrigerator to chill for 1 hour.

5 After 1 hour, remove the dough to a floured surface. Use a rolling pin to roll the dough out to an approximately 10-inch (25.5cm) circle. (You do not need to be exact. Just eyeball it.)

6 Using a pizza cutter or sharp knife, cut the dough into 2-inch (5cm) pieces. (They will be uneven when cutting around the edges of the circle.)

7 Place the pieces onto a parchment-lined baking sheet, cover with plastic wrap, and refrigerate while you're making the apple filling.

TO MAKE THE APPLE FILLING

1 Combine the apples, maple sugar (or molasses, if using), cinnamon, salt, lemon juice, and lemon zest in a large bowl. Toss to combine and then set aside.

2 Add the butter to a 10-inch (25.5cm) cast-iron skillet (or other ovenproof pan). Melt over medium heat. Once the butter has melted, add the apple mixture. Cook the apples for approximately 10 to 12 minutes or until they release their juices and begin to soften.

3 Mix the apple juice and cornstarch together in a small bowl until there are no lumps. Add the mixture to the skillet. Bring the apple mixture up to a boil and then immediately turn the heat down to medium-low. Simmer until the sauce is thickened, about 2 to 3 minutes.

4 Remove the skillet from the heat and place on a heatproof surface. Press on the apples with the back of a wooden spoon to flatten them into an even layer. Set aside.

TO MAKE THE PANDOWDY

1 Preheat the oven to 400°F (204°C).

2 Remove the dough pieces from the refrigerator and place them, in no particular pattern, on top of the apple mixture in the skillet. (They can overlap, and there can also be openings where you can see down into the apple mixture.)

3 Mix the cinnamon and cane sugar together in a small bowl to prepare the topping. Set aside.

4 Brush the dough pieces with the egg wash.

5 Sprinkle the dough pieces with the cinnamon and sugar mixture.

6 Place the skillet on the middle rack of the preheated oven. Bake for 15 minutes.

7 After 15 minutes, carefully remove the skillet from the oven and place it on a heatproof surface. Using the back of a spoon, press down on the crust, breaking it in different places and allowing the apple juices to seep up on top of the crust.

8 Return the skillet to the oven. Continue baking the pandowdy until the crust turns a golden brown and puffs up slightly, about 15 minutes.

9 Transfer the skillet to a wire rack and allow it to cool for at least 10 minutes. Scoop out a portion of the apples along with the crust into a bowl. (Add an optional splash of cultured cream for a creamy treat.) This dessert is best eaten the day you make it.

Easy Sourdough Bread Pudding with Dried Fruit

Bread pudding is a very old-fashioned recipe, probably dating back to the eleventh century, but it is still popular today. Frugal home cooks then (and now) knew that whenever there was leftover or stale sourdough bread around, it would not go to waste. Instead, it would be turned into a tasty bread pudding. And no one would ever know that it was made from nothing more than scraps!

This bread pudding recipe is one my mom was fond of making whenever she had collected enough bread scraps. She would store pieces of uneaten bread in the freezer, and once it looked like she had enough to fill a baking dish, she would get to work. This is not an overly sweet bread pudding since my mom would only use a small amount of sugar. But it's high in protein thanks to all the eggs, which makes it a tasty breakfast substitute for scrambled eggs and toast. Topped with some sweetened creamy vanilla glaze, it makes a perfect dessert and one that was a favorite of President Thomas Jefferson, the third president of the United States.

PREP TIME: **2 HOURS**
BAKE TIME: **45–60 MINUTES**
TOTAL TIME: **APPROXIMATELY 3 HOURS**
YIELD: **8–10 SERVINGS**

INGREDIENTS

1 cup raisins or dried currants (or other dried fruit cut into bite-sized pieces)

¼ cup apple juice (or water)

1 tbsp butter, softened

10–12 cups stale sourdough bread, torn into bite-sized pieces

10 large eggs (room temperature)

¼ cup unrefined whole cane sugar (see **Cook's Notes**)

3 cups whole milk (room temperature)

1 cup heavy whipping cream (room temperature)

1 tbsp vanilla extract

1 tsp ground cinnamon

For the creamy vanilla glaze (optional)

2 cups whole milk

4 egg yolks (see **Cook's Notes**)

2 tbsp vanilla extract

¼ cup unrefined whole cane sugar

1 tbsp all-purpose flour

Reserved apple juice or water (from soaked fruit)

1 Add the dried fruit and apple juice to a small bowl. Set aside to soak for at least 1 hour.

2 Use the butter to grease a 9-inch x 13-inch (23cm x 33cm) baking dish. (Make sure the dish is well buttered. Use more butter if necessary.)

3 Place the torn sourdough bread pieces into the baking dish.

4 After the dried fruit has had time to soak, drain off the remaining juice or water and reserve it for the optional creamy vanilla glaze. Sprinkle the rehydrated dried fruit across the top of the bread. Set aside.

5 In a large bowl, whisk together the eggs and unrefined whole cane sugar, then whisk in the milk and cream along with the vanilla extract and cinnamon. Whisk very well until the mixture is smooth and creamy in appearance. (This mixture is your custard.)

6 Pour the custard over the bread in the baking dish. Use a spatula to press down on the bread to ensure the custard covers all the pieces. Allow the bread cubes and custard to rest for at least 1 hour while the bread begins to absorb some of the custard. (If you have the time, wrap the baking dish well and refrigerate it overnight. It will be even better!)

7 After 1 hour, preheat the oven to 350°F (177°C).

8 Place the baking dish on the middle rack of the preheated oven. Bake the bread pudding for 45 to 60 minutes or until golden brown on top. The bread pudding will puff up in appearance. If you touch the top with a spatula, it should spring back slightly, indicating that it should be done. You can also insert a knife in the center. If it comes out clean, it is cooked. (If at any time the bread pudding is browning too quickly on top but has not finished cooking, tent it with aluminum foil.)

9 While the bread pudding is baking, make the creamy vanilla glaze (if using) to top the bread pudding. In a saucepan over low heat, gently warm the milk. In a medium bowl, whisk together the egg yolks, vanilla, unrefined whole cane sugar, and flour. Add in the juice or water reserved from soaking the fruit and whisk until combined.

10 Slowly add the egg mixture, little by little, to the warmed milk while whisking constantly. Once all the egg mixture is added to the milk, continue whisking until the sauce thickens but is still pourable. Once finished, set aside, but keep warm. When the bread pudding is ready to be served, transfer the creamy vanilla glaze to a pitcher and serve it alongside the bread pudding. (The glaze is best when poured on the bread pudding while it is still quite hot.)

11 When the bread pudding has finished baking, remove it from the oven and transfer it to a heatproof surface. Allow the bread pudding to rest for 5 minutes and then top with the warm vanilla glaze (if using). Serve warm.

12 Bread pudding is best consumed the same day it is made, but leftovers can be wrapped well and refrigerated for 2 to 3 days. To rewarm, place on a baking sheet lined with parchment paper and warm gently in an oven set to 200°F (93°C).

COOK'S NOTES

Other optional whole sweeteners: In place of unrefined whole cane sugar, you can use ¼ cup of maple sugar for a delightful flavor that will be perfect paired with dried apples if you make this bread pudding in the fall.

Storing egg whites: When making the creamy vanilla glaze, do not discard the egg whites. Instead, freeze them individually in ice cube trays and then transfer them to a freezer-proof bag or container. Whenever you have a recipe that calls for egg whites (such as a meringue), just allow the egg whites to defrost and continue with the recipe.

Sourdough Cinnamon Rolls with Homemade Cream Cheese Frosting

Cinnamon rolls have to be one of the most decadent desserts or, dare I say, breakfast treats! But even these wonderful rolls can sometimes overdo it on the sweet, which drowns out the cinnamon. This is where sourdough comes to the rescue by offering a touch of tartness. Plus, the cream cheese frosting provides a welcome tang when melted on top of the hot rolls to create the perfect complement to the sweet cinnamon filling.

PREP TIME: **15 MINUTES**
RESTING TIME: **1 HOUR 30 MINUTES**
FERMENTATION TIME: **12–18 HOURS**
RISE TIME: **3–4 HOURS**
BAKE TIME: **20–25 MINUTES**
TOTAL TIME: **APPROXIMATELY 17–24 HOURS**
YIELD: **12 CINNAMON ROLLS**

INGREDIENTS

For the dough

1 cup fed sourdough starter

1 cup whole milk

1 large egg

4 tbsp butter, melted (plus extra to grease the baking dish)

2 ¾ cups all-purpose flour

½ cup whole spelt flour

¼ cup unrefined whole cane sugar or maple sugar

1 ½ tsp fine ground sea salt

2 tsp olive oil, divided

For the filling

1 cup unrefined whole cane sugar or maple sugar

¼ cup all-purpose flour

2 tbsp ground cinnamon

¼ tsp fine ground sea salt

1 tbsp unsalted butter, melted

For the cream cheese frosting

1 cup full-fat cream cheese (preferably homemade)

½ cup unsalted butter

½ cup maple syrup or honey

1 tsp vanilla extract

⅛ tsp fine ground sea salt

1 In a medium bowl, whisk together the sourdough starter, milk, egg, and melted butter. Set aside.

2 In a large bowl, mix together the all-purpose flour and spelt flour along with the sweetener and salt.

3 Make a well in the dry ingredients and then pour in the sourdough starter mixture. Mix very well until all the flour is moistened and the dough takes on a shaggy appearance. Cover the bowl with a towel and set aside to rest at room temperature for 20 minutes.

4 After 20 minutes, remove the towel. Using a wet hand, firmly grasp the dough from the underside and pull it up and over itself. (This is called the *stretch-and-fold method*.) Rotate the bowl a quarter turn and repeat this process. Rotate the bowl a quarter turn 3 more times, repeating the stretch-and-fold method with each quarter turn rotation. This completed process is called a *set*. Repeat this set 4 more times at 15-minute intervals (covering the bowl after each set) for a total of 5 sets.

5 Cover the bowl tightly with plastic wrap or a lid and place it in the refrigerator to allow the sourdough to ferment overnight for at least 12 hours. (18 hours is better.)

6 After the fermentation time is complete, remove the bowl from the refrigerator and let the dough come up to room temperature, about 1 hour.

7 Grease a 9-inch x 13-inch (22cm x 33cm) ovenproof baking dish with butter. Set aside.

8 While the dough returns to room temperature, make the cinnamon filling. In a medium bowl, mix all the filling ingredients together. (It will take on an appearance like wet sand.) Set aside.

9 Once the dough has returned to room temperature, punch it down in the bowl, scoop it out of the bowl, and then place it onto a gently floured flat surface. Grease your hands with the remaining 1 teaspoon of olive oil and then begin flattening the dough, patting it down into a rectangle until it measures approximately 14 inches x 20 inches (36cm by 51cm). (This rectangle will be slightly larger than the standard home cook's baking sheet, also called a half-sheet pan.)

10 Spoon the filling onto the dough, and spread it evenly over the entire surface, leaving ½ inch (1.25cm) of exposed dough along just one 14-inch (36cm) edge. (This side will be used to seal the roll.)

11 Starting with the other 14-inch (36cm) edge with the filling, carefully roll the dough into a log. (As you roll, the log will flatten slightly and begin to lengthen by a few inches. This is normal.) If the dough sticks to the surface at any time, use a bench scraper or spatula to loosen the dough.

12 When you reach the other edge of the dough that has the ½ inch (1.25cm) of exposed dough with no filling on it, gently press down across the entire roll of dough to seal it with the exposed edge of dough with no filling on it. Adjust the roll so that the sealed edge is on the bottom.

13 Cut the log into 12 even slices and then place the slices into the prepared baking dish. Cover the dish with a flour-dusted towel and let the rolls rise until they have doubled in size and look very puffy, about 3 to 4 hours depending on the temperature in your kitchen.

14 About 30 minutes before the rolls finish rising, preheat the oven to 400°F (204°C) and place the oven rack in the middle position.

15 Place the baking dish on the middle rack in the oven and bake the rolls for approximately 20 minutes or until they appear golden brown.

16 While the rolls are baking, make the cream cheese frosting by combining all the ingredients in a medium bowl. Mix until they reach a smooth and creamy consistency.

17 Once the rolls have finished baking, remove the baking dish from the oven and place it on a heatproof surface. Allow the rolls to cool for 5 minutes before spreading the frosting over the top of the rolls. (Alternatively, allow the rolls to cool to room temperature and then spread the frosting if you prefer a firmer frosting.)

18 These rolls are best enjoyed the day they are baked. However, any leftovers can be wrapped well and refrigerated for up to 1 week. When ready to enjoy, they are best if simply unwrapped and allowed to return to room temperature.

Pioneer Wedding Molasses Stack Cake

This may be a traditional Appalachian wedding cake, but it can also serve as a real treat for any special occasion. And the best thing about this cake is that it can be made up to two days in advance and will actually be better for it than if it was served immediately! Legend holds that these stack cakes could become quite tall as the bride's family began to collect all the cake layers brought by family and friends to the wedding. But we'll stop at five layers so that the cake will be manageable to slice but still be filled with plenty of apples to be utterly delicious!

PREP TIME: **15 MINUTES**
COOK TIME: **45 MINUTES TO 1 HOUR**
BAKE TIME: **15 MINUTES**
TOTAL TIME: **APPROXIMATELY 1 HOUR 30 MINUTES**
YIELD: **8 SERVINGS**

EQUIPMENT

5 (9-inch/23cm) round cake pans (see **Cook's Notes**)

INGREDIENTS

2 ½ cups whole wheat or whole spelt flour

2 cups all-purpose flour (plus more for dusting)

½ cup unrefined whole cane sugar or maple sugar

1 ½ tbsp baking powder

1 tsp baking soda

1 tsp fine ground sea salt

½ cup molasses

Approximately ½ cup buttermilk, homemade or store-bought (see **Cook's Notes**)

½ cup butter (1 stick), melted and cooled

1 large egg

Powdered sugar, for dusting (optional)

For the apple filling

5 cups packed dried apples (any variety), cut into 1-inch to 2-inch (2.5cm to 5cm) pieces

1 cup unrefined whole cane sugar or maple sugar

1 tsp ground cinnamon

1 tsp ground ginger

6 cups apple juice

TO MAKE THE APPLE FILLING

1   Combine the ingredients in a medium saucepan over high heat. Bring the apple mixture up to a boil and then immediately turn the heat down to low. Let the apple mixture simmer, stirring the mixture frequently, until the apples appear rehydrated and tender.

2   After about 45 minutes to 1 hour, the juice should have reduced to the point where the apple mixture appears darker and thicker in appearance (like applesauce or apple butter with big chunks of apples). If not, allow it to simmer a bit longer.

3   Remove the mixture from the stovetop to a heatproof surface and allow it to cool.

TO BAKE THE CAKE LAYERS

1   Preheat the oven to 350°F (177°C).

2   Grease the cake pans with butter and then cut circles of parchment paper that can fit into the bottom of each pan. Place the parchment circles into the cake pans, grease the top of the parchment paper, and use all-purpose flour to lightly dust the interiors of the cake pans.

3   In a large bowl, whisk together the whole wheat flour, all-purpose flour, unrefined whole cane sugar, baking powder, baking soda, and salt.

4   In a medium bowl, mix together the molasses, buttermilk, melted butter, and egg. Whisk until the ingredients are completely incorporated.

5   Make a well in the dry ingredients and then pour in the molasses mixture. Mix well with a wooden spoon until the mixture looks like cookie dough. (Important! You want this dough to be very malleable and easy to flatten between the palms of your hands.) If the dough appears quite stiff, add extra buttermilk, one tablespoon at a time, until the dough reaches a smoother consistency.

6   Divide the dough into 5 equal pieces. Take 1 piece of dough and set it aside while you cover the remaining 4 pieces with a damp (lint-free) towel, such as a flour-sack towel.

7   Lightly flour your hands and then place the first piece of dough into one of the prepared cake pans. Flatten it into the bottom of the pan as evenly as possible, filling the entire pan. Next, take a fork or a toothpick and poke small holes all over the flattened dough. (This will allow the steam to escape while baking to keep the layers flattened, which is what you want.) Continue this process with the remaining pieces of dough until all five cake pans are filled.

8   Place the cake pans into the oven and bake for approximately 15 minutes. Depending on the size of your oven, rotate the pans from front to back or from top rack to lower rack halfway through the baking time.

9   Keep an eye on the cake layers as they bake from this point forward. You do not want them to be overbaked. The layers won't rise much as they bake, as they would with a traditional cake batter. Instead, what you are looking for is that when you touch the baked layers, they feel firm.

10 Once fully baked, remove the cake layers from the oven and transfer them to a heatproof surface. Allow the cake layers to cool slightly.

TO ASSEMBLE THE CAKE

1   Once you can handle the cake pans comfortably, remove the first cake layer from its pan, peel off the parchment paper, and transfer the cake layer right side up to a large cake plate or cake stand. Spread a layer of the apple filling over the top of that cake that is sufficient to completely cover the cake layer. Continue stacking and topping the remaining layers until you've stacked the final cake layer. (When you stack the fifth and final cake layer, do not top it with any apple filling.)

2   Wrap the cake tightly with plastic wrap around the sides and top to keep out as much air as possible. Refrigerate for 2 days.

3   Once you unwrap the cake, top it with some of the apple mixture, if any remains, or simply dust it with powdered sugar (if using). Slice to serve. (A serrated bread knife works best to cut the cake.) (See **Cook's Notes**.)

···················· **COOK'S NOTES** ····················

What if you don't have five cake pans? If you do not have five cake pans, you can bake these cake layers in batches. All the dough does not need to be baked at the same time.

What if you don't have buttermilk? If you do not have buttermilk, you can substitute whole milk to which you have added 1 tablespoon of lemon juice. Buttermilk or milk curdled with lemon juice serves as somewhat of an insurance policy to ensure that your cake layers come out perfectly every time.

When to serve: This cake is best served once the apple mixture is allowed time to soften the cake's layers. If you plan to serve this cake the same day, make it in the morning to serve in the evening. But if you can wait 2 days before cutting it, all the better! The longer you wait, the softer and more flavorful the cake layers will become.

Chapter Fourteen
TRADITIONAL COMFORT FOOD MEALS

BRINGING TOGETHER ALL YOU'VE LEARNED

As you've worked your way through this book, honing your skills on your traditional foods journey, I hope you have developed a skill set that will help you easily prepare a variety of nutritious homemade foods. Now it's time to take everything you've learned to start creating comforting and complete meals that you, your family, and your friends can enjoy.

In this chapter, I share a selection of my favorite comfort foods, some of which I discovered while living here in the Texas Hill Country. First, we'll start with the easy way to roast a chicken, which is my ultimate comfort food. With this quick version, we will spatchcock the chicken to allow it to cook faster. If the word *spatchcock* is new to you, it simply means that we will cut out the backbone of a whole chicken, allowing us to flatten it on a baking sheet or in a roasting pan. Cooking a chicken this way moves the process along much quicker than when roasting a whole chicken left intact. Once you learn to cook a chicken this way, it'll become one of your weeknight go-to dinners.

After we spatchcock a chicken, we'll go on a bit of a culinary tour, including learning how to make the perfect New Mexican chile con carne with a nutrient-dense twist. And I'll certainly share with you some delicious Tex-Mex and German specialties that are steeped in the rich history of the local area where I live. Plus, on the lighter side, I have a few simple fish dishes to share that you can put on the table in around 30 minutes!

In Search of Traditional Chile con Carne

When I was growing up, I enjoyed running errands with my dad on Saturdays. Once we finished the outside chores, we would climb into the car and head into town. The best part of our day was when we stopped to have lunch at a little cafeteria in the basement of the Sears and Roebuck store. Our order was always the same because we both enjoyed it so much: chile con carne with a side of saltine crackers. It was a combination of ground beef, beans, and tomatoes, with an assortment of spices, and it was delicious!

When I came to Texas, I was pleased to discover that chili, as it is simply called here, is the state dish of Texas. (But some argue it should be barbecue!) Most of the time, it's heavy on the meat but with no beans. Now there's nothing wrong with that since technically, the traditional dish chile con carne (as it is called and spelled in New Mexico) translates to "chiles with meat." And whenever I have had chili in Texas, it's always delicious, whether made with or without beans.

When my family and I traveled to New Mexico with my father-in-law, he took us to a delightful town called Mesilla. What now seemed to me to be a small town was one of the larger towns in the Southwest between San Diego, California, and San Antonio, Texas, in the 1800s. We stayed in Mesilla to enjoy dinner, and it turned out that the building in which we dined was rich in history. It was not a restaurant back in that day, but instead it was the Corn Exchange Hotel, and this hotel was a regular stop for the Butterfield Stagecoach Line!

As I opened my menu, I saw something described as red chile con carne, and I ordered it immediately. This dish was made with cubes of beef mixed in a red chile sauce. The New Mexican red chile pepper flavor was outstanding! But it was made even better by the fact that the chile was ladled into crispy corn tortillas that had been shaped into three little bowls. Every time my family and I visited New Mexico after that, we made a point of stopping at that restaurant. And every time, I order the chile con carne!

I've done my best to recreate all the wonderful flavors—both Texan and New Mexican—in the chile recipe I share. And thanks to all the delicious spices in a traditional chile con carne, it becomes one of the best places to add in nutrient-dense ingredients without anyone being the wiser. For example, you can include nutritious organ meats in this recipe to enjoy the meats' benefits without having to prepare them as a standalone dish that might be new to many palates.

You Say "Tamale," I Say "Tamale Pie"

If the word "tamale" is new to you, it's a traditional Mexican dish that dates back thousands of years! Today, it can be eaten all year long, but it is most popular during the Christmas season, beginning with the Feast of Our Lady of Guadalupe on December 12 to Three Kings' Day on January 6. My husband introduced me to tamales, which he grew up enjoying in El Paso during holiday festivities.

A tamale is a dish made with masa, which is a dough made from nixtamalized corn that is filled with various meats, beans, or cheese and then usually wrapped in a corn husk and steamed. When I first learned of this dish and how the masa was prepared, I was fascinated by the word "nixtamalized." I quickly learned that it is a traditional method for preparing corn so that its full nutritional profile can be released and easily absorbed by our digestive systems.

As a traditional foods cook, I loved learning all about this recipe. The nixtamalization process places dried corn kernels in a solution of water and the mineral lime (food-grade lime) in a large stockpot and leaves the mixture to soak overnight. The next day, the kernels are rinsed well, covered with fresh water, and then brought to a boil to cook the kernels until they are soft. The corn is now ready to be ground into a paste called *masa*, which is used to make tortillas and tamales. Today, this process is streamlined for us because we can buy masa harina, a corn flour, already prepared for us, that makes the process of preparing the masa for tamales a bit easier.

However, a tamale pie is something different from a tamale. Food historians believe tamale pies originated in Texas in the early 1900s. Records dating back to this period show Texas students in home economics classes were learning how to make tamale pies, and this dish even made its way onto the school cafeteria menus of that time. But what exactly is it? You can think of a tamale pie as a deconstructed tamale that is easier to create than the traditional tamale. You can make it for a quick weeknight meal, but it still captures all the wonderful flavors of a tamale. All your ingredients go into a frying pan and are sautéed before being topped with a cornbread batter made with masa harina or cornmeal. We'll take this cornbread batter one step further by using some of our sourdough discard to make the batter, which makes for a tasty complement to the cornmeal.

Sauerbraten—a Texas Hill Country Tradition

Although Mexican cuisine and barbecue tend to dominate the Texas culinary scene, there is one other popular traditional cuisine enjoyed by most Texans, specifically here in the Hill Country. In the mid-1800s, German immigrants began to settle in different parts of Texas, including Galveston, Houston, and San Antonio. But those who traveled beyond San Antonio discovered the beautiful and rugged, Texas Hill Country. They eventually settled and built a town that was christened Friedrichsburg in 1846. Today, it is known as Fredericksburg, and this charming little town is recognized as having some of the best German restaurants in Texas, serving the tastiest sauerbraten I have ever had.

Every German family probably has their own version of the traditional sauerbraten recipe, and I am sure all are equally delicious! Sauerbraten is a slow-cooked dish often made with an inexpensive beef rump roast that is slowly simmered with a delightful mix of spices to create a flavor reminiscent of gingersnap cookies.

German hausfraus and immigrant pioneer housewives living in the Texas Hill Country needed a few shortcuts when it came to thickening their sauerbraten sauce. Traditionally in Germany, lebkuchen cookies are often used to thicken the sauerbraten sauce. But many recipes for sauerbraten in the United States suggest crumbling some gingersnap cookies into the sauce, as they are easier to find at a local grocery store. However, we are going to forgo the cookies when we make our version. Instead, we will use powdered ginger, juniper berries, and a bit of a whole sweetener to create a delightfully sweet and tangy sauce for our roast, which we will simmer till it is fork-tender and easy to slice.

The Lure of Fish

If pioneers were blessed to live near a river, they always had their fishing gear handy. Even those in wagon trains made sure to bring fishing gear with them. One of the favorite meals of wagon train travelers along the Oregon Trail was salmon. They often fished for it along the river they followed on their journey through Idaho and into Oregon.

I'm sure the salmon was a welcome treat compared to their usual fare of beans and rice, cornmeal mush or cornmeal pancakes (called *johnny cakes*), hardtack, jerky, and potatoes. I can only imagine how delicious fresh-caught salmon cooked over an outside fire must have been. Especially after a diet of cornmeal mush!

Although the pioneers on the Oregon Trail fished for salmon, they often traded for salmon from the Native People of the Pacific Northwest. These people consumed salmon in abundance and considered it a gift of food from their creator. I always find it fascinating when studying traditional cultures to learn how so many of them seem to intrinsically understand—as through a collective memory from their ancestors—the right foods that would lead to robust good health. We can learn so much from studying what foods traditional cultures all over the world consume.

Although not out on the trail, I share with you a tasty and easy way to cook salmon right in your own oven. You can make and serve it in about 30 minutes. It's a true one-pan dinner since you will bake the salmon and veggies together tossed in your homemade ghee. It makes for a delightfully hearty meal as salmon is a fish high in fat—and an especially important fat. It is rich in omega-3 fats, which support brain and heart health.

And for a lighter fare but still filling and tasty, we'll cook up a fillet of sole that was one of my mom's favorite dishes to make. To this day, she still calls it her favorite

brain food. Sole is high in protein and a good source of vitamins B6, B12, and D, which are important for cardiovascular and neurological health, as well as supporting a healthy immune function. And better yet, sole supports brain development and brain health. So, as always, my mom was right. Sole is brain food! Panfrying sole in ghee and then serving it with lots of fresh lemon wedges and a tartar sauce that you will make using your homemade mayonnaise simply doesn't get any better! Even those fussy eaters will be drawn to this scrumptious dish.

The Easy Way to Master Making Traditional Wholesome Meals

When it comes to creating an efficient up-and-running traditional foods kitchen, the secret is to master the few basic meals that I share here and then build on them over time. As you have come to the end of this book, you already have all the skills you need in your kitchen toolbox (or should I say "recipe box") to create the basic pantry staples needed to build your menus. In this chapter, I share six traditional meals that you can easily become proficient in preparing. You can rotate through these during the course of a week and then start all over again.

Once you find that you can prepare these meals with ease, you can begin to put your own spin on them by varying the vegetables or the herbs and spices that you use. As you become comfortable with customizing the recipes, keep in mind that each of these recipes has its roots in a different traditional culture. And that's the good news because although different, most traditional cultures have a lot in common. For example, once you master how to make a sauerbraten, switching up the ingredients to make an American-style pot roast, an Italian stracotto, or a Mexican carne guisada is easy. If you don't have any beef on hand, you can use a pork roast. And if you don't like pork, you can use chicken and make a cacciatore. These are all classic traditional recipes that allow for the easy interchange of ingredients to keep you full and satisfied indefinitely!

Let's face it, chile con carne might be my favorite, but chile is one of those foods you can use with an assortment of meats, including poultry, to create a tasty meal. And by tweaking the ingredients ever so slightly, you can transform the makings of any chile recipe into a soup or a stew. Next thing you know, you'll use some of your fish to create a cioppino fish stew reminiscent of what the Italian immigrant fishermen, who lived along the San Francisco coast, made.

It's About Using What You Have on Hand

It's all about looking at what you have on hand and then referring to the assortment of dishes created by traditional cultures, including what our ancestors made with what they had available. You don't need to be fancy or use ingredients that are hard to find. Simple, fresh ingredients that you source locally mixed along with various pantry staples that you made homemade, can create some of the best meals you've ever had. As modern pioneers in the kitchen, we are often starting with basic traditional recipes but

reinventing them in any way we want based on the bounty of local flavors distinct to where we live.

For example, when it comes to switching up your tamale pie, you have countless variations to choose from. You can sauté pretty much anything you want in a cast-iron frying pan. You can even go completely meatless, relying on beans and rice for the base, or just a simple mix of vegetables, such as when making a French vegetable ratatouille. And no one says that you have to pour on a cornbread topping. I have been known to simply grab some of my sourdough discard and pour that right on top with little else added!

When salmon is unavailable, but halibut is, cook it the same way and you will have created an entirely new dinner selection to add to your repertoire of menus that you can keep track of in your kitchen journal. And when it comes to panfrying fish, you have many possibilities. You can panfry pretty much any fish, with the simple whitefish varieties being some of the tastiest. You are in no way limited to sole in the recipe. The simple recipe I share can be applied to cod, haddock, flounder, and trout—just to name a few.

There is no right or wrong way to make traditional meals. What I share with you is simply the easy way. I never want you to be overwhelmed when it comes time to prepare and serve a traditional meal. That is why I am often fond of saying, "If you don't have this, then use that." This is the beauty of these recipes. These are foods that traditional cultures have been making for centuries. And each culture has put their own spin on what started as a basic formula, a basic blueprint to prepare simple food while maximizing its nutritional availability. Now it's your turn to create your own traditional favorites!

Keeping Kitchen Life Simple

Overall, the recipes I share with you in this chapter are relatively easy. However, I completely understand that sometimes we can all start to feel a little overwhelmed with the pressures of everyday life and are too tired to follow a recipe—easy or otherwise. In those cases, remember what I mentioned early on in this book ... just start with a roast chicken. Over time, you will find that a roast chicken is one of those meals that can become quite routine, and that's a good thing since you'll be able to make a roast chicken for dinner, knowing that you've made a healthy and traditional-food meal without having to think about all the possible recipe combinations.

Once you master making a roast chicken, you'll be able to easily make this warm and delicious dish to comfort you, your family, and your friends. The familiar aroma of a plump chicken roasting in the oven will lift everyone's spirits. Throw some veggies into the roasting pan, and you've made the quintessential one-pot meal. It's comfort food at its best! And in this chapter, I share a technique to make a roast chicken in 45 minutes. So now you have easy combined with fast. Nothing could be better or tastier than that!

A Final Word

Charlotte Mason was an educator who taught a generation of home educators in the late 1800s to early 1900s how to enlighten the whole child, the whole person, through the use of what she called "living books." When she coined this phrase, she did not provide a specific list of books, but provided a paradigm for what type of books would meet this standard.

These "living books" were so much more than just pages filled with text. Instead, a living book was one Miss Mason described, and I paraphrase, as being filled with imagination and originality. It was a book that stayed with you long after reading it. This book gave you a glimpse into the time when it was written and a peek into who the author was at their core.

I'm not sure if Miss Mason would have classified cookbooks as living books, but I have tried my best to bring the topic of traditional foods alive for you as we've worked through this book together. I hope this book will serve as much more than a cookbook to you and that it will be a lifelong manual and companion to help you on your traditional foods journey. You'll be able to reference this book time and time again to assist you in creating your own modern pioneer kitchen.

If I have come only the slightest bit close to creating a living book, it is thanks to you, my sweet friend and reader, for joining me along this trail. And although we are not presently on an overland trek in a covered wagon, creating traditional foods in our home kitchens is certainly a culinary adventure for us modern pioneers! And it's a journey I am grateful to be on with you.

Spatchcock Chicken

You can bake this easy chicken dinner in about 45 minutes so that you can enjoy a whole home-cooked chicken any night of the week! Plus, there is a good chance that you will have leftovers, which can be great for using in a soup or for making chicken salad sandwiches. But most important, don't forget to save all the bones and any scraps for using to make your next batch of Roast Chicken Bone Broth (p. 48).

PREP TIME: **5 MINUTES**
COOK TIME: **45 MINUTES**
TOTAL TIME: **50 MINUTES**
YIELD: **4–6 SERVINGS**

INGREDIENTS

4lb (1.80kg) whole chicken

Fine ground sea salt

Freshly ground black pepper

Crushed red pepper (optional)

2 medium sweet potatoes, peeled and each cut into 8 wedges

2 medium yellow onions, peeled and quartered with root intact

8 medium carrots peeled, halved, and cut into 2-inch (5cm) pieces

¼ cup ghee, melted

1   Place the oven rack in the middle position and preheat the oven to 425°F (218°C).

2   Remove the giblets from the cavity of the chicken and then cut out the backbone of the chicken using kitchen shears. Save the backbone and giblets (except for the liver) in a scrap bag for making bone broth. (The liver can be cooked in a small skillet for a cook's treat or a dog treat.)

3   Place the spatchcocked chicken breast-side down on a baking sheet pan or roasting pan. Season generously with salt, black pepper, and crushed red pepper (if using).

4   Flip the chicken over so it is breast-side up. Using your hands, firmly flatten the chicken until you hear the breast bone crack and then tuck the wing tips under the chicken.

5   Scatter the sweet potatoes, onions, and carrots around the chicken on the sheet pan. Drizzle the chicken and the vegetables with the melted ghee and season everything with additional salt and black pepper. (I generally don't sprinkle red pepper flakes on the top side of the chicken.)

6   Place the chicken into the preheated oven. Bake for approximately 45 minutes or until chicken skin is golden brown and the juices run clear. Insert a meat thermometer next to the meatiest part of the thigh. If the temperature is 165°F (74°C), the chicken is fully cooked. (I prefer to roast chickens to an internal temperature of 180°F [82°C] so that the dark meat is not pink or rubbery.)

7   When the chicken is cooked, remove it from the oven and place the baking sheet pan or roasting pan on a heatproof surface. Transfer the chicken to a cutting board, and using a sharp knife, cut the breast in half, then cut off the wings, legs, and thighs. Transfer the chicken pieces, potatoes, onions, and carrots to a serving platter. Bring them to the table and enjoy!

Cast-Iron Skillet Texas Tamale Pie with Sourdough Cornmeal Topping

This is one of my favorite dinners to make when I have to clean out my refrigerator or freezer. One of the best things about this version of a tamale pie is that it's a very clever way to use up some of your sourdough discard. This is the perfect meal to soothe the souls of modern pioneers who strive to create a no-waste kitchen!

PREP TIME: **10 MINUTES**
COOK TIME: **20 MINUTES**
BAKE TIME: **25 MINUTES**
TOTAL TIME: **55 MINUTES**
YIELD: **6 SERVINGS**

INGREDIENTS

For the tamale pie filling

2lb (907g) ground chuck

1 medium yellow onion, chopped

1½ tsp fine ground sea salt

1 tbsp ancho chile powder

2 tsp ground cumin

2 tsp ground coriander

1 medium green bell pepper, stem and seeds removed, chopped

1 cup whole kernel corn (frozen or canned)

1 (14.5oz/411g) can diced tomatoes (or an equal amount of home-canned tomatoes, crushed)

1 cup tomato sauce

½ cup beef bone broth

For the sourdough cornmeal topping

½ cup cornmeal or masa harina

2 tsp baking powder

1 tsp fine ground sea salt

1 tsp baking soda (optional) (see **Cook's Notes**)

1½ cups sourdough starter discard

3 tbsp melted butter, cooled

3 large eggs, lightly beaten

1 cup grated Monterey Jack cheese

½ cup grated sharp cheddar cheese

1. Place the oven rack in the middle position and preheat the oven to 400°F (204°C).

2. In a 10- or 12-inch (25.5cm or 30.5cm) cast-iron skillet or other ovenproof skillet, brown the ground chuck along with the onions. If desired, drain off some of the fat the meat releases.

3. Once the meat is browned, add the salt, ancho chile powder, cumin, and coriander. Stir the mixture well. After a few minutes and once the spices are fragrant, add the bell pepper, corn, tomatoes, tomato sauce, and bone broth. Bring the mixture up to a boil and then turn it down to medium. Simmer for approximately 10 minutes, allowing some of the liquid to evaporate and the flavors to blend together.

4. While the meat mixture simmers, begin making the sourdough cornmeal topping by whisking together the cornmeal, baking powder, salt, and baking soda (if using) in a medium bowl.

5. Add the sourdough starter discard, melted butter, and eggs to the bowl. Mix well.

6. Turn off the stovetop burner and pour the topping over the mixture in the skillet. Top with both grated cheeses and then transfer to the preheated oven. (Alternatively, you can mix the cheeses into the topping.)

7. Bake for approximately 25 minutes or until the topping is puffed and the cheese is melted and golden.

8. Transfer the skillet to a heatproof surface and allow it to cool for 10 minutes before serving.

9. Well-wrapped leftovers will stay fresh in the refrigerator for 2 to 3 days or in the freezer for 2 months. To reheat, place on a baking sheet in a preheated 350°F (177°C) oven for approximately 20 minutes until warmed through.

····· COOK'S NOTES ·····

Why add baking soda to the sourdough cornmeal topping? Baking soda will help reduce the sour taste of the sourdough discard topping if you prefer a milder flavor.

Budget-Friendly Southwestern Chile con Carne

To make this chile con carne, we'll use an inexpensive cut of meat, but it won't lack in flavor thanks to the combination of peppers used to make the red chile sauce. Plus, we are going to push the nutrient envelope, so to speak, by grating a bit of beef liver into the sauce. (No one will ever know it's there because of the bountiful flavor of the chiles!)

Although you will need to source dried chiles to make this recipe, it's worth it. The flavor difference between a sauce made with dried chiles versus store-bought chili powder mixed with tomatoes is significant. And using dried chiles is very traditional. Although I was not raised cooking Mexican or Tex-Mex food, I try to be as traditional as possible when recreating these types of dishes, and I like to think that my attempt at imitation is the highest form of flattery!

PREP TIME: **30 MINUTES**
SOAK TIME: **25–30 MINUTES**
COOK TIME: **1½–2 HOURS**
TOTAL TIME: **2 HOURS 30 MINUTES TO 3 HOURS**
YIELD: **8 TO 10 SERVINGS**

INGREDIENTS

For the red chile sauce

12 dried chiles (Guajillos, New Mexican, Pasillas, or Ancho)

1 medium yellow onion, peeled and chopped

4 cloves garlic, peeled and chopped

1 tsp cumin

1 tsp coriander

2 tsp fine ground sea salt

½ tsp freshly ground black pepper

5–6 cups beef bone broth

For the chile con carne

¼ cup all-purpose flour

2 tsp fine ground sea salt

½ tsp freshly ground black pepper

4–5lb (1.80–2.23kg) chuck roast cut into 1-inch (2.5cm) cubes

¼ cup lard

½ cup frozen beef liver, grated

2 (14.5oz/411g) cans diced tomatoes (or the equal amount of home-canned tomatoes, crushed)

Masa harina (nixtamalized corn flour) (optional) (see **Cook's Notes**)

Fine ground sea salt and black pepper, to taste

TO MAKE THE RED CHILE SAUCE

1 Put on a pair of disposable gloves or clean dish gloves to protect your hands.

2 Using a sharp knife, cut off the stem of a dried chile pepper and then make a slit lengthwise down the center of the pepper. Open the pepper along the slit and use the knife to scrape out the seeds and veins. Place the pepper in a large heatproof bowl. Repeat the process with the remaining peppers.

3 Once all the peppers are seeded, boil water in a tea kettle and then pour it over the peppers until they are covered. (If they float, place a heavy plate in the bowl to hold the peppers under the water.)

4 Allow the peppers to soak between 25 and 30 minutes to rehydrate them to the point where they are soft and pliable. (See **Cook's Notes**.)

5 Remove the peppers from the soaking water and then add them to a blender along with the remaining sauce ingredients (except the bone broth). Pour just enough of the bone broth into the blender to cover the other ingredients. Begin blending until the ingredients are puréed, adding more bone broth as needed. This will take about 4 to 5 minutes.

6 Once you have a smooth sauce with a pourable consistency, pour it through a mesh strainer placed over a bowl to strain out any solids. (If you find the sauce is on the thicker side and not draining quickly through the mesh strainer, add more bone broth to help "wash" it through.) Set aside.

TO MAKE THE CHILE CON CARNE

1 Combine the flour, salt, and pepper in a medium bowl. Add the meat cubes and toss to coat.

2 Heat the lard in a large Dutch oven placed over medium-high heat. Once the lard is sizzling, add the meat in batches. (Do not crowd the meat in the Dutch oven.) As each batch browns, use a slotted spoon to remove it to a platter. (If needed, add additional lard and allow it to come up to a sizzle.) Set aside.

3 Once all the meat is browned, add the beef liver to the Dutch oven and toss quickly to brown.

4 Add the red chile sauce, diced tomatoes, and the browned meat, along with any drippings. Increase the heat to high and bring it up to a boil. Stir well, turn the heat down to the lowest setting, and cover the Dutch oven. Allow the meat to simmer in the sauce for 1 ½ to 2 hours or until it is very tender. (Periodically check on the meat to make sure there is sufficient sauce in which the meat can simmer. If the sauce ever becomes too thick, add additional beef bone broth.)

5 After 2 hours, if the sauce is of a consistency you like, taste the sauce and add additional salt and black pepper if needed. The chile con carne is ready to be ladled into individual serving bowls.

6 If you want to thicken the sauce, it's traditional to use masa harina. Start by mixing 2 to 3 tablespoons of masa harina with approximately ¼ to ⅓ cup of beef bone broth to make a slurry. Add this slurry to the sauce and stir well as the chile con carne continues to simmer and the sauce reaches the consistency you like.

·················· COOK'S NOTES ··················

Reserving the cooking water from the peppers: Some chile con carne recipes will call for reserving the soaking water to use when making the chile sauce, but I generally do not do this because I prefer to use bone broth to add extra nutrition. Also, sometimes the soaking water can have a bit of a harsh flavor. Taste your soaking water first to decide if you want to use it in place of the bone broth.

Where can you find masa harina? Masa harina is available in the baking aisle at most large grocery stores. However, if you can't find it, you can make a slurry with all-purpose flour and beef bone broth.

Traditional Sauerbraten with Raisins, Honey, and Ginger

The Texas Hill Country offers a wide variety of Mexican and Texas specialties, and when combined, they have become Texas' own unique cuisine referred to as *Tex-Mex*. But it might surprise you to learn that the Texas Hill Country, specifically a town called Fredericksburg, has an abundant selection of German restaurants, each one better than the next!

Whenever I am in that town, I always look forward to enjoying traditional sauerbraten. Now, as with many traditional recipes, I'm sure every family has their favorite version. But the recipe's main signature is tender beef immersed in a sweet and tangy sauce. I have recreated my version of traditional sauerbraten here for you, and I recommend that you serve it with your homemade sauerkraut and fermented red cabbage for a delightful meal.

PREP TIME: **48 HOURS**
COOK TIME: **APPROXIMATELY 2 HOURS 20 MINUTES**
TOTAL TIME: **APPROXIMATELY 50 HOURS**
YIELD: **6–8 SERVINGS**

INGREDIENTS

For the marinade

1 cup apple cider vinegar

1 cup apple juice or apple cider

1 large yellow onion, sliced

Zest and juice of 1 lemon

10 whole cloves

5 whole juniper berries, crushed

4 bay leaves

1 (3-inch/7.5cm) Ceylon cinnamon stick, broken into pieces

6 whole peppercorns

2 tsp fine ground sea salt

2 tbsp whole sweetener (see **Cook's Notes**)

For the sauerbraten

3 ½–4 pound beef rump roast

2 tbsp ghee or beef tallow, divided

2 cups beef bone broth

½ cup raisins (dark or golden)

2 tbsp all-purpose flour

1 tsp ground ginger

¼ cup pourable honey

1. In a deep bowl, mix together all the marinade ingredients. Place the rump roast into the bowl and turn it around several times to saturate it with the marinade. Cover the bowl tightly with a lid or plastic wrap and refrigerate for 48 hours, turning the rump roast over in the marinade every 12 hours.

2. After 48 hours, place a large Dutch oven over medium-high heat. Add 1 tablespoon of ghee or beef tallow.

3. Once the fat melts and begins to sizzle, transfer the rump roast to the Dutch oven. Brown on all sides for approximately 15 minutes, turning the meat every few minutes to ensure the meat does not burn on any side.

4. Pour all the marinade over the rump roast along with the beef bone broth and the raisins. Bring the mixture up to a boil. Scrape up any brown bits that may have formed on the bottom of the Dutch oven and then immediately turn down the heat to the lowest setting.

5. Place the lid on the Dutch oven and allow the rump roast to simmer for approximately 2 hours. When done, the meat should be tender and easily pierced with a fork, but it should be intact and not fall apart.

6. Transfer the meat to a platter and keep it warm in an oven set to 200°F (93°C).

7. Place a colander or mesh strainer over a medium heatproof bowl. Pour the liquid from the Dutch oven through the colander or strainer. Set the liquid aside and discard the solids.

8. Return the Dutch oven to the stovetop over medium heat. Add the remaining ghee and the flour. Cook until the flour turns golden brown, about 2 minutes. Add the ginger and stir well to incorporate.

9. Pour the strained liquid from the bowl into the Dutch oven. Bring the mixture up to a boil, stirring constantly, allowing the liquid to thicken slightly.

10 Once the liquid has thickened slightly, turn the heat down to its lowest setting. Add the honey and stir well to incorporate and gently warm through. (This is the sauce.)

11 Remove the rump roast from the oven. Using a sharp knife, cut the roast against the grain into ½-inch (1.25cm) slices. (See **Cook's Notes.**)

12 Pour some of the sauce over the slices of meat on the platter. Place the remaining sauce in a pitcher to serve on the side.

13 Leftovers can be stored in an airtight container and refrigerated for 2 to 3 days. Sauerbraten is best rewarmed on the stovetop in a skillet along with the sauce.

········· COOK'S NOTES ·········

What is the best whole sweetener to use in a sauerbraten marinade? When making a sweetened marinade for beef, your best options are unrefined whole cane sugar, coconut sugar, or maple syrup. (If you use maple syrup for the marinade, you'll use 3 tablespoons instead of a ¼ cup.) Maple sugar is terrific too, but because it tends to be expensive, you should reserve it for those dishes where its flavor can shine through, such as with the baked salmon recipe.

What does cutting "against the grain" mean? When you slice a beef roast of any kind, you will notice lines running across the meat. This is the grain. When you slice the meat, cut it in the opposite direction than the grain. Your cut will make an X pattern with the grain when you slice the meat. This will make the slices of meat more tender and easier to chew, and will keep the meat slices neatly intact for serving.

Panfried Breaded Whitefish with Homemade Tartar Sauce

When it comes to eating any type of whitefish, this is my husband's all-time favorite way to have it prepared. I usually use sole, but this recipe will work with any other mild-tasting white fish. What makes this extra special is serving it alongside your homemade tartar sauce. Or you can do as we do in our household, and slather the tartar sauce across the fish right when it comes out of the pan. The heat melts the tartar sauce a bit, turning it into a creamy, sweet, and tangy sauce.

PREP TIME: **5 MINUTES**
COOK TIME: **30 MINUTES**
TOTAL TIME: **35 MINUTES**
YIELD: **4 SERVINGS**

INGREDIENTS

½ cup all-purpose flour

2 large eggs

1 cup plain bread crumbs

1 tbsp mix of dried herbs (see **Cook's Notes**)

½ tsp fine ground sea salt

½ tsp freshly ground black pepper

2 tbsp ghee or clarified butter

4 skinless sole fillets, approximately 6–8 ounces each

2 medium lemons cut into wedges (to serve)

For the quick-and-easy tartar sauce

¾ cup mayonnaise (preferably homemade)

¼ cup chopped bread and butter pickles (preferably home canned)

Zest and juice of 1 lemon

Fine ground sea salt and freshly ground black pepper, to taste

---

········· COOK'S NOTES ·········

What are the best dried herbs for seasoning fish? When it comes to panfrying fish, a variety of herbs can complement the gentle flavor of most white fish. Herbes de Provence or an Italian seasoning mix are two of my favorites. But if you prefer to keep things very simple, you can just use one dried herb such as chives, dill, parsley, or thyme.

---

1 Make the tartar sauce by mixing together the mayonnaise, chopped pickles, lemon zest, and lemon juice in a medium bowl. Season to taste with salt and pepper, if desired. Cover and place in the refrigerator until ready to serve.

2 Set up an assembly line of three plates. Put the flour on the first plate; next, whisk the eggs in a small bowl and pour them onto the second plate; on the third plate, mix together the bread crumbs, herbs, salt, and pepper.

3 Place a well-seasoned cast-iron skillet over medium heat. Place the ghee or clarified butter into the skillet and allow it to melt. (The clarified butter will offer a milder flavor than the ghee.)

4 Pat the first piece of fish dry and dredge each side of the fish in the seasoned flour. Shake off any excess. Next, dip the floured fish into the egg and allow any excess to drip off. Lastly, dip the egged fish into the bread crumbs, pressing the crumbs into the fish and coating each side generously.

5 Take a pinch of the bread crumbs and toss it into the skillet. If it sizzles, place one piece of fish into the skillet and panfry on one side for 3 minutes or until golden brown. (Cooked sole or any white fish will break apart easily when flipped, so use a wide fish spatula or two traditional spatulas for this job.)

6 Once turned over, allow the fish to cook for an additional 3 minutes. Once cooked, transfer the fish to a plate and place the plate in a warm oven set to 200°F (93°C).

7 Continue the process until all 4 fillets have been panfried. Serve immediately with lemon wedges and the homemade tartar sauce on the side.

8 Panfried fish is best consumed the day it is cooked, but leftovers can be stored in an airtight container for 2 to 3 days in the refrigerator. Warm gently on the stovetop in a dry skillet set to low heat. Serve with the tartar sauce on the side.

Sheet Pan Baked Salmon with Maple Sugar Glaze and Roasted Vegetables

This is probably one of the easiest fish dishes to make, but definitely one of the tastiest. And it's all pulled together on a simple baking sheet pan, which makes cleanup a breeze. Something to keep in mind when cooking salmon is that it can be like cooking a steak: some folks like it rare, while others like it well done, and still others like it somewhere in between. I am in the well-done camp, but if you prefer it rare, don't worry; I share an easy tip below to help you know when to take it out of the oven.

PREP TIME: **5 MINUTES**
BAKE TIME: **APPROXIMATELY 25 MINUTES**
TOTAL TIME: **APPROXIMATELY 30 MINUTES**
YIELD: **4 TO 6 SERVINGS**

INGREDIENTS

1 wild-caught Alaskan sockeye salmon whole fillet (approximately 24 ounces)

1 tbsp coarse ground sea salt

1 tsp freshly ground black pepper

½ tsp crushed red pepper (optional)

⅛ cup maple sugar

4 tbsp ghee

1 large yellow onion, peeled and cut into 8 chunks

2 cups cherry tomatoes

2 medium yellow summer squash, cut into 1-inch (2.5cm) pieces

2 medium zucchini, cut into 1-inch (2.5cm) pieces

Fine ground sea salt and black pepper, to taste

1. Line a baking sheet pan with aluminum foil or parchment paper.

2. Place the whole salmon fillet on the baking sheet pan.

3. Evenly sprinkle the salt, black pepper, and crushed red pepper (if using) over the salmon. Evenly sprinkle the maple sugar over the salmon.

4. Take 1 tablespoon of ghee, divide it into 4 small dollops, and evenly distribute them across the salmon.

5. Place the onion, cherry tomatoes, yellow squash, and zucchini on the baking sheet pan surrounding the salmon. Dot all the vegetables with the remaining ghee. Sprinkle the vegetables with salt and pepper, if desired.

6. Place the oven rack in the middle position and put the salmon into the cold oven. Turn the oven on and set it to 400°F (204°C).

7. After 25 minutes in the oven, check the salmon. It should be well done or approximately 145°F (63°C) on a meat thermometer. If you don't have a meat thermometer, flake the salmon with a fork. If it feels firm, flakes easily, and is no longer translucent, it's done. If not, return it to the oven and allow it to cook for an additional 5 minutes.

8. If you prefer your fish be cooked less than well done, you will want to start checking it after 20 minutes. If you have a meat thermometer, rare to medium-rare salmon will be in a range from 115°F to 125°F (46°C to 52°C). If you flake it with a fork, it will look translucent and be somewhat darker in color in the center. Cooking salmon to 135°F (57°C) is considered perfect by most diners. The salmon will still appear translucent when flaked, but will no longer have that darker color interior. (See **Cook's Notes**.)

9. Once the salmon is cooked to your liking, transfer it to a serving platter. Toss the vegetables together while on the baking sheet pan and then transfer them to the platter, placing them all around the salmon. Serve immediately.

················· COOK'S NOTES ·················

What is the right internal temperature for cooked salmon? There are different opinions about the right internal temperature at which salmon should be cooked to be the most flavorful. The United States Food and Drug Administration (FDA) recommends that salmon be cooked to an internal temperature of 145°F (63°C), and that's also the temperature I prefer.

Index